THE HISTORY OF THE
HOROSCOPE

THE HISTORY OF THE
HOROSCOPE

DAVID OVASON

SUTTON PUBLISHING

First published in the United Kingdom in 2005 by
Sutton Publishing Limited · Phoenix Mill
Thrupp · Stroud · Gloucestershire · GL5 2BU

British Library Cataloguing in Publication Data
A catalogue record for this book is available from the British Library.

ISBN 0-7509-3897-8

Save in those cases where a specific archive, library or museum is specified, all the illustrations in this book are derived either from the astrological collection of the author, or from Topfoto, Edenbridge. The full-page figures have been made from colour transparencies in the collection of Topfoto.

Typeset in 11.5/15pt Garamond.
Typesetting and origination by
Sutton Publishing Limited.
Printed and bound in England by
J.H. Haynes & Co. Ltd, Sparkford.

Contents

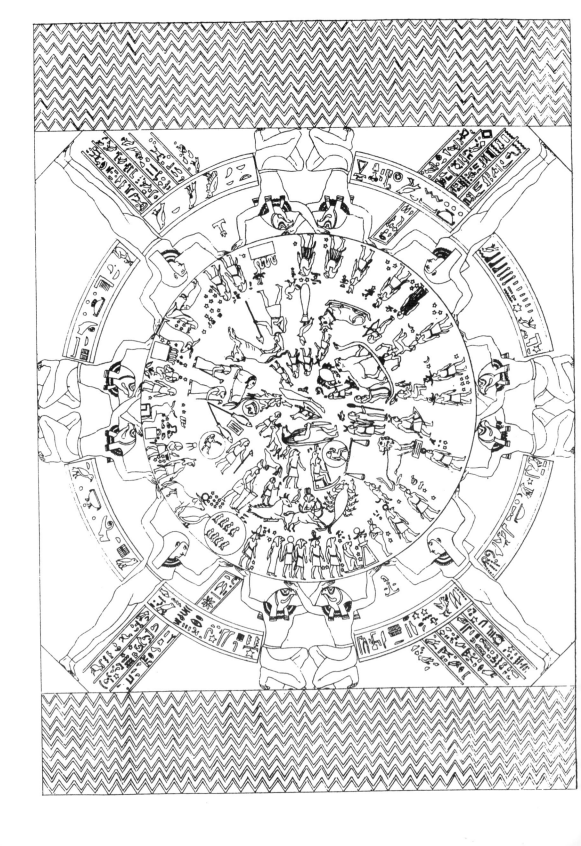

CHAPTER 1

Introduction

For Astrology wants its History as much as any other part of Philosophie; It being the onely *Via Regia*, to its perfection, and all other wayes but by-wayes.

Joshua Childrey, *Syzygiasticon Instauratum* (1653), f. A4

The streams of Western esotericism meander gently back in time, until they lap against the fertile banks of the ancient Nile. While the earliest personal horoscope known to scholars is from ancient Babylon and was cast for a day in April 410 BC, it seems that the astrologer–priests of Egypt had used non-personal horoscopy for over two thousand years before this date.[1]

The zodiacs of ancient Egypt, in such places as Esna and Denderah (opposite page), are by far the oldest to have survived into modern times. Many of these images – whether painted on papyrus, plaster or wood, or whether carved in enduring marble – were derived from ancient horoscopes, calculated for a particular moment in time and space. These horoscopes were not erected to assess the destinies of human beings. The ancient Egyptian astrologer–priests were rarely interested in such matters: their vision encompassed vast expanses of time, which dwarfed into insignificance the normal lifetimes of men and women. The Egyptian priests, who understood the need to regulate human endeavour to the structures and strictures of the heavens, were interested in determining the precise moment that cosmic ages began. They were intent on establishing the slow displacement of the stars, in order to ensure that their temples reflected cosmic patterns and harmoniously united heaven with earth. This is why so many of the surviving Egyptian horoscopes point to the beginning of what is now called the Sothic Period – that vast cycle of time, begun when the star Sirius, or Sothis, rose heliacally over the horizon, at almost the same time as the Sun.

We now know that some of these Egyptian horoscopes, and the many copies that found their way into later temples, go back nearly five thousand years. In the twentieth century, the Irish astrologer Cyril Fagan suggested that a number of surviving zodiacs in Egypt relate to the beginning of the Sothic era, in 2767 BC.[2]

It is not without significance that the earliest horoscopic diagrams known to man are linked directly with Sirius. For the Egyptians, it was a star that not only heralded the beginning of a new age; it was one to which they oriented the long tunnel-like processionals of a few of their temples. The ancient Egyptian hieroglyphic for Sirius △⁎𓏤 incorporated the image of the obelisk (the giant needle, or gnomen, so often used for measuring solar shadows) alongside the five-pointed *sba* star.[3]

Light was the spiritual keynote of Sirius. When its first rays irradiated the dark passageways of a temple, so that the star became visible in the sacred adytum, the experience was akin to the renewal of cosmic life: it was as though the goddess had descended in an aureole of light to take charge of her own temple, built to honour her name. Even today, something of the thrill of this cosmic mystery may be felt as one experiences the sunrise play its annual magic with such ancient buildings as Mnajdra in Malta, the tumuli of Loughcrew in Ireland, or Stonehenge in England – all of which were designed to reflect in a meaningful way the cycles of the heavens, and all of which are the near-lost relics of ancient astrologies.[4]

While it is always tempting to hark back to the prehistoric wonders of architecture, in search of solar and stellar magic, we might like to consider a modern example. In the War Memorial in Melbourne, Australia, the remembrance stone dedicated to those who fell in the First World War has been so sited that, at a certain time, a ray of sunlight, admitted from a hole in the roof, strikes the centre of the stone.[5] The time of the event is the eleventh hour of the eleventh day of the eleventh month. I wonder if those who established this light magic knew how intimately it was linked with astrology. On the day in question, and in the years following the end of the First World War, the Sun was on the beneficial star Zubeneschamali, which is traditionally held to confer blessings, good fortune and benefits.

In ancient times, the star *Sept*, or Isis-Hathor (as the Egyptians called Sirius), was believed to be a living being – a goddess. The goddess Sept could mingle her light with that of her father Ra, when they streamed down the narrow processional of a temple. 'Radiant rises this golden one, above the forehead of her father, and her mysterious form is before him', proclaims a text relating to the viewing of the rising Sirius, seen from the roof of the temple at Denderah.[6]

Several temples were oriented to Sirius in ancient times, but what is of interest to us is that the Temple of Hathor at Denderah, which housed some of the most magnificent zodiacs of the ancient world, was rebuilt and oriented towards Sirius about 700 BC.[7] The rebuilding seems to have become necessary to accommodate changes in stellar positions.

The frescoes, painted coffin lids and marble slabs that bear images derived from the Sothic proto-horoscope were designed for temples and burial places. They had little, if anything, to do with every-day life, or with the living. The temples of old were esoteric centres, with access restricted to priests and initiates: these centres were designed to serve the needs of the Mysteries, which fed the spiritual life of the ancient worlds with their mysterious cults of the dead. Perhaps this is why, when Egyptian zodiacal imagery is transferred from Egyptian soil, it looks out of place, in worlds concerned chiefly with the living.

The amazing 'Egyptian' zodiac, painted in 1893 by the American artist John Singer Sargent for Boston Public Library, certainly looks out of place and out of time. Perhaps the cold light of the north does not do justice to such exuberant Egyptian imagery (figure 1).[8] Perhaps the exotic symbolism is foreign to the North American culture.

One might imagine that so pagan a theme, which incorporates the bull-headed Moloch with the goddess Astarte on either side of a zodiac, has little to do with modern consciousness, and has no place in a modern library. However, the theme was chosen intentionally by Sargent, who sought to project the idea that all history – even modern history – streams back to pagan sources.

The imagery of Sargent's zodiac savours more of the Art Nouveau style than of anything reminiscent of ancient Egypt. Indeed, were it not for the Egyptian hieroglyphic 🔲 on the outer periphery of the zodiac, we might even conclude that it had nothing to do with Egypt at all.⁹ The hieroglyphic in the cartouche is one of the names of Horus, the Sun god, whose radiant disk hovers over the head of the demon-bull, Moloch, and radiates its forces into darkness. The Egyptian Horus is sometimes casually described as the Egyptian equivalent of the Sun-god, but Horus was more than this, for he interpenetrated all the planetary gods of the ancient world. His name is interwoven into the names of the planets. He is Hor-akherty, or Horus of the Horizon, in one of the names of Mars. Hor-wep-sheta, or Horus the Revealer of Secrets, was a name of Jupiter. Hor-pa-ka, Horus the Bull, was a name for Saturn.

In Sargent's Boston zodiac, the solar disk of this multilayered Horus overlays that arc of the zodiac now called Gemini, the sign of the Twins. The Egyptian hieroglyphic *heter*, meaning 'twins', included an ideogram of two men holding hands: 𓀀𓂝𓀀 The vestigial drawing was still used in Graeco-Roman times, when Gemini was called Na-hetru, and was sometimes figured as a letter H (representing two uprights or humans, bound together). Almost certainly, it is to this letter that we may trace our own modern sigil, or graphic symbol, for Gemini ♊.¹⁰

Many medieval drawings of the Gemini twins continued this notion of a pair of conjoined uprights. In some cases, the two upright twins shared a single body (left). In later times, as the lax sexual mores of the fifteenth century entered into astrology, the twins were portrayed as male and female, still sharing bodies, though on a more carnal level, as, for example, in the central arc of the three zodiacal images to the right.¹¹

We should not be misled by demoted imagery of this kind, for its ancestry was originally esoteric. One of the charms of the Geminian nature is the particular character of his or her self-love, which, Narcissus-like, evokes the mirror image. However, on a much deeper level, the Geminian nature reflects the bipolarity of the brain – it is the coming together of the left and right side of the brain which makes the spiritual activity of thinking possible.¹² In the so-called 'zodiacal man' (the melothesic figure), Gemini rules the 'pairs' of the human body – externally, the arms; internally, the lungs. The ancient imagery of Gemini was designed to reflect the fact

that all humans have a physical form which is frontally symmetrical, and that this symmetry serves a cosmic purpose. The Geminian nature is usually mentally adroit and youthfully clever: at its best, it is creative, often in the realm of literature, where it is proficient in thought processes involving the balancing of the contrasts reflected in the bipolarity of the brain. These wonderful characteristics are born of the peculiar cosmic bipolarity, celebrated in many astrological and mythological traditions, relating to the Twins, one of whom is immortal, the other mortal.

In preparation for painting his magnificent Boston images, Sargent researched Egyptian and Babylonian mythology, even travelling to Egypt during this period. However, it is unlikely that he wished merely to paint on the ceiling of this public library a purely pagan imagery. It seems more likely that he was intent on transforming the pagan zodiac and its attendant imagery to serve a Christian theme. It is this impulse which explains why Sargent painted the radiant disk of the Sun as though it were in Gemini.

When the earliest known Egyptian horoscopic diagrams had been designed, in 2767 BC, to mark the heliacal rising of Sirius, the star had been in Taurus.[13] However, by the time the massive marble planisphere had been carved on the ceiling of the temple of Osiris at Denderah, Sirius had moved, by the phenomenon we call precession, to Gemini.* It was still in this sign during the lifetime of Jesus Christ. Thus, for all its obvious pagan symbolism, the Boston zodiac points to the beginning of the New Age of Christ.

By electing to place the Sun in the hands of the cosmic Twins, Sargent was touching upon one of the deepest mysteries of Christianity. The new Sun was visualised as a gift, being handed by the spiritual world to mankind. On one level, the pair of children represented the union of the mortal and the immortal in Christ, who uniquely combined the living God with the living man.[14] This duality, or bipolarity, was that recognised by the Church Fathers in respect of the two-fold nature of Christ. It was identical to the mystic duality familiar to the Greek and Roman mythologisers, who traced the Twin stars of Gemini to Castor and Pollux, the mortal and immortal, respectively. The mythology seemed to reflect the numerology of Gemini, the sigil which besides being a version of the Roman numeral II, is also a vestigial drawing of a portal, through which one might enter the higher world, beyond the threshold of familiar life.

Just as Sirius might be said to herald the civilisation of ancient Egypt, so, Sargent argues (through the medium of his painting), Sirius heralds the civilisations associated with Christianity. Perhaps this is why, in the Boston zodiac, the circle of the zodiac is obscured until the segment of Gemini emerges, dominated by and illumined by the Sun: it is as though Sargent is reserving his symbolism for the era of Christianity. The following signs – the crab of Cancer, the lion of Leo, the woman of Virgo, the scales of Libra – are now visible in the lighted circle, as the top diagram, opposite, demonstrates.

The hidden arc of Sargent's zodiac appears to hint that the past is obscured, while the visible arc proclaims that the Christian future is clear. In terms of the drift of the stars, measured by

---

*   Technical terms not discussed in context are examined in the Glossary on p. 249.

precession, it will take almost ten thousand years for Sirius to appear to slide forwards to the same degree in Libra as it occupied in Gemini. In terms of this imagery, the painted zodiac is essentially Christian, and thoroughly esoteric.[15] It hinted at a Christian way of life – a Christian epoch – that would last for over ten millennia.

It is possible that Sargent's interest in the esoteric element of his zodiac stemmed from his familiarity with another secret of the star Sirius. Sargent could hardly fail to have known that, on the day the new age of the American civilisation began, Sirius was also rising with the Sun.[16] On 4 July 1776, when the Declaration of Independence was proclaimed in Philadelphia, the Sun was in the same degree as the star Sirius. The horoscope for this great event is given below.[17]

Something of the deep significance of this chart will emerge as we study horoscopes and learn more about their symbolism. For the moment, however, it is sufficient to observe that the star Sirius is marked alongside the Sun, represented by the encircled dot, towards the top of the figure.

This placing evoked an echo of a new age, a new beginning, such as had been observed by the Egyptian priests in their studies of epochs and cycles, relating to Sirius. A similar new epoch had been celebrated by the Roman poet Virgil during the first century BC. Virgil's words are from an *Eclogue* that was interpreted by many as a prophecy of the coming of the Child Jesus.[18] Whatever the identity of this child, some of Virgil's words from this poem eventually found their place as one of the Latin mottoes on the Great Seal of the United States of America as *Novus Ordo Seclorum* (A New Order of the Ages). It is certainly not without significance that, on the reverse of the Great Seal, this motto is scrolled beneath the image of a pyramid – the great symbol of ancient Egypt, for whom the most important star was Sothius, or Sirius.

In 1935, this potent imagery was transferred to the dollar bill, and, since then, has been absorbed daily into the subconscious of all Americans (below). For the moment, we might like to reflect on the notion that the five-pointed star, which is the root symbolism of the American nation, is supposed to have been derived from the star Sirius, which the Egyptians called Sept.

This is not the only link afforded between modern America and ancient Egypt: the five-pointed *sba*, or star, of the ancient Egyptian priests has survived the ages, to find a new role as the pre-eminent symbol of America.[19]

We shall examine the horoscopes for the Declaration, later. For the moment, we can use the chart above to learn about one of the most important terms in horoscopy. In most British and American horoscopes, the ascendant is represented to the left of the figure; in the Declaration chart (on page 5) it is marked with the abbreviation, **Asc**. This ascendant marks the most powerful single degree in the horoscope – it is the insistent indicator of the intrinsic personality of the native. The ascendant degree is among the most rapidly moving of all points in the horoscope: depending upon latitude and the time of year, the degree of the ascendant changes by 1 degree every 4 minutes. It is the true index of the 'type', the measure of the unique personality and destiny within the chart, the very pivot on which the meaning of the horoscope hangs. While the ascendant is usually taken as the indicator of the zodiacal sign (thus, ascendant in Scorpio, for instance), we shall discover later that astrologers also take the ascendant as a reference to a specific degree (thus, ascendant in 5 degrees of Scorpio).

The majority of horoscopes are drawn up with the ascendant cusp marked with either an abbreviation or a sigil. The most frequently used abbreviations are **A**, **As**, **Asc**, and so on. In

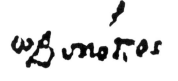

medieval charts, the Latin *Oriens* (east, or, literally, 'point of rising') was often used. Only rarely in modern horoscopy are sigils used to denote the ascendant.[20] However, one surviving ancient sigil is derived ultimately from a contraction of the Greek, *horoskopos*, which originally referred not the horoscope in the modern sense, but to the ascendant degree. It consists of a union of three letters – the Greek *rho*: ρ, *omega*: ω and *kappa*: κ each derived from the word *horoskopos*. The example left (with the

Greek equivalent above it) is from a page of Greek astrological abbreviations copied by the Italian humanist Angelo Politian (1454–94), a professor of Latin and Greek at Florence University, who had a deep interest in astrology.[21] For anyone familiar with the philosophy of sigillization, this symbol is extraordinary, for it plainly represents the three-fold nature of man. The *rho*, with its vestigal head, represents thinking. The *omega*, with its open symmetry of balance, represents the breathing rhythm of the human being, and hence the realm of feeling. The *kappa* seems to be striding out, in imitation of walking, and represents the capacity of the will life to engender motion, and activity. As a whole, the sigil represents the three stages by which man is linked with the spiritual world. The spiritual activity of thinking (in the head) is mediated by the emotional realm (in the heart), and is translated into action by the somatic will life.

This sigil for the ascendant captures the creative essence of the human being – that a man or woman may translate invisible thought into action, on to the material plane. The ascendant is that mystical point, where extension from invisibility into the realm of time and space takes place: it is the birthing point not only for the individual, but also for all ideation. This ancient sigil reminds one of the tremendous importance ascribed to the ascendant, the point of self, the pivot of the soul, the point of intersection between the spiritual space of the higher world and the sequence of time that distinguishes the lower world.

If we examine the chart for the United States we observe that, in its most simple form, it consists of a circle enclosing a basic cross: ⊕ The four arms of the cross are called *angles*. The ascendant is one of the 'angles'. It is also called the eastern point because it marks the point of sunrise.[22] As the chart for the United States suggests, the tendency in modern times is to locate the ascendant degree on the right-hand arm of the figure.[23]

There are three other angles in the chart, besides the ascendant (below, marked AS). One marks the Midheaven (that is, the MC, or *Medium Coeli*); another marks the western horizon or descendant (DC), the point where the Sun begins to sink below the horizon. In many medieval charts, this is the *Occidens*, or west, literally, 'the killing place of the Sun' – marking the place where the Sun appears to die. Another angle marks the lowest part of the heaven, called in medieval Latin *Imum Coeli*, usually now abbreviated to IC.[24]

These four angles draw across the cosmos the great cross on which the horoscope is hung. This zodiacal cross combines the things of the Earth represented by the horizontal line, which symbolises the horizon) with the things of spirit (the vertical line, which symbolises the descent of spiritual forces into the material realm).[25] This cross is especially visible in the circular figure I have elected to use here as an example horoscope.

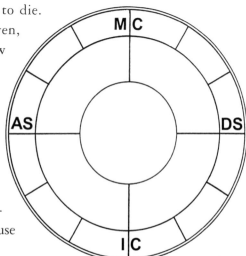

Sargent's zodiac on the ceiling of the upper floors of Boston Library (figure 1) is not a horoscope. However, it *was* designed to symbolise a precise moment in time and space, which is the essential purpose of any horoscope. Sargent's zodiac marks the period of the birth of Christ, when Sirius was in Gemini.

As we have seen already, Sargent's ceiling zodiac calls to mind another ceiling zodiac, of ancient Egypt. This was designed (almost certainly copied from an earlier prototype) and put *in situ* while Christ was on the earth. It is the marble planisphere set in the ceiling of the shrine of Horus at Denderah (see figure at chapter opening). This is accessed by narrow flights of stairs and corridors leading directly along the south–north axis of the building to the roof of the Temple of Hathor. The ceiling planisphere is frequently called a zodiac, though it is far more than merely a zodiac. The astrologer Cyril Fagan, who specialised in sidereal zodiacs, claimed that the distribution of planets, and other factors in the carving, points to the precise date 17 April 17 AD.[26] In his view, the planisphere is a pictorial horoscope, set in durable marble.[27] Someone familiar with the symbolism of Egyptian astrology can easily pick out the twelve signs of the zodiac, the known planets, and a number of constellations and stars – the very language of horoscopy.

Those unfamiliar with the rich imagery of ancient astrologies might be inclined to argue that the Denderah planisphere does not resemble a horoscope in any way at all. Shortly, when we have learned a little more, I will return to this objection. Horoscope or not, the fact is that, when examined closely, the zodiacal images on the planisphere are revealed as corresponding closely to those familiar to modern astrologers. Below, I have picked out the twelve zodiacal figures from the inner circle of the planisphere, and placed them inside a circle of zodiacal figures derived from a popular work on astrology published in the early twentieth century.[28] In each case, the resemblance is beyond reasonable doubt.

Interspersed among the Egyptian zodiacal twelve are images of several fixed stars, including Sirius. In the Egyptian hieroglyphics, Sirius was first represented as a dog – a prototype of the modern name, Dog Star. Later it was called Isis Hathor, and represented in the form of a cow with disc and horns. At Denderah, the star is represented in this latter form, and is located in the second concentric register of images, towards the bottom of the circle (figure opposite chapter heading above). As a representative of Isis Hathor, the star figures as the sacred cow of Hathor, recumbent in a boat: above its head is the five-pointed *sha* star.

By now, it must be evident that modern horoscopy has is origins in remote antiquity, and is steeped in the ancient lore of the Mysteries. The simple truth is that, in modern times, when-ever we cast or read a horoscope, we are indulging in the last vestiges of a Mystery lore that seems to be well over five thousand years old. This long expanse of time might encourage us to claim astrology as being among the most ancient of the sciences, but in making such a claim, we should not be misled into error. As the historian Anthony Grafton has pointed out in one of the finest books on late medieval astrology, the astrological tradition does not form a seamless continuum.[29] An astrologer of the Egyptian period would not be able to make much sense of a horoscope drawn up in the sixteenth century, or in the twenty-first century, no more than a modern astrologer, who is not specialist in such things, can make much sense of horoscopes drawn up in ancient times.

In spite of these differences, there exists a basic alphabet which unites most of the astrologies we shall encounter in this book. In the next few paragraphs I shall sketch out some of the more important elements of astrology, in so far as they relate specifically to the graphic structure of the horoscope – that is, to the familiar figure, which is divided, first into a grand cross, then into twelve segments. Any reader who feels the need for a fuller understanding of the horoscopes to which I refer is recommended to study one of the available textbooks or introductions to elementary astrology.[30]

Few charts of modern times portray the zodiac as a series of images in the manner of the Egyptians. The twelve images of the zodiac are now represented by sigils, specialist graphic symbols, most of which may be traced back to Graeco-Roman astrology, and even to the demotic texts of Egypt. However, in their modern forms, these sigils are not much older than the fifteenth century.[31]

Below, I have arranged the twelve zodiacal sigils in four columns, to indicate the related Element, of Fire, Earth, Air and Water, to which the signs belong. These Elements help determine the primal natures of the signs: Fire is exuberant and active; Earth is placid and sustaining; Air is communicative and loquacious; while Water is sensitive and emotional.

Fire Signs		Earth Signs		Air Signs		Water Signs	
Aries:	♈	Taurus:	♉	Gemini:	♊	Cancer:	♋
Leo:	♌	Virgo:	♍	Libra:	♎	Scorpio:	♏
Sagittarius:	♐	Capricorn:	♑	Aquarius:	♒	Pisces:	♓

The Elemental groups of three are called *triplicities*. For example, Leo is one of the Fire triplicities.

After learning to recognise these sigils, it will be worthwhile examining the medieval images on the opposite page. These combine the Latin names of the signs with their equivalent images (that is, zodiacal pictures) and sigils, as used at the beginning of the sixteenth century.[32] If the Egyptian priests were unable to read the twelve sigils for the signs, it is fair to say that they would probably recognise the corresponding twelve images.

In modern times, the seven planets personified (more exactly, deified) in the Denderah planisphere are also represented as sigils, some of which are of Graeco-Roman origin. To these have been added a few sigils intended to depict the so-called 'new' planets and asteroids, discovered since astronomers have had access to powerful telescopes. The standard modern sigils for the planets, and the four main asteroids, are given below.

The Sun	☉	The Moon	☽	Mercury	☿	Venus	♀
Mars	♂	Jupiter	♃	Saturn	♄	Uranus	♅
Neptune	♆	Pluto	♇	Ceres	⚳	Vesta	⚶
Juno	⚵	Pallas	⚴				

In some astrological systems, we find the following variants:

Uranus	⛢	Pluto	♇

These sigils for the twelve signs, ten planets and four asteroids are the near-universal sigils of astrology – the basic alphabet of the art. These are the letter-forms that have been in use from at least the sixteenth century, when our present story of the horoscope opens.

There are three further important horoscopic sigils, which represent neither zodiacal sign nor planet, but which are significant pointers in personal charts. Two sigils represent what are traditionally called *Caput* and *Cauda* – the Latin for head and tail of the celestial Dragon. These sigils are vestigial drawings of the two points where the path of the Moon cuts through the path of the Sun. These points are called the nodes of the Moon. Caput Draconis is rendered ☊ while Cauda Draconis is ☋. The two are linked with a dragon because, in the distant past, it was believed that the path of the Moon was akin to the long serpentine body of a dragon. In some systems, the creature was called *Atalia*, a word probably related to the Assyrian *atalû*, meaning 'eclipse'.[33] The dragon *Atalia* is supposed to swallow the Sun from time to time, thus bringing about what we now call solar eclipses.

Mythology apart, the nodes called Caput and Cauda are linked with the phenomenon of eclipses, which, when operative, have a deep effect on the life of the native. At those times when eclipses do become operative in a chart, unforeseen factors eclipse (as it were) conscious life: in this way, they bring about conditions which are nowadays sometimes called karmic – karma being the welling up of darkness or light from depths within the human psyche that are normally inaccessible. We shall study the effects of eclipses in many charts in the following text.

The northern node of the Moon was said to mark the place of the head (Caput), which has a beneficial effect. The southern node was said to mark the place of the tail (Cauda), which has a deleterious effect. In the engraving to the left, two serpents are wrapped in union below the zodiac, the head and tail of each meeting in Sagittarius and Gemini.[34] It is no accident that the seventeenth-century engraver of this image portrayed two serpents, each with a Caput and Cauda, resting on opposing signs of the zodiac. The heads of the serpents rest upon Gemini and Sagittarius for a highly symbolic reason, which we shall examine later.

The third non-planetary sigil is the one that denotes Fortuna – properly *Pars Fortuna* – represented as a small encircled cross ⊕. The Fortuna is a projection, from the ascendant of the horoscope, of the same arc of the zodiac which separates the Moon from the Sun, usually measured along the zodiacal sequence. At this stage, we do not need to know any of the complex sub-rules that determine its placing. The significance of Fortuna is interpreted differently by different schools of astrology, but it does appear to indicate, from its house position, the area where one is most likely to succeed, in a material sense. Symbolically, the Fortuna – sometimes called simply Fortune – may be viewed as being the power of the Sun and Moon, brought to earth as a gift for the native.

As this book is not intended to be a treatise on astrology, I will not set out the traditional interpretations of the potential planetary and nodal positions in the signs. However, it is as well to note that astrological tradition teaches that the nature of each planet and node changes in accordance with the sign in which it is placed. For example, as a general principle, the heavy planet Saturn reveals elements of control in the life of the native, and points to the things that frustrate the smooth working of the ego, as well as to the underlying fears of the native. When Saturn is in the earthy sign Taurus, the native tends to be cautious and patient – to a point where others may see the individual as being rather dull, and unresponsive to outer stimuli. The underlying fear marked by Saturn in Taurus is lack of resources. In contrast, Saturn in the fiery sign Leo limits the intrinsic creative joy of the Leonine, so that the native usually finds it hard to enjoy life, and often has real problems with the products (that is, the 'children') of his or her life. Since it is the nature of Leo to stand out (or at least to imagine itself as standing out, and being somehow 'different'), Saturn in Leo projects an underlying fear of mediocrity. Each of the planets has attached to it a similar series of associations, based on the sign it occupies.

In just such a way are the influences of all the planets tempered by the signs in which they are located. As we pursue the history of the horoscope, we shall find that there are several other factors that expand or limit the actions of the planets: however, the planet-in-sign meanings are fundamental to an understanding of the horoscope.

Since we have glanced at the chart for the beginning of the United States of America (see page 5, above), it will be as well to examine it here, if only to offer some practice with the sigils for planets and signs we have just examined.

If we look towards the top of the figure, we see that the Sun is in 13 Cancer. At that time, the star Sirius was also in 13.00 Cancer: however, the actual degree occupied by the star is not marked in the chart. Three other planets are in Cancer. Reading clockwise, these are Mercury, Jupiter and Venus. Continuing down the arc, we encounter Mars and Uranus, in Gemini. At the bottom of the chart, we see (still reading clockwise) the Moon in Aquarius, Cauda, or the Dragon's Tail, in Aquarius, and Pluto in Capricorn. Higher in the arc, we see Saturn in Libra, Neptune in Virgo, and Caput in Leo.

A third set of symbols may be read in our modern chart for the United States. In the centre is a mesh of criss-cross lines that symbolise 'aspects'. These lines denote various angular relationships between the planets. Not all the aspects recognised by astrologers are operative within the Declaration chart; however, the most important ones are as follows:

Aspect Name	Sigil	Angle
Opposition	☍	0 degrees when exact
Conjunction	☌	180 degrees when exact
Trine	△	120 degrees when exact
Square	☐	90 degrees when exact
Sextile	✳	60 degrees when exact
Semi-square	L	45 degrees when exact

Sesquiquadrate	⚼	135 degrees when exact
Quincunx	⚻	150 degrees when exact
Semi-sextile	⚺	30 degrees when exact
Quintile	Q	72 degrees when exact
Bi-quintile	BQ	144 degrees when exact
Tredecilis [sesquintilis]		108 degrees when exact
Decilis [semiquintilis]		36 degrees when exact

Each of these aspects has a different 'influence' on the planets it involves. For example the trine tends to enhance the harmonious working of the involved planets. In contrast, the square brings difficulties and tensions. We need not concern ourselves here with these influences: they will be revealed, where necessary, in the following text.

Aspects is one of the many interesting flotsam and jetsam words which so distinguish the English language. When we show our moods on our face, then we may properly describe this as an aspect of ourselves: the Latin *aspectus* was linked with how we show our face, with what we might call 'the mien', the appearance we present to the world. In just this way, the aspects of the medieval astrologers revealed the faces and moods presented by the planets – tempered by the relationships they hold with each other. For example, if the Sun were to find himself in the difficult square aspect to Saturn, then the face of the Sun would, so to speak, be darkened by this contact.

The moods of the planets, expressed through aspects, are related to the age-old theory of the four Elements. If you consider the angles involved in the aspects, then you will note that planets in a harmonious trine are expressing themselves through signs which have communal Elemental natures, such as Fire, or Water, and so on. Planets in the tension of square are in mutually antagonistic signs, contrasting (for example) Fire with Water, and so on. In the Declaration chart, Mars (in 21 Gemini) is *almost* in trine with the Moon (in 25 Aquarius). Technically, they are both within *orb* of the trine. Both Gemini and Aquarius are Air signs. A key-level interpretation of a harmonious relationship such as this suggests that the energy of Mars is realised by the harmonious contact with the Moon, and is given the impetus to achieve its goals and ambitions easily: the psyche is optimistic. Here we have an example of how an aspect between a pair of planets is translated into the mien or personality of the native, even if, in this case, the 'native' is a nation.

Finally, within the sample chart are to be observed the eight dividing lines that run across the main circle, between the four angles. These lines mark the house cusps, indicating (as some maintain) the boundaries of a distinct house within the horoscope. Even in its non-specialist usage, this word 'cusp' came into the English language by way of thirteenth-century astrology. When translating the works of Arabic astrologers, the scholar, John of Seville, cast around for a word that would act as the equivalent of the Arabic *watad*, which means 'peg' or 'pin'.[35] At length, John decided on the Latin *cuspus*, meaning 'sharp point', which he visualised as pinning down the twelve houses in space and time, much as the *watad* of old could be used to pin down a tent in the desert sands.

There are twelve such house cusps in all, each house bearing a relationship to one of the twelve zodiacal signs. Below are marked the house divisions, in both a circular and in the quadrate chart favoured by medieval astrologers. Starting from the first house, and moving in a widdershins direction, the houses have the following general significance.

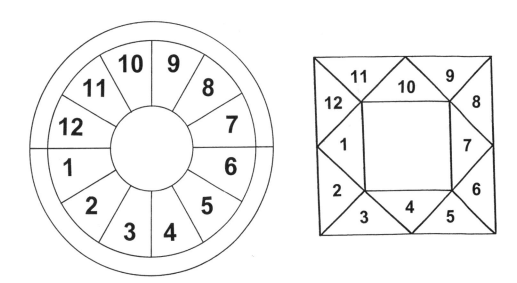

First house. Of the nature of assertive Aries, this is the personal house, where one may study the drives of the ego and related selfish impulses. It is the house of beginnings – offering an index of the ideas or ideations that lead the native to begin projects.

Second house. Of the nature of materialistic Taurus, this is the house of possessions – the things that support or adorn the ego. It rules personal earnings and money, and the native's attitudes to how enterprises are to be supported, once begun.

Third house. Of the nature of alert and nervous Gemini, this house rules short-term communications, such as letter-writing, telephone calls, e-mails and so on, as well as demands made on the native from a close quarter. It is also an index of the manner in which a person speaks, of his or her acting ability, and tendency towards histrionics.

Fourth house. Of the nature of protective Cancer, this house rules the beginnings of life itself – hence, it rules the home, where protection should be at its most loving. It offers an index of how – with what limitations and encouragements – the native passed his or her childhood.

Fifth house. Of the nature of exuberant Leo, this house rules all creative activities, self-expression, as well as the 'products' of such creativity activity – that is, as works of art and children. It is sometimes an index of whether or not a native is likely to complete projects.

Sixth house. Of the nature of critical Virgo, this house rules activities devoted to others – work, commitment, service and so on. It is the house of health and personal hygiene. It is sometimes said that the urge of the sixth house is to tidy up the chaos left by the activities of the previous house of Leo.

Seventh house. Of the nature of harmony-loving Libra, this is the house of relationships, formal or otherwise. It is an index of marriage, of the partner sought out by the ego, and of the general image of the 'other' – it often marks the impulse towards freedom from the tyranny of the first house. It is also the house of legal enmities – where clarity of thought enters into relationships that might otherwise drown in emotionality: this is the incursion of the head-force of Aries into the emotional realm of Libra.

Eighth house. Of the nature of penetrating Scorpio, this is the house of intense involvements, of new beginnings arising from old endings. Hence, it deals with legacies, and with money gained legitimately from others, offering new opportunities. The house is an index of attitudes to death and the afterlife.

Ninth house. Of the nature of wisdom-loving Sagittarius, this is the house of distant communications and aspirations. It rules travel to (and life in) foreign places, intellectual exploration and deeper studies. It is sometimes called the House of Education – and is linked especially with extra-mural education – with life as an educative process.

Tenth house. Of the nature of coldly aspirational Capricorn, this is the house of ambitions and of planned attainments, such as careers. It governs things far removed from the home, and relates to the expression of the ego in the outer world; it offers an index of how the native treats those above and below on the social scale.

Eleventh house. Of the nature of detached Aquarius, this is the house of group endeavours – of hopes and wishes, in a less personal and more social sense. It governs aspirations of a political and reforming kind, only loosely connected with personal ambitions. It offers an index of how the native will respond to working in groups.

Twelfth house. Of the nature of sensitive Pisces, this is the house of awareness of others, and of the ability to sacrifice for others. It is an index of the psychic and unconscious strivings. Just as the first house rules beginnings, so the final house rules endings. This is why the house is sometimes called the 'House of Sorrows', even though not all endings are sorrowful. It should really be called the 'House of Completions'.

Unfortunately, there has never been firm agreement among astrologers as to precisely what the house cusps signify. Some astrologers insist that the cusps mark the boundaries of the house. Other astrologers claim that the cusps mark the centre of the house, and are thus indicators of the most powerful influence relative to that house. This latter argument has some validity, if we consider the ascendant as being coterminous with the first house cusp. The ascendant, being the most powerful indicator of personality, may reasonably be interpreted as marking the centre, rather than the beginning, of the first house.

This major difference in interpretation need not concern us greatly at this point. The truth is that, beyond the issue of where houses begin and end, there is a far deeper issue of *how* the cusps are determined, in a mathematical sense.

There are at least a dozen different systems in use among modern astrologers for calculating the positions of the intermediate cusps. Some of these systems are based on divisions of time, others on divisions of space. That the horoscope should be divided into twelve areas, marked by cusps, is an essential part of astrological doctrine: how these divisions are made has been a matter of contention almost since the early days of astrology. Ptolemy seems to have followed a system whereby the twelve houses consisted of 30 degree arcs, starting at the ascendant. This method, now called Equal House, is used by some astrologers today, even though it is frowned upon by the majority of experienced practitioners.

In attempting to visualise in graphic form the three-dimensional nature of the solar system, astrologers have recognised that four great cosmic circles are involved in the projection of the heavens. As a generalisation, we may say that one circle measures the position of the earth in the cosmos: this is the equator, which divides the globe of the earth into north and south. Extended into space, this equatorial division is called the Celestial Equator. Another circle measures the path of the ecliptic, or zodiacal belt. The two points of intersection of these great circles are called the zero points of Aries and Libra: it is from the former that the tropical zodiac of twelve signs is measured, starting in time at the vernal equinox. A third great circle measures the horizon. A fourth circle is projected into the heavens as a great circle at 90 degrees to the Celestial Equator: this is called the Prime Vertical. Astrologers recognise that, in order to represent the twelve houses in a valid way, a geometry must be devised to reconcile these different great circles so that what is essentially cosmic (that is, zodiacal) can be represented stereographically in earthly terms, as houses. The twelve-fold division of the ecliptic must be projected, by geometric means, to the Celestial Equator, in order that it might be reflected in the horizon specific to the place of birth.

Since accurate tabulations of a number of house systems are readily available, this specialist division of horoscopy need not unduly trouble the non-specialist. The published tables permit the astrologer to access a number of different systems of house division, without a knowledge of the three-dimensional geometry involved in their construction. Even so, an approximate idea of the issues at stake is essential for understanding the stereographic projection that lies behind the horoscope.

For the sake of graphic simplicity, the diagram below illustrates a projection of only half the heavens. One must visualise the east point (the zero point of Aries, here marked 1) as being raised towards the spectator. The plane of the Celestial Equator (here marked CEL. EQ.) is divided into twelve equal segments (of course, only six are shown in the diagram). Lines that are initially at right angles to the Prime Vertical are drawn through each of these divisions on the Celestial Equator. These lines are then projected on to the plane of the Ecliptic Circle. The points of intersection form the cusps of the houses. These are marked by numbered circles, in which number 1 represents the east point, or ascendant: this is the cusp of the first house. Number 2 represents the cusp of the second house, and so on. Since, in this diagram, only seven divisions of the Celestial Equator are visible, one must imagine the completion of the remaining five, on the hidden side of the globe. These hidden house cusps are obtained by projecting the visible cusps diametrically: thus, the cusp of the twelfth house projects to form the cusp of the fifth house, and so on.

This particular system of house division – the projection from the Prime Vertical – was proposed in the sixteenth century by the German astrologer Regiomontanus. There are many such systems in use today; we shall encounter others in the horoscopes reproduced in this book, including those of Campanus and Placidus. The various methods of constructing houses have a profound influence on how charts are analysed.

We may see this influence at work in a comparison of two different house systems for a single horoscope. Below, left, is a horoscope of the Roman emperor, Nero, cast by the Italian astrologer Junctinus in the sixteenth century: this was calculated according to the Regiomontanus system of house division, discussed above. Alongside is a manuscript version of Nero's chart cast in the same century by the Italian, Cardan; this was calculated according to the ancient equal house system (all the cusps are marked as being on 20 degrees).[36]

If we examine the two charts carefully, we see that the Regiomontanus stereographic projection places Jupiter in the sixth house. However, in the equal house system it is well and truly in the fifth. Jupiter in the sixth is reflected in the native's capacity to serve others in a helpful and loyal way. In contrast, Jupiter in the fifth tends to make the native more selfish, and expands love of sports, personal pleasures, and the wish to speculate (sometimes through gambling). This contrast offers a fine example of how different house systems can change the meaning that may be ascribed to a chart.

One thing that will surely have struck anyone, who has already glanced at the illustrations in this book, is that there exists a wide variety of different chart forms, not all of which consist of

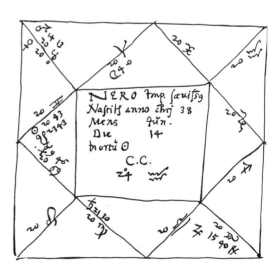

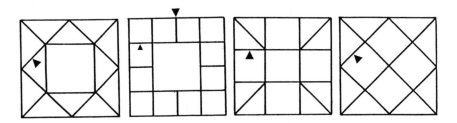

quadrate or circular charts with twelve house divisions. The sixteenth century (from whence our own study begins) inherited a wide range of figures or schemas into which horoscopic data could be inserted.[37] The most extensively used was the quadrate form, which was itself subject to several variations. Some of the quadrate patterns are set out above, with an arrow pointer indicating the most usual position of the ascendant. The earliest forms of the quadrate second from the left usually had the ascendant at the top (in accordance with Arabic convention), but in later medieval usage the ascendant was normally to the left, as marked here with a smaller arrow. The quadrate was at times subjected to plurification, involving two or more sets of data within a single group of quadratures.[38] The most complex of the western series are the compound horoscopes of the fifteenth-century astrologer Richard Trewythian, some of which incorporate three sets of data constituting a quadruple horoscope nestling into a single graphic quadrate, with the appearance of a maze.[39]

Circular charting was less common in medieval astrology, though some outstanding examples have survived. Usually, variations arose from the manner in which the circle was subdivided to set out the twelve houses. Left, is one variant of a medieval circular chart cast for shortly before sunset on 17 April 1487.[40] It was intended to celebrate the raising of the author Conrad Celtes as Poet Laureate by Frederick III, Elector of Saxony, one of the great patrons of literature and learning in the medieval period.

In this chart, the house spaces are organised around a pointed cross. The disadvantage of this graphic form is evident from the chart itself: the space within the 'cross' is too cramped to contain adequately the potential planetary contents. We observe that the block-maker has forgotten to include Saturn (which should be in 22.30 Sagittarius). One interesting detail may be seen to the bottom right, where the astrologer has represented sigils depicting two planets

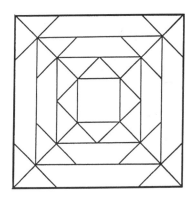

in a square aspect □♃♀ . The sigil for the square is easily identified, as is the final sigil for Venus, but the sigil in the middle is more obscure. In fact, it is the most widely used medieval sigil for Jupiter. Its presence in this woodcut reminds us that, towards the end of the fifteenth century, the wide range of available sigils was regularised to approximately those forms which are now used. It is rarely that one finds, in a single chart, different sigils for the same planet, as in this case.

Some circular charts reveal their true significance only when they have been completed. For example, the sixteenth-century circular chart below (left), which resembles a sort of sunburst, may seem to be nothing more than a curvilinear form of the standard modern chart system. However, when it is completed, with zodiacal and planetary positions (to the right), its meaning is revealed. This chart form was designed to suggest the motion associated with the revolution of the heavenly spheres, depicted in the horoscope: these spheres (sometimes confusedly called orbs) carried each of the individual planets, together with the great wheel of the zodiac, around the earth. This chart was cast for the afternoon of 10 March 1491, in Leipzig.[41] In those days it was believed that Jupiter had rule over the zodiacal sign Pisces. Since the Sun is in Pisces, this probably explains why the figure supporting the horoscope is a personification of the planet Jupiter.

Certain systems of charting derived from the European continent are not drawn up in a graphic form pre-divided into houses. These consist of a circle, or a series of simple concentrics, graduated with the 360 degrees, into which the house cusps and the positions of the zodiacal signs are marked, with each individual charting. An example of this type of horoscope is given on page 224: the fiducial degree to the right is not the ascendant degree but the so-called zero degree, marking the beginning of Aries.

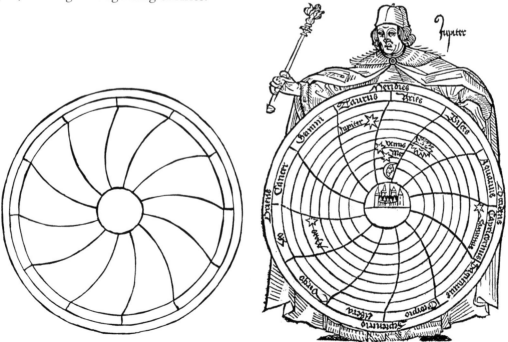

Not all astrological systems were based on a sequence of twelve houses. As we shall see later, some charts, derived from ancient medical astrology, involved eight-house systems and even sixteen-house systems. A striking non-medical example of the latter is the chart calculated by the astronomer Tycho Brahe for the appearance of the great Nova of 1572 (see page 67).

The really important thing about a horoscope cannot always be seen in a chart. The horoscope is a sort of mask behind which the historian – like the astrologer – must fumble for meaning, if he or she is to understand the rationale behind it. This mask – the visible form of the horoscope – is sufficiently arcane for most people. Indeed, the majority are so taken by the mask that they do not even imagine that it is in fact a front for something else much more profound in content.

So far, we have seen that the horoscopic mask is of a triple nature. We have the four angles, which are further subdivided into triads by means of cusps. We have the groupings of planets and signs. And we have the aspects. These make up the visible appearance of the horoscope, which I have called the mask. Beyond and behind the horoscopic mask lie numerous invisible factors of tremendous importance to the astrologer.

The most powerful of the 'invisibles' are the fixed stars. In the arcane tradition, it is said that certain fixed stars have the propensity to lift up the native to greatness, while others have the power to push him or her down into the gutter. However, some stars perform both functions, at different stages of human life. Almost without exception, genius in an individual is marked out by one or other of the fixed stars, rather than by any other single factor in the horoscope.

Unlike the planets and signs, not all the fixed stars have convenient sigils to denote their presence. When an astrologer wishes to reveal the presence of an important star in a chart, he tends to write the name of that star into the appropriate place in the horoscope. In certain late medieval texts and horoscopes a number of sigils were used to denote a limited number of stars, but these sigils have fallen into desuetude.[42] In modern times, as indeed after the sixteenth century, astrologers intent on pointing to specific stars in a chart usually mention them, not in the chart itself, but in the analysis attached to the horoscope. We shall study a fine example of this in connection with the chart of Pope Paul III on page 52.

In some instances, astrologers would indicate the presence of an important fixed star by inserting, into the relevant part of the chart, an asterisk or the name of the star itself. A pertinent example is the chart alongside, of the unfortunate King Louis XVI of France. We shall deal

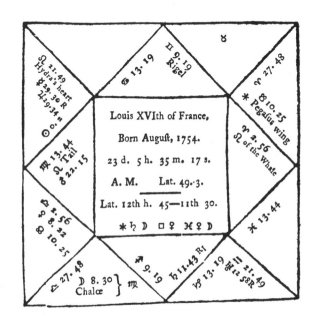

Louis XVIth of France,

Born Auguſt, 1754.

23 d. 5 h. 35 m. 17 s.

A. M.   Lat. 49.·3.

Lat. 12th h. 45—11th 30.

with this particular chart later; it is sufficient here to observe that no fewer than six stars are named in the figure, from the powerful Rigel to the star Algenib, in the wing of the flying horse, Pegasus.

The term 'fixed star' is, of course, a misnomer: it is nothing more than a throw-back to the remote past, when even the planets were called stars. Medieval astronomers distinguished the cosmic role of the planets by calling them *errantes*, or wandering stars, and contrasted them with those that seemed fixed. Since those remote days, the term 'fixed stars' has become both archaic and inaccurate, although even the great seventeenth-century astronomer Kepler at times referred to the planets as stars.[43] Nowadays we know that the fixed stars have motions infinitely more rapid than those of the planets. The movement of Rigel, set in the giant Orion, and visible near the MC of the chart of Louis XVI (overleaf), is not among the most rapid in the heavens, yet it is receding from our solar system at a speed of over 10 miles per second. There is nothing quite so illusory to ordinary vision as the skies.

The widespread assumption that there exists, somewhere, a corpus of knowledge called astrology which has always been practised uniformly by astrologers is profoundly in error. As must be evident from what we have seen so far, the truth is that there has always been a vast range of astrologies, rather than a single astrology. Each society adapts the various lores of astrology to fit its own needs and to reflect its own cosmological vision. We might almost go so far as to suggest that there are as many astrologies as astrologers.

The earliest surviving attempts to set down, in book form, an account of the rules and traditions of astrology may be traced back to Alexandrian Egypt, in the second century of the Christian era. Modern historians have traced to this place and time a number of important astrological texts by such authors as Claudius Ptolemy and Vettius Valens. However, it is known that much earlier compilations of horoscopic lore had been written, and that most of these have been lost. There are indications that horoscopic astrology was taught much earlier than the second century, in Greece.[44]

During the medieval period, when the modern form of the horoscope was being laid down, it was sincerely believed that there was only one source for the ancient tradition. So highly regarded was this single source that, by a happy coincidence of names, he was, for some time, identified as a pharaoh, and portrayed wearing a crown.[45] This pseudo-royal was the second-century BC Alexandrian, Claudius Ptolemy, author of the Greek *Tetrabiblos*, or 'Four Books' on astrology. The shadow of Claudius Ptolemy has lain for eighteen hundred years over Western astrology; one could easily construct a history of astrology from the standpoint of how later astrologers either followed Ptolemy or rebelled against him: no astrologer since his day has been able entirely to throw off his influence.

The ideas Ptolemy scavenged from the libraries and dustbins of the ancient world have totally dominated the view of what astrology was, is and should be. In view of this, it comes as something of a shock for us to realise that Ptolemy did not leave behind a single horoscope to adorn or explain his methods or theories. It comes as an even greater shock when we realise that

Ptolemy seems not to have been a practising astrologer, and did not always understand some of the things about which he felt constrained to write in his seminal books.

Against this critique of our heritage, we must make some assessment of what Ptolemy did leave of value in his transmission of ancient ideas. For all his weaknesses, the truth is that each time we contemplate a modern horoscope, we cannot help but see it through the eyes of this ancient non-astrologer.

The most simple of all the graphic forms in the modern horoscope – the outermost circle, or the outermost square – may be traced back to Ptolemy's theories, many of which antedate Ptolemy himself. The fact that the majority of modern horoscopes are encircled by the tropical zodiac is partly due to what Ptolemy wrote almost two thousand years ago. From the several systems available in Alexandrian Egypt, Ptolemy had adopted the tropical zodiac – the zodiac of the twelve equal-arc signs – associated with the mathematician Hipparchus, who set the beginning of the zodiac against the vernal equinox. In some respects this tropical zodiac was Ptolemy's most important contribution to the practice of astrology, for it was by his route that the zodiac was widely adopted in Western astrology. This adoption has been so effective that, nowadays, only specialists recognise that there are other possible zodiacs available to horoscopists.

Of almost equivalent importance is the tradition handed down by Ptolemy concerning the natures of the constellations and the fixed stars. It was Ptolemy who established the method of evaluating the power of fixed stars: he recorded that their power for evil or good was best expressed in terms of a planetary equation. Ptolemy equated the influence of the stars with various combinations of planets: thus the star Canopus was viewed by Ptolemy as the equivalent of a second Saturn and Jupiter, and representative of what the ancients revered as the most powerful of planetary conjunctions. This Ptolemaic tradition was continued into late medieval celestial globes and star maps, and survives in the star lore of modern times. For example, in the

globe designed by the van Langren brothers in 1589, the constellations were marked with one or more planetary sigils to indicate the natures of each asterism (right).[46]

Beneath the name Argo Navis are the sigils for Saturn and Jupiter, indicating that the chief stars in Argo exude the influence of these planets. The name *Canobus* on the violin-like oar of Argo is a version of Canopus favoured by Ptolemy: faithful to the sigils marked under the name

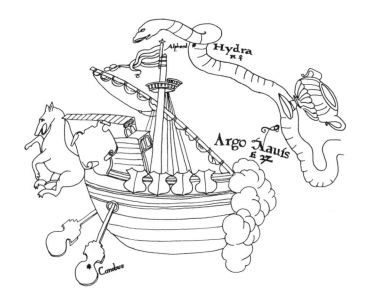

of the constellation, Canopus is still ruled by Saturn and Jupiter, and is regarded as favourable for those who wish to make journeys by sea. Canopus has also been seen as a perversion of dark Saturn with sensual Jupiter, as an impulse towards promiscuity and a violent death. Whenever the star fell on the same degree as a planet or nodal point in a horoscope, its dire effects would be felt in the life of the native. For example, the magnetic Dutch dancer, courtesan and seductress, Mata Hari, who was executed by firing squad as a German spy during the First World War, had Canopus in conjunction with her Venus, the ruler of the feminine sensuality for which she was famous.[47]

Another notion that Ptolemy encouraged, and which had been widely applied in earlier astrologies, was that one could cast charts for inanimate or inchoate entities, such as metropolitan cities and even cultures.[48] Thus, in insisting on the importance of the position of the ascendant, Sun and Moon at the founding of metropolitan cities, Ptolemy sanctioned the method used in modern astrology for casting the chart for the United States of America at the moment of the Declaration of Independence (see page 5 above).[49]

Beyond these simple principles, astrology has changed almost beyond recognition over the past two thousand years. The star lore has survived, though vastly expanded with the naming and numbering of a myriad more stars than Ptolemy could have counted, let alone named. The systems of houses have changed from the equal house system proposed by Ptolemy, and many such systems now flourish under a dozen or so different names. Ptolemy's proposed methods for computing and predicting the future have also changed – most have become far more sophisticated and complex.

Eclipses have been regarded with awe in every age and it is scarcely surprising that by the time of Ptolemy the effects of eclipses were being related to personal charts. The astrologer Balbillus, who cast charts for the first-century AD emperor, Claudius (with whom he visited Britain, attached to the XXth Legion), and who later served his less benign successor, the insane Nero, became involved in the politics of eclipse lore. Indeed, one detail of his life acts as a commentary on the two attitudes to eclipses that still persist into our own day, the official and the astrologic.

Claudius was not the first Roman general to worry about the effect that eclipses had on the superstitious Roman armies. Previous attempts had been made to explain to the soldiery that eclipses should not be objects of fear, but these had not always achieved satisfactory results.[50] When Balbillus computed that a solar eclipse was shortly due to fall on Claudius' birthday, he sensed danger and advised Claudius to issue a proclamation. Thus, in 45 AD, a Roman emperor made a serious attempt to explain the mystery of eclipses in a public proclamation. He not only announced the fact of a coming eclipse, but specified just how long it would last, and gave the reasons why the Sun would appear to be blotted out for that period.[51]

Balbillus, more knowledgeable about such matters than Claudius, must have been laughing quietly to himself. He knew that when a solar eclipse falls on the Sun in a personal horoscope, then, no matter how that eclipse is explained away, change of some kind is bound to ensue. An astrologer familiar with the chart of Claudius might well blame the eclipse for the events that followed. Claudius' profligate young wife Messalina started an affair with Silius, whom she then bigamously married without the Emperor's knowledge. For this she was executed, thus giving Claudius the chance to marry his niece Agrippina, who poisoned him less than eight years later to make room for her detestable son Nero.

That modern astrologers can relate these unseemly events to the horoscope of Augustus is due to the Balbillus family, who cast the charts that were preserved by astrologers interested in personal destinies and in history.[52] Perhaps more famous was the prediction (attributed to the astrologer father of Balbillus, Thrasyllus) that Nero would achieve two great things: he would become emperor, and he would kill his own mother. It is largely thanks to the activities of this family of astrologers that the horoscopes of these remarkable and corrupt rulers of Rome have come down to us.

It was during the medieval period, which was so deeply influenced by Arabian astrology, that the lore of eclipse interpretation came into its own, to become one of the most important assets of horoscopy. An enormous number of medieval horoscopes are concerned with the effects of eclipses. Clearly, the solar eclipse depicted in the fifteenth-century woodcut, right, is dramatised – the two people on earth are pointing with some consternation at the blacking-out of the Sun, visible on 20 July 1487.[53]

The delightful floral device which marks the sixth degree of Leo (where the eclipse occurred) reminds us that it is only recently that special sigils have been proposed to depict solar and lunar eclipses, respectively.[54] It is evident from the diagram that the important thing was the degree in which the eclipse took place. It was this degree (and, because the eclipse involved an alignment of the Sun, Moon and Earth, the *opposite* degree) on which astrologers seized to wring meaning from eclipses. Ptolemy had emphasised the power of the eclipse preceding birth, but, by the medieval period, eclipses were held to be important at *any* stage of life – and were even regarded as indices of death. In all cases, the principle remained the same: the eclipse degree would wield a powerful influence in any horoscope wherein the same degree was occupied by a planet, node or angle.[55]

These ideas have survived the centuries, albeit in amended forms, but they are used in modern times only by a handful of astrologers. After the death of Princess Diana in 1997 a host of articles was published that dealt with her horoscope. However, few of these articles pointed to a cosmic truth which would have made Ptolemy or Balbillus nod knowingly.[56] Less than forty-eight hours after Diana's death, an eclipse occurred, which was intimately interwoven into her horoscope.[57]

The existence of different astrologies may be traced to the very beginning of the Ptolemaic tradition. There can be no greater contrast to the work of Ptolemy (with his lack of references to specific horoscopes) than that of his near-contemporary, Vettius Valens, who also lived in Alexandria. The two astrologers were, as one modern historian recognised, 'poles apart'.[58] However, the main difference in their approach was that, unlike Ptolemy, Vettius practised both as an astrologer and as a teacher of the art, in a school which he had set up for this purpose.

With Vettius we have immediate access to horoscopes, one of which is given below left (the diagram alongside will be explained shortly). This chart was cast for 23 February 97 AD, at about 4:00 PM. Vettius tells us that the *horoskopos* (H) was in Leo.[59] The chart, cast by astro-computer, corresponds closely to the descriptive text given by Vettius Valens in the first century of our era, save that Jupiter was not in Aries, but in Scorpio.

The astrology of the first century was markedly different from that practised today, and, for this reason the chart introduces us to unfamiliar terms. For example, Vettius tells us that the *Part of the Demon* (which seems to have been of great importance in early Graeco-Roman astrology) was in Scorpio. The sigil he used for the *Daimon* was ♅, and is represented in the diagram alongside the horoscope. The *Daimon* marked a beneficial degree, obtained by projecting the arc between the Sun (SU) and Moon (MO), from the Ascendant (A), asymmetrically to the Part of Fortune (for construction, see the diagram alongside). In the case of this particular horoscope, the *Daimon* fell in 17 Scorpio. Another important event recorded in

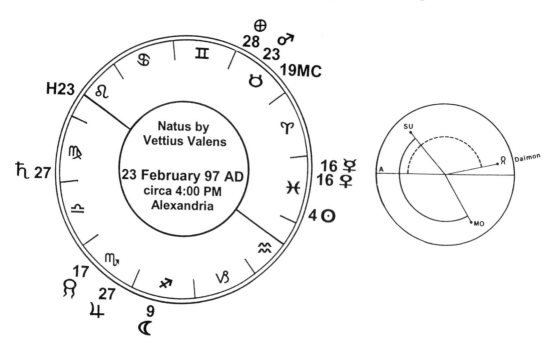

the chart, and one relating to something no longer used in modern astrology, was the position of the first full Moon after birth. This would occur on 16 March, and fall in 25 Virgo, very close to Saturn.

Vettius tells us little about the native himself save that he met his end by being beheaded. The fact that Saturn was on the star Spica, and Mars on Rigel, should have ensured a successful enough life. However, because Vettius deals in an astrology which is essentially foreign to us, we cannot read the chart in the way he would have done. For example, he tells us that the *Part of Death* was in Sagittarius, in the same sign as the Moon. This *Part of Death* was in an inferior aspect to Saturn (in Virgo), which was itself in the sign of the next full Moon. Extrapolating from these factors, it might perhaps be possible to work out the unpleasant fate of the native, but it is extremely difficult to get into the mind of an astrologer who uses terms with which we are not intimately familiar. As a matter of fact, a modern astrologer would observe that the Moon was very close to the fixed star Facies, the nebula in the face of the Archer, Sagittarius. This star *does* posit a violent death, but unfortunately we do not know whether Vettius had Facies in mind when he wrote his astro-analysis.

Vettius' seminal work, *Anthologiae*, offers 123 similar charts, each either illustrating a teaching point or acting as an exemplum.[60] His text includes reference to conception charts and horary astrology, which seem to have had a long ancestry prior to being used by Vettius. Perhaps most important was his record of the system of directions (designed for offering a glimpse into futurity) which appears to have been widely used in classical times. Vettius gives several accounts of making predictions from natal horoscopes, one of which – the chart of the Roman emperor Nero, which was probably borrowed from the Balbillus family – has survived into several modern astrological anthologies. All in all, his *Anthologiae* is among the most comprehensive treatises on horoscopy to have come down to us from the ancient Greek world: it offers striking evidence that the astrology of the ancient world was very different from that practised in the post-medieval world.

Since our history starts at the beginning of what may be described as 'modern' history, at the inception of our own Renaissance-based Western civilisation, it may be as well to glance at a sample horoscope from that period. In so doing we shall be able to take stock of what we have learned about horoscopy in general. It will be instructive to examine a chart entitled by its anonymous astrologer (no doubt set on impressing his client, the father of the child), 'a horoscope of a remarkable and rare kind'. It is the chart of a son born to Ambrosius Glandorp, on 28 May 1542, in Brunswick (now Braunschweig), in Germany.[61] Although this is a manuscript chart, only a little

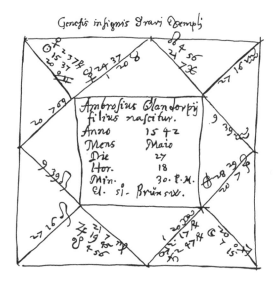

effort is required to work out the sigils: perhaps the only one that might give any difficulty is the form for Scorpio, which is a vestigial drawing of a scorpion ♏.

In the original chart, one observes that the birthday is given as 27 March. However, when the figure is adjusted to take into account methods of contemporaneous German time-keeping, the date proves to be the equivalent of 28 March. The chart was erected by the *Modus Rationalis*, or Regiomontanus house system, which we examined in some detail a little earlier. In the sixteenth century this was the most popular of all available house systems, both on the Continent and in Britain.

The most noticeable thing in the chart is the conjunction between Mars and Saturn, in Scorpio. Mars is further strengthened by being in its own sign (Scorpio). The sigil ℞ after the two planets means that they are retrograde, or seeming to move back along the zodiacal path. Both planets are in the creative fifth house, associated with Leo. They are in trine aspect to Caput (4.56 Pisces). As the astrologer recognised, the warmth of Mars does not mingle easily with the cold of Saturn, but the conjunction does help make the native hard-working and self-reliant. The medieval astrologer rightly saw this conjunction as one of the factors against which the parents would have to guard: he recognised then (as a modern horoscopist would recognise now) that the conflict between Mars and Saturn generally points to an issue of discipline. Saturn in Scorpio strives to develop emotional control and self-discipline. Mars in Scorpio is usually intensely given over to the emotional life of passions, and to disciplining (that is, to manipulating) others. If over-disciplined in childhood, the native can become rigid in outlook.

A modern astrologer would observe that Venus is quincunx (150°) with both Mars and Saturn – an aspect that is likely to add further strain on the native. However, the astrologer who cast this chart, presumably around 1542, would not have known about the quincunx aspect as it was one introduced to astrology by Kepler in the early seventeenth century.

Although Jupiter is in detriment (that is to say, in the sign opposite to that which he rules) and weakly square to the Sun, it is angular to the IC, and therefore immensely powerful. It is also trine to Mercury, both planets being sextile to the ascendant. Save for the detriment and the square aspect, these factors are beneficial. Jupiter will give a clear and practical mind, which will augment and spiritualise the otherwise slow and practical nature of Mercury in Taurus.

The one thing which a modern astrologer might be prepared to ignore when reading the chart is the weak opposition between the Sun and the Moon. The opposition is almost 9 degrees away from being exact. However, in keeping with medieval practice, the anonymous astrologer was undaunted by this wide orb, and seems to have regarded the opposition as a factor worth taking into account. One thing is certain – this astrologer did not take into account the effects of the fixed stars. The ascendant is on Procyon, which in 1542 was in 19.23 Cancer. This star, the mortal of the Twin stars, tends towards violence and disaster.

In ancient times astrology was merged intimately with the Mystery wisdom and, in its pure form, was the domain of initiates. Something of this aloofness in astrology has lingered on through the ages and it is not surprising that we should still encounter, from time to time,

figures which can only be called crypto-horoscopes. Certain images are designed to incorporate astrological data (usually in horoscopic form) in a manner which obscures the true astrological purpose, or design, from the uninitiated. A very simple example of this may be seen in the sixteenth-century woodcut by Albrecht Dürer, on the previous page.[62]

The woodcut appears to portray an image of the naked Urania, holding a simple armillary sphere, dominated by a zodiacal band. Among the uppermost segments of the zodiac – all of them in the higher half of the zodiac – are sigils for the planets, as follows:

	Moon		Mercury		Jupiter		
TAURUS	♉☽♀	GEMINI	♅☿☉	CANCER	♋♃♄	LEO	♌♂
	Venus		Sun		Saturn		Mars

Such an arrangement of planets in signs suggests that this woodcut might well be a horoscope for a specific time. If we hunt around in old ephemerides, or tables of planetary places, we will eventually discover that only one time during the past few hundred years corresponds to this arrangement of planets. On 9 June 1504, the Moon and Venus were in Taurus, Sun and Mercury were in Gemini, Jupiter and Saturn were in Cancer, while Mars was in Leo. That is to say, Dürer's distinctive woodcut of Urania was actually intended as the equivalent of a horoscope.

The German printer Martin Landsberg frequently published crypto-horoscopes in his almanacs and news sheets. These images would probably have been recognised by his contemporaries as astrological puzzles, but it is unlikely that those unfamiliar with medieval astrology would recognise them as horoscopes. The woodcut below shows three sets of figures. It is headed (in Latin) 'Figure for the Eclipse of the Sun'. Given the date of the almanac in which the image appeared, this must have been the solar eclipse of 1488.[63]

The seated figure to the left is Jupiter, holding his wand of office. His unorthodox seat is a huge fish, so we take it that this is a reference to Jupiter in Pisces. The more complex image to the extreme right seems to portray the lame Saturn (identified by his crutch and serrated scythe), leaning for support against the bowman. We must presume that this portrays Saturn in Sagittarius. The scary image in the centre represents the sign Cancer, in its guise as a crayfish. The solar head, which covers the body, implies that the image relates to the solar eclipse in Cancer. We are aided in this surmise by the Latin inscription, *prope caudā draconis*, which means 'close to the tail of the dragon'. This suggests that the solar eclipse would have taken place near to Cauda. That much is graphically confirmed by the dragon's tail, knotted ominously below the crayfish, and its frightful head rearing above the bowman.

The clues offered by Landsberg are sufficient for us to work out the precise moment to which his enigmatic design points. At 04:18:40 AM, on 9 July 1488, in Leipzig (where Landsberg printed his almanacs), a solar eclipse occurred in 25.41 Cancer, just over 1 degree from Cauda (in 27.09 Cancer). At this time, Jupiter was in 23.08 Pisces, and Saturn was in 29.11 Sagittarius.

By now, it is likely that the reader will have learned something of the basic alphabet of astrology, and have noted that (much to the confusion of non-astrologers) certain factors at work in a chart are not always represented in visible symbols. From what we have learned, we should be well on our way to being able to make sense of the form and symbolism of a horoscope, if only in terms of such visible factors as the planets, signs, houses and so on. However, at this point we must turn to a more complicated side of horoscopy, which may require some readers to consult the glossary from time to time. The underlined words in the following paragraphs are intended to alert the reader to the fact that these terms are included in the glossary (on page 249).

One popular misunderstanding about horoscopy is that an astrologer needs to cast only one horoscope in order to prepare a thorough and complete reading of the native's personality and destiny. Nothing could be further from the truth. The process of constructing and studying the potential within a horoscope usually requires several distinct stages, each demanding a separate chart, or series of charts.

The general procedure is for the astrologer to cast a preliminary horoscope, which is then subjected to a series of techniques (called rectification techniques) in order to ensure that it is a correct figure for the native. Once this rectified chart has been obtained, the astrologer may then subject it to one or more of several techniques designed to explore the future potential within the figure. These techniques include what are called directions (involving the directing of given planets or nodes to specific points, as measurements of time) and revolutions, or revolution charts. This technique involves moving the Sun forward (that is, revolving) to the same place in the zodiac as it occupied at birth. The chart cast for that moment is the revolution. However, in modern astrology the investigation of future potential is generally limited to a special kind of directions, called progressions. This technique requires that the planets, nodes and angles be moved forward to specified times in the life of the native, from which it is possible to assess unfolding potential. This is as true for modern astrology as for that of the past: towards the end of the twentieth century the astrologer Ronald C. Davison mentioned the 'vast array of possible charts' which could be engendered for any given year when attempting to work out future events. He proposed that four basic charts were required for each year under consideration, and that each of these should become the basis of additional charting to reveal their potentials – a minimum of eight charts for every year of life.[64]

The methods used in modern times are only tenuously related to those used in ancient horoscopy. Thus, in some surviving medieval records, culled from the astro-readings of proficient astrologers, we find an extensive sequence of charts. Among these are the initial tentative nativity (cast for the time given of birth, and sometimes called the *aestimativa*, or 'estimated chart'), along with a related chart, cast for the previous full or new Moon, or eclipse (sometimes called the *figura deliquium*).[65] This was cast to determine the <u>animodar</u>, with the intention of establishing an accurate horoscope, which was usually called the *figura rectificata*. Another technique of rectification that was popular in medieval horoscopy was the Trutina of Hermes, usually referred to as the <u>trutine</u>. A further rectification method might be applied, according to what was called *per accidens* – that is, by adjusting the chart so that it would reflect the timing of known events in the life of the native – an early form of progressions. Once the accurate horoscope (the *figura rectificata*) was established in this way, the astrologer might then begin to study the future, by means of the potential within the chart. He might calculate a number of revolution charts for the following years of life. From each of these revolutions, the astrologer was usually able to make predictions pertaining to the specific year for which it was cast. During the medieval period, revolution charts were used extensively by the more proficient practitioners. For example, the sixteenth-century French astrologer Michel Nostradamus cast at least fourteen revolutionary charts for his client, the German industrialist, Hans Rosenberger.[66]

On the page opposite, I have constructed a series of six charts marking a rational sequence and designed to reveal this complex process. The series begins with the first estimated birth chart ('Time as given'), and continues through to a progression for the rectified chart. These six charts will help us form a clearer understanding of what the phrase 'casting a horoscope' really means in serious astrology. For ease of reading, I have represented these charts in the now-familiar circular format. They have not been plucked out of the air, without any thought for a historical horoscopic process: the first four figures may be compared with the extraordinary manuscript quadrate charts cast in the fifteenth century for Francesco Giucciardini.[67]

Chart 1 shows the horoscope cast for the time and place given – in this case, for 2:18 AM on 6 March 1482, at Florence, Italy.

Chart 2 shows the nearest full or new Moon to the birth – this is sometimes (wrongly) called an 'eclipse chart', a syzygy chart (more properly) an animodar chart. The astrologer requires this figure so as to apply the rule of the animodar, which depends upon the position of the last syzygy prior to birth. In some medieval chartings, only the position of the Moon is given in this chart, as it is the only important factor.[68] In the second figure, the solar–lunar opposition took place on the day before the birth, on 5 March 1482, at 11:04:30 AM local time, Florence. The animodar

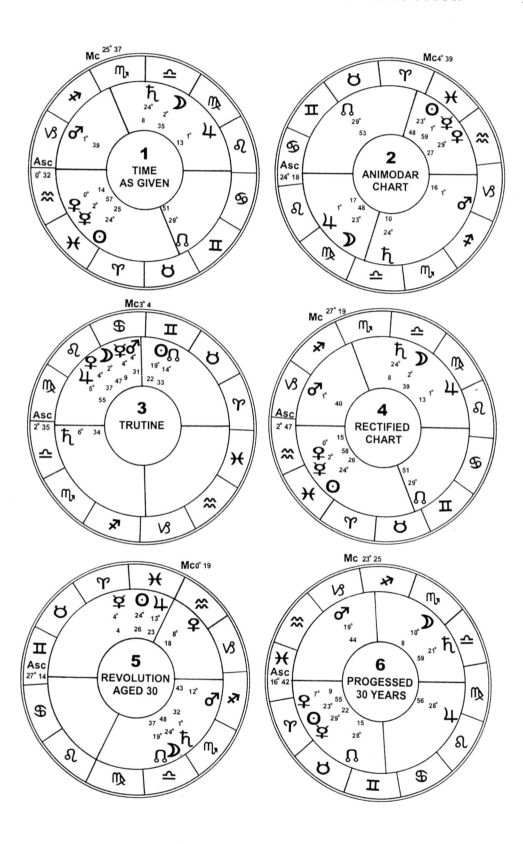

is rarely used in modern astrology, as the rules upon which it relies depend upon astrological concepts (such as the planetary *dignity*, and lordships) that are now regarded as archaic.

Chart 3 shows the first calculation relating to the trutine, pertaining to the approximate period of conception (that is, about nine months prior to the birth). The word 'conception' was often used in medieval horoscopy, and the impression given to the uninitiated is that these charts relate to the moment of conception in its biological sense. However, there is no evidence that anyone really believed that this moment marked the actual point of conception: the name was a convenient figment. For this reason, modern astrologers prefer to describe it merely as 'a certain epoch'. In modern astrology, a more sophisticated series of rules, serving the ancient trutine, is called the Prenatal Epoch. In its simplest formulation the law of the trutine says that the degree of ascendant or descendant at birth marks the position of the Moon at this epoch. Since the ascendant or descendant at this epoch is identical to the place of the Moon at birth, it is possible to adjust the birth chart to accommodate this fact. In this particular case, the Moon of chart 1 (in 2.35 Libra) marks the ascendant in 2.35 Libra (chart 3), on 1 June 1481, at 11:12:55 AM, local time. At this moment, the Moon was in 2.47 Leo.

Chart 4 shows the previous trutine chart, now accommodated into a rectification. The lunar position in chart 3 is adjusted to form an ascendant of 2.47 Aquarius. This adjustment moves the Moon of chart 4 to 2.39 Libra.[69] From this ascendant, we can calculate the time of birth (that is, the *rectified* time of birth) was at 2:25 AM on 6 March 1482.

Chart 5 shows the revolution chart, cast for the 30th birthday – literally for the solar birthday. The Sun is in the same degree and minute as it was at birth (that is, in the rectified chart 4), but all the other planets and the angles have changed. Revolution charts of this kind are read as pertaining to the future year of the native. (This revolution has been cast for Florence, but see the note on page 113.)

Chart 6 shows a progressed chart for the 30th birthday. Following the astrological convention of regarding each year as being the equivalent of one day, the progressed chart represents the astrological factors at play in the life of the native on 6 March 1512. It offers a dramatic contrast to the revolution in chart 5: in the latter, the Moon is in Libra, while in the progressed chart it is in Scorpio. In fact, there is no agreement between the two charts, even though they are held to pertain to future events to be experienced by the native in the same year.

Undoubtedly, the deepest gulf between astrologers of the past and those of modern times is to be found in their view not of the horoscope, but of what the horoscope represents. For the ancients, the horoscope was a sign of the activity of the gods – a belief which seems to have been entirely lost in recent centuries. At the beginning of our own era, the astrologer Vettius Valens lamented that he did not live in former times, when the true initiates occupied themselves with the sacred science. In those lost days, which Vettius so regretted, the love of the initiates for the Mysteries was so great that they frequently left the earth below, and in their deathless souls became 'heaven walkers', mingling personally with the divine beings.[70] The path of true astrology led directly to heaven, where one rubbed shoulders with the gods.

In the days of Vettius Valens, horoscope-making was still part of the Mystery lore. The astrological writings of those earlier times always took it for granted that the planets were living beings, overlooked by mighty angels. They had no doubt that the zodiacal powers were living creatures, a notion that is hinted at in the Greek etymology of the word zodiac, which is linked with the idea of living entities. For the ancients, the cosmos itself was a vast, interrelated and incomprehensible being. To some extent this idea of the planets and signs as living beings continued into late medieval astrology: for example, the French astrologer and prophet, Michel Nostradamus, incorporated into his astrological verses the lore of the 'living beings' called the planetary angels, or Secundadeians.[71] These were the mighty rulers of the planets, who ruled, in a prescribed sequence, periods of history during which they left the stamp of their own spirituality on the world of man. This vision, of an earth serviced by mighty cosmic beings, faded shortly after the sixteenth century, and through this loss astrology was weakened, as it was divorced from its underlying concept of the cosmos as a living being.

The severance of modern mankind from this living vision, and from both the Mystery wisdom and the spiritual vision of the stellar world, was symbolised in the discoveries of Copernicus, published in 1543, at about the same time that Nostradamus was writing the first of his predictive verses. Unwittingly, by displacing the earth as centre of the cosmos, the great Polish astronomer dislodged something of the ancient spirituality from the vision of Europeans and their descendent Americans. Because of Copernicus, our own intellectual and somatic worlds have been severed – we know something about the cosmos intellectually, but we cannot support this with our first-hand vision and experience. In our somatic life, and in our perceptions, there is always the sunrise, never the earth-set that the Copernican intellectual viewpoint premises. In this sense, therefore, the horoscope is a reminder of a former vision, one in which the intellectual and the somatic had not been separated.

The American writer Henry Miller (whose horoscope is displayed later in this work) once voiced a most perceptive *aperçu* concerning astrology and the human soul. 'Sometimes,' he wrote, 'I think that astrology must have had its inception at a moment in man's evolution when he lost faith in himself.'[72] Undoubtedly Miller was right. When man's contact with the spiritual realm was severed, man began to lose faith in his own spirituality, and in the world. If we can learn anything from the Egyptian zodiac-horoscopes of the pre-Christian era it is surely that astrology must have had its inception at a time when mankind had a different conception of what spirit is, far removed from that he holds to now.

Seen in this light, each modern horoscope is a record of an attempt to find faith once again in our own spirituality, and in our relationship with the cosmic realm beyond. The quotation at the head of this Introduction might be read as voicing the opinion of a seventeenth-century practitioner that astrology is in need of a history, in the sense that the present book is a history. However, this was not the case. The highly original English genius, Joshua Childrey, was really expressing his view that astrology is in need of the *service* of history. He argued that, for astrology to prosper, there is a need for a dated record of events and births, which would offer a useful testing ground for the art. Childrey was right to clamour for such a useful historical record, yet the quotation is also valuable for its ambiguity. Astrology must be seen for what it is — a sequence of interlocking astrologies, each enmeshed in different views of the cosmos and man. A history of horoscopy should reveal the truth behind the bewildering complexity of these astrologies. Astrology and horoscopy, which in recent centuries have fallen so deeply into venal disrepute, are really attempts to understand both the riddles of the cosmos and the riddles of mankind. Any such daring undertaking certainly deserves a history.

CHAPTER 2

The Sixteenth Century

How, maps of persons?
Ben Jonson, *Epicoene, or the silent Woman*, v. i. 22

The Elizabethan, Simon Forman, was not a great astrologer, yet his place in the history of sixteenth-century astrology has been assured by his autobiography and astrological diaries, which are among the most interesting of the century.[1] In 1573, Forman began an awkward part-time education at Oxford University while acting as a servant to John Thornborough, who was to find easy and steady preferment in the Church, ending his days as the Bishop of Worcester. Forman did not take a degree – he was of humble origins and too poor to enrol as a full student – but there is little doubt that he would have walked through the FitzJames Arch in Merton College and admired the remarkable stone carvings of the zodiacal signs set in the vaulting.

This late fifteenth-century arch was one of the wonders of Oxford, with the image of Pisces (below) specially adapted to reflect the symbolism of the single dolphin, which was emblazoned on the arms of Richard FitzJames, who designed and built the edifice. The twelve carved zodiacal images are still in place, and still intrigue visitors to the college. Casual observers – and even casual historians – have concluded that the zodiacal decorations represent a horoscope, but this is not the case.[2] However, it is true that, in accordance with the practices of the time, a horoscope was cast to determine the moment when the building of the arch should commence. This foundation chart was erected for 12 March 1497. The quadrate chart, cast for this moment, had originally been painted on glass quarries, in a window of the lodgings of Warden FitzJames. Unfortunately, the glass was among that destroyed by Warden Lydall, almost two hundred years after the foundation date.[3]

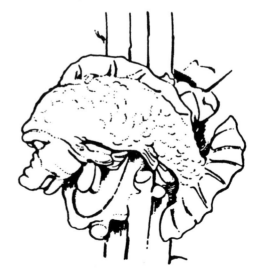

A copy of the painted glass chart has survived in a book written against astrology by the sixteenth-century author John Chamber. Ironically, it is now one of the many reminders of the importance of astrology in the intellectual life of Oxford during the fifteenth and sixteenth centuries.[4] This horoscope is shown below, alongside a modern version, cast for the equivalent time, on 12 March 1496. One observes that the medieval chart gives the year 1497, and that the modern equivalent is given as 1496, a discrepancy that relates to calendrical issues stemming from the *Mos Anglicanus*, which we shall discuss later in connection with the chart of the Oxford scholar Robert Burton.

The Merton zodiac and the related horoscope both contain profound secrets. The significant thing is that the most important single degree in the chart – the ascendant – is in Cancer. The importance of this sign is reflected in the orientation of the arch itself. One passes through the arch, and into Fellows Quad, under the gaze of Cancer the Crab, which has been placed central to the southern archway. The esoteric significance of this direction has almost been lost in modern times, but in the early Renaissance astrologers were familiar with the writings of Porphyry, who had insisted that all human souls were born into the world through zodiacal Cancer.[5] In terms of this symbolism, each time one passed though the Merton arch, one was, so to speak, being born anew, redeemed, as it were, by the power of this remarkable sign, the keeper of the Gate of Birth. This gate is sometimes called the Gate of Cancer, at others, the Gate of the Moon. The meanings are much the same as the Moon is ruler of zodiacal Cancer and the notion was that the pre-natal soul passed through the orb of the Moon, before descending to the earth to take up a body compounded of the elements.

It is probably too much to conclude that the Merton zodiac sparked off Forman's passion for astrology. Although he could easily have begun his astrological studies while at Oxford, it would not be until 1579, ten years after his unhappy and humiliating experiences at the university, that he began openly to practise medicine and magic – both arts in which knowledge of astrology was then indispensable. Clearly, he had learned astrology some time

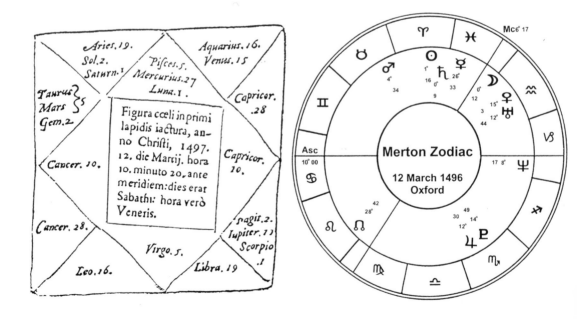

prior to this, but it was in that year that he chose to work as a healer and astrologist – a course of life which, in the early days at least, ensured that he 'could have no justice nor law'.[6]

Forman's contemporary, John Dee, was educated at St John's in Cambridge and later became one of the founding Fellows of Trinity College, Cambridge. There is a mystic numerology involved in this accident of education, for the Trinity is reflected in the sigil △, a form of the Greek letter *delta*, which has the sound-value *dee*, and which Dee sometimes used as a cipher signature. As he reminded us in several of his writings, this trinity is more than a three, for *delta* is the fourth letter of the alphabet: thus, the three is merged with the four to make the mystic seven, and to form the arcane symbol for man: 🜨.[7] Although Dee does not spell it out for us, the fourth sign of the zodiac is Cancer: thus the sigil is representative of the great mystery of how spirit (three) becomes enmeshed in matter (four) to make a living human being (seven).

Much earlier than Forman, Dee found himself with a somewhat unsavoury reputation as a magician, which he had first acquired with his ingenious and successful staging of a flying scarabaeus beetle in a play performed in the great hall at Trinity. In the dramatic opening moments of a production of Aristophanes' comedy, *Peace*, Dee arranged for the citizen–hero, Trygaios (who was anxious to reach the celestial realms of Zeus), to be carried high over the heads of the audience by an astonishing flying beetle.[8] It was felt that such an achievement could not be the work of a mere engineer, but was necessarily that of one who had resorted to black magic.

The flight of the scarab might appear to be rollicking good mechanical farce, yet it was more than that – both for Aristophanes and for Dee, and presumably for some of those who witnessed the event. The idea of a man mounted on a scarab takes us back to the ancient Mysteries of Egypt, in which the scarab was Kheper 🪲 the zodiacal sign Cancer.[9] The flight was nothing more than a typical Aristophanean sacrilegious play on the sacred Mysteries, here relating to the nature of birth.

During his later years, in what was the consummate sixteenth-century work on esoteric astrology, Dee returned to the idea of the scarab, but within a less sacrilegious framework. While discussing 'the most secret mysteries' of the physical world in his astonishing *Monas Hieroglyphica* of 1564, Dee referred to the egg as a model of the cosmos.[10] This, he tells us, was the egg of the eagle that had once been a scarab beetle, which lived in a cave. Dee has no need to explain the cave – it is the same as that described by Porphyry in his esoteric work *The Cave of the Nymphs*. One entrance to the cave is the Gate of Birth, accessed through Cancer; the other is the Gate of Death, accessed through Capricorn. It is evident that as a student in Cambridge the youthful genius John Dee was evoking the same esoteric astrology as the designer of the Merton arch zodiac.

Dee survived the early reputation for necromancy born of this play with the flying scarab, and went on to become the greatest mathematician of the age. Eventually, he gained the confidence of Queen Elizabeth I herself, and acted as her private adviser and astrologer. The miracle is that contemporaries so different in outlook and social standing as Forman and Dee should have met at all.

At 12:40 PM, on 26 July 1604, Simon Forman went to dine with John Dee at the house of a Mr Staper.[11] It was typical of Forman to record in his diary the beginning of such an enterprise. He was a work-a-day astrologer, dependent on his art for his living, and the meeting must have held far more promise for him than for Dee.

Both astrologers would have known that the powerful conjunction of Saturn and Jupiter in Sagittarius, which had recently caused several tracts and books to be penned, was still operative.[12] More specifically, as Forman stepped over Staper's threshold he would have known that Mars was rising in Scorpio, along with the beneficial star Princeps. Perhaps he had arranged this precise time himself, for the operative degree fell in his second house, the ruler of money.

This meeting of contrasting astrologers almost encapsulates the splendid age that had just come to a close. Elizabeth I of England, who had frequently consulted Dee on matters spiritual and astrological, had died in the previous year. Both Dee, who had served her, and Forman, who had served some of her courtiers, had been astrologers in the sixteenth-century mode, and now, as a new age dawned, were almost figures of fun. In less than six years, they would be dead – both leaving behind unsavoury reputations, save among a handful of specialists.

John Dee died in such isolation that even his date of death is no longer known for certain. Next to 26 March 1609 in his diary, someone had drawn the cipher **Jno** Δ alongside the sketch of a skull. While he was on his deathbed, his daughter Katherine had taken away his books, which, being discovered by Dee later, broke his heart and, quite literally, killed him.[13]

Forman died on 8 September 1611, leaving his 'secret manuscripts' and horoscopes to his student, Dr Napier, from whom they were acquired by Elias Ashmole, through whom they finally came to the Bodleian Library, in Oxford.[14] A year or so later, Forman's memory was to be execrated by Chief Justice Coke during the trial of the murderers of Sir Thomas Overbury in the Tower. During the hearings Coke had exploded with anger at the deceased Forman. It is said that one of the astrologer's autograph notes, exhibited to the court, listed the names of several high-born ladies and identified those whom they secretly loved. Having opened the paper, Coke refused to admit it in evidence: the first on the list was Lady Hatton, his own wife.[15] Coke's injustice continued to taint the reputation of Forman until modern historians gave him a second hearing.

In his day John Dee had been the most learned man in England. He had travelled throughout Europe on behalf of the state and (more personally, and even more secretly) as an ambassador of Rosicrucianism. As a personal friend of Queen Elizabeth, he was acquainted with the mightiest in the land. On one famous occasion, at the command of the Queen, delivered by Robert Dudley, Dee accepted the responsibility for choosing a suitable election to mark the coronation of the Queen.[16]

In contrast to John Dee, Simon Forman was a self-educated man, more perceptive and cunning than learned, who had been imprisoned more than once for his shady activities. Forman was by no means a nonentity – he, too, had mingled with the famous, though, to judge from his diaries, these were more of his own rough-and-ready sort than those with whom Dee was accustomed to rub shoulders. Forman might have known Ben Jonson, for the poet used the astrologer's name in one play during Forman's lifetime and, after his death, in yet another. In *Epicoene*, Ben Jonson mentions Forman by name, and later fools around with the idea of horoscope-making as being the equivalent of mapping human beings. The topicality of the joke is perhaps lost on the modern reader, but in the early seventeenth century men still thrilled to the mysteries of maps and map-making, which were revealing a new and romantic world.[17]

Dee and Forman had entirely different attitudes to astrology, but both knew their own horoscopes well. The nativity that Dee cast for his own birth is preserved in the Bodleian Library (below).[18] Dee does not appear to have left any notes on the significance of his chart, but his self-assessment of his greatness is hinted at in the fixed stars he included. Antares is on the ascendant, where it is supposed to bring honours and riches, as well as spates of violence. The binary Arista is on the tenth house cusp, promising unexpected honours and advancement beyond even the hopes of the native.

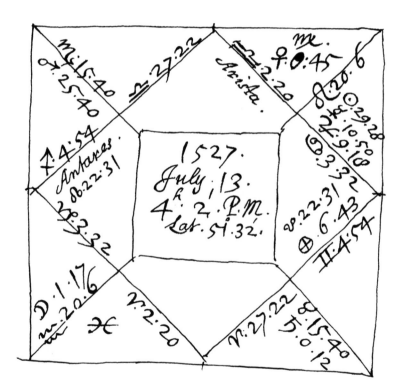

His reluctance to add a reading to the chart does not mean that Dee was incapable of making such an analysis. The chart he drew up for his former pupil, the soldier-poet Sir Philip Sidney, was followed by a 62-page astro-analysis, in which he predicted a wonderful career up to 1576. In that year, Sidney would be in grave danger, from sword or fire. As it happened, the prophecy was fulfilled, for Sidney was severely wounded in the thigh while fighting at Zutphen. He died on 17 October 1576, a few minutes before a solar–lunar opposition.[19]

In some ways, it is quite extraordinary that Dee should have been able to predict this fatal event from the chart. The placing of Mars, from which he calculated the prediction, was out by almost a degree.[20] So far as it is possible to determine, from the several progressions left by Dee, the operative influence in Sidney's thirty-first year was the trine between the progressed Sun and Mars. In the natal chart, the two had been in square. In the progressed chart, Mars was in opposition to Saturn, and the IC (18.33 Taurus) was on the killing star Algol (in 1554, on 18.32 Taurus). More than once, Dee reveals his reliance on the stars in interpretation, and it is probably this progression which he has in mind when discussing Algol.[21] Accurate in detail or not, Dee's beautifully drawn geniture of Sidney, and the long analysis to which he subjected it, is entirely different from the charts and readings scribbled down by Forman.

Although Forman kept a diary and a notebook of cases, he had the habit of casting charts with dangerous abandon, and scribbling near-illegible commentaries on scraps of paper. His charting was not altogether accurate and one often feels sorry for those who received his advice on the basis of such horoscopy. Inevitably, he treated his own birth chart differently. In his *Autobiography*, Forman recorded with great precision the moment of his birth, at 9:45 PM on 30 December 1552, in Quidhampton. Forman was not overly honest, and I find myself wondering about the authenticity of the time. As given, the chart offers Jupiter on the ascendant – something to be desired by all and sundry – but it is more likely that Mars was on the ascendant. Either way, Mars was close to the fixed star Alphard, notorious for its connection with sexual power.[22] This would go a long way to explain Forman's obsession with sex, about which he has no hesitation in writing in his autobiography. At every possible opportunity he had sexual relations with his female clients (married or single), with friends, servants and casual acquaintances. It is partly this detail of Elizabethan life that makes his autobiography such a compelling read.

The meeting of Dee and Forman was almost prophetic. The contrast between Dee and Forman could symbolise the two different kinds of astrology that would be practised in England for the next few centuries. In a sense, it would be the mercurial and venial type, beloved of Forman, that would dominate horoscopy during those centuries, yet it was generally the isolated and learned horoscopy, practised by Dee, that introduced much-needed reforms into the art. Unfortunately, while Dee had many admirers, no one continued his astrology: indeed, so far as it is possible to tell, no one has even studied his astrology in depth, general interest being confined to his dabbling with the Occult. In contrast, the type of astrology practised by Forman has continued to this day, in the hands of the semi-learned, the charlatans and those who serve the press with pseudo-horoscopy.

When, towards the end of his life, the sixteenth-century Italian astrologer Jerome Cardan reflected upon events he had witnessed during his lifetime, he recorded his delight that he had been born into the century 'in which the whole world became known'.[23] He had witnessed the expansion of the European horizon – the Americas had been explored, from Brazil as far as New France, the vast country that we now call Canada. But of all the developments in which Cardan delighted, paramount was that of 'the typographic art ... a rival, forsooth, of the wonders wrought by divine intelligence'. Cardan's sense of history was acute: it was the invention of printing that was to influence and mould the direction that astrology would take over the next five hundred years.

As a consequence of the development of printing, certain arbiters were introduced into the art of astrology. There was a move to standardise the representation of charts and the use of astrological sigils. For example, shortly after the invention of printing, the several forms used until that time as sigils for the Sun were rejected in favour of that still in use today. The earlier sigils, which were derived from short-forms for the Greek word *helios* ☌ ☌ ☌ and those derived from alchemical theory ☉ ☉ were relinquished in favour of a solar sigil ☉ which may be traced back to the hieroglyphics of ancient Egypt. For the first time, horoscopes were drawn up in forms and sigils which modern astrologers can read with little difficulty.

However, this 'universal' horoscopy had its inbuilt limitations. Because a modern astrologer is able to make sense of the graphic sigillisation of the sixteenth century, he or she may be inclined to believe that the chart can be interpreted in accordance with the same rules contemporaries used. This is far from being the case. If anything, with the invention of printing, and the freedom of communication to which this gave rise, more and more personalised forms of astrology were developed: horoscopy became more opaque and complex than ever before. Because of this, it is a brave historian who undertakes to interpret a chart of that period without first having access to a detailed analysis written by the astrologer who cast it.

A good example of how different a sixteenth-century horoscope can be, in comparison with a modern one, may be seen in a copy from a manuscript chart now in the British Library.[24] This chart enables us to understand why one historian, Hilary Carey, should have lamented that

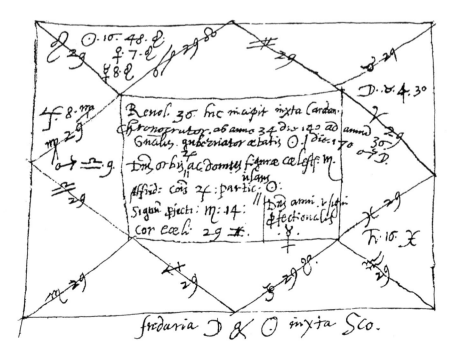

'mediaeval scientific astrology was fiendishly difficult'.[25] This difficulty does not stem merely from the complexities of dog Latin and extensive abbreviations favoured by medieval astrologers, nor even from the multitude of now-archaic terminologies one encounters in virtually every manuscript horoscope of the late medieval period. The main difficulty arises from the fact that, in former times – perhaps more so than in modern times – astrological terms were often 'personalised' by astrologers, and, all too often, were made to mean what they wanted them to mean.

Were it not for the plethora of information contained within the inner quadrate, we might imagine that we could interpret this chart in accordance with the traditional rules of modern astrology. However, the moment we examine the lines of text within this quadrate, we realise that we are dealing with an astrology that is foreign to that with which we are now familiar, in modern times. The chart is replete with obscure terminologies and is an interesting example of just how far removed from modern horoscopy sixteenth-century astrology could be.

Although no *natus* is mentioned in connection with this manuscript figure, research into ephemerides of the period enables us to establish that it was cast for 31 July 1553. Among the Latin phrases within the inner quadrate, we find the following specialist terms, which I examine in the order they appear, reading downwards, from left to right.

The opening word, *Revol*, or *Revolution*, tells us what kind of horoscope this is. The first line, which is a key to the horoscope, translates, 'Here begins the revolution for the 36 year, according to [the method] of Cardan'. A revolution chart is cast for a given future year, according to the moment when the Sun is 'revolved' to precisely the same degree as it had held in the radical chart.[26] The chart proves to be a revolution for a birth that had occurred on 31 July 1517.[27]

The *Chronocrator* is a measure, or marker, of time. In astrology, the term is applied to one of the planets – most usually to the so-called 'superior' planets, Saturn, Jupiter and Mars. In this case, the text tells us that the chronocrator is that connected with the period from the 34th year and 140 days, to the 36th year and 170 days – the period being examined in the chart. The period set out here (approximately) from the age of thirty-four to thirty-six, fell under the rulership of Mars.[28]

The *gubernator aestatis*, or the governor of age, is the planet said to relate to the period of human life under question in the chart. At first, it is tempting to assume that the term refers to the *alcocoden* (of Arabic astrology) – the planet that determines the length of life. However, such a question really has no relevance to a revolution chart, for the *alcocoden* may only be determined by reference to the radical chart. In view of this, we must assume that the term refers to the Ptolemaic system of Seven Ages, whereby each of the seven planets was accorded a distinct rule over a specified period in the life of the native. The Sun was regarded as the ruler of the period from twenty-three to forty-two years of age.[29] The period, from the approximate thirty-fourth to the approximate thirty-sixth year, falls firmly under this time-frame ruled by the Sun. Thus, the entire revolution chart falls under the Sun.

The fourth line distinguishes two Lords. *The Dns orbis [dominus orbis]*, or the 'Lord of the Orb', is specified as Jupiter. By the early sixteenth century, the term 'orb' was already archaic when applied to the planet itself, rather than to the orb, deferent or revolving 'wheel', which was supposed to carry the planet. The Lord of the Orb is the equivalent of the Planetary Ruler, or Planetary Lord of the Horoscope (more usually, in English astrology) the 'Lord of the Geniture'. (It is from such terminologies that horoscopy derives the general term 'Lordships'.) There was much argument in astrological circles as to which rules properly determined this Lord. In the ancient Graeco-Roman tradition, which passed into certain streams of medieval horoscopy, the Lord of the Geniture was the ruler of the sign into which the Moon moved subsequent to the birth. In this case, the Lord would be Mercury (as the Moon next passes into Gemini). Clearly, this ancient rule was not being applied here. Another method of determining the Lord of the Geniture was to select that planet with the most dignities, determined by rather complex rules, based on the relative position of the horoscope, in sign and house, aspects received, and so on. In this particular chart, Jupiter is designated Lord because he has the most dignities. Jupiter is rising in the sign Virgo and is angular. Furthermore, it is in harmonious trine to the mutable Moon. Those who followed one or other of the Arabic astrologies would call this Lord the *Almuten*.

The *Dominus figurae coelestis*, or 'Lord of the celestial figure' (that is, Lord of the chart itself) is in this case Scorpio. Even by the first half of the sixteenth century, the notion that a 'Lord' could be a zodiacal sign was being dispensed with. However, the distinction being drawn here is between a planetary ruler, which is a planet, and the Lord of the Figure, which is a zodiacal sign. In terms of modern astrology, the distinction has no meaning and, in this case, it is a powerful reminder that we are dealing with a highly personalised astrology. We must hazard a guess as to why, in this particular chart, Scorpio is being emphasised as a Lord. It is probably connected with the fact that Scorpio was the ascendant in the radical chart.

The phrase 'conjunction of Jupiter *particularis* to the Sun' involves a highly specialist terminology no longer used in astrology. The shortest of the three measures of time involving Jupiter or Saturn, which was a period of twenty years, was called either *minimus* or *specialis*.[30] The unidentified astrologer seems to be using the term *particularis* within such a context, and pointing to the effect of the conjunctions between Jupiter (the Lord of the Horoscope) and the Sun (itself the determinant in the revolution). In the chart itself we can see that the Sun is approaching another beneficial conjunction with Jupiter.

Pfects is a contraction of *Profectus*, a term which seems to have come into astrology during the twelfth century.[31] Profections refers to the technique of directing movable points in a chart at a predetermined arc per year in order to reveal future trends. The measure of the arc sometimes varied from astrologer to astrologer, but it was usual for this to be a 'sign' of 30 degrees. In annual profections, the natal ascendant was moved forward a whole sign for each year – thus moving forward in twelve-year cycles. In monthly profections, a single sign represented a single month. The selection of the starting point for this profection of a sign was determined by the subject matter of the intended enquiry or prediction, and is determined mainly by the readings of the houses: thus, a question relating to the wife of a subject, or to his marriage, was profected from the house of marriage – the cusp of the seventh house. In terms of astrological theory of the period, only the radical chart could offer a valid basis for profections.[32] From the figure before us, it is not at all clear how the astrologer obtained 4 Scorpio by profection.

Cor Coeli means literally 'the heart of the heavens'. This is one of several medieval terms denoting the *Medium Coeli* (or Midheaven). In this particular case, the tenth-house cusp is 29 Gemini. However, since this is an equal house charting, the cusp degree of the tenth is the same as that on the ascendant. The degree of the *Cor Coeli* is not always identical to that on the cusp of the tenth: however, in this particular case an ascendant of 29 Virgo will give an MC of 29 Gemini at latitudes in northern Italy.

Dominus anni, or Lord of the Year, is a term reserved for a revolution figure, and is sometimes also used in ingress charts, cast for the opening of the seasons. In this particular case, the Lord of the Year is said to be Mercury. The Lord of the Year is determined by means of an estimate of relative dignities. In this case, Mercury is determined Lord because it is the ruler of the signs on both the ascendant and the tenth-house cusp.[33] Furthermore, Mercury is suffused by the impulse of Venus (with which it is in conjunction) and by Mars (with which it is in sextile aspect).

At the bottom of the chart, the phrase *foedaria Luna et Sol* means 'union, or compact between Moon and Sun'. This is the equivalent of the modern technical term syzygy, or eclipse. Of course, no eclipse has been symbolised in the chart itself. The line of text, detached from the main quadrate, signals a Ptolemaic doctrine which is, to some extent, still recognised in modern horoscopy. According to this teaching, when an eclipse takes place, the degree in which it falls is accorded a temporary empowerment, or strength. The eclipse nearest to the birth of a native engenders such a sensitised degree in the chart – a degree that will be operative for the entire lifetime of the native. In this particular case, the next conjunction (syzygy) of Sun and Moon in Scorpio (*iuxta Sco.*), would be on 6 November 1553, in 23.23 degrees of that sign. This degree would mark an important sensitive point in the chart, and would have a consequent effect on the life of the native, whenever it was subject to tenancy by other planets.

The emphasis within the inner quadrate for this chart is on Lordships, or hierarchy of planetary rulers, determined by specially formulated rules which have little or no application in modern astrology. This realm of Lordships – so important to medieval astrology – lost favour as the sixteenth century progressed. Indeed, by the early nineteenth century the English astrologer James Wilson was minded to dismiss the entire edifice of Lordships as 'ridiculous', and the theory of dignities, on which the Lordships were based, as 'all nonsense and absurdity'.[34] Unfortunately, the publication of this view was tantamount to dismissing an astrology that had been regarded as valid for almost a thousand years.

Jerome Cardan was the first European astrologer to collect and publish a number of charts in book form.[35] His first work in this field included exactly 100 nativities. On the top row of the opposite page, I reproduce two horoscopes from Cardan's book. These are the nativities of the Italian chiromancer Barthèmy Cocles and the great physician–anatomist Andrea Vesalius.[36]

The collection included a personal revolution chart for the age of thirty-five, and his own conception chart.[37] On the bottom row, is a portrait of Cardan alongside a chart he cast for his

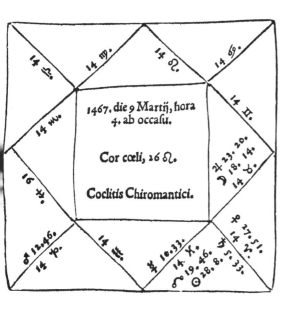

1467. die 9 Martij, hora 4. ab occasu.

Cor cœli, 26 ♌.

Coclitis Chiromantici.

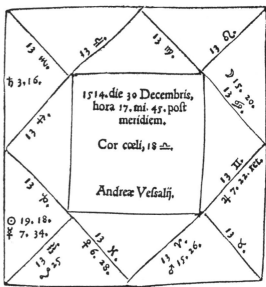

1514. die 30 Decembris, hora 17. mi. 45. post meridiem.

Cor cœli, 18 ♎.

Andreæ Vesalij.

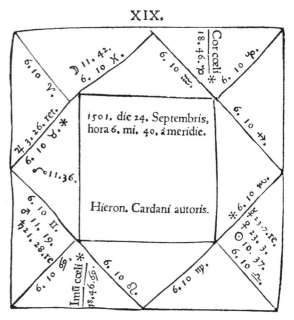

XIX.

1501. die 24. Septembris, hora 6. mi. 40. à meridie.

Hieron. Cardani autoris.

own nativity. One observes the proximity of Jupiter to the ascendant – an indication of how Cardan would survive the numerous difficulties and vicissitudes of his life, brought about mainly by the square between the Moon (11.42 Pisces) and Mars (11.19 Gemini). The chart is cast according to the equal house system and offers us an opportunity to see how the Midheaven is not always equated with the tenth-house cusp. In this case, the tenth house is 6.10 Aquarius, while (as the chart records) the *Cor Coeli* is 18.46 Capricorn.

Cardan, born at the very beginning of the sixteenth century, is among the more interesting astrologers of the age. His father, a well-known scholar and a friend of Leonardo da Vinci, had encouraged his son to study medicine.[38] In his choice of this profession, he was like many astrologers of that particular century (including Michel Nostradamus), who used medicine as a secure base for a later study of astrology. Cardan became one of the most famous doctors in Milan – later, his reputation is said to have been second only to that of Vesalius in the whole of Europe. Like his near-contemporary, the Florentine artist Benvenuto Cellini, Cardan left a racy autobiography, from which we learn a great deal about the conditions of the times.[39] In 1570, when he was well established as a professor of medicine at Bologna University, he was arrested by the Inquisition on charges of heresy – some say, for having cast the horoscope of Christ (which he certainly had done on at least two occasions), and for implying that the events surrounding His life and death could have fallen under the influence of the planets. Cardan was forced to recant and to abandon teaching. Ironically, after he was released from the Inquisitor's prison he was adopted as a special friend by Pope Pius V (a comparison between the charts of Cardan and Pius is of deep interest).[40]

The Italian astrologer and palmist, Luca Gauricus, was the second astrologer to publish a collection of genitures, in which he assembled and commented upon over a hundred and sixty charts.[41] However, the most important of such collections of genitures was that published in 1573 by the Florentine astrologer, Francesco Giuntini, whose Latinised name was Junctinus. This enormous work, which was an extensive and detailed commentary on the astrological writings of Ptolemy, contained over four hundred charts. Below are two charts from this collection. These are the nativities of the Polish astronomer, Nicolas Copernicus, and that of Mary, Queen of Scots.[42] In the chart for Copernicus one notes the platic trine between Mercury and the Moon, which is a classic example of a well-developed and sensitive intellect. However,

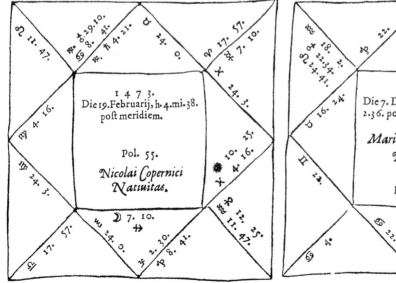

as is often the case with genius, the true influence is not represented in symbolic form within the figure. In 1473, Mercury was in the same degree as the fixed star Alpheratz. (In 1473, Alpheratz was in 6.56 Aries, 14 minutes from exact conjunction with Mercury.) Traditionally, this gives an active mind and one that develops pioneering work that brings the native into prominence. The native will write on science.[43]

As one of the above charts has suggested, during the sixteenth century there was an impulse to relate astrology and palmistry. Cocles, besides being a leading chiromancer, was a well-established astrologer; Gauricus practised both arts with equal success. Given this background, it is not surprising to find a number of astrologers attempting to show that the structure of the human hand was paralleled by factors in the corresponding birth chart. The German astrologer, Joannes Rothmann, published a number of quadrate charts at the centre of which were images of the hands of the natives (below).[44] His main purpose was to point to similarities between the hand structure and the natal chart.

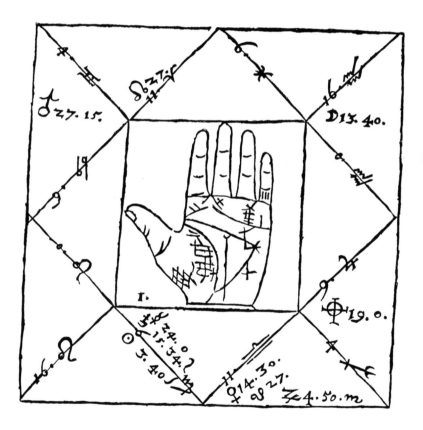

In reference to the example above, Rothmann pointed to the three vertical lines on the lower joint of the little finger. These, he insists, reveal the domination of Mercury, the giver of wit and 'commendable behaviour'. These lines are reflected in the placing of the planet Mercury, which is in its own house (Virgo, on the fourth-house cusp) and therefore an indication of mental ingenuity.

Although such innovations as astro-palmistry were explored in the sixteenth century, it is the more conservative side of astrology that must be emphasised — that side of the art which served the ruling classes. An examination of the published writings of the important astrologers of that period carries us firmly into the courts of Europe, where some of the horoscopes which they cast for their royal patrons are still preserved in manuscript form in various private or public archives. If we follow such astrologers as Luca Gauricus and Nostradamus, we are led to the several courts of Catherine de' Medici in France. If we enquire into the work of the Danish astrologer, Matthias Hacus Sumbergius, we are led to the charts he cast for the dour and serious-minded Philip II of Spain, who kept his own horoscope in a bedside book, now in the Royal Library in Madrid. If we seek the horoscopy of the German astrologer Nicholas Kratzer, we find ourselves in the court of Henry VIII, where Kratzer served as astronomer, horologer, cosmographer and astrologer, and (unwittingly) as a prototype for his more famous near-equivalent, John Dee, who worked for Henry's daughter, Elizabeth I, in a similar vein.[45]

I shall examine one or two sample charts from these royal stables, shortly. Meanwhile we should study a chart of the most important royal personage in the first half of the sixteenth century, Philip II. A large number of horoscopes for the birth of Philip have survived as it was essential that the character and futurity of so important a monarch were known, if only to his enemies. For example, when Philip visited London as the consort of Mary Tudor, John Dee (who was introduced to Philip) was required to cast his horoscope. Among other important astrologers who were required to cast Philip's chart were Junctinus, Luca Gauricus and Johannes Stadius.[46]

The excellent Danish astrologer, Sumbergius, also cast the chart, at Philip's own request. This was seemingly intended for Philip's eyes only, as it was preserved by him and remained for a number of centuries in the Escorial, Philip's esoteric mausoleum–palace.

Having cast the estimated chart, Sumbergius then adjusted it, or, as he wrote on the figure itself, *rectificata per Animodar & Conceptionem* — 'rectified, according to the Animodar and the time of Conception'. His purpose was to ensure that the star, Caput Herculis, was rising on the ascendant. Unusually — and no doubt to impress his royal client — Sumbergius wrote in the name of the star alongside the ascendant. There were strong mythological, political and symbolical reasons why Philip II should have been linked with Hercules, for, in order to evoke powerful mythologies, Philip was sometimes eulogised as the Hercules of the North. Unfortunately, there seems to have been no valid astrological reasons for this link. The star, which is the *alpha* of the constellation Hercules, was also known as Ras Algethi. Even taking precession into account, this suggests that Sumbergius was playing fast and loose with the star, and with his client's ascendant. For example, in 1583, about fifty years after Philip was born, Junctinus located the star Ras Algethi in 8.44 Sagittarius.[47] Ras Algethi was nowhere near the ascendant in Philip's chart, and it was erroneous of the astrologer to link Philip's ascendant with this star of Hercules. However, Sumbergius was by no means the only astrologer to dislodge the stars in order to stroke the ego of a needy or powerful client.[48]

This understandable involvement with the royal courts of Europe, and with the aristocracy within those courts, was only one aspect of sixteenth-century astrology. It is this aristocratic side of astrology that has tended to be preserved, due to the literacy and influence of the royal circles. Yet there was a vast undercurrent of a more popular astrology, designed to serve ordinary people such as seamen (ever anxious about their safety in pirate-infested and storm-scourged seas), soldiers (anxious about their prospects in coming wars), and a whole bevy of womenfolk perpetually anxious about their loved ones, their lovers and their husbands – the last often suspected of infidelity, or of being lost or dead in distant lands or seas.[49] Simon Forman's diary offers an extraordinary cross-sectional view of these lower strata of Elizabethan society, and it is fitting that we should glance at a chart he cast for a female client with whom Shakespeare may have been in love (see page 72).

In the heyday of arcane symbolism a number of non-astrological works made use of horoscopes as diagrams. An outstanding example of this is the figure used as a surround for the portrait of the *duc* de Nevers, Louis de Gonzague, on the title page of a book published in 1588 (below).[50] The portrait (like that of his wife, which appears on the same title page) is said to

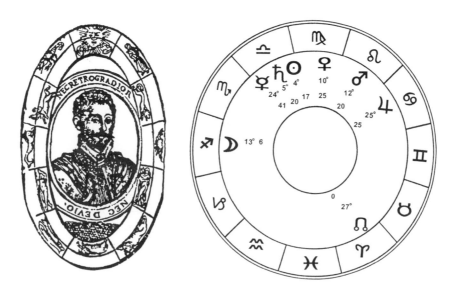

have been drawn for the wood-cutter by the English miniaturist, Nicholas Hilliard.[51] The oval surround contains the twelve signs of the zodiac, along with a tenth-house Sun, in Libra. The cunning double oval band is clearly designed to permit the insertion of the planets against the appropriate signs. The chart alongside is cast for the birth of Louis de Gonzague. The symbolism of the printed chart was intended to serve as much more than merely a blank horoscope: it was designed to illustrate the force of the Duke's personal motto: *Nec retrogradior nec devio* (neither am I made to go backwards, nor do I deviate). The point is that neither the twelve signs of the zodiac nor the Sun can go retrograde – nor can they deviate from their allotted paths. The zodiacal signs themselves mark out a path, which is followed faithfully by the Sun.

The first decades of the sixteenth century were of special interest in the history of horoscopy. It was during this period that the argument between the Arabists and the traditionalists came to a head. The nub of the argument among practitioners concerned which of the two streams of astrology was most valid for the purposes of horoscopic prediction – the Arabic or the Ptolemaic.

During the sixteenth century, the Arabic horoscopy was popular among several of the astrologers working in the papal courts – especially at that of Pope Paul III, who was to become one of the great supporters of both astronomy and astrology.[52] Given that, during the first three-quarters of the sixteenth century, Islam was thundering loudly at the very gates of Europe, it is quite astonishing to see just how Arabised was the astrology used by those practitioners working in Rome. For example, in 1548, when the astrologer Marius Alterius was struggling (unsuccessfully, as it happened) with his own version of Paul's chart to work out how many years the Pope would continue on the throne of St Peter, he quite openly quoted such Arabian astrologers as Almansor, Albubater, Messahala and Albumasar.[53] Towards the end of Paul's life,

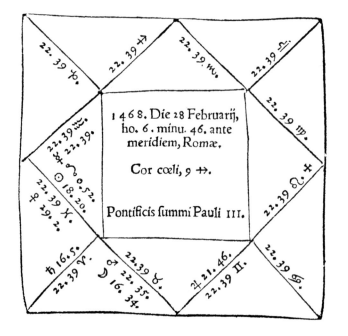

Juana de Aguilera cast solar revolutions based on the Pope's radical chart, revealing in his interpretation a fondness for Haly Abenragel.[54] Against this background, the chart cast by Jerome Cardan for Paul III (left) is interesting because of the prominence he gave to fixed stars – a tradition which owed a great deal to the Arabic astrologers, as so many of the star names indicate.[55]

Cardan's reading is of great interest to historians of astrology, for two main reasons. First, he used several now-defunct names of certain stars. Second, his text offered a refreshing insight into the complexity of medieval star lore. For example, we learn from the text that Cardan is prepared to link Jupiter not merely with one individual star (as would happen in modern astrology) but with no fewer than four stars and star groups – surely a most difficult combination from which to abstract meaning. Below, I give the relevant Latin section relating to the horoscope followed by a translation. The words contained within square brackets are my own interpolations, necessary to make sense of the text for a modern reader.

SAturnus cũ præcedente flexus piſcium, magnitudinis quar tæ, naturæ Saturni, & parum Mercurij.
Iupiter cum dextro Orionis humero, magnitudinis primæ, naturæ Martis & Mercurij: & cum dextro aurigæ humero, ma= gnitudinis ſecundæ, naturæ præcedentis: corpore autem iunctus ſummitati clauæ Orionis magnitudinis quintæ, naturæ Iouis & Saturni: atcჳ quartæ ſtellæ adiacentium cornu boreali tauri, ma gnitudinis quintæ, naturæ Martis, in uia lactea.
Mars eſt inter Vergilias, ſunt autẽ naturæ Martis & Lunæ.
Luna eſt cum cauda arietis, magnit: quartæ, naturæ Veneris.
In Occidentis angulo eſt regulus, ubi & Iouis ſextilis.

Saturn is with the preceding star in the spine of Pisces, of the fourth magnitude, and of the nature of Saturn with a little Mercury.

Jupiter is on the right upper arm of Orion [Betelgeuse, which is now situate on the right shoulder]: it is of the first magnitude, and has the equivalent nature of Mars and Mercury. [Jupiter is also with the star] on the right arm of Auriga [Menkalinan, the beta of Auriga, now situate on the right shoulder]: it is a star of the second magnitude, and of the same nature as the preceding star. But the body [of the planet] is joined to the very tip of the cudgel of Orion, which is of the fifth magnitude, and of the nature of Jupiter and Saturn. [Jupiter is also with] the four stars [125, 132, 136 and 139] running along the northern horn of Taurus [that is, El Nath]; these are of the fifth magnitude, of the nature of Mars, in the Milky Way.

Mars is in the Vegilias [Pleiades], which are of the nature of Mars and Moon.

The Moon is with the tail of Aries [probably the epsilon of Aries], of the fourth magnitude, and of the nature of Venus.

On the descendant is the star Regulus, wherein it is of the influence of Jupiter sextile.[56]

There is a certain degree of overkill in the representation of these stellar influences, and it is not clear which influences are deemed to predominate.[57] Even so, the translation reveals just how important the tradition of fixed star interpretation was held to be in medieval astrology.

In contrast to the influential following of the Arabist astrology which flourished under Paul III, it is interesting to study the work of Valentine Naibod. It is a pity that Naibod is remembered now only for his famous measure (used in predictive astrology – see below), as his studies of Ptolemy were both forthright and instructive. Relevant to our own study, Naibod rejected the notion of ingress charts based on the vernal equinox – not because this was an Arabic invention, but because he preferred eclipses as the basis for prediction. He argued that eclipses were not only 'valid, but easier to determine [mathematically]'.[58]

The sixteenth-century fashion which led astrologers to publish their own horoscopes was indulged in by Naibod. His personal chart is reproduced below, along with dramatic proof of his fidelity to the old tradition of Ptolemaic astrology, which is a graphic representation of the now-archaic theory of sign-listening relationships, for which there is a word in Greek but no suitable translation in English. According to Ptolemy, certain signs were *Imperantia* (or 'commanding'), while others were *Obedientia* (or 'obeying'). For example, from this diagram we see that Cancer is a commanding sign, which is listened to, or obeyed, by Sagittarius.[59] Ptolemy had introduced these terms in his *Tetrabiblos*, but he had not related the two terms to the zodiacal decans, or three-fold divisions of the signs, as had Naibod in his diagram.

Although a great champion of Ptolemy's astrology, Naibod seemed very anxious to 'improve' on the writings of the Alexandrian. Far more influential than this diagram of relationships was his treatment of Ptolemy's method of prediction. For a useful and valid measure of future time, which could be used in prediction, Ptolemy had proposed a measure that is now known as 'a degree for a year'. Naibod famously refined this tradition by proposing an adjustment, so that one degree of arc should be regarded as the equivalent of 1 year and 5 days.[60] Within a short time, Naibod's Measure had replaced that of his hero, Ptolemy.

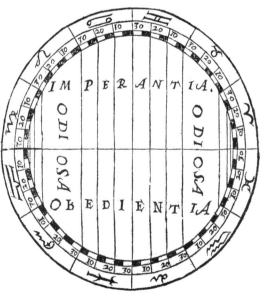

Many astrologers of the sixteenth century, including Naibod, were painfully aware that their tables were not sufficiently precise to serve certain functions. For instance, most of them recognised that the precision required to determine the moment of the annual solar ingress into the so-called zero degree of Aries was beyond the remit of late medieval charts. For this reason, some astrologers rejected the validity of such charts, which were frequently used as the basis for annual predictions.

As we shall discover below, even the great astronomer Tycho Brahe was unable to produce really accurate tabulations of the planetary positions. I have no wish to suggest that Tycho Brahe was an inept astrologer; rather, I wish merely to point to the nature of sixteenth-century tabulations. By modern standards, the planetary tables in use – especially those for Mercury – were insufficiently accurate for really precise horoscopy, and, in these terms at least, many charts were doomed to predictive failure.

The sixteenth century was especially rich in horoscopy. The following selection of horoscopes from the period has been designed to reveal something of the more influential charts, and theories, that distinguished the period. The charts range from the work-a-day horoscopy of practising astrologers to the high-flown sophistication of chart-encoding that was much loved by Renaissance scholars.

THE ANGELUS DEGREES

Although initially published towards the end of the fifteenth century, the imagery relating to John Angelus' work on zodiacal degree symbols poured over into the horoscopy of the following century.[61] Angelus (sometimes referred to by his German name, Engels) claimed no originality for his text, admitting that he was merely transmitting material from a manuscript penned by the thirteenth-century astrologer Pietro d'Abano.[62] His system was based on interpreting the degree rising on the ascendant in terms of a related 'degree symbol'. In other words, Angelus revealed what he took to be the individual significance of each of the 360 degrees of the zodiac. He expressed these meanings in short and pithy sentences, which were later accorded simple illustrations.

His published work reproduced a horoscopic form for each of the 360 degrees. Interspersed with these were twelve intriguing woodcut plates. At the top of each are three images of what we would call decans, and what Angelus called *facies* (faces) – the three 10° arcs of the relevant zodiacal sign. In our example (overleaf), this sign is Pisces, as indicated by the image at the centre of the plate. As the text of the first 'face' (top left) indicates, this is given over to Saturn. The face indicates a person who is full of anxiety, has many thoughts of journeys or of moving from place to place, and of seeking after substance and food. The second face is given over to Jupiter, and is a face in which the person is of high mind, and is involved with great and high things. The third face is Mars, and relates to fornication and physical love (*amplexationis*), through great delight with women.

Prima facies pisciū est satni
ꝫ est anꝛietatis:cogitationū
multarum:itinerū mutandi
se de loco ad locū ingrendi
substantiam ꝫ victum.

Secunda facies est iouis
ꝫ est apꝛeciandi se multū:
voluntatis alte:peteⁿdi ac
intromittendi se de rebus
magnis ꝫ altis.

Tercia facies est martis:et
est fornicationis ꝫ amplexa
tionis:magne delectationis
cum mulieribus ꝫ diligendi
quietes.

Ascendūt duo viri vnum caput
habentes.

℃Domo litigiosus erit
ꝫ instabilis.

Uir in terra sedens.

℃Rusticus erit.

It is in the lower part of the plate that we are presented with the degree symbols proper. The degrees in question are those placed inside the first house, as marking the ascendant degree. Thus the two quadrates at the bottom of the figure are intended to mark the degree readings for the first and second degrees of Pisces, respectively.

The symbol accorded the first degree of Pisces is of two men with a communal head. The degree symbolises a troublesome and unstable man (it is not at all clear how the curious one-headed pair of figures relates to this reading). The second degree is portrayed as an image of a man sitting on the earth: it symbolises a man of a rustic nature – in fifteenth-century parlance, a serf or a simple-minded fellow.

The exotic charm of these examples belies the complexity of the book itself. The work was among those condemned by the faculty of theology at the university of Paris in the middle of the century.[63] However, as we shall see in a later chapter, the Angelus system of degree symbolism took on a new lease of life towards the end of the nineteenth century.

AN INGRESS CHART OF GAURICUS

If Naibod was prepared to condemn ingress charts as useless for predictive purposes, Luca Gauricus was not. In his ephemeris for 1533, he published an ingress chart for the coming year which, if the attached reading were to be taken seriously, promised death and destruction for a good part of Europe.[54] The chart is reproduced below, and is a good example of just how inaccurate ingress charts could be in the sixteenth century.[65] It is a reminder of how right

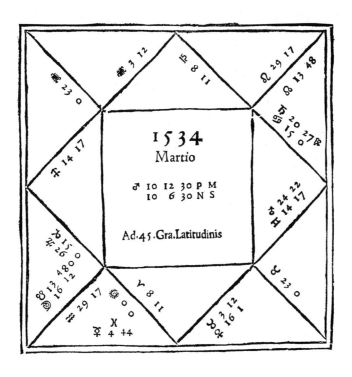

Gauricus' contemporary, the Flemish astrologer Albert Pigghe, was when he condemned extant ephemerides as insufficiently accurate to determine the precise moment of the four ingresses.

According to the planetary distribution at the ingress, Gauricus foresaw 'horrible tumult of arms … fires, rapes, depopulations, along with terrible epidemics', and, 'as the Arabs were wont to say', much fornication and little marriage. The reading was dire and, thankfully, only moderately accurate in its prophecy of coming events. In the course of 1533, Henry VIII of England declared himself Supreme Head of the English Church, and nudged aside the Pope to scoop up his revenues. In the year under analysis, the girl Elizabeth was born, daughter to Henry, and one who would become the greatest English queen of all time. These events in England caused scarcely a ripple in Europe itself. The war between Lübeck and Holstein against Denmark and Sweden was a remote if bloody affair. That Suleiman the Magnificent captured Baghdad in the same year merely added to the entrenched European fears of Islam. Any astrologer who cared to cast a revolution for Suleiman would have realised that his Sun, which stood in the same degree of the Sun in the chart for Venice, was under intense pressure from Saturn.[66]

The implications of Muslim expansion would not become evident for a few more decades. Otherwise, life went on in its accustomed, if insecure, way. What charms us about this particular chart is not its success or otherwise as an instrument of prediction, but that it contained certain specialist terms of enduring interest to historians of astrology.

THE CHRISTOPHER HATTON HOROSCOPE

Christopher Hatton, who is said to have danced his way into the favour of Queen Elizabeth I, was born at Holdenby, 6 miles from Northampton, in 1540.[67] Under the Queen's patronage he became a key player during the heady period of Elizabethan expansion. His friends included the sea-dog, Drake, the scholar, Dr John Dee, and all the important politicians of the day.

Our present interest in Hatton revolves around the fact that a surviving panel portrait, painted in the 1580s, contains what appears to be a personal horoscope (figure 2).[68] We observe that the zodiac circle is represented as equal house, with no cusps marked. This implies that the time of the supposed birth was not known to the astrologer, who therefore symbolised the eastern point at the vernal equinox. The position of the Sun, at the very top of the circle, would suggest that it is a midday natus.

In the concentric within the zodiacal circle, and beneath the feet of the planetary personifications, are painted precisely formulated zodiacal degrees and minutes. Under the zodiacal section given to Capricorn is a personification of the Sun carrying a staff, above which is a splendid radiant sunburst. The degree beneath the figure is no longer complete, but it is possible to read … 0.16 s. (the abbreviations s., sc. or scv. stand for *scrupulus*, the equivalent division of time as a minute). Alongside is the personification of Mercury, with a winged helmet, and caduceus; below, it is possible to read gr. 14 … (*gradus*, or degree 14 …). The figure alongside this, and still in the segment of Capricorn, is Jupiter, with a wand of office.

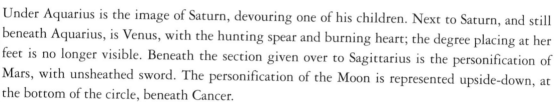

Under Aquarius is the image of Saturn, devouring one of his children. Next to Saturn, and still beneath Aquarius, is Venus, with the hunting spear and burning heart; the degree placing at her feet is no longer visible. Beneath the section given over to Sagittarius is the personification of Mars, with unsheathed sword. The personification of the Moon is represented upside-down, at the bottom of the circle, beneath Cancer.

To facilitate a reading of the planetary figures, I have reproduced above drawings of the six planetary images in the upper part of the chart. One may be forgiven for assuming that the planets, so carefully painted into the zodiacal circle, are intended to represent the horoscope of Sir Christopher Hatton. However, this is not the case. In 1540 (the year of Hatton's birth), Saturn was in Libra, Jupiter in Virgo, and Mars in Aquarius. The planetary figures given in the horoscope did not relate to planetary positions in the actual heavens for several years on either side of 1540.

The only time in the entire life of Sir Christopher Hatton when there was a correspondence between the seven painted planets and those in the skies was on 12 December 1581. The correspondence between the surviving degree positions in the painting and the actual positions held by planets on 12 December 1581 are set down (below) in tabulated form. The question marks indicate either that the information once on the painting is no longer legible, or that it was not brushed in when the painting was made. The date 12 December 1581 signifies the only day during the entire sixteenth century when the planetary positions corresponded to those given in the painting. Since the Sun has just entered Capricorn on that day, and the Moon is nearing the end of Cancer, the date could not be adjusted, even by so little as a day.

Planet	Painting	Positions on 12 Dec. 1581
Saturn	24.[?] Aquarius	24.43 Aquarius
Jupiter	22.55 Capricorn	22.48 Capricorn
Mars	17.33 Sagittarius	17.54 Sagittarius
Sun	[?].16 Capricorn	00.44 Capricorn
Venus	[?] Aquarius	07.09 Aquarius
Mercury	14.[?] Capricorn	20.16 Capricorn
Moon	[?] Cancer	28.18 Cancer

We may search the known details of Hatton's life in vain for an explanation of the importance accorded to this date in the portrait. The year 1581 followed the return of Drake after his incredible voyage of circumnavigation of the world. One of Drake's ships had been named *Christopher*, in honour of Sir Christopher Hatton.[69] In 1578, during the voyage and while off the Magellan Straits, Drake changed the name of his own flagship from *Pelican* to *Golden Hind*. Once again, this renaming was done 'in remembrance of his honourable friend and favourer' – Hatton's cognisance was a golden hind (this may be seen as a crest on the arms, to the top right of the painting). Hatton had put money, as a speculation, on Drake's secret trip. Later, in 1581, the spire of St Paul's – the 'Luck' of London – fell in a wild storm. Sir Christopher was one of the two officials delegated to see to its refurbishing. Apparently, as the reconstruction began, one contemporary suggested that the *Golden Hind*, now a popular attraction in the port, should be raised and set on the broken tower as a suitable replacement symbol for the spirit of London. Thus the year did prove to be an eventful one for Hatton, but there is no special event – no promotion, for example – that would reveal why an artist should have painted his portrait inset within a horoscope for that specific day in 1581.

In fact, the painted horoscope proves to be a revolution chart, cast to reveal the tenor of Hatton's future. It was a reasonable time to erect a revolution, as Hatton was on the point of entering his forty-second year. In astrology, this year is regarded as a climacteric – a most significant year in relation to the life.[70] Not only was it an important septenary year (6×7), but, according to Elizabethan numerology, it was held to be linked with a historical epoch. All in all, the forty-second year was believed to mark a most important development in the life of any man or woman.

The painting has been ascribed to the workshop of William Segar, but the name of the astrologer is unknown. However, there was one contact which Hatton did have with astrology in that year. Among Hatton's many friends was John Maplet, who dedicated to Hatton his book on astrology in that year, 1581.[71]

That the chart itself is intended as a mystery of time is reflected in the symbolism on the back of the painted panel. The front of the panel relates to a specific day, while the back of the panel, dominated by the image of a wing-footed Tempus, points to time in general. The theme of mortality is reflected in the portrayal of one of the three mythological sisters of Fate, Lachesis, who cuts the thread of life – or, as the inscription on the panel puts it, *Lachesis Trahit*. Furthermore, the long Latin passage, headed *Tractatus de Tempore*, deals with time: this has been identified with a Greek epigram, and is certainly involved with themes relating to time that were popular during the Renaissance.[72]

All in all, the picture is among the most arcane zodiacal works produced in Elizabethan England, but this is not the place to examine in detail the symbolism of this two-sided panel. However, it is worth mentioning that the figure of the astrologer, to the right of the bottom register in the painting, points with his stick (*virga*, in Latin) to the sign Virgo, on the celestial sphere. No doubt this is intended as a sly reference to the Virgin Queen, Hatton's personal friend. Perhaps this friendship, or love, is hinted at in a major deviation of the symbolism in this zodiacal strip, on the celestial sphere. Following the sign Virgo, we do not find the sigil for the next sign, Libra, but the sigil for Venus, the planet of love.

Perhaps there is a real mystery about this planet, Venus. As we have seen, when people are attracted to each other, there is usually some communality in their charts. Elizabeth I and Christopher Hatton were no exception: the fact that Elizabeth could elevate him from comparative obscurity to the most important position in England has something to do with their charts.

Because of this revolution chart, we can calculate that Christopher Hatton was born on 12 December 1540, at about 2:15 PM. If we compare the chart cast for this birth with that of Elizabeth, we find some interesting communal degrees. One of the planets involved in these communalities is the Venus in Elizabeth's chart: she had been born between three and four in the afternoon, on 7 September 1533, in London.[73] Hatton's Cauda is on Elizabeth's Venus:

Cauda in chart of Hatton:	03.6 Libra
Venus in chart of Elizabeth:	03.49 Libra

THE MINI-HOROSCOPES OF NOSTRADAMUS

Although Michel Nostradamus is now chiefly remembered for his extraordinary prophecies, his sixteenth-century contemporaries regarded him as a proficient astrologer. 'To the most famous erudite man, pre-eminent in virtue, Michel Nostradamus, doctor in medicine and in astrology, my incomparable and venerated master', began the German merchant Lorenz Tubbe, in a letter he addressed to the savant, on 1 January 1560, concerning his own chart.[74]

Surprisingly, none of the original manuscript horoscopes cast by Nostradamus has survived. Until fairly recently, the only horoscopes undoubtedly in his hand were those that appeared as woodcut prints in his published almanacs.[75] However, a few years ago a collection of copies of his letters, in Latin, French and Greek, was discovered, among which were a number of copies of horoscopes he had cast for clients and friends.[76] The letters and charts were preserved, partly at the instigation of César, Nostradamus' son, in the library of the famous scholar, Peiresc. The modern historian, Dupèbe, is of the opinion that the letters and nativities were copied in the second half of the sixteenth century, with a view to publication.

A copy of such a chart for the German industrialist Johannes Rosenberger is reproduced overleaf, alongside a 'translation', with accurate positions for the given time. This chart reveals how Nostradamus (or, at least, the copyist) indicated the planetary positions in Roman numerals. The figure serves as a useful record of a horoscope that was rectified by events in the life of the native (that is, as Nostradamus put it, *per accidentia rectificato*).[77]

We can learn a great deal about sixteenth-century astrology from the horoscopes and personal letters, which passed between Nostradamus and his clients. We learn of Nostradamus' penchant for solar revolutions as an aid to prediction (for example, he drew up at least fourteen solar revolution charts, for predictive purposes, on behalf of his client, Rosenberger).[78] We learn of

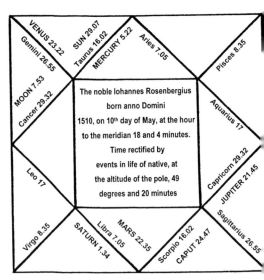

The noble Iohannes Rosenbergius born anno Domini 1510, on 10th day of May, at the hour to the meridian 18 and 4 minutes. Time rectified by events in life of native, at the altitude of the pole, 49 degrees and 20 minutes

Nostradamus' tendency to use only quadrate charts. We note that when the birth time was unknown, he would use a local midday chart, rather than a solarscope, cast for the moment of sunrise. We learn, furthermore, that he is inclined to use the *Modus Rationalis* house system of Regiomontanus, and the ephemerides of Stöffler. Revealed are the extraordinary pressures put on Nostradamus to cast charts for individuals, at a time when he was deeply preoccupied with his personal studies and writing, and, from his own letters, we sense his private indignation at such importunities. It is made clear that many of his clients cannot fully understand his analyses, suggesting that he wrote these with the same learned obscurity as he penned the famous prophetic quatrains. We learn that Nostradamus wore a finger ring, on which were carved symbols of his own personal birth chart.[79]

I shall not dwell on the horoscope copies preserved in this collection, for there is nothing in them which is either original or indicative of the genius of Nostradamus: indeed, many of them have been transmitted in a terrible state of inaccuracy. Rather than dealing with the charts themselves, I will touch upon that element within the horoscopy of Nostradamus which is unique to this enigmatic astrologer.

Nostradamus is the only astrologer known to me who had the ability to cast predictively accurate horoscopes for events centuries in the future. No word has yet been coined for this unique ability, but if it were, then it might be something like *praeterhoroscopy* –'beyond horoscopy'. There are few more astounding examples of this complex and difficult art than in the miniature horoscopes Nostradamus cast for events that would unfold in the troubled eighteenth century, over three hundred years after his own death.

As early as 1555, Nostradamus had foreseen the coming of the guillotine in the eighteenth century, the mass murders in the major French cities, the carnage in such towns as Lyon, and especially in Paris, where a spectacle of horrors was displayed daily, and where the French King and Queen, Louis XVI and Marie Antoinette, were murdered in public.

After contemplating this unwelcome future for his beloved France, Nostradamus decided to write a prophetic verse about the coming events. He cast around for a method by which he might encode in the verse a record of the precise year in which the horror would begin. At length, while writing the prophetic verses he decided to adopt a technique which he had used several times: he resorted to astrology, and constructed what can only be described as a 'mini-horoscope'. In his verse, Nostradamus described a planetary relationship which he foresaw would occur on the first day of 1789. The entire quatrain, reproduced from the 1557 edition of his verses, is given below.[80]

> **Faulx à l'eſtan ioinĉt vers le Sagitaire,**
> **Et ſon hault A V G E de l'exaltation:**
> **Peſte famine, mort de main militaire,**
> **Le ſiecle approche de renouation.**

For all they are almost incomprehensibly obscure (even for a fluent reader of French), the first two lines prove to be astrological in nature. They read and translate:

> Faux à l'estan, joinct vers le Sagitaire,
> Et son hault AUGE de l'exaltation:

> [The scythe in the pond, joined near Sagittarius,
> And his high fixed-point of exaltation.]

The most arcane term in the two lines is the word AUGE, which (for the moment) I translate as 'fixed-point' – though, in simple language, an 'auge' is really a bucket fixed on a revolving water-wheel to scoop up water. Nostradamus had set out the astrological conditions in a sort of code which only a person familiar with sixteenth-century astrology might unravel. However, if we examine the lines in the light of astrological symbolism, they do begin to reveal some hint of their meanings.

As the sixteenth-century woodcut overleaf indicates, the scythe (*Faux*) is the attribute of Saturn: the pond (*l'etang*) is probably a reference to the water sign Pisces, for fishes swim in ponds.[81]

It seems that Nostradamus has in mind a future time when the planet Saturn will be in Pisces. Further, the line seems to hint that Saturn will be in conjunction (that is, *joinct*) with some other unnamed planet.

I must examine the specialist term *exaltation* with some trepidation. First, it has a specialist meaning in astrology – in the astrological tradition a single degree is said to mark the exaltation of a particular planet. The traditional degrees are:

Sun	Moon	Mercury	Venus	Mars	Jupiter	Saturn	Caput
19 ♈	3 ♉	15 ♍	27 ♓	28 ♑	15 ♋	21 ♎	3 ♊

The term *AUGE del'exaltation* has an even more specialist sense in sixteenth-century astronomy. The sixteenth-century Scottish astrologer James Bassantin had used the term several times in a work that he dedicated to Nostradamus' patron, Catherine de' Medici. However, this work did not appear in print until 1562, some years after Nostradamus had published the quatrain. Almost certainly, Nostradamus learned the term either from Bassantin directly, or from some precursor to the book, with which I am not familiar. It is unlikely that Bassantin invented the word.

Although a Scot, Bassantin wrote his work directly in French. One consequence is that – especially in the technical parts – his meaning is not always clear. Evidently, the Auge is a point which may be fixed in relation to the planets.[82] In Bassantin's book is a magnificent plate which seems to be a map of the heavens but which turns out to be a volvelle, or circular diagram, placed over another diagram and pinned at the centre so that it will revolve upon its own centre.[83] On the circumference of the movable part are small pointers, distributed at irregular intervals (Figure. 3). Each of these is marked with one of the planets, while one has been labelled

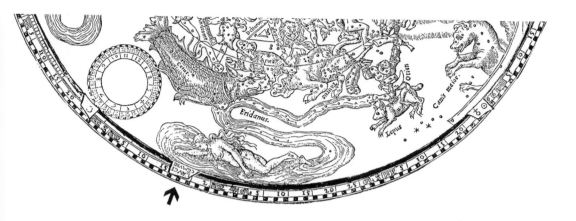

by Bassantin as *L'Auge Comuni* or 'the communal Auge' – a kind of communal pivot. This latter is marked on the circumference of figure 3 (and in the detail above) with the pointer, ↓. If we make use of this Auge volvelle, we discover an odd thing. When we move the inner part of the volvelle on its fixed centre, so that the Saturn rests over 7 degrees of Pisces, then the pointer for *L'Auge Comuni* rests exactly on 15 degrees of Cancer. As we saw above, this latter degree is traditionally termed the exaltation degree of Jupiter. Thus the Auge is in Jupiter's exaltation. No doubt, this is the secret of Nostradamus' line. I have reproduced above the relevant section of the volvelle, cut from the whole figure to show the *Auge Comuni* resting on 15 Cancer, the exaltation of Jupiter.

Nostradamus' line now makes perfect sense. He is writing of a future time when Saturn – the slow marker of time – will be in 7 degrees of Pisces. Perhaps he has in mind that, on this future occasion, Saturn will also be conjoint (*joinct*) with another planet.

As Nostradamus had foreseen in 1555, the new age of 1789 did begin with cosmic conditions that reflect the first two lines of his quatrain. At the very beginning of that year, on 1 January 1789, Saturn was in 7 degrees of Pisces. It was conjunct with the Moon. Right is the horoscope for this day and time, cast for Paris: it is entitled *Vulgar Event*, because this is one of the names that Nostradamus gave to the coming French Revolution.

This chart reveals that Nostradamus had constructed his mini-horoscope in verse in order to indicate the year 1789, which he foresaw as the most difficult year in the entire history of France.

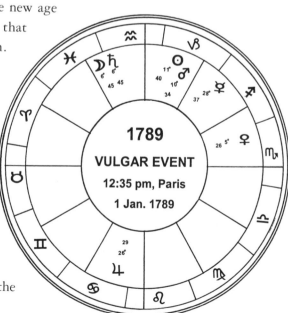

THE CHART OF SIMEONI

Among the files of recently discovered letters to Nostradamus is one dated 1 February 1556, written by the historian and esotericist Gabriel Simeoni, who was then living in Florence.[84] I refer to this letter, which reveals the two authors to be close friends, because the personal chart of Simeoni has survived, if only in a curious form.

The horoscope is part of the title-page illustration for Gabriele Simeoni's work of 1558 and is among the more interesting exemplars of this type of semi-arcane horoscopy.[85] I have reproduced it below, alongside a modern rendering of the horoscopic content. At times, I have found myself wondering if the original chart, which formed the basis of this enigmatic figure, was cast for the Florentine by Nostradamus.

Simeoni's own medallion portrait is at the centre of the oval zodiacal band, which is so arranged that the cusp between Aries and Taurus is exactly at the top. The planetary figures are disposed in lively personifications among the architectural forms that frame the zodiac. Each planet is linked with an attribute that reveals the sign it occupies. Starting from the top, we see Mercury (with the caduceus) resting on the lion: to his right is Venus, to his left, Apollo, suggesting that all three planets are in the sign Leo. In front of the pilaster to his right is Mars with buckler and spear: he is standing on the crab, a sure sign that the planet is in Cancer. In front of the pilaster to the left of Simeoni is the huntress Diana: this goddess stands on a scorpion, an indication that Venus is in Scorpio. At the base of the image, Saturn and Jupiter hold up cartouches bearing their corresponding signs: Saturn, with his scythe, is in Virgo, while crowned Jupiter is in Sagittarius.

There can be no doubt that the illustration is a formal representation of Simeoni's personal horoscope. This is of historical importance as, to date, scholars have been sure only of the year of Simeoni's birth, in Florence.[86] From the data contained within this title page, we can now be certain that he was born on 24 July 1509, shortly after sunrise. The modern chart above, cast for this time, indicates why this is the only possible date: the planet Mercury was just about to leave Leo at that time, and the Moon had only just entered Scorpio. Simeoni knew enough about astrology to realise that if he presented images of the planets in the signs, this would be sufficient for an astrologer with access to ephemerides for 1509 to establish exactly at what time he was born.

This arcane chart has found its way to other title pages in the published works of Gabriele Simeoni: another striking example of zodiacal imagery graces that of his 1559 translation of Ovid.[87]

TYCHO BRAHE'S NOVA CHART

It was not until the seventeenth century that the circular chart gradually came into its own, in a number of different divisional guises. However, during the sixteenth century a number of impressive circular horoscopes did appear. A distinctive example is that cast by the Danish astronomer, Tycho Brahe, for the appearance of the Nova of 1572 (below), which helped shake astronomy free of its medieval roots, by dispelling the long-held Aristotelian teaching that the heavens were immutable.[88] It is far from easy to pin down in time the appearance of a nova so Tycho adopted the convention of giving its position at the moment of the solar eclipse on 5 November 1572. As the chart below indicates, the eclipse occurred at night, in 23 Scorpio: at that moment, the nova was visible almost directly overhead, and could be seen even in daylight.

The form of this chart is distinctly stellar, and it was no doubt designed to reflect the nature of its contents.[89] Furthermore, the chart contains sixteen houses, rather than the traditional twelve. Even so, Tycho has emphasised the great cross formed by the angles, and has merely divided the third, fifth, eighth and eleventh houses. It is not easy to make sense of this division. The truth is that the eclipse fell in 23.31.34 Scorpio. At that time, at the latitude of Hveen (Uraniburg), where Tycho was working, the ascendant was 17.36 Cancer. However, Tycho's chart shows an ascendant of 27 Cancer, yet accurately gives the rounded-off degree for the eclipse.

While a house system with as many as sixteen houses may be surprising, it was by no means unique. Very likely, it was derived by Brahe from the medical horoscopic tradition. In what is sometimes called iatro-astrology, or iatromathematics, it was commonplace for doctors (who were usually also astrologers) to cast charts to reveal what were called critical periods, during illness, in both eight-house and sixteen-house figures. We shall examine two forms of these decumbiture charts in connection with the seventeenth-century astrologer Nicholas Culpeper (see pages 99–100).

In the nova chart are one or two interesting sigils. The form for Scorpio is less a sigil than a pictograph ♏. We also note that Tycho has invented his own sigil ☾ to represent the solar eclipse, which fell in 23 degrees Scorpio, and which he appears to have used as the basis for timing the appearance of the nova.[90]

The eclipse sigil had no particular agreed form until the late nineteenth century, and the sigils ☌ ☍ denoting the solar and lunar eclipses, respectively, were not universally adopted until the twentieth century. From time to time, individual medieval astrologers invented sigils for their own use, or even proposed sigils publicly, but for reasons that are obscure these were not universally adopted. A good example, from the fifteenth century, is the ☉ used in the horoscope for the eclipse of 20 July 1487, when the solar eclipse fell in 05.44 Leo (below).[91]

The sigil is nothing more than a vestigial drawing of a partial solar, with the body of the Sun partly obscured by the dark of the Moon. One observes that in this chart, the medieval sigil for

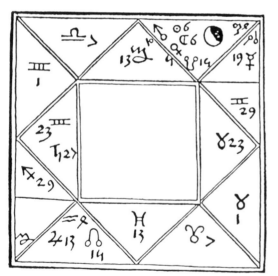

Leo ♋ has been used to denote the cusp. (Note also the distinctive sigil for the sign, Scorpio ♏.)

Being more of an astronomer than an astrologer, Tycho Brahe did not fail to emphasise in the nova chart his own particular interest: he located, with remarkable accuracy, the positions of several stars. Thus Hircus (now better known as Capella), Rigel (here represented as *Sinister pes Orion*) and Arcturus are marked in the horoscope, the last one distinguished by a graphic star, perhaps to indicate its proximity to Cauda: *Arcturus* ✳

THE PUBLIC HOROSCOPE OF ROBERT BURTON

Few horoscopes are openly displayed in European churches. However, one famous exception is that of the sixteenth-century scholar, Robert Burton, which forms an integral part of the symbolism of his memorial tomb in Christ Church, Oxford. It is claimed that this marble horoscope, mounted by his brother William to the right of his bust effigy (see below), was copied from one that Burton cast personally, and rectified by the trutina and animodar.[92]

Burton's most famous work was *The Anatomy of Melancholy*, which, in keeping with the Saturnine influence that dominated Burton's life, has been described as 'the most sententious book ever written ...'[93] Even if we did not possess the attestations of his contemporaries, we would quickly learn from this work that Burton was deeply interested in astrology. Burton set out the basic horoscopic structure of the chart in a passage from his *Anatomy* in which he reminds us that he rarely travelled far from Oxford and his beloved books.

I never travelled but in map or card, in which my unconfined thoughts have freely expatiated, as having ever been especially delighted with the study of cosmography. Saturn was lord of my geniture, culminating, etc., and Mars principal significator of manners, in partile conjunction with mine ascendant.[94]

What Burton claimed of his horoscope is true of the marble figure. Saturn *was* culminating (that is, moving close to the cusp of the Midheaven), and it was certainly the dominant planet ('lord') of the chart. Mars was in close conjunction with the ascendant of the chart. To account for his predisposition towards medicine – that is, towards being an amateur physician – Burton mentioned that he had Jupiter in his sixth house.[95] Burton's fleeting comments on his geniture are precisely noted, and always to the point, no doubt a reminder of his vast erudition in the field of horoscopy.[96] A copy of the chart from the memorial is given overleaf, alongside a modern rendering. This copy was made before the original memorial horoscope was recently vandalised.

The horoscope, incised with lines picked out in black against the light-coloured marble by some form of *niello*, is of the quadrate form and is, in some respects, the most mysterious horoscope to have survived from the seventeenth century. It is mysterious partly because there is no relation between the data in the inner quadrate and the planetary configurations in the outer

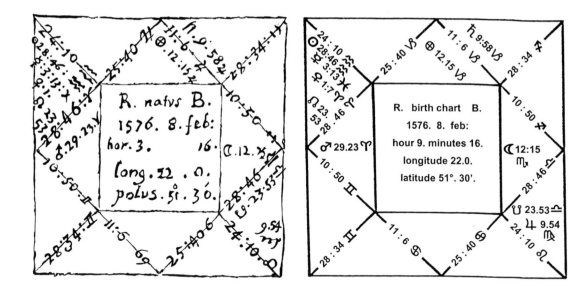

sections. As may be seen from the chart on the next page, the inner quadrate gives as date of birth 8 February 1576.[97] However, the planets displayed do not correspond to this date: they correspond to 8 February 1577.

The immediate conclusion, drawn by someone unfamiliar with the complexities of European calendrical systems, might be that Burton had his date of birth wrong, and that therefore the horoscope is incorrect. The date and time of Burton's birth were dutifully recorded in a sort of genealogical 'Book of the Burton Family'. This specifies that Burton was born at 9 AM on 8 February 1576.[98] However, if he had been born in 1576, then Saturn would not even have been in Capricorn, and near the MC – the placing which Burton himself regarded as being so important ('Saturn was lord of my geniture, culminating …'). The seeming confusion in the years may be understood in terms of certain calendrical changes.

One direct aim of the Gregorian reform of the calendar, promulgated by papal bull in 1582, was to restore the vernal equinox to 21 March. It was one of the most bitterly contested reforms in the history of Europe, and one that was not universally adopted until the Bulgarian Church accepted it in 1968. Although the edict famously removed ten days from the calendar, in order to adjust the vernal equinox, the reform also changed the beginning of the year from 25 March back to 1 January. This former reckoning was first called the *calculus Florentinus*, and later the *Mos Anglicanus*, 'the custom of the English Church': it was not finally dispensed with until 1751. It is to this confusion, pertaining to the origin of the year, that we must trace the contradictions in the Burton horoscope. It is worth emphasising this curiosity of late medieval dating systems if only because it points to one of the many difficulties facing astrologers attempting to cast charts for dates recorded during that period. If Burton had not left his own manuscript horoscope, it is more than likely that later astrologers, working from extant records of his birth and unfamiliar with the intricacies of calendrical changes, would have come up with a chart that was hopelessly inaccurate.

Besides the horoscopes drawn up in Burton's hand, two early versions of Burton's chart have survived. There is a manuscript version, probably cast by John Aubrey, in a manuscript *Collectio Geniturarum*, in the Bodleian Library, Oxford.[99] There is a well-known copy of Burton's chart (published as the horoscope of 'Henry Burton') in a work by the astrologer John Gadbury (right).[100] These two charts have one thing in common, something which is not found in the memorial horoscope. The final line in the inner quadrature reveals the most recent and future aspects of the Moon – a survival of the practice, requisite in horary charts, of indicating whether or not the Moon was void of course.

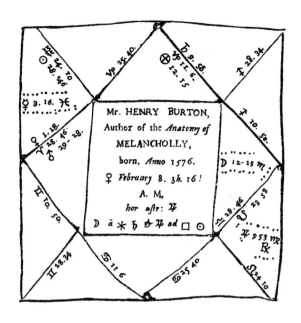

Most historians and astrologers, who have taken an interest in Burton's horoscope, have pointed to the fact that Burton is supposed to have predicted the time of his own death.[101] In the absence of his own notes or progressed charts, it is always difficult to form an opinion of how an astrologer would have directed a chart to gain a glimpse of the future. However, one example of how Burton might have perceived that 1640 would be dangerous to him could have been by his directing the Sun to a powerful evil fixed star.[102]

An analysis of the most popular methods of predicting the future during the late fifteenth century, and into the following century, is beyond the remit of this present work. It is probably sufficient to say that the majority of astrologers of that century used the art of directing planets set out by Argolus, popularly called Argol in astrological literature.[103] We know that, in the calculation of charts (and probably also in directions), Burton made use of the remarkably accurate tables drawn up by Tycho Brahe.[104]

Medieval astrologers were often alerted to important transits by their familiarity with revolution charts. Working along the lines of a revolution cast for 1640, Burton might have been alerted to the transit of the all-important Saturn over the radical prior eclipse in his natal chart, which point Ptolemy valued so highly. This eclipse fell on 24.18 Aquarius/Leo. The transit of Saturn was exact at 4:54:32 PM, on 8 March 1640. At that moment Saturn was in 24.18 Aquarius, conjunct with Mercury in 25.13 Aquarius. The lunar nodes were exactly across the MC–IC axis. On the day of death on 25 January (the time is not on record) Saturn was in orb of this position. Furthermore, the transiting Moon was in opposition to the radical Saturn. Saturn was in close orb to the radical prior eclipse line, in 24.18 Aquarius. The benign planets Venus and Jupiter were exactly conjunct, in 29 Capricorn, and therefore exactly square to the malefic radical Mars, in 29 Aries.

A CHART CAST BY SIMON FORMAN

In his surviving notebooks Simon Forman recorded that the beautiful Emilia Lanier consulted him on an astrological matter on 13 June 1597.[105]

Emilia was not the only contact Forman had with someone who knew Shakespeare. Shortly after 1600, Shakespeare took up lodgings with a Mrs Mountjoy, on the corner of Silver Street and Mugle Street, in London. By a curious chance, at this time Mrs Mountjoy was already one of Forman's clients: on 22 November 1597 she had consulted him about the loss of a number of things from her purse. Presumably the consultation was satisfactory, for she returned on several occasions to seek his astrological advice.

Emilia was the daughter of Baptista Bassano and Margaret Johnson, the father being from a family of Venetian musicians who had served as the court of Henry VIII. Emilia had been born in about 1569, but the early death of her father led to her undoing. By the time she began to consult Forman she was already unhappily married to Alfonso Lanier. She had been the mistress of the old and wealthy Lord Hunsdon, Henry Carey, the Lord Chamberlain, who had maintained her in considerable style: she had also given birth to his child, named after him.

These footnotes to history reveal an extraordinary secret for, according to the historian A.L. Rowse, the beautiful Emilia was the dark lady of Shakespeare's sonnets.[106] Forman's diary reveals that he was himself smitten by Emilia, and made every attempt he could to seduce her.

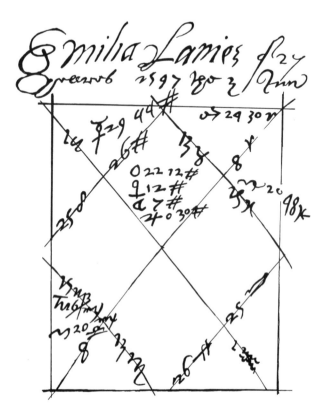

The lady disappointed him – she permitted free and intense petting, but refused intercourse.

The horoscope for the question put by Emilia to Forman on Friday 13 June 1597 (see chart alongside) is very instructive, but for surprising reasons.[107] By the standards of the day, it is a fairly ordinary horary question. Emilia has asked about the likely profit her husband might gain from his sea voyage to the Azores, under the command of Essex (this was actually a voyage of piracy against the Spanish).

Now, the fact is that when drawing up this chart Forman radically miscalculated the position of Mercury – the very planet from which it would be most suitable to estimate profit and loss. In his chart, Forman placed

Mercury in 29.44 Gemini – yet, on the day in question, it was in 04.15 Cancer. No matter what response Forman gave to Emilia's question, it is unlikely to have been correct, from an astrological point of view.

CARDAN'S HOROSCOPE FOR THE BIRTH OF JESUS

Jerome Cardan's work on genitures makes it clear that he had developed a novel approach to horoscopy – one that did not really become established practice until the late nineteenth century. Cardan began to check the reputation and professed achievements of individuals against their personal horoscopes.[108] The historian Lynn Thorndike elaborated on this approach – especially in regard to Cardan's comments on the German astrologer Regiomontanus, of whom Cardan had a very poor opinion, and whom he considered to be a plagiarist.[109] Whatever the underlying professional piques, Cardan's method marked the first signs of what may be called a scientific approach to horoscopy.

A number of historians have suggested that Cardan's undoing was the horoscope of Christ, which he cast during the 1530s and published in 1557. The Church, supported by its Mafia-like Inquisition, could not conceive of Christ as participating in human nature (for all He was said to be both Man and God), and it was a tenet of belief that natal astrology dealt only with human nature. For some churchmen, the suggestion that Christ had been subject to planetary and cosmic influences seemed heretical.[110]

Cardan's imagined theological sin was one thing, but the horoscope was another: there was no possibility of its being accurate. Even by the sixteenth century, scholars recognised that the birth of Christ did not take place on the night of 24 December (or, as Cadan put it, in *IX Calendis Ianuarii*). Nor could it have taken place in year 1 (*anni initium*), as Cardan recognised in another version of the chart he cast for the birth of Christ.[111]

The literature pertaining to the birth of Jesus Christ is too extensive for us to survey here.[112] However, in 1933 the German historian Holzmeister constructed a tabulation of 100 scholarly sources, revealing that the proposed date for the birth of Jesus, as speculatively published by scholars and ecclesiastics, was spread over a period of twenty years, between 12 BC and 9 AD.[113] The most favoured year was 3 BC, while most modern authorities placed the birth in 7 BC.

Although this means that the chart cast by Cardan (right) is of little value as an actual horoscope, it is useful for us to study the sort of chart that he was prepared to argue as

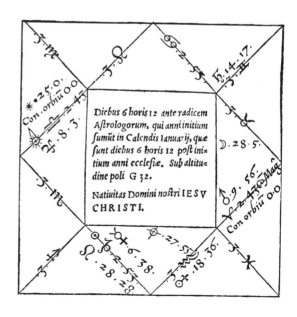

Diebus 6 horis 12 ante radicem Astrologorum, qui anni initium sumūt in Calendis Ianuarij, quæ sunt diebus 6 horis 12 post initium anni ecclesiæ. Sub altitudine poli G 32.

Natiuitas Domini nostri IESV CHRISTI.

valid for the incarnation of God.[114] Such chartings formed an important stream in sixteenth-century horoscopy.

The chart has some interesting elements: note, for example, the curious symbol meant to denote the presence of a comet, which crosses the ascendant line in 02.43 Libra. This comet was included because Cardan believed that the Star of Bethlehem, which was reported as moving from east to west, guiding the Wise Men to the new-born Child, was nothing more than a comet.

The eight-pointed star above the comet is (typical of Cardan) a reference to a fixed star, which happens to be Spica, the star in the lap of Virgo, which has for centuries been associated with Jesus. It is true that, around that first Christian year, the star which Cardan called *spica Virginis stella* (the modern Spica) was very close to 02.43 Libra, which Cardan had specified as Christ's ascendant. Earlier astrologers had made much capital out of this degree, for it fell in the first decan (a ten-degree division, or third part) of Libra, the traditional image for which was of a pure virgin, feeding a child. This, many astrologers maintained, was an image of the Virgin Mary.[115]

Although he does not show it in the chart, Cardan emphasises that the star Hercules (one of the names of Pollux) was on the Midheaven, and that this star – an equivalent of a second Mars in the chart – was associated by many authorities with martyrdom.[116] As the chart demonstrates, around the supposed time for the birth of Christ the two chronocrators, or planetary markers of time, Saturn and Jupiter, were trine in Air signs, while Venus (in the Air sign Aquarius) was trine to Saturn. This triple arrangement formed what has since been termed a 'grand trine' – one of the fortunate indications in a horoscope. These trines, which involved 'the most resplendent' (*fulgentissimo*) Venus, boded well, and heralded the birth of a remarkable man – or, as Cardan put it, 'the most glorious God had embellished the horoscope with the best and most wonderful disposition of the heavens imaginable'.

However, at a time when it was frowned upon to predict the death of the Pope, or of the majority of Europe's kings and queens, Cardan probably overstepped the mark when he tried to find the anaretic, or killer, in the chart of the Son of God. Cardan looked into the figure in order to determine when this person would meet the cruel death promised by the opposition between Mars and Jupiter so dangerously close to the angles. To date this event, he progressed the Moon, and found that, during Christ's thirty-third year, the Moon would be conjunct with the dark Saturn.[117]

The chart was cast for a date we know to have been incorrect, yet it has remained famous because of its subject, and because of the consequences to which it is supposed to have led. Versions of the chart have been repeated – usually without reference to the primal source – in a wide number of astrological texts.[118] Once the power of the Inquisition had waned, it became almost a commonplace for astrologers to cast the nativity of Christ, in accordance with which-ever date and time they imagined the great event might have taken place.

As a matter of fact, the popular notion that Cardan was undone by his chart is itself suspect. Cardan was not arrested and imprisoned by the Inquisition until 1570, almost sixteen years after the chart was published, and though the horoscope may have played a small part in his downfall, the Inquisition appeared to have been more interested in his many other heresies, supposed or otherwise.

Cardan had merely been following a well-established astrological tradition: few astrologers had doubted that the human side of Christ, immersed as it was in space and time, would have been subject to stellar influences. They argued that, for the expiatory death of Christ to have any spiritual value, he would have had to descend into a human body, and to have become subject to the planetary influx in the way of ordinary men.

In fact, the earliest Western charts for the imagined 'birth of Christ' were frequently derived from the traditions of Arabic astrology, within which there was no danger of heresy. In the West, the most widely known of such horoscopes was that cast by Albumasar, which was usually transmitted in a text associated with Albertus Magnus.[119] This chart was often misunderstood by Western astrologers, for it was not intended as the horoscope for Christ's birth in the conventional sense; rather, it was an ingress chart, representing the moment of the vernal equinox for the year in which the Saturn–Jupiter conjunction occurred. Supposedly marking a new era, the chart was cast for 23 March 25 BC.[120] However, some charts allegedly cast for this time are so inaccurate as to be of little value.[121] It is evident that Albumasar believed that Jesus had been born in 14 BC, for he cast a second chart for the birth, based on the moment of the vernal equinox for that year.

The horoscope of Jesus Christ lifts us out of the confines of the sixteenth century, even though it was during this time that the chart caused the most perturbation. The important fourteenth-century astrologer Pierre d'Ailly was a cardinal, but this did not prevent him from incurring posthumous censure in 1631, when the papal bull of Urban VIII condemned the practice of casting the chart of Christ – thus rather foolishly handing the horoscopic tradition over to Protestant astrologers. D'Ailly's chart is reproduced overleaf, alongside a later version of the horoscope by Morin. The d'Ailly version serves as yet a further reminder of just how inaccurate medieval tables could be.[122]

This fifteenth-century edition of the chart gives both the planets and the signs in words rather than in sigils. The chart is cast for 4 January 1 AD, to give a Virgoan ascendant. Mercury is out by 10 degrees, but the worst offender is the Moon, which was in 05.08 Libra at that time, but which was given by d'Ailly as being in Taurus.

Interest in the chart continued into the seventeenth century. For example, in 1602 the astrologer Maestlin had lectured publicly at Tübingen university on the horoscope of Jesus Christ. On the basis of his own chronological researches he concluded that Jesus must have been born about 4 BC – a date which is now widely accepted by modern chronologists. Later in the century, the French astrologer Jean-Baptiste Morin proposed a chart which relates to the year

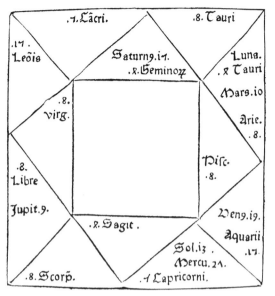
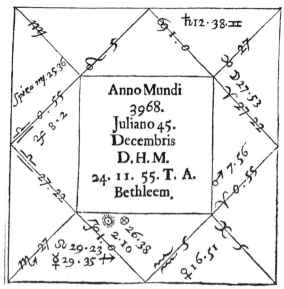

1 BC (or, as he put it, the year 45 of the Julian calendar).[123] This is reproduced above, alongside the d'Ailly chart.

In his preamble to this chart, Morin had made an intriguing analysis of all the nativities for Christ known to him (including the infamous Cardan chart), and justified his own on horoscopic grounds.[124] He argued for the strength and relevance of the chart on the grounds that Jupiter is in the first house, in trine with Venus, herself Lady of the Horoscope. Mars is in opposition to Mars. Saturn (in trine to Jupiter) is in the ninth house (the house proper to Jupiter), which gives the greatest possible leaning towards religion. Give or take a degree or so, the horoscope is remarkably accurate.

A famous chart, calculated in 1668 by John Butler, seems to have been a reworking of that cast by Morin. Butler's chart was copied in its turn in an elaborate engraved chart by Ebenezer Sibly in 1790, with an ascendant of 01.26 Libra (see opposite).[125] At least Sibly's version makes no bones about the fact that the chart relates to the Christ Child born according to Matthew's Gospel, rather than the one born according to Luke's Gospel. Not only is the star very much in evidence, shining directly upon the Child, but Sibly's caption mentions 'the Eastern Astrologers' who worshipped Jesus, referring specifically to Matthew 2.[126]

It is particularly hard to summarise the nature of sixteenth-century astrology. However, one thing is quite evident – it was a European phenomenon, with the charts and astro-analyses written in a universal Latin that would be recognised from the bottom of Italy to the top of Scotland. Over the following centuries, this universality was gradually lost, and national – even regional – forms of astrology were established, much to the confusion of later historians.

It is the nature of the beast that historians tend to judge the achievements of a period from written records. For this reason, the popular astrology of poor-quality horoscopy and magical

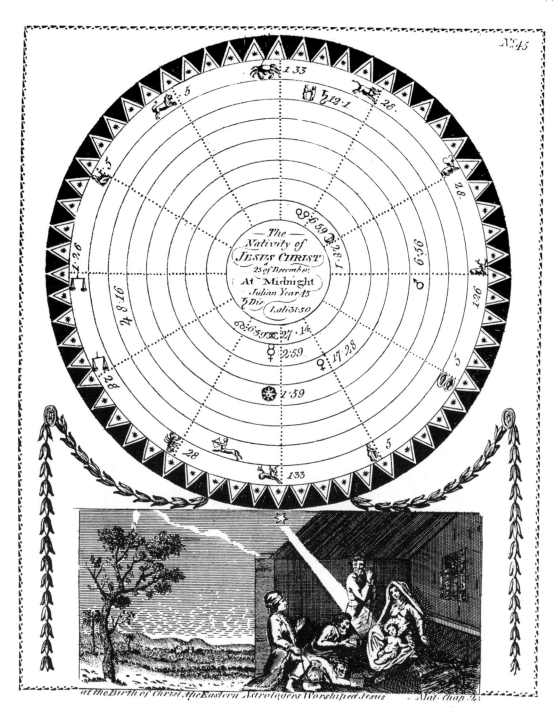

Nᵒ 45

The
Nativity of
JESUS CHRIST
25 of December
At Midnight
Julian Year 45
♄ Die   Lati 31:30

at the Birth of Christ, the Eastern Astrologers Worshiped Jesus   Mat. Chap. 2.

charms which must have dominated the sixteenth century is all but lost to us. In contrast, much of the horoscopy of the royal and papal courts and universities has been preserved, which means that we are inclined to misread the history of the art as one reserved for the scholarly and wealthy. Even contemporaries of that scene showed a similar disposition. In 1563, the puritan Laurence Humphrey had lodged a complaint that astrology was being 'ravened, embraced and

devoured' by the nobility.[127] Perhaps he saw this as a disease of the ego – an intense interest in that selfhood which horoscopes were supposed to reveal. However, there was an unrecognised social reason why astrology should have been held in such high esteem in that century. One reason why astrology was enjoyed and encouraged by the ruling classes is that the cosmoconception behind the art premised a model of stability which was beneficial to the state, and therefore to their own political position. During the century, astrological doctrines formed an integral part of the educated person's vision of the universe, even though polemics in politics and religion were often waged by way of horoscopy and astrology. The basic diagrams of the art, such as the woodcut below, which depicts Queen Elizabeth as a sort of sky-goddess Urania with power over the great planetary orbs, proposed a harmony in which the Greater World was reflected in the Lesser World. It symbolised that all things had their ordained places.

The huge mass of peasantry would probably have had no understanding of the macrocosm, yet – almost to a man – they would have recognised that everything (including themselves) had a place in the world. They would sense that, no matter how distressing this place might be, it was probably best not to disturb the holy golden chain of being, which had been wrought by God. Those at the top of the chain had good reason to ensure that its golden links stayed firmly in place. Astrology was itself a further symbol of the golden chain. Properly used, it would ensure that its history emphasised the more important side of horoscopy – that touching on the life of the royal courts, nobility and people of repute.

CHAPTER 3

The Seventeenth Century

. . . no sooner has he learn'd the Mystery to *Set a figure*, but he fancies himself, a whole Sphear above *Tycho Brahe*, or *Fryar Bacon*; and is more proud of the knack of finding *Part of Fortune*, than *Columbus* of discovering the new *golden world*.

William Ramesey, *The Character of a Quack-Astrologer: Or, the Spurious Prognosticator Anatomiz'd* (1673), third page in unpaginated text

In 1981, a long-lost astrological diary was discovered in the William Andrews Clark Memorial Library in the University of California. This diary had been written by Samuel Jeake, a merchant who had lived during the latter half of the seventeenth century in Rye, a seaside town in southern England.[1] Interspersed with the text were a large number of horoscopes and a proliferation of astrological references to events in Jeake's own life. There is little doubt that the discovery was a most important event for historians of astrology: the diary reveals the mind of a man who had an almost scientific urge to validate the truths of astrology, and who made every attempt to incorporate up-to-date concepts into his astrological work.[2] In some respects, this urge to settle astrology on well-tested ground, by means of experiment, was the keynote of the seventeenth-century art at its best.

All the books dealing with Samuel Jeake as an astrologer insist that there is an engraved horoscope on the façade of his former storehouse in Mermaid Street, Rye, Sussex.[3] We know from his diaries that, in 1689, he cast a foundation chart to determine a suitable time to commence building the wool storehouse, which was later called Jeake's House. Indeed, Jeake went to the trouble of copying the horoscope for this propitious moment into his diary. Opposite, is a copy of this chart, alongside a drawing of Jeake's storehouse, in its modern restored form. From this diary we learn that Jeake personally laid the foundation stone for the building, at the appropriate cosmic moment.

If foundation stone ceremonies and horoscopes are designed to ensure the durability of buildings, then this ceremony, which related the building to the heavens, certainly worked: the storehouse has survived through numerous transformations and vicissitudes. After its first phase as a wool store, it became a school and, later, a dwelling house. It was near-derelict when the American novelist Conrad Aiken purchased it in 1924, and fitted it out as a suitable venue for his friends, among whom were T.S. Eliot, E.F. Benson, Radclyffe Hall and

the artist, Paul Nash. Converted yet again, Jeake's House now serves as part of a modernised hotel.

On the façade of the building, at the level of the second-floor window, a square stone is inset into the wall. This is large enough to contain a quadrate chart, which would have been legible from the road. However, I am disappointed to report that if there ever had been a horoscope mounted in the square, it must have been removed many years ago.[4]

As a matter of fact, a historian of astrology knowing something of Jeake's background would be surprised if, in 1689, he had publicised a horoscope in the form of a stone carving. Jeake had endured many tribulations because of his Nonconformist religion, and it is unlikely that he would have been advertising his 'magical' art in so public a way. Jeake was certainly obsessed with astrology, yet some of his astrological notes were written in code, and some of the horoscopes he recorded seem to have been intended for his eyes only, or for the eyes of the more famous English astrologer, Henry Coley, whom he knew personally. Furthermore, it is clear from Jeake's own diary that he was apprehensive about the whole business of casting foundation charts like the one that was supposed to adorn his wool-store. Jeake was a Nonconformist – a Puritan – and such a form of astrology as 'elections' lay uneasily with his sect.

In the seventeenth-century climate of witchcraft fears, electional astrology was believed by some to smack of magical practice.[5] This probably explains why Jeake pointed out that he had cast the chart only as a matter of 'experiment', and certainly not with any real confidence that *Artificials* (things built by the artifice of man) could be subject to the heavens, as were God's creatures. His mentor Henry Coley had insisted that astrologers should judge only 'Lawful' questions – even though he did include among these such things as elections.[6]

Perhaps there never was a stone horoscope on the façade of the wool storehouse in that cobbled street in Rye, yet the story introduces us to an astrologer of fine capability and deep learning, whose work deserves to be more widely known, as a representative of late seventeenth-century English astrology. Jeake was one of a small number of English astrologers who made serious attempts to set the art on a reformed and tested foundation. He is one of the few English astrologers who is known to have studied in depth the massive and reformative work, written earlier in the century by the French astrologer, Morin de Villefranche, and to have introduced into his own work some of the proposed reforms.[7]

Jeake may be regarded as truly representative of the pioneering astrologers of the seventeenth century. The best-known English practitioner, William Lilly, had shown no real interest in reform, and seems to have put all his energies into the practice of an astrology that involved him in few doubts, and which brought him considerable wealth. John Gadbury, only slightly less well known than Lilly as an astrologer, had shown an interest in reforming astrology, but was sporadic in his attempts to introduce actual reforms. However, Gadbury had set out his position clearly when he wrote, 'one real experiment is of greater worth ... than one hundred pompous predictions'.[8]

Jeake's 'experiments' probably did owe something to the new scientific spirit that was permeating English intellectual life, in the latter half of the century. It is evident that astrology did have some common ground with astronomy and mathematics, wherein such scientific research was notably being applied. However, astrology was uniquely concentrated on a prognostic methodology which owed little to either of these two disciplines, and which made it remarkably impermeable to the scientific method. It is in horoscopy that we see astrology as a unique tool, honed to utility by centuries of use, and employed as an instrument of interpretation that carried it well beyond the premises of astronomy and mathematics. By the time our history begins, in the late medieval world, astrology stood as an independent art – that world would have used the word *scientia* – which owed its calculative method to mathematics, but which owed its forms of interpretation to no other discipline than itself. The unique contribution made by English astrology during the seventeenth century has been dealt with in a penetrating and scholarly manner by the modern historian Ann Geneva. She concludes that the astrology of the seventeenth century was a unique divinatory and prognostic art, embodying centuries of tradition.⁹ However, amid the myriad astrologers who practised during the seventeenth century, such voices are few and far between. Few astrologers were interested in reform, so much as in mastering and using a tradition which seemed, on the whole, to work as a prophetic tool.

We are inclined to see the history of astrology in terms of our own prejudices. These prejudices, which tend to laud the scientific method, were not rampant in the seventeenth century even though, during that time, new attitudes to science were being forged on Baconian principles. In the seventeenth century, different prejudices were formative. Then the underlying urge (indeed, the struggle) of astrologers was not to prove that their art was somehow scientific, but that it was compatible with Christian belief. The astrologer William Lilly wrote the defining book of the century as a shameless compilation of earlier works: it was an anthology of traditional beliefs, rendered more acceptable to his readers by the title, *Christian Astrology*. It is significant that there was little in this work which pertained to Christianity: indeed, almost everything in the book dealt with an astrology that was just about as pagan as that promulgated by Ptolemy, a millennium and a half earlier. Even the well-known reformers of the age were more interested in Christian reformation than anything we would now call scientific. As we shall see, the influential French astrologer, Jean-Baptiste Morin, was more intent in fitting the art into a strait-jacket of Catholic orthodoxy than in turning it into a 'science' – no matter how we attempt to define this elusive term. In a sense, Jeake was being more Christian in his approach to astrology in feeling uncomfortable about election charts, which savoured of 'magic', than Lilly, who made extensive use of such a method of charting in his magnum opus. Jeake, already marginalised in society by virtue of his Nonconformist religion, was among the few astrologers of the period who sought to subject his art to a method, and who was prepared to check, on a near-experimental basis, the techniques then in widespread use.

There is no greater contrast between the charts which Gadbury published in his *Collectio Geniturarum* (1662) than those laboriously collected and checked by Jeake, perhaps with publication in mind. Gadbury had merely borrowed from other astrological sources a selection of charts of well-known individuals, like that of 'Henry Burton' which we examined on page 71. Jeake, on the other hand, cast the charts for more than 150 people whom he knew personally (mainly from within Rye itself), and drew up an essential list of personal 'accidents', which he attempted to relate to these charts. His approach to the art was essentially experimental in spirit. His obsession with his own solar revolution for 1687 was an extension of his interest in attempting to discover the rules governing astrological investigation and cosmic causation or, as he put it, 'Astrall Causes'.¹⁰

If astrological sigils are anything to go by, there is more astrology in the house opposite the modern hotel that once served as Jeake's storehouse. Hartshorne House, a massive, fifteenth-century half-timber-frame dwelling, had come to Samuel Jeake as part of the dowry due on his marriage to his child-bride, Elizabeth Hartshorne. Since those days the house has carried a confusion of names, the relevance of which depends upon the period one has in mind. Confusingly, it is really the true Jeake's House, for it was here that Jeake and his family lived. However, before Jeake came into possession, by virtue of marriage, it was called Hartshorne House; its former owner had been headmaster of Rye Grammar School. A century after Jeake died, it was renamed The Old Hospital, for it served the military in this guise during the Napoleonic Wars.

I am not sure how old the iron door knocker mounted on the main door of this house really is, but it is in the form of the sigil for zodiacal Aries: ♈. This resemblance may be nothing more than a happy accident, yet the fact is that Aries was a sign that seemed to follow Samuel Jeake wherever he went, and whatever he did. Aries was exactly on the Midheaven of his horoscope, cast for 4 July 1652, at 6:15 AM, in Rye.[11] When, twenty-eight years later, Jeake cast a chart to determine the best moment to approach Mrs Hartshorne about a possible marriage to her daughter, Jeake ensured that Aries was on the seventh house (the house of marriage), and that Cauda was in precisely the same degree of Aries as Caput in his own birth chart.[12] Six days later, when he cast a chart to determine the best time to actually propose marriage to the girl, he ensured that Aries was on the same seventh house.[13] Later still, on 1 March 1681, when he – now twenty-nine years old – married the young girl, the disruptive planet Uranus was in Aries. When Jeake drew up the chart for this happy union, his hand seems to have slipped, and his usually exquisite charting was marred: he seems to have placed Venus in Aries, but then corrected it, to place the planet of love in Taurus.[14] Two days afterwards (as Jeake recorded, in code) the marriage was consummated. The troublesome Uranus was now in 18.34 Aries.

Jeake's astrological analysis of the 'accidents' in his life – though unfortunately left unfinished at his death in 1699 – is among the more astonishing astrological documents of the seventeenth century. It was, among other things, an attempt to explore the accuracy of Naibod's Measure of Time (see page 54) and Morin's method of calculating directions, for the purpose of predictive astrology.[15]

Jeake's death came at the very end of the seventeenth century, yet he belonged to a stream of astrology that may be traced back to the beginning of that century. Jeake was one of the large group of astrologers who appear to have learned their preliminary astrology from the writings of William Lilly – in this case, by way of Lilly's friend and amanuensis Henry Coley.[16] William Lilly had been taught astrology by John Evans, a curate of Enville, Staffordshire and later rector of Littleton-on-Severn, Gloucestershire, who, as an Oxford graduate, also offered tuition in Latin, Greek, Hebrew and mathematics.[17] It is unlikely that Jeake had personal followers and students. His son and namesake seems to have been more interested in building flying machines than in exploring astrology.

Perhaps because of his mercantile background, Jeake was extremely methodical and precise – he paid great attention to ensuring the accuracy of his horoscopes: in some respects, he was more careful than either of his English mentors. Both Coley and William Lilly were frequently careless in the way in which they cast and interpreted charts, especially those of the horary kind, which were usually of such importance to the querents. Jeake's charts are a delight, for they are as accurate as the tabulations of the day would permit.

The charts in Jeake's manuscripts are worthy of close analysis, in so far as they reflect the astrologer's near-scientific attempts to study, through the medium of planetary influences, the incidence of accidents in his life. What in his diary may appear to be excessive self-absorption with such minutiae as financial transactions, physical accidents and periodic illnesses, are actually a consequence of his attempt to establish a 'history' against which he could seek a celestial cause for such mundane events. Nowhere in this diary are there horoscopes quite as interesting as the three he cast relating to the negotiations leading up to his marriage.

The earliest of these horoscopes was cast for the moment of his first approach to the mother of the fourteen-year-old girl he wished to marry. In the related diary entries we are permitted an insight into just how complex – and just what hard-driven bargains – were arrangements regarding dowry. The second chart is cast for the moment he proposed marriage (and was accepted). The third chart (below) is for the moment of his marriage: the event took place on a dull day, yet, as he records, 'The Sun shone out just at tying the Nuptial Knot'.[18] So far as the astrology of the moment was concerned, Jeake had done his work well: it was a propitious chart for matrimony, and there was only one darkling planet that might pose a threat.[19] However, our interest does not lie in the success or otherwise of the marriage, but in certain details of the chart itself.

Almost all the interesting details are found in the inner quadrate. The top word *Riæ* relates to the place, Rye, where the couple were married – and, indeed, where they lived. The date, *Martii.*

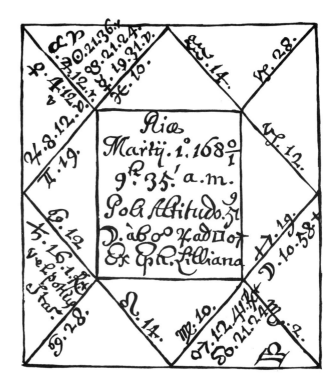

1°. 1680 $\frac{0}{1}$ (1 March 1681), is written in the form designed to show that this date is given according to the Julian calendar, at a time when the Gregorian calendar had been widely accepted in the rest of Europe. The time, *9h. 35'. a.m.*, is recorded with practised precision: at 9:35 AM, Jupiter would be rising – an important beneficial astrological factor, for planets near the ascendant are generally believed to exert their influence over the entire chart. The words *Poli Altitudo 51 g.* (altitude of the Pole 51 degree) is the approximate equivalent of latitude: Rye is actually on 50.57 North.[20]

The fifth line raises so many interesting questions that I will come to it after dealing with the final line, which runs *Ex Eph. Lilliana*. This latter is an abbreviation indicating that the data in the chart have been abstracted from the ephemerides published by William Lilly. The data of the fifth line are represented mainly in sigillic form. This translates, *Moon {moving} from opposition to Jupiter {and moving} towards square of Mars*. The importance of this line is that it records Jeake's attempt to ensure that the Moon is not 'Void of Course', a term used of a planet (particularly the Moon) when it is not forming an aspect during its journey through the rest of the sign wherein it is placed. A planet void of course is claimed to indicate that the business in hand will come to no good. As William Lilly wrote in a book with which Jeake was familiar, 'do you carefully observe whether she be void of course yea or no; you shall seldom see a business go handsomely forward when she is so'.[21] What is of interest to the historian of astrology is that this term is properly used only in relation to horary questions. This chart may well have been an 'election' – that is, a chart drawn up to elect a propitious moment for the marriage – but it could not have been a horary chart, raised in response to a question. The fact that Jeake inserts this void of course data in all the charts known to us suggests that he is applying rules proper to horary astrology both to personal horoscopy and to elections.[22] The implication – not confined to the horoscopy of Jeake – is that the boundaries between horary and genethliacal astrology had become blurred in the seventeenth century.

Later, when contemplating his marriage horoscope, Jeake did not appear to be especially happy. In his diary he related the chart to his own natus, and saw in the new relationship some good, some bad. The planet Jupiter, which he undoubtedly elected to be rising over the horizon so that it would bring success to the marriage, is, as he admits, 'cadent detrified & opposed by the Moon'.[23] He saw other aspects, involving Mars, as a threat to children of the marriage (a threat which was actually realised). However, having listed the pros and cons of the horoscope for which he was assuredly responsible, he rounded off his analysis in the spirit of a business man who had cannily paid attention to Jupiter. He noted that, through the marriage, he came into immediate possession of about £800 of his wife's portion (dowry), with other sums to follow, as agreed. Time and again, in this diary the merchant overshadows the astrologer.

One reason why I have begun this study of seventeenth-century astrology with an account of an astrologer who is little known, other than to specialist historians, is that Jeake was entirely representative of the best sort of astrology that was practised during that century. Because he was a man of means, relieved from the day-to-day pressures that beset most seventeenth-century professional astrologers, he had time to consider his charts, to ensure their accuracy, and to reflect upon their meanings in a manner harassed professionals could normally ill afford.

Professionals were under different pressures, as the astrology of the period performed an important social service. Astrologers were the popular – in some cases, the sole – recourse for people going through what we would now call an emotional crisis. For a few pennies, a poor villager could have access to a learned and skilled confidant, someone who would be able to guide the supplicant with a knowledge well beyond the confines of astrology itself. As we have seen, the kinds of question brought to astrologers in the course of an average day are recorded in the diaries of more than one English astrologer: the preserved charts and astro-readings provide an illuminating insight into the troubles and injustices that beset the ordinary people of the time. In some respects, justice was not always forthcoming for those of limited means, in seventeenth-century courts. Illnesses all too frequently proved painful, were unrelieved by narcotics, and serious ones were often fatal. Wars were conducted in a world almost bereft of stable lines of communication, and even ordinary trade was subject to a multitude of vicissitudes, including inclement weather, poorly built and poorly managed shipping, piracy and unsafe roads. It was this level of insecurity in their lives which produced the troubled questions that the common folk, the soldiers, sailors and traders brought to their counsellors, the astrologers.

The increase in seafaring that occurred with the establishment and development of the American colonies served to intensify the need for horoscopy. The Atlantic crossing was especially dangerous, and many horoscopes have survived dealing with questions relating to journeys by sea, between the colonies and the West Indies. Francis Crow, who wrote critically against astrology, pointed to the widespread dependence on the art among seamen. He spoke from experience, for he had spent some years on Jamaica – in his opinion an island 'too much addicted to Judicial Astrology' – and he had observed with chagrin that sailors seldom 'set out to Sea without consulting the Oracle of a Star-gazing Astrologer for lucky Dayes, and happy Stars'.[24] John Gadbury was sufficiently aware of the needs of the island to publish a special table of houses, 'to serve the Meridian and Horoscope of Port-Royal', the island's capital.[25]

There is no reason to believe that the seafarers of Jamaica were any different from those in other places, but it is interesting that the capture of the island from the Spanish in 1655 became something of a *cause célèbre* among English astrologers. The astrologers were excited by the fact that the taking of the island, by Admirals Penn and Venables, was viewed, from an astrological standpoint, as marking the birth date of the new English colony there.[26]

There seem to have been no types of horoscope that were not called for by a society under such expansive tensions, and beset by religious strife. The most popular astrologer, if by no means the best in terms of proficiency, was William Lilly, who (like most jobbing astrologers) cast charts of the horary kind to discover lost objects, hidden treasures, the whereabouts of murdered bodies, the truths behind lovers' claims, the destiny of souls thought to have been lost at sea or in war. At the same time, he would turn his hand to casting charts for famous people, including Charles I and Charles II and, during the Civil War and Interregnum, of Cromwell and his followers, with whom he had sided.

It was an age when virtually all educated men had some knowledge of astrology, and one in which most individuals took its doctrines seriously. We cannot believe everything that William Lilly wrote in his *Autobiography*, yet it is evident that he must have cast well over two thousand charts a year. Lilly was a big fish, but he was only one fish in a well-stocked pond. It was an age when the demand for astrology, as a way of revealing cosmic patterns and spiritual meanings, far outstripped its resources, and made a fertile ground for charlatans, as the lament of William Ramesey, quoted at the head of this chapter, suggests.

The impulse towards popularisation, encouraged by such men as Lilly and John Gadbury, was perpetuated well into the century by those whom they taught or influenced. So rich is this period in astrology that it is especially difficult to represent its breadth and depth by reference to a handful of horoscopes. However, if we are to attempt to set down the spirit of the art implicit in this popularisation, then it is right to say that seventeenth-century astrology, for all its involvement in codifications and meaningful obscurantism, represented an honest attempt, by a small number of astrologers, to reject those elements in the Ptolemaic tradition that had proved wanting, with an eye to reforming their art. This unexpected impulse, towards what we might loosely call a 'scientific' approach, may have been part and parcel of the intellectual ethos of the period, but it was one that was to lend a distinctive quality to some of the horoscopes produced in that century. Shortly, we shall glance at some of the more enduring names among those astrologers who were inclined to promote a reformation of their art.

The use of astrological references in both drama and literature, which had been one of the hallmarks of sixteenth-century culture, continued alive and well throughout most of the following century. The poet John Dryden had been deeply interested in astrology and his knowledge of the art spilled over into his poetry and plays, peppering their texts with allusions that are sometimes opaque to those who have not studied the subject.[27] In this, Dryden was not much different from other scholars and writers of his age, for, as the historian Kenneth Young has pointed out, the men of the sixteenth century could be at once astrologers and believers in experimental science.[28] However, even in the sixteenth century, few poets would prepare to write a major opus (such as *Annus Mirabilis*) by casting a horoscope to determine a suitable time to begin the work.[29]

Dryden was a sufficiently skilled horoscopist to predict from the chart of his eldest son, Charles, that the latter would meet an accidental death in his thirty-third year. The prophecy proved correct: in the predicted year (1704), Charles was drowned at Datchet while swimming across the Thames.

The horoscope of the poet himself has survived in two manuscripts in the Bodleian.[30] They both present compelling evidence of Dryden's interest in the art, as the Sun is in 26.17 Leo and therefore in the astrologer's arc (see pages 182–3). The most powerful thing in the chart (at least for a modern astrologer) is the conjunction of the Moon (23.55 Taurus) with Pluto (23.48 Taurus), both in close square to the Sun. The contact between the Moon and Pluto can often bring an interest in matters of the occult, and even make the native sensitive to paranormal experiences – as Dryden undoubtedly was at times.

While the sixteenth century had seen the heyday of crypto-horoscopy, this art did survive into the seventeenth century. A good example is from the middle of the century, even if it does refer to horoscopic conditions in the previous one. In the engraving of 1651, on the opposite page, Ptolemy is shown leaning back beneath the pans of a balance which is held

by Urania (her body studded with stars, and the zodiacal belt as her cincture), the personification of astrology.[31] Each pan depicts a cosmic system, that of Copernicus on the left, and that of Tycho Brahe to the right. In the skies, on either side of the hand of God (identified by the Hebrew) are putti, symbolic of the planets. With the exception of the Sun, the planets in their hands are designed to reveal the truths shown by the telescope. To the right, the curious form in the hands of the top putto is intended to represent Saturn and its rings. The second putto down, representing Jupiter, holds a globe that reveals the distinctive striations, and its satellites.

From our point of view, the interesting thing is that amid this plethora of symbols that seem to flatter astronomy, the circular diagram at the feet of Urania, representing the concentric orbs of the Ptolemaic system, seems to be a crypto-horoscope. If we conceive the figure in reverse (as it would have been engraved), then it is very close to representing the appearance of the heavens in November 1543.

On 24 November of that year, the Moon was in conjunction with Jupiter, as indicated in the spheres diagram. With one small exception, the disposition of the planets was exactly as shown below.

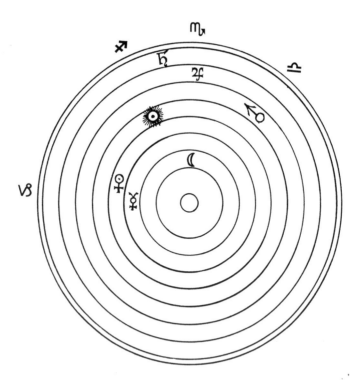

Reading from left to right, Mars was in Libra, Jupiter was in 18 Scorpio (with the Moon), Saturn was in 26 Scorpio, the Sun was in the next sign, Sagittarius. As indicated in the spheres, Mercury and Venus were in the same sign, but the order should be reversed for the entire sequence of planets to marry completely with the representation in the spheres diagram. It is tempting to believe that the disposition of the planets was intended to point to the year 1543: this was not only the year in which Copernicus died, but it was also the year in which his long-awaited *De Revolutionibus* was finally published.

The seventeenth century was a dynamic period for astrology, especially in England. During that century the favoured method of house division changed, both in England and on the Continent. The finest house tables had been inherited from the sixteenth century and were usually based on those attributed to Regiomontanus, but had actually been developed in the eleventh century.[32] The initial popularity of these tables was due mainly to the activities of the seventeenth-century English astrologer, John Partridge, who wrote in favour of both the Placidean house system itself, and of the system of directions favoured by Placidus.

One cannot explore seventeenth-century astrology for long without encountering Placido de Titis, the supposed designer of the Placidean house system, which, until recently, dominated modern astrology. He was a monk, a professor of mathematics at Pavia University, and personal astrologer to Archduke Leopold William of Austria. Although his influential system of house division has been criticised by many astrological practitioners and mathematicians, it was widely used during and after the mid-seventeenth century.[33] One rarely noted influence which Placidus exerted on seventeenth-century horoscopy was his teaching that aspects were not themselves influenced by the signs in which the relevant planets were found – rather, they were to be calculated in terms of the 360 degree circle, as though the signs had no meaning. This teaching was in contrast to the well-established tradition, which tended to interpret aspects in terms of elemental factors, derived from the signs. It is certainly one of the characteristics of seventeenth-century horoscopy that it concentrated upon aspects to the detriment of the influence of planets-in-signs, which are nowadays so much in vogue.

The astrologers of the seventeenth century collected horoscopes on a much wider scale than those of the sixteenth century. Many of these collections have been published, but a great number still remain in archives and public libraries, in manuscript form. Among these is a manuscript in the Bodleian collection, dated 1677.[34] It comprises an astonishing array of charts, which includes those for Tycho Brahe, Robert Burton, John Dee, Kenelm Digby, John Dryden (cast by John Gadbury), John Evelyn (cast by Henry Coley), Matthew Hales, Edmund Halley, Thomas Hobbes, Wenceslas Hollar, Robert Hooke, Titus Oates, William Penn (the Quaker reformer and colonist who founded Pennsylvania), William Petty, Philip Sidney, and Christopher Wren. The collection included a version of Brounker's sixteen-house chart, with a twelve-house variant, both containing fixed stars.[35] Overleaf, I give the charts of William Penn and of the Czech artist, Wenceslas Hollar, based on data culled from this manuscript. The charts will be welcomed by historians, as the time of Penn's birth does not appear otherwise on record and even the day of Hollar's birth has been recorded as unknown by some art historians.[36]

The seventeenth century saw the introduction into horoscopy of an entirely new range of aspects. Ptolemy had written of five aspects, and these had been in use for many centuries. However, by the mid-seventeenth century, these five were being called the 'Old Aspects', or

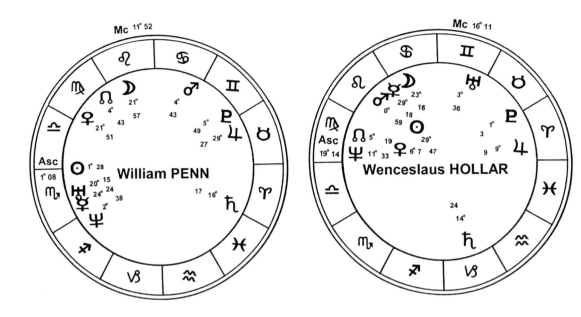

'Radiations'. This term seems to have been introduced after the mathematician, John Kepler, proposed the adoption of two new aspects, the Semisextile (or Dodectile) and Quintile. By the last quarter of the century, a further six aspects had been described and added to the new pair. In place of sigils, the new aspects were usually represented by letters or abbreviations.[37]

Biquintile [Bq.]	144 degrees	Decile [dcc.]	36°
Quincunx [Vc.]	150 degrees	Quintile [Q]	72°
Semiquadrate [S]	45 degrees	Semisextile [SS]	30°
Sesquiquadrate [SSq]	135 degrees	Tredecile [Td]	108°

To these we can add the 'whimsical Aspects', of Octiles, Vigintiles, Quindreiles, 'and the like', which the English astrologer, Joshua Childrey, wanted to get rid of in 1652.[38]

With so many aspects now available, seventeenth-century horoscopy was beginning to take on a visible complexity that would probably have worried Ptolemy and his followers. Statistically, it had reached a point where it was virtually impossible for a planet not to be in aspect with at least one other planet. In many cases, single planets were involved in a whole bevy of aspects, which required great perseverance to combine their influences meaningfully within a reading.

The predictive side of astrology was especially open to the researches of reformers. There seemed to be few doubts that horoscopic prediction was possible – the only argument was about which of the many techniques available had proved to be the best. Setting aside the vexing questions of what precisely one meant by the term 'day' or 'year', and dismissing the issues surrounding which of the great circles should be used in astrological prediction, the most popular systems were those involving the so-called 'day for a year' method of progressions. The majority of predictive methods of this kind required conversion of time measured against the rotation of the earth to sidereal time (or stellar time). It was for this reason that standard books on astrology furnished conversion charts – tables for Right Ascension, calibrated against zodiacal time. Equally popular as a predictive technique was that of solar returns – the revolution charts of the kind we examined in Chapter 2 – which involved casting a chart for the moment the Sun returns to its original natal longitude in the year under scrutiny.

The large number of ephemerides published in the seventeenth century should not blind us to the difficulties that contemporary astrologers experienced in obtaining accurate tables, as a basis for their computations. It is true that, as the century progressed, these tabulations were improved, yet they never attained the reliability of modern tables. Even as late as 1780, the first American eclipse expedition – mounted under Samuel Williams to study the total eclipse of the Sun in 4.55 Scorpio, on 27 October at Penobscot, Maine – was unable to locate the path of totality due to the unreliability of the tables at their disposal.[39]

Not so much a problem for seventeenth-century astrologers themselves yet often a serious difficulty for historians is the variety of different time systems in use in that century. In some systems, the twenty-four-hour day was conceived as beginning at noon; in others it began at sunrise. In yet other systems, the time was given as AM, with the difference subtracted from the noon-time – which in theory was always measured as local noon-time, and therefore a great variable, from city to city. Indeed, throughout Europe there seems to have been no consensus as to what an hour really was. The monastic system of dividing the day into two periods, one beginning at sunset and ending at sunrise, and the other beginning at sunrise and running through to sunset, persisted in various astrological systems. The first twenty-four-hour clock built in Britain was that constructed by Dutch clockmakers in 1386. Even this northern horologium was called the 'Italian Clock', since the day it marked ended and began at 'dusk' – that is to say, half an hour after sunset, in the Italian manner. Since dusk is a variable phenomenon, this was a most unreliable time, even though, at Westminster, it was at least measured by the last of the twenty-four strokes of the bell which marked the half-hour after sunset.

I mention this fourteenth time system because it persisted for some centuries, and figures in many horoscopes of the sixteenth and seventeenth centuries. The astrological tradition of planetary hours (see page 117) was initially dependent upon this monastic division of day and night into two periods of twelve 'hours', the so-called 'artificial' divisions. In this system, the nocturnal series were rarely of the same duration as the diurnal.[40]

There are no available tabulations designed to unravel the complex differences in time systems and the only arbiter is experience, and knowledge of history and chronologies. In some cases it is still difficult for astrologers to determine which time system was used. For example, even as late as the early nineteenth century, nautical records in ships' logs still adhered to a dating period that was twelve hours in advance of official calendar time. Thus the battle of Trafalgar, which was fought in the afternoon of 21 October 1805, is recorded in the log of HMS *Victory* as having been fought on the 22nd.[41] According to such naval records, Nelson died on the latter date, yet if an astrologer computing the great seaman's death chart were unwittingly to use this date, he or she would construct inaccurate charts. On the day of that historically significant battle, there were five planets in Libra – Moon, Mercury, Sun, Saturn and Uranus. On the fatal afternoon of that same day, Saturn (20.12 Libra) was on the Mercury (19.47 Libra) of Nelson's birth chart.[42]

William Lilly's book, *Christian Astrology*, based on a wide familiarity with traditional material as expounded by continental astrologers, had a refreshing influence on the development of the art in the seventeenth century. It was the first serious attempt in English to set out the rules of astrology in a manner that could be understood by all those possessed of a modicum of mathematics. However, Lilly appears not to have been particularly interested in reform: he worked easily and competently with the techniques inherited from the Ptolemaic tradition. Perhaps, like others, he recognised the shortcomings of the available tables, but he showed little interest in reforming the welter of traditions available to him.

Lilly was not alone: few astrologers of this period saw the need for a reform of the art, and even fewer actually committed themselves to participating in such reform. Even so, the names and works of a small group of reforming astrologers have survived.[43] Lilly's arch-enemy, John Gadbury was the most famous of those who became involved in the reformation of astrology. The obscure ecclesiastic Joshua Childrey carried reformation so far that it went beyond the comprehension of most practising astrologers. Dr Francis Bernard dedicated a great deal of his time attempting to establish a relationship between astrology and various social mutations (see pages 108–9).

John Goad's incessant search for patterns in human behaviour, epidemics, misfortune and the weather, led him to keep a detailed diary for about thirty years – a record which he extended backwards to 1500 by means of events recorded by others. His undertaking was nothing less than a sophisticated – and ultimately unrewarded – experiment in astrology, for by means of his detailed records he sought to establish earthly patterns, the meaning of which (he believed) lay in celestial patterns. In his attempts to develop a new kind of astrology, which had relevance to earthly mutations, Goad must have been the most advanced of all those seventeenth-century astrologers intent on reforming the art.[44] Goad's published work is densely packed with information, but from our point of view it is disappointing: while it contains much data, and involved a great deal of horoscopy, it is not illustrated with horoscopes. The historian, Keith Thomas, has rightly noted that John Goad was one of the earliest writers to observe that suicide rates vary according to the time of year.[45]

Experimentation is the key to understanding the best seventeenth-century astrology. Some astrologers of the period developed experimental attitudes that questioned and breached many of the Ptolemaic traditions and, in some cases, resulted in graphic forms for which interpretative keys have been lost.[46] For example, the experimental basis for the quadrate chart with sixteen houses is now hard to fathom, unless its origins are to be found in the charting of crises, an approach used by doctors familiar with astrological principles. If the horoscope cast by Brouncker (the future first President of the Royal Society) for Charleton (the future

President of the College of Physicians) had been provided with explanatory notes, then these have been lost. All that remains is an intriguing astrological mystery.[47]

In the absence of explanations, it is quite impossible to establish how Brouncker would have interpreted the chart, from a translated version, copied from a standard chart cast by Broucker (right).[48] We shall examine certain of the experimental attitudes behind seventeenth-century astrology in some of the following sections. Before looking at some sample charts, it will be as well for us to examine a seventeenth-century chart in detail to see something of the nature of the horoscopy of the period.

WALTER CHARLETON
horoscope cast by
BROUNCKNER
Reduced from sixteen houses
to the traditional twelve.

12 February 1620
12:18 PM

Few seventeenth-century horoscopes have been subjected to the same depth of analysis as that of King Charles I of England, who had been born in 1600. In 1659, Gadbury published a book which dealt solely with the horoscope of the unfortunate King.[49] Besides providing the natal chart, his survey included a number of annual revolutions, and a death chart for the moment the King was beheaded in Whitehall, in 1649. Overleaf is the natus, alongside the death chart, cast by John Gadbury.

The depth of Gadbury's analysis reveals very clearly the nature of seventeenth-century astrology. It is typical of that period's charting that some of the words in the figure are in English, others in Latin, and yet others in Greek. The poorly penned Greek in the third house is meant to spell out Μικρός Κουταράτος ('Little lance-bearer'), which is one of the names for Spica. Perhaps, in this case, Gadbury was displaying his learning, for the version of the name was rare, having come into astrology by way of a recent study by Ismaelis Boulliau of the fourteenth-century astronomer Georgius Chrysococca.[50] It is not easy to determine why Gadbury inserted the name: in 1600, Spica was in 18.12 Libra, and thus nowhere near either the cusp of the third, or the Moon, as Gadbury had claimed.[51] The Latin at the bottom of the inner quadrate (*à vac. ad* ✴ ☉*.*) really belongs to the horary tradition, yet it had become usual during the seventeenth century for astrologers to insert such data in genethliacal figures. The abbreviated and sigillated line indicates that the Moon was without aspect at the moment of birth, but was moving towards a sextile with the Sun.

Gadbury's analysis of the King's chart is prefaced by a complete speculum of all factors of importance in the horoscope. Alongside the horoscope he furnished a list of the antiscia (the singular of which is *antiscion*), the contra-antiscia, and a fairly complete speculum for the birth

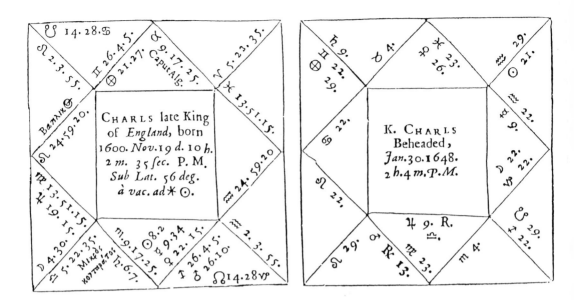

chart. Gadbury uses the word antiscion in its Ptolemaic sense, as being the cosmic reflection, across the axis of Cancer–Capricorn, of any given planet, or node. Because, in the natal chart of the King, Saturn is in 6.7 Scorpio, its antiscion is 23.53 Taurus. One observes that the antiscia are not tenanted places – no bodies occupy the degrees indicated. At best, they may be regarded as shadow areas, or reflections, even though the influential Italian astrologer, Antonio Bonattis, wrote of the planetary antiscion degree as 'vibrating' to the planet it mirrored.[52]

Gadbury's charting lists the major directions of the ascendant, MC, Sun, Moon and Fortuna, for every year of the King's life. It is this listing of important directions for every such year, which reveals why Gadbury had been so careful to list the antiscia and contra-antiscia for the chart. In seventeenth-century astrology, directions to these were considered to be of the greatest importance in the unfolding of planetary and nodal potential.

Gadbury also adds a diagram that would make little sense to a modern astrologer, but which was a fairly run-of-the-mill diagram in his day. This is a list of point systems for the fortitudes of the planets in the horoscope. It had become a commonplace for textbooks on astrology to display tables of 'Essential Dignities', similar to the one above (see entry for Dignity in the Glossary). The assessment of the dignities that could be accorded to a planet was among the most complex of all operations in late medieval astrology, and we are fortunate that the entire system was so thoroughly reformed in later centuries as to be virtually banished from modern practice. Dignities could be calculated according to sign position, placing within the horoscope (relative to angles, and also to specific houses), and in accordance with certain divisions of signs (sometimes called faces, and at other times decans), as well as specific degrees, as exaltations. In addition, there were dignities if the planet was in its own sign – for example, when the Sun was in Leo. The planets could also be strong in other ways – for example, when swift in motion, in beneficient angles with the benefics (Jupiter and Venus), and in close conjunction with beneficient fixed stars. Balanced against these plus points were a number of negatives. For xample, there were detriments and falls for the planets, which detracted from the values of the lignities. For example, the Sun was in detriment in Aquarius, and in its fall in Libra – the sign pposite to Aries, where it was strong by virtue of being in its own house, and so on. In some strological systems, specific points were given for each essential dignity, and points were ubtracted for the debilities, such as detriments and falls. It is this point system that is lemonstrated in Gadbury's simple analytical figure (above). Mars scores the most points (or testimonies'), for the planet is in its own term (25–30 Sagittarius), it is exactly cuspal to the ifth, trine to the ascendant, and so on.

> *Jupiter* is Lord of the Eighth House, as he go-
> verns the Fishes which descend thereon , and he is
> in ♍ in his detriment. But ♂ being Lord of the
> Fourth, and having Triplicity in the Eighth, and in
> Quartile to ♃ also,may be admitted Anareta,(*e.i.*) *He was*
> the interficient or killing Planet. The Lord of *very sub-*
> the Ascendent is in ♐ with *Cor Scorpii* , a violent *ject to a*
> fixed Star of the first magnitude ; which is one te- *death:many*
> stimony of a violent death. The Lord of the Eighth *arguments*
> squared by ♂ , and the Eighth House also, from a *thereof.*
> violent Sign , is another argument of a violent
> death. *Cor Leonis*, or the heart of the Lyon in the
> Ascendent, and *Caput Algol* in the Tenth House ;
> *Venus* Lady of the Tenth, in ♂ with ♂, in □ of ♃,
> and ♄ casting an ☍ to the Tenth from fixed Signs,
> are most assured arguments of a violent death.

From the long and detailed analysis of the chart, the most informative reading is that relating o the judgements made concerning the eighth house, which has the popular title 'the House of Death'. Gadbury gives no fewer than four good astrological reasons why Charles should have net a violent end (above).[53] These are set out in the language of seventeenth-century astrology, nd, to be fully appreciated, require a commentary.

First, 'Jupiter is Lord of the Eight House …'. After making the point that Jupiter is weak (in ts detriment) because it is in Virgo, Gadbury turns to the square between Mars and Jupiter: it s this aspect that forms the background to his claim that Mars is the killing planet, or anaretic. With Mars in 26.10 Sagittarius and Jupiter in 19.15 Virgo, the orb of 7 degrees would be egarded by most modern astrologers as pointing to a weak square. However, in terms of eventeenth-century astrology, this orb is quite acceptable. Again, in modern terms, Mars (in 6.10 Sagittarius) could not itself be said to have 'triplicity' in the eighth. However, what Gadbury claimed is that the sign Scorpio, which Mars rules, was in the same triplicity (that is, the Water triplicity) as the eighth-house cusp: this allegiance is sufficient to reflect on Mars, and draw its influence to the House of Death.

Second, 'The Lord of the Ascendent is in Sagittarius ...'. Gadbury makes much of the fact that the Sun (Lord of the ascendant) is with the violent star, Cor Scorpii. However, he did not indicate graphically the position of this star in his chart. Better known nowadays as Antares, it was in 4.08 Sagittarius during 1600.[54] This means that it was almost four degrees from the Sun (8.02 Sagittarius) – an orb too wide for modern acceptance, yet one that satisfied seventeenth-century horoscopists.[55] For Gadbury, the contact would imply a violent end: the star is renowned for causing headstrong behaviour, which leads to the native's own undoing.

The third conglomerate, 'The Lord of the Eighth squared by Mars ...', is seen by Gadbury as yet a further indication of a violent end. The square between Mars and Jupiter is mentioned a second time, but in the context of the eighth house being ruled by a 'violent Sign'. While this last term is scarcely ever used in modern astrology, it does appear in many seventeenth-century texts. Technically, a violent sign is one that is the house or exaltation of a malefic planet. Now Sagittarius (in which Mars is placed) is not itself a violent sign, even though it is true that Mars squares the eighth house: it is possible that Gadbury is reflecting on the fact that the eighth house is associated with Scorpio, the eighth in the zodiacal sequence, which *is* a violent sign.

The fourth conglomerate, 'Cor Leonis, or the heart of the Lyon ...', relies heavily on a reading of fixed stars. Gadbury tells us that Cor Leonis is on the ascendant: indeed, he has marked the cusp with the Greek name for the star, Βασιλικος, meaning 'ruler' or 'king'. As he admits, in another part of the analysis, 'the Regal Star *Basiliskos*, or heart of the Lyon ... [is] directly Horoscopical'.[56] In 1600, Cor Leonis (now usually called Regulus) was in 24.12 Leo, and thus in the same degree as Charles' ascendant. In the stellar tradition, the star brings great honours and wealth, but final violence. Having pointed to this incipient violence, Gadbury then refers to the most violent star in the skies – that is, to Algol ('Caput Alg.') in the tenth house. In 1600, Algol was in 20.39 Taurus, and over 11 degrees from the cusp of the tenth: however, in the seventeenth century, the presence of such a powerful star in a house was seen as irradiating that house with its stellar influence. Developing on this dire placing, and in order to illustrate its ramifications throughout the chart as a whole, Gadbury points out that the Lady of the tenth house (that is, Venus, ruler of Taurus) is conjunct with the malignant Mars (itself in square with Jupiter). This same tenth-house cusp is under further pressure from the malign Saturn (in the violent sign, Scorpio), which is in opposition (6.07 Scorpio) to the tenth cusp, in 9.17 Taurus. After something of an astrological over-kill, Gadbury affirms that these factors offer an assured argument for a violent death.[57]

As we have seen, Gadbury had already offered his readers a glimpse into the King's future by way of directions, for each year of the King's life. Once he had completed his analysis of the radical chart, Gadbury turned his attention to the other favoured technique for investigating the future – the use of revolution charts. He drew up and published revolutions for each of the last eleven years of the King's life. Gadbury does not say whence he derived the time for the execution of the King. However, the time is not exactly the same as that mentioned by modern historians.[58]

It is a curious fact that for all the care he exercised in marshalling the astrological evidence for the life and death of his King, Gadbury missed the most surprising thing about the death chart. At the time of death he gave, the Moon was in 22 Capricorn. This was precisely the degree of the antiscion of the Sun, in the radical horoscope. In spite of this, Gadbury's extensive reading of the chart offers one of the most thorough and representative examples of horoscopy in the seventeenth century.

The following selection of charts, intended as representative of seventeenth-century astrology, falls lamentably short of this purpose mainly because the century was so rich in its astrologies and horoscopy: perhaps as many as sixty charts would be insufficient to illustrate the variety of horoscopy in this astonishing period. Given the space, I would have chosen to include the chart of Wallenstein, drawn up by the great Johann Kepler. This chart, and its extensive reading (with annotations by Wallenstein), is notable for several reasons: it throws light on Kepler's own approach to astrology (for example, on his disdain of houses), and it is one of those rare charts that was rectified at the request of the native.[59] Wallenstein knew enough about astrology to realise that the original time he had given Kepler was inaccurate, when measured against events. Accordingly, in 1624, he returned the horoscope to Kepler, asking him to amend it so as to accommodate predictions, then in error by one or two years. The amendment was only 6 minutes and 30 seconds, yet this was sufficient to satisfy both the astrologer and his client.

Again, had space permitted, I would have elected to incorporate many more charts by William Lilly – for example, the eclipse charts for the Dark Year of 1652, that of 11 August 1645, in which he predicted the death of Charles I, and at least one of his many charts for mock Suns, which Lilly connected (by macrocosmic analogy) with rebellion against the Crown.[60] I would have dealt with several of the charts mentioned in passing by Ashmole, in his diaries – for example, the intriguing horoscope he cast, at 6:08 AM on 18 December 1681, for the rat talisman he had constructed to protect the kitchen of his neighbours, the Tradescants, from the vermin – or, even the more conventional (though none the less remarkable) charts discussed by one modern historian in an article on the golden age of predictive astrology.[61]

Perhaps of greater interest to the historian is the wide range of figures available in the text mentioned by John Aubrey in a letter to Anthony Wood, regarding his collection of nativities of learned men, which he and Ashmole were assimilating from as many as forty earlier works on astrology.[62] I would also have enjoyed analysing the elaborate charts of the herbalist–astrologer, Nicholas Culpeper, alongside interesting modern attempts to rectify the same figure. Of special interest in Culpeper's chart was his appearance in court, on 17 December 1642, on a charge of witchcraft. His natal chart, and the progressions for this painful time, are reminders that the pursuit of astrology was conducted under the infamous Witchcraft Statute of 1563, in which legal boundaries had been poorly drawn, and echoes of which continued to resound in anti-fraud legislation, in Britain and North America, until the twentieth century.[63] Another Culpeper chart I might have glanced at was that he cast for the 'Black Monday' solar eclipse of 29 March 1652, from which he argued the invasion of Europe by the Turks, the fall of Kings and Popes and the introduction of a new order of things.[64] Culpeper was not the only doleful prophet of the times, and we have a delightful vignette of terrified souls sealing up windows with pitch and cowering under their bedclothes as the time of the eclipse drew near.[65] The charts of Culpeper would also have given us an opportunity to examine the so-called 'Decumbiture charts' – those cast for illnesses, often employing the eight-house system of houses, related not to the twenty-four hours of solar motion, but to the lunar crisis 'hours'.[66] To cover another interesting approach of seventeenth-century astrology, I would have elected to study in detail the heliocentric charting of William Hunt, who was intent on producing what he purposely called 'diagrams', which were horoscopes according to the Copernican system – a late development of the methods espoused by Childrey.[67] In particular, I would have enjoyed discussing the diagram Hunt cast for 'sunset' (properly speaking, of course, in a heliocentric system this should be 'earth-rise') on 11 June 1695.[68]

I have discussed only two charts from the rich manuscript tradition (see pages 114–16). Had opportunity presented itself, I would also have elected to reproduce and discuss at least fifty of these, as being useful for the astrologer and for the historian, the latter of whom is generally unaware of these treasure-troves of data, so relevant to seventeenth-century history.

SOME HOROSCOPES OF WILLIAM LILLY

There are few well-executed portrait paintings of the seventeenth century that include horoscopes. However, one exception is the anonymous picture in the Ashmolean, Oxford, which portrays the astrologer William Lilly holding in his left hand the revolution chart for his forty-fifth year. The horoscope is quadrate, and in the inner square are the two Latin words, *non cognunt*. The words, adopted by Lilly as his personal motto, are from a phrase of some antiquity, meaning 'The Stars do not compel'. The truncated phrase is imbued with the refreshing notion that although we may read in nativities the outlines of a person's fate, there is, somewhere, a freedom from this seeming determinism, and the human will is not a mere figment of the imagination.[69]

William Lilly was one of the more colourful astrologers of this colourful and tortured century. He was born in a thatched cottage in Diseworth, Leicestershire, the son of a land-owning farmer. The timber-frame house still survives, across the road from the thirteenth-century Church of St Michael and All Angels, where Lilly was christened, within days of his birth, on 1 May 1602. One version of the horoscope is given opposite, carefully framed in the house system of Regiomontanus, which Lilly recommended to his students.[70]

The chart is from a collection published by Lilly's sparring partner, John Gadbury. In his notes to the chart Gadbury claimed, rather spitefully, that Lilly 'hath pretended himself to have two several Nativities'.[71] This sentence alone reveals some of the animosity that existed between the two most famous English astrologers of the century. They had been divided first by politics, and then by the Civil War. Lilly was a Parliamentarian – an adherent of 'New Model Astrology', as one Royalist astrologer put it, rather tartly. Gadbury was one of the King's men.[72] However, the tension between the two went much deeper than such political allegiances: unbeknownst to either of them, it was reflected in the planetary tensions of their horoscopes.[73]

Lilly cast charts for almost every stratum of society, and even acted as a sort of roving propagandist for the Parliamentarians during the terrible Civil War that tore in twain England, and many English families. In one of his astrological works, he famously

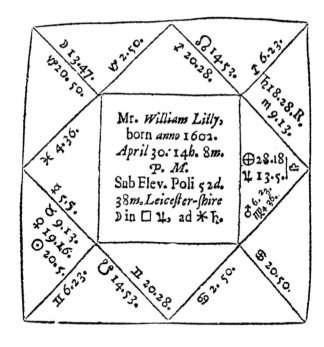

portrayed Oliver Cromwell as a bull: no disrespect was intended, for Cromwell was born with Sun, Mercury and Venus in Taurus.[74] Below is a reproduction of the bull hieroglyphic itself alongside a chart for the birth of Cromwell, as cast by Gadbury, who ascribes to the Aries ascendant 'this prodigious Natives Desire of Soveraignty and Rule, and of the Tyranny he used when he ruled …'.[75]

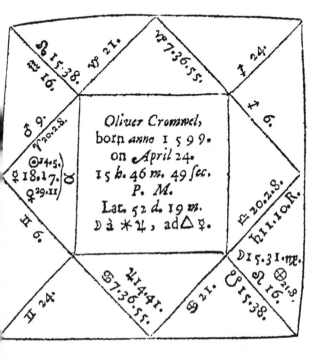

A good many of Lilly's horoscopes – especially those cast as horary charts – concerned the lives of ordinary people, and reveal much about the fears and expectations of seventeenth-century England. However, with the outbreak of the Civil War, Lilly began to expend a great deal of his energy in support of the Parliamentarian cause against the King. During this time, many of his charts and pamphlets were directed towards showing that Charles I would meet a violent death.[76]

In reading the analyses of the horary readings, which Lilly published in several of his books, we are left with a feeling that he enjoyed horary astrology much more than the exercise of genitures.

It is astonishing just how varied were the chart forms used in the sixteenth century – especially so in connection with horary astrology. On the opposite page are six sample charts, all cast by Lilly. Reading from left to right, and starting at the top, the charts relate to a question of whether the husband or wife shall die first; a query as to the victor at the battle of Alsford, in March 1644; a question whether a certain lady would marry the gentleman she desires; a query as to whether Canterbury would be hanged or beheaded; a question as to whether or no a man would obtain a certain parsonage he desired; and a question as to whether a sailor husband was alive and, if so, when he would return home.[77]

Save in those cases where he is dealing with political issues (especially with questions arising out of the Civil War) his analyses are without guile and are usually astrologically adroit. The ease with which he takes so complex a thing as a horoscope and subjects it to analysis, in order to answer the questions of his clients is quite astonishing, and, in a lesser astrologer, might be regarded with some suspicion.

Although some horary rules spilt over into genethliacal astrology, it would be foolish to imagine that a horary chart might be subjected to a similar kind of analysis as a geniture. It would be even more foolish to believe that, without the sort of notes that Lilly and certain of his companions left regarding the horary art, a modern astrologer would be able to make sense of most surviving horary charts. Horary astrology is rooted in a mesh of specialist astrological laws, many of which now seem unbelievably complex.

For example, if we consider Lilly's ruminations on the question relating to the parsonage (page 103, bottom left), we see a type of astrology that is not only entirely foreign to that practised in modern times, but also different from that practised in relation to sixteenth-century genethliacal astrology. Lilly concluded that the man would not obtain the parsonage he sought. He based this conclusion on several factors, some of which he lists and few of which would have any value in modern horoscopy. For example, Mars is not Lord of the ascendant, and Moon is not in the ninth. Saturn does not translate the light of Jupiter to Mars. There is no reception between Jupiter and Mars. Furthermore, as the Moon is separating from a trine of Mars, and applying to an opposition to Mercury, Lilly concluded that a letter, or information, would shortly wholly destroy the querent's hopes. Events proved as Lilly had foreseen, and the man did not obtain his desires.

Terms such as 'translate the light', and 'reception' were sometimes used in late medieval genethliacal astrology, but they remain firmly entrenched as specialist terms in horary

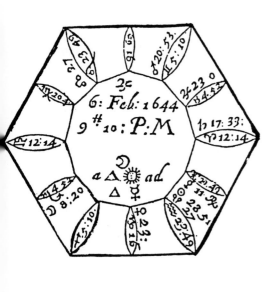

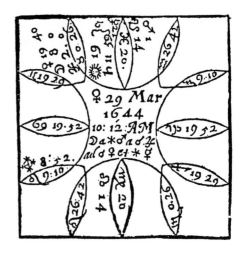

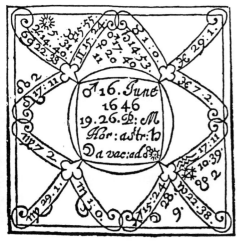

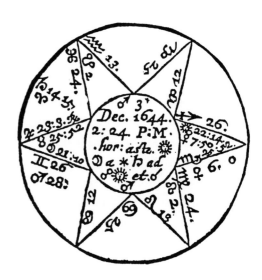

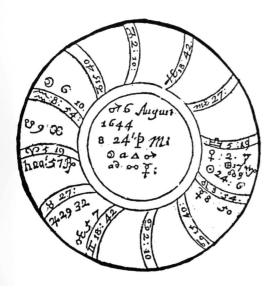

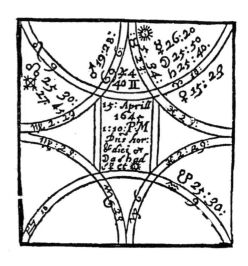

astrology.[78] 'Translation of light' occurs when a light planet, such as Mercury, separates from a heavier planet, such as Mars, to another heavy planet, such as Saturn. In this movement, the lighter planet is said to 'translate' (that is, carry) the virtue of the former planet to the latter.[79] 'Reception' is a term used to denote the circumstance whereby two planets are in the sign of each other's dignity: for example, when the Sun in Aries is in reception with Mars in Leo.[80]

Below, I shall examine another case history for a horary horoscope cast by William Lilly. Only through examination of such case histories will we be able to glimpse just how abstruse are the rules behind seventeenth-century horary astrology.

On 28 December 1644, a London merchant enquired of Lilly about the well-being of a ship – was it 'sunk or living?' The resultant chart is given below.[81] This was the sort of question that was frequently put to astrologers during the sixteenth century. It arose from the shortcomings of the seventeenth-century insurance system, which would not provide cover for ships until there was some danger that they were lost. Evidently, the merchant posing the question had been unable to obtain insurance, as it was widely believed that all the vessels on that voyage had been shipwrecked.

Lilly inspected the chart and came to the conclusion that the ship was not lost: it had been in danger, but would shortly return.[82] As he predicted, so it proved. The ship's affliction, or delay, was signalled by the square of Saturn to the ascending degree. From Cauda, in the ninth house (the house of long journeys), Lilly concluded that she had suffered some affliction during her trip – some 'bruise, leak or damage' near her breast – the place being indicated by Aries, occupied by Saturn (Aries rules the face in the human being, but, in terms of horary charts, the front part or prow of a ship).

The Moon is the lady (or ruler) of the ascendant, and is strengthened by being in the sign of her own exaltation. Furthermore she is under benevolent aspects of an applying trine (a trine in process of construction) from both Sun and Moon. From this, he concluded that the ship, and all those who sailed on her, would be safe.

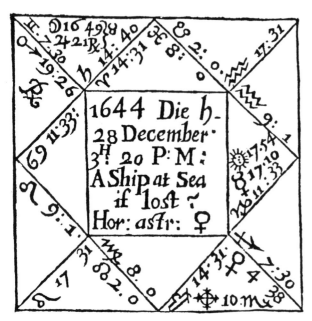

In order to determine the present whereabouts of the vessel, and whether there would be news of it, Lilly next considered the placing of the Moon. She was in the eleventh house, in a southern sign, but in an eastern quarter of heaven, verging towards the south. Her application to the trine of Mercury (which planet was in a south sign and near the western angle) convinced Lilly that the ship was presently south-west from London. It was 'upon our own coast, or near those which lie betwixt

Ireland and Wales'. Because the Moon was in the eleventh house (a place of retreat and comfort), and in a fixed sign, Lilly judged it to be safe in harbour. Because the trine between Moon and Mercury would shortly be exact (that is, 'partile'), he concluded that there would shortly be news, or a letter – if not by that very night, then within two days. Such a letter did arrive, and what he had claimed concerning the ship was shown to be correct.

As for the goods aboard the ship, Lilly looked into the second house, which marks finance and substance. The Lord of the second house was the Sun (ruler of Leo). Since the Sun was in harmonious trine to the Moon, Lilly estimated that the merchant would not lose financially by the venture. The antiscion of Jupiter falls in 9 degrees of Leo, 'the very Cusp of the second house, while the antiscion of Mars falls upon the degree of the Ascendant: these two should be taken as good testimonies of the safety of the vessel'.

The Moon is applying to (that is, moving towards) Jupiter. The application of the Moon to any fortunate planet gives reason for hope. By virtue of its rulership over Aquarius, Jupiter is Lord of the tenth, which governs such matters as trade and commerce. Because Jupiter is retrograde, Lilly recognises that the matter would be brought to an end relatively quickly, by the approach of the Moon. As Lilly predicted, so it would happen.

THE HELIOCENTRIC CHARTS OF CHILDREY

In England, the most revolutionary of the seventeenth-century astrologers was Joshua Childrey, born at Rochester on 20 October 1625. He was educated at Magdalen College, Oxford, and worked for some years as a schoolmaster in Faversham. Eventually, he was appointed Archdeacon of Salisbury Cathedral, later serving as the rector at Upwey (now Upway), where he died in 1670. Among his astrologer friends were Samuel Hartlib and Vincent Wing, of whom we shall hear more later.[83]

In his short lifetime, Childrey gained some fame for a compilation of natural histories of Britain, but it is his experiments with astrology that interest us here, and which reveal him to be well ahead of his time. Among his most astonishing conclusions was that astrology should be brought into line with post-Copernican astronomy, by replacing it with a heliocentric horoscopy.[84]

Some historians claim that the earliest use of heliocentric positions in horoscopy was undertaken by the eighteenth-century French astrologer, Henri de Boulainviller. Certainly, Boulainviller was an original thinker, and an outspoken critic of Ptolemaic astrology: there is no doubt that he regarded the theory of heliocentric planets as an entirely new astrological doctrine, and one which he himself had discovered.[85] However, it is a matter of historical record that Joshua Childrey had personally experimented with the heliocentric system for some years prior to 1653, when he published the first heliocentric charts, in an ephemeris. So satisfactory were the results of these heliocentric experiments that Childrey recommended that all horoscopes – whether genethliacal, horary, interrogational or revolutionary – should be cast in the same manner.[86]

As far as I can tell, only four of Childrey's heliocentric charts have survived: the one alongside, from the 1653 ephemeris, is probably the earliest heliocentric horoscope to have been published in Europe.[87] Just for the record, the complex calculations for this chart were undertaken not by Childrey in person, but by his friend the mathematician Richard Fitzsmith, who published an almanac in 1654, and who was also a friend of John Gadbury.[88]

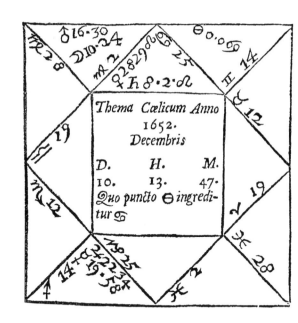

There is, of course, no Sun in the heliocentric chart, but the planet Earth is represented, in the ninth house, by means of the sigil ⊖. In his earlier work on heliocentric astrology Childrey had proposed that the earth should be symbolised as a black circle.[89] In making this suggestion he was following the post-Copernican tradition, as may be seen from the diagram of the world system of Tycho Brahe (below), which depicts the black-circle Earth at the centre of the Moon's orbit: ☽.[90] We have already encountered a version of this *Systema Mundanum Thyconicum* in the left-hand pan of the balance held by Urania in the image on page 89, above.

However, in the ephemeris of 1653, Childrey had adopted one of the alchemical sigils for the Element Earth ⊖, with the idea that this should represent the physical earth itself. In the same chart (above), the earth is depicted as being in the zero point of Cancer. The Latin at the foot of the inner quadrate, *Quo puncto* ⊖ *ingreditur* ♋, is an extension of the date and time above, and means, 'at which point the Earth enters Cancer'. The fact that the chart is illustrating a view-point for beings on earth, of an event that could not possibly be experienced on earth, points to one of the inherent difficulties with heliocentric charting.

One observes that the normal rules of horoscopy are ignored in the chart. Venus and Mercury revolve around the Sun. This means that, in a geocentric chart, these three bodies are limited in the extent of arc by which they may deviate from each other. This restriction does not apply in a heliocentric chart. In the chart alongside, we see Mercury in Capricorn and Venus in Virgo:

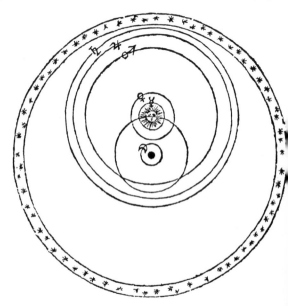

the Sun is not portrayed in a heliocentric chart, just as the Earth is not directly portrayed in a geocentric. In both cases, Sun and Earth are to be visualised, respectively, as being at the centre of the chart: sometimes, in heliocentric charts (and indeed, sometimes in geocentric ones) the respective bodies are inserted diagrammatically, as a matter of form, but always at the centre of the relevent charts.

Childrey's *Syzygiasticon* appears to be a slight work – an ephemeris, with ingress charts for the four quarters – yet in terms of astrology it is one of the most remarkable ephemerides ever published. The work proclaims an entirely new approach to astrology – not merely in terms of the heliocentric method, but also in terms of a scientific methodology. Childrey proposes setting up a history and chronology of 'all the signall occurrences in Empires, Kingdomes, States, etc. with their times (as near may be) were with all convenient brevity digested into Books'.[91] These would form the basis for the checking of historic events against the new heliocentric astrology which Childrey has proposed. Not only planetary considerations will be weighed against this history. A list of previous eclipses, 'calculated for some ages past ... [with] their place in the Ecliptique', should be compiled, and a history of comets should be written, together with a list of 'all new Stars', by which the cosmic effects may be measured against earthly events.[92] In particular, Childrey recommends that 'all grand extremities of weather' that have been recorded by historians should also be gathered together 'and compared with the Aspects of the heavenly bodies'.[93]

Childrey was entirely revolutionary – almost iconoclastic – in his approach to the art. In effect, he recommended that the following staples of horoscopy be dispensed with, as superfluous to his new heliocentric system: exaltations, triplicities, terms, faces, the Part of Fortune, combustion, and retrograde motion. It is a tribute to Childrey's insight that four from this list have been omitted from most modern astrologies, while retrogradation is now held as being of questionable value in interpretation.[94]

The 'new' astrology left by Childrey's massive rejection of tradition would depend mainly on a pair of interrelated aspects, planets in signs, and Lordships. Furthermore, astrologers would be required to consider aspects to the Moon, which (he reminds us) has a different centre within the heliocentric system. His most surprising deviation from tradition was his insistence that the astrologer should predict from the conception chart, rather than from that cast for birth. Finally, as the sample heliocentric chart above left indicates, Childrey would begin the year at the winter solstice, rather than at the vernal equinox.

Childrey was particularly keen to establish the rhythms behind the movements of tides: indeed, he was one of the first to realise that tides are governed by multiples or submultiples of the tropical year.[95]

As we have seen, Childrey was not the only astrologer of the period to recognise that the Ptolemaic astrology was in need of reform. Indeed, many intelligent men and women of the last half of the century had concluded that astrology was essentially a pagan art. Furthermore, they recognised that it was not 'scientific', in the sense that it had never been subjected to methodical testing. The word scientific had not yet acquired the near-deific connotation of modern times, yet it was felt by many people – including astrologers – that the art was ripe for a new examination, and that all those things which were found wanting should be relegated to the scrap heap of history. Joshua Childrey was prepared to act on his ideas by attempting a practical reform of the art.

A HOROSCOPE OF FRANCIS BERNARD

Among the seventeenth-century experimenters was Dr Francis Bernard, who concentrated on the horoscopes of cities and whose work has survived in a number of collected nativities and commentaries. One of these collections includes the chart which Bernard cast for the outbreak of the Great Fire of London, which he dated to 1 September 1666, in the early hours of the morning.[96]

Bernard's technique was to treat cities as though they had a natural history and were, like human beings, subject to 'accidents', or events. In this case, he was convinced that the Great Fire was one of the *accidentia* arising from the chart he cast for the City of London.[97] Just as it is sometimes possible to construct a valid horoscope for a birth of unknown date and time, from a study of the accidents encountered by the native, so, Bernard argued, it was possible to discover the horoscope of a city, the chart of which was either forgotten or had never been established. He constructed a history of fires in London, from 1212 onwards, and from this built up what he regarded as a convincing chart of the city.[98] Curiously, he wrote to William Lilly about his discovery only two years before Lilly himself famously predicted the Great Fire of 1666.

This 'prophecy' was made in the form of a 'hieroglyphick' in which Lilly represented London as an image of Twins hanging over a great fire. This woodcut was rendered slightly arcane by Lilly's recognition that London is ruled by Gemini, the Twins.[99] One really interesting thing about this woodcut was that Lilly cunningly placed alongside the Twins an empty quadrate chart, suggesting that, in time to come, someone would be able to insert the planetary positions relating to the conflagration that would destroy 436 acres of the city.

The horoscopic data from Bernard's fire-diary (above) are derived from one of

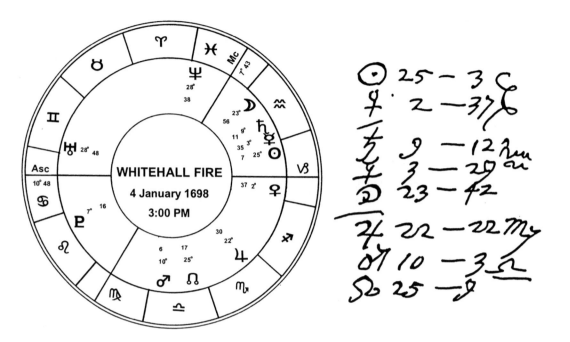

his manuscript notebooks now in the British Library.[100] With the hindsight offered by history, we may be inclined to examine the entry for 2 September 1666. However, we can learn more from a lesser-known London fire, that which destroyed Whitehall in 1698 (above). Bernard has grouped the planets in a manuscript notation horoscope that was widely used among specialists during the seventeenth century, especially in their personal notebooks. Above, I give a modern horoscope for the event, cast for 3:00 PM. It will be seen that the related manuscript data were tolerably accurate: Jupiter alone is out by a little over a degree.

When Dr Bernard died in 1698 his library, with its books in Greek, Latin, Italian, Spanish, German, Dutch and English, was sold at auction. The published list suggests that Bernard must have owned the most astonishing private collection of astrological books in seventeenth-century England.[101]

SOME CHARTS OF MORIN DE VILLEFANCHE

Although England proved to be the place where seventeenth-century astrology flourished, one powerful influence that would help change horoscopic interpretation came from France. This was the work of the astrologer, Jean-Baptiste Morin de Villefranche, who wrote with all the precision and system of a medieval Schoolman. Possessed of a thorough knowledge of practical astrology, he was enthused by a powerful urge to Christianise astrology, at about the time when the official Christian hold over the art was itself weakening. With remarkable intellectual dexterity, Morin succeeded in this Christianisation without changing much of the pagan Ptolemaic tradition.

Morin should be remembered by historians of science as the first person to discover a valid method of determining longitude. Unfortunately, acknowledgement of his extraordinary achievements in this area was thwarted by the pernicious influence of Richelieu, in consequence of which Morin's contribution was not officially recognised by the Royal Council until after the death of the French first minister, in 1642.[102] In his analysis of his own personal horoscope, Morin offered an interesting planetary explanation as to why Richelieu should have been his 'secret enemy'.[103] Later, I shall examine two charts cast by Morin that relate to the life of Richelieu.

Morin's primary message was that a new astrology was needed, and that this new art should be a simplification of the systems known to practitioners. This renewal should be marked by a return to the basic principles set out by Ptolemy, or even (in Morin's ill-founded view) by a mythological pre-Ptolemaic astrology. Of course, this is by no means the whole truth behind Morin's massive and scholarly book on astrology, yet the attempt made by him to systematise and simplify the complex tradition resulted in its acquisition of an accessible and rational-seeming form of astrology.

Like so many astrologers, Morin had trained initially as a physician: unusually, he gave up medicine because he did not approve of the excessive blood-letting then popular in conventional treatments. Morin recorded that he was introduced to astrology by a Scotsman then living in Paris, William Davison. An astrological prediction which Morin made shortly before 1617 concerning his employer, the Bishop of Boulogne, proved to have been accurate. As a result, his reputation as an astrologer was widely bruited, and he was consulted by many influential individuals, including those in the royal court. In 1638, when the birth of the future *Grand Monarque*, Louis XIV, drew near, his father, Louis XIII, specifically commanded Morin to be cloistered in the royal apartments so as to cast a precise horoscope for the birth of his son.[104] Ultimately, all charts (even the rectified versions) of Louis XIV owe their data to Morin. The

example left is from a book dealing with the chart, published in 1680.[105] It differs only by a few minutes from that given by Morin.[106] Those unaccustomed to reading seventeenth-century charts may have some difficulty disentangling the sigils in the second house:

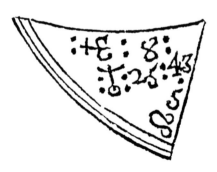

Reading from the top, the three entries are: Sagittarius 8° on cusp of second; Mars in 25° 43′ Sagittarius; Caput in 5° Capricorn. One observes that the time of birth (23.03 PM) is given for the time system then used in France, where the day began at twelve noon. The abbreviation S:N: after the date stands for *Seigneur Notre*, which is the equivalent of 'the year of Our Lord'.

Few astrologers would have foreseen from this chart that, on the death of his father, and before the child was five years old, he would have become king.[107] Morin gained favour in the royal court and it is known that he later cast horoscopes to determine the most satisfactory times for various royal events and embassies, though he was never appointed royal astrologer.

Morin's major work was so monumental in scope that it is impossible to deal with adequately in a restricted space. However, some of his proposals were ahead of his time, and have found their way into many forms of modern astrology. Among these we might include his approach to the significance of the ascendant. Morin emphasised, above all other factors, the degree on the ascendant. He held this degree to be more important than even the Lord of the ascendant, or than any planet in the ascending sign. In the context of seventeenth-century astrology this was a revolutionary idea, yet the paramount importance of the degree is taken for granted in modern times.[108]

Morin's book was intensely Christian. The concept of the Trinity of the Godhead, so important to seventeenth-century Catholics, permeated his book, in which he adopted the Paracelsian triad of occult worlds – the Elemental, the Ethereal and the Celestial – as a pertinent analogy for the Trinity. In terms of astrology, these corresponded approximately to the earthly, the planetary and the zodiacal (the latter merged with the realm of fixed stars).[109] This attempt to unify the Christian Trinity with the occult ternaries led Morin to adjust the astrological traditional itself, by subdividing the twelve houses into four sets of ternaries. He concluded that, just as the twelve signs of the zodiac were regulated by four great triangles (the Elemental triangles that mark out the quadruplicities), so the houses should be similarly arranged. The four domiciliary trigons were arranged by him in the schema alongside.

One of the triangles from the above four he called the 'trigon of Passions'. This trigon incorporated the twelfth house, with its emphasis on the sufferings that assail the native during and towards the end of life – hence, illnesses and enemies. The eighth house was linked with the final passion or suffering, which is death itself. According to Morin, the fourth house corresponded to the parents. This last amendment to the tradition is fundamental. In the

Ptolemaic astrology inherited by the West, the fourth house was the exclusive domain of the mother, while the tenth house was that of the father. It is in regard to the religion – engendered change for this house that Morin reveals the ultimate background to his system of domiciliary trigons. The house is linked with the material suffering of birth itself – that is with incarnation and with the moral suffering imposed on those born by Original Sin. Here, the parents are revealed as being linked with the primal parents, the archetypal Adam and Eve. These associations, with a somewhat idealised pristine parenthood, and with the notion of birth as suffering, reveal the domiciliary trigons as a result of an attempt to present the houses from a point of view of the Trinity of the Godhead.

The structure of houses proposed by Morin is intensely Christianised: it is no accident that the ninth house, formerly linked with philosophy, exploration, education and travel, has become, in the hands of Morin, a representative of 'Life in God', the *vita dei* of the contemplatives.

It is in his study of the houses that Morin is most irritating. He suggested that the knowledge of the twelve houses (and presumably that of the twelve signs) was revealed to Adam, who passed it on to posterity by way of the Cabala. This astonishing view of the history of astrology seems to hinge on his recognition that the sephiroth of the Cabalistic Tree were themselves equivalents of, or reflections of, the twelve signs, and of the twelve houses. Perhaps Morin had been persuaded into this view by the writings of the English Rosicrucian, Robert Fludd, who had published elaborate diagrams relating the Tree to the twelve signs.[110]

Some modern historians have had difficulties explaining why, and on what astrological grounds, Morin sought to change the interpretation of houses. As we have seen, in his proposed system he held that the fourth house, rather than pointing merely to the mother, should point to *both* parents. However, he took this reform further and proposed that the fourth should govern 'the animate, or living, possessions of the native', such as servants and domestic animals. The reason behind this adjustment to the traditional system has not been recognised with sufficient clarity by historians of astrology. The fact is that Morin was partly influenced by the tradition of horary astrology, in which the fourth house was already established as 'the House of the Parents'. As John Evans, who taught William Lilly astrology, had written within a horary context:

> By the fourth which is called the House of Parents, wee judge of Fathers, Houses, Lands, and ancient heritages, (but not always of those that are dead) and of Gardens, Woods, Pastures, & all things immovable, as of Castles, and other like things, and what may happen after death.[111]

For reasons which he never made clear, Morin was merging the horary and the genethliacal traditions. However, the fundamental reason behind this change is to be found in Morin's own search to rationalise and systematise astrology within a Christian framework.[112]

It has become a convention among modern historians of science to point to Morin as the last of the great French astrologers. The argument has been put forward that he could not find a publisher for his magnum opus, *Astrologia Gallica*, because the interest in astrology was on the wane, or because the Latin in which it was written was no longer the language of astrology or scholarship. It is certainly true that the royal decree prohibiting the practice of astrology and promulgated with the connivance of the French statesman, Jean-Baptiste Colbert, seems to have driven Morin into isolation. At all events, from about 1626 Morin began work on his magnum opus: an undertaking that was delayed by civil war in France, and which did not come to fruition until after his death. However, it is unlikely that any of these reasons for the delay in publication are sound. It is more likely that Morin could not find a publisher for his book simply because it was so critical, and because so many of his ideas flew in the face of the traditional art, as it was practised in his day. As the historian, Lynn Thorndike, has observed, Morin found so many faults with the astrology of everyone else that it is doubtful whether he himself would have found many followers.[113]

There was one division of astrology where Morin's great learning did provide a new impetus. His commentary on the methods of revolution charts was sufficiently concise to influence the development of this predictive technique in years to come. Morin pointed out that solar revolution charts could not have been accurate in the past simply because the tables formerly available (especially the Alfonsine tables) were not sufficiently reliable as a basis for such calculations: they could be as much as 20 or 30 minutes out. However, he argued that by now ephemerides had become sufficiently accurate for revolutions to be regarded as valid, and the whole art could be examined in a fresh light.[114]

One question raised by Morin – perhaps for the first time by a well-informed astrologer – concerned for which *place* the revolutionary chart should be cast. It was normal for such solar charts to be cast for the place of birth, but Morin proposed that for the time of a futurised chart to be accurate, then the place in which that event had occurred should be taken into account. For a revolution to be valid in time it had to be equally valid in space.[115] This explains why the revolution charts which Morin cast always indicated a place or latitude that the native was known to occupy at the time of the specific revolution. For example, the birth chart overleaf (left) was drawn up by Morin for his enemy, Cardinal Richelieu. Alongside is the solar revolution for Richelieu's fifty-seventh year (1641) cast for the more northerly latitude of 50 degrees, which, Morin tells us, is for the locality of *Ambianus* (Amiens), in Picardy.[116]

When contemplating the revolution of 1641, Morin recognises just how terrible was the opposition of Saturn, from the tenth house, to the satellitium of Mercury, Sun and Mars, in the fourth; it was in the following year that Richelieu died. One observes that the locality for this revolution chart of 1641 should have been the city of Lyon (Morin calls it by its Roman name, *Lugdunum*), at latitude 45 degrees. Morin tells us that, at the time the revolution became valid, Richelieu was in this city overseeing the decapitation of two of the Cinq-Mars conspirators, who had planned to kill the King.[117]

Nativitas Joan. Armandi Du Pleſſis
Cardinalis Richelii.

Revolutio.

230. 58.

332. 24.

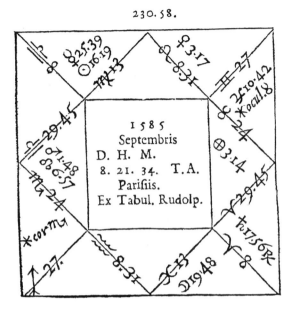

1585
Septembris
D. H. M.
8. 21. 34.   T.A.
Pariſiis.
Ex Tabul. Rudolp.

1641
Septembris
D. H. M.
8. 11. 0.   T.A.
Ambiani
Latit. 50.

A FOUNDATION CHART BY FLAMSTEED

Among the several famous surviving election charts relating to the foundations of buildings in the seventeenth century is one cast by Flamsteed, the first Astronomer Royal and the founder of Greenwich Observatory. The original chart, now preserved in Cambridge University Library, has been copied many times and has been published in a number of astrological works.[118]

Fittingly, the chart was erected by Flamsteed to determine a suitable time for the foundation of the Observatory. The most satisfactory election for this great event was for 10:03:14 PM on 10 August 1675. It was a curiously late time for such an enterprise. However, as we shall see, there was a very good reason why Flamsteed was prepared to wait for 17 degrees of Sagittarius to be on the ascendant. In almost every other respect, the moment was wisely chosen. The Lord of the Horoscope, which Flamsteed would probably have called the 'Almuten', was in its own sign, within 8 degrees of the

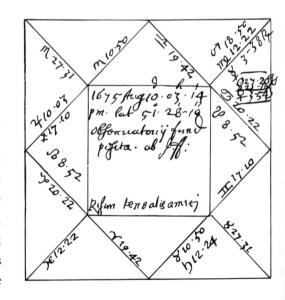

ascendant. Perhaps most interesting is the fact that Flamsteed elected a day in which the Sun was within the astrologer's arc (see pages 182–3).

Generally speaking, the chart is fairly accurate: the major deviant is Saturn, which was actually in 11.57 Taurus. As the astrologer Pearce has pointed out, the fortunate star Spica was on the Midheaven (though Flamsteed did not mark the star on the chart).[119] As a matter of fact, in 1675, Spica was in 19.18 Libra, and the correspondence between this degree and the Midheaven suggests that Flamsteed must have chosen the curious time for the laying of the foundation stone purely in order to ensure that this star was placed on the MC.[120]

At the bottom of the inner quadrate are the three Latin words *Risum teneatis amici* (you should restrain your laughter, friend), which Pearce has ascribed to 'some learned astronomer hostile to astrology'. However, if the writer were an astronomer, then he must have been one familiar with anti-astrological writings. The three words are part of a phrase quoted by the learned and unfortunate Elizabethan, Henry Howard, Earl of Northampton, in a book written against prophecy and judicial astrology. The full phrase (derived from lines by the Roman poet, Horace) was *Spectatum admissi risum teneatis amici*, which means something like 'If you have not seen it for yourself, friend, then you should restrain your laughter about it'.[121] As a suitable election for a foundation, it was thwarted by a factor well beyond even Flamsteed's knowledge. At the time he proposed the election, Cauda (which Flamsteed placed in 08.52 Cancer) was in exactly the same degree as the yet undiscovered Pluto!

Cauda on 10 August 1675: 08.36 Cancer
Pluto on 10 August 1675: 08.18 Cancer

Flamsteed had developed an interest in astrology during his youth and is one of the many individuals of the period who owed their enthusiasm for the art to William Lilly. It is said that Flamsteed first attracted Lilly's attention when the young man sent him astronomical data. Recognising the youth's potential, Lilly arranged for him to meet the influential astrologers Jonas Moore and George Wharton.[122]

Flamsteed seems to have had considerable experience with foundations and foundation charts. For example, he was among those who attended the laying of the foundation stone of Sir Christopher Wren's magnificent Greenwich Hospital. The diarist, John Evelyn, who was present at the event and who appears actually to have helped Wren lay the first stone, mentioned that Flamsteed observed the punctual time with his instruments.[123] The chart for this event demonstrates just how intent astrologers could be on providing a relevant election for a building. The rulership of Virgo over hospitals and nursing is catered for astrologically, by allowing Jupiter and Mars to be in this sign. Similarly, the concern with surgery was reflected in the presence of both Caput and the Moon in the sign Scorpio, which rules invasive surgery.

There was a certain irony in the fact that during the laying ceremony, one of the workmen grazed his fingers against the gravel support and some drops of blood fell on the stone. Astrologically, this ominous event might be explained by the fact that Mars was directly overhead, on the Midheaven and – what was then unknown to any astrologer of the period – was in direct opposition to Neptune, the ruler of liquids:

Mars on 30 June 1696:   29.00 Virgo
Neptune on 30 June 1696:   28.47 Pisces

THE HOROSCOPE OF ELIAS ASHMOLE

We can learn a great deal about the nature of seventeenth-century astrology from the horoscope which Elias Ashmole cast for his own birth. This chart, reproduced in figure 4, is a modern graphic 'translation' of the original, now in the the Bodleian Library, Oxford. A translation of this kind permits one to study the fixed stars with their modern names, rather than with the medieval names used by Ashmole. Furthermore, a translation offers one an opportunity to adjust the precessional positions of these stars within the zodiac (relative to 1617): this is necessary, as the precessional positions given in the original manuscripts were not always accurate. The zodiacal positions of planets and cusps are derived from a modern computerized version of the birth-time. As an aid to the reader, the same horoscope is given, in a small format, below.

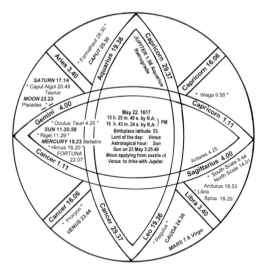

Not only was the manuscript chart drawn up with great care, but it also includes an astrological overkill of fifteen fixed stars, each marked with the sidereal position and each referenced into the chart. By modern standards, these stellar insertions allow too wide an orb, yet they do appear to be valid in the context of seventeenth-century astrology. At the bottom of the chart are useful lists of planetary latitudes and of antiscia and contra-antiscia.[124] The degrees on the cusps indicate that the *Modus Rationalis* was used for the houses.

The top line of the inner data suggests that Ashmole was born on 22 May 1617 at 15:25:49 PM in Lichfield. This contradicts the date given by the greatest student of Ashmole, Josten, who gave the date as 23 May 1617.[125] However, the first line in the chart relates to a time system that is no longer used in the West, but which was often used in seventeenth-century charts. As we shall see, the data in the horoscope relate to a birth on 23 May 1617.

Within the inner data section of the chart, there are certain terms that permit an insight into the nature of seventeenth-century astrology. It may seem trifling for us to examine terms which are now obsolete, yet the fact is that these were taken very seriously by the astrologers of the period and are an integral part of its horoscopy. Indeed, it is only by reflecting on the meaning of such terms that we will be able to understand just how different was their astrology from that of today.

I shall deal with the dates and time systems shortly. First, I would like to glance at two terms towards the bottom of the data. In the original, these abbreviations were *Dns. diei. (Venus)*, and *Hor. astr. (Sun)*. In my version of the chart, the terms are translated as 'Lord of the day: Venus', and 'Astrological hour: Sun'. These terms relate to planetary rulerships that are specific to the day of birth.

The 'Lord of the Day'. This is a statement of the ruling planet, the name of which is enshrined within the specific day of the week. Friday (the day on which the birth took place) is the day ruled by Venus. It is this planet which is supposed to suffuse the entire horoscope – it points to the presiding deity (for Venus was a planetary goddess) ruling the horoscope. It is true, as both Ashmole and Lilly recognised, that the dominant planet within the chart itself was Mercury, but it is Venus that lends her softness and feminine intelligence to Mercury, and indeed to all the other planets in the figure.

The 'Astrological Hour' has nothing to do with the ascendant, or *Horoscopos*; rather, it is an important hour that is determined by specific rules, which take the Lord of the Day as a starting point. The rules for determining this Lord point to a long-archaic system which measured the commencement of the day as at sunrise. Its antiquity is especially emphasised in the data for this chart which, as we shall see, insist on measuring time from two different fiducials – from noon time, and from midnight.[126]

One of the clearest expositions of the astrological hour is that given by William Lilly, whose instructions we shall now examine. The earth is divided horizontally by darkness and light: that part of the skies which is in daylight (regardless of the time of year) is called an 'Artificial Day', and is divided into twelve equal 'hours', which are rarely of an hour's duration, and which are called 'Planetary or unequal Astrological hours'.[127] Similarly, that part of the earth in darkness is divided into twelve equal 'astrological hours'.[128]

Each of the hours is allocated to one of the seven planets. The first hour is said to be ruled by the Lord of the Day – in this particular case by Venus, the ruler of Friday. The daylight planets are then allocated rulers in the specific order of:

Venus	Saturn	Sun	Moon	Mars	Mercury	Jupiter

This rulership series is directly derived from the sequence of days in the week. When the seventh planet has been reached, the sequence begins again. With Venus as marker of the first hour, Mars appears on the last 'hour' of the day. The sequence continues below the western horizon (in this case with Mercury), and begins the rulership sequence of the twelve hours of the night. Following this sequence, one arrives at the last hour of the night, which is shortly to become the first hour of the day. This hour is ruled by the Sun.

Despite the benign reputation of the Sun in astrological circles, the hour of the Sun was not highly regarded by medieval astrologers: it is generally an unfortunate hour, 'unless [for] making Applications to great Persons'.[129] Traditionally, it is not a good hour in which to invest money, or to attend on the female sex. Nor is it a good hour in which to begin a building. The entire programme of interpretation of the planetary hours is slanted towards horary astrology, and should never have been introduced into natal horoscopy. This much was admitted by the astrologer, Henry Coley, when he pointed out that the planetary hours are of great antiquity in astrology, but that they are not to be regarded as having the same interpretative strength as a well-constructed election chart which is in sympathy with the nativity of the querent.[130] Indeed, Coley was one of the astrologers of the period who was keen to see the whole apparatus of the hours dispensed with, as an invalid part of astrology.[131]

The true birth day in the Ashmole chart, according to the modern frame of reference, is recorded in the third line from the bottom. This marks the arc of time (3:25:49) traversed by the Sun on 23 May, presuming time to have begun at midnight. The time in the second line is based on the measurement of a day commencing local time midday, measured not by clock time, but by the transit of the Sun over the Midheaven. Within this frame of reference, the day of 22 May will not be completed until the end of the revolution on the following midday, when 23 May will begin.

One interesting thing about the Ashmole manuscript chart is that it makes use of three seemingly different time systems. The first two involved the date 22 May 1617, simply because the fiducial of time is midday. The first of these times is given as 15:25:49, which relates to the passage of time elapsing after the transit of the Sun over the Midheaven: this time measurement must not be confused with the twenty-four hour clock. Later, in the penultimate line, the equivalent time for the date of birth, 23 May, is recorded: in this, the position of the Sun on 23 May is recorded as 3:25:49. This is a time arc equivalent of the movement of the Sun after its transit of the local Imum Coeli, rather than the Midheaven.[132] Under this system of time measurement, the birth was recorded for the following day.

The number of fixed stars included in the manuscript horoscope is something of a puzzle. The placing of Antares, and even of the South and North Scales, on the cusp of the seventh, may be explained in terms of their proximity to the cusps themselves – even though a much wider orb is in play than is usually regarded as acceptable in the seventeenth century. For example, the North Scale is 10 degrees from the cusp and, in terms of the astrology of the time, would be regarded as effective. On the other hand, there is no apparent explanation for the inclusion of the two powerful stars, Spica and Arcturus, in the middle of the sixth house. The one possibility is that Ashmole was prepared to accept the stellar influences working through the antiscia. However, the star Wega, in 9.58 Capricorn, lies neither on an antiscion nor on a contra-antiscion.

Ashmole has marked into the chart the names of fourteen fixed stars. One observes that ten of these are from the medieval tradition, known to scholars as 'the fifteen stars' – a list that ascribed special sigils, jewels, and other associations to that number of special stars.[133] It is tempting to imagine that Ashmole was including in his chart only stars from this medieval tradition. However, this proves not to have been the case. There are exceptions in the chart which indicate that Ashmole was familiar with the methods used by astrologers, in respect of stellar readings: for example, the beneficial star Rigel is recorded, even though it was not among the fifteen, precisely because it was in the same degree as Ashmole's Sun, and therefore strongly operative within the chart.

Seventeenth-century astrology had taken much of its enthusiastic impetus from attempts to reform certain aspects of the Ptolemaic tradition. Among the most energetic and thoughtful of the English reformers had been John Gadbury, who, over a period of ten years, had collected some ten thousand birth charts in order to study specific effects, yet towards the end of his life even Gadbury despaired of his efforts at reform. In 1703, he admitted in a letter that, while he could not altogether 'Renounce, or bid Good Night to Astrology', he no longer felt in a position to defend many of its doctrines which he had previously accepted and used.[134] It was a sad letter, no doubt written under the influence of Saturn, during the penultimate year of a long life, 'the brink of the Grave being become the Desk we write on'. However, the truth is that the efforts towards reform *did* leave their mark on astrology, even if these were not felt until the following centuries.

CHAPTER 4

The Eighteenth Century

Astrology is too noble an Art to be slightly studied; and Pity it is, that it should fall into an ignorant or prophane Handling, as (the more is the Pity) of late Years it often hath, to the great Scandal of the Science itself, and the Reproach of the heavenly Bodies, those illustrious Subjects thereof.

Henry Season, *Speculum Anni: Or, Season on the Seasons, For the Year of our Lord* (1776), p. C3ʳ–C3ᵛ

The forecourt of the British Library in London is dominated by a giant statue of the seventeenth-century scientist, Isaac Newton, entitled *Newton after Blake*. Sculpted by Eduardo Paolozzi and unveiled in 1997, the design was influenced by a colour print that had long fascinated Paolozzi – the print *Newton*, made in 1795 by the English painter–poet, William Blake.[1]

Both the modern statue and Blake's print portray Newton seated, leaning over somewhat uncomfortably while constructing a geometric design on the ground with a pair of dividers. Viewed from a side elevation, the statue and the print are very similar, though Paolozzi's three-

dimensional figure is robotic, with heavy bolts through his joints, suggestive of an artist's lay figure. Unlike Blake's near-classical naked figure (which was influenced by one of Michelangelo's frescoes), Paolozzi's is mechanical in appearance, yet some of the divisions and slices into the body suggest a cosmic symbolism. The head is treated as though it were a celestial hemisphere, with semi-gores marking great circles, as though the skull were itself a model of the heavens. The division of the head, into left and right, is emphasised by strong verticals through the forehead and chin.

No doubt Paolozzi regarded the scientist Newton and the artist Blake as supreme examples of British genius, and therefore a suitable combination of science and art to mark so prestigious a site as the British Library. However, it is unlikely that even Paolozzi would have recognised the extraordinary astrology behind his choice of subject.

One astonishing astrological fact helps us understand the fascination that William Blake had with Isaac Newton. Although born over a century apart, the two great men were astrologically related. Both the artist and the scientist have had their horoscopes cast and interpreted by leading astrologers.[2] A comparison of their two horoscopes reveals they both had in common a number of zodiacal degrees.[3]

Newton's Neptune was in the same degree as Blake's Jupiter – indeed, the two planets are within a minute of each other:

Neptune in chart of Isaac Newton:	00.58 Sagittarius
Jupiter in chart of William Blake:	00.59 Sagittarius

Newton's Mercury was in the same degree as Blake's Pluto:

Mercury in chart of Isaac Newton:	20.58 Sagittarius
Pluto in chart of William Blake:	20.07 Sagittarius

Newton's Saturn was in the same degree as Blake's Uranus:

Saturn in chart of Isaac Newton:	19.54 Pisces
Uranus in chart of William Blake:	19.18 Pisces

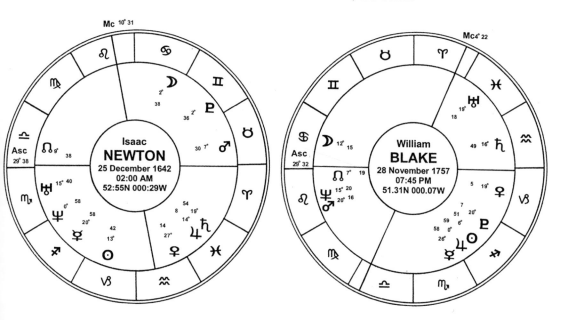

The communalities are astonishing. As we have already learned, even a single communal degree is something like a cosmic sign that two individuals will relate together in some way. Two individuals, cosmically related in this way, are generally pulled towards each other in a powerful unconscious urge to interact. In this case, the attraction was massive, for no fewer than six planets yoked together the two individuals through space and time.

Given this cosmic pressure, we find it easier to understand the peculiar fascination that Newton exerted over William Blake. The latter wrote about Newton, painted his picture and adopted him as a symbol of a particular form of consciousness, which he termed 'materialistic'.[4] In fact, Blake had a highly distinctive – even unique – view of Newton's achievements, as we might expect of his dark and penetrating Pluto, resting on the Mercury of the scientist. Blake (perhaps unfairly) maintained that Newton's vision was both materialistic and dismissive of spirituality: Blake argued that Newton reduced even sunlight – that most magical and spiritual of phenomena – to a stream of particles. In a word, according to Blake, Newton dismissed from science all the invisible spiritual hierarchies, and with them the centre of their adoration – God.

Paolozzi was born of Italian immigrant parents at 4:30 PM on 7 March 1924, in Leith, near Edinburgh.[5] We should not be surprised to find that his chart is intimately related to those of Newton and Blake. His Moon was in the same degree as the Caput in Newton's chart:

Moon in chart of Eduardo Paolozzi:	10:30 Aries
Cauda in chart of Isaac Newton:	09.38 Aries

One of the distinctive characteristics of Paolozzi's natal chart was the conjunction between the Sun and Uranus in Pisces. No doubt this contributed to his interest in mutilated and sectioned human forms, but it is also a conjunction which links his chart with a planet in Blake's horoscope. The conjunction is as follows:

Sun in chart of Eduardo Paolozzi:	16.51 Pisces
Uranus in chart of Eduardo Paolozzi:	17.28 Pisces

Now, in terms of astrological theory, a conjunction is sufficiently powerful to expand the orb of influence. In this case, instead of the maximum permitted orb of influence being 18.28 Pisces (that is, 17.28, plus 1 degree), the conjunction expands it to 19.28 Pisces. This means that the conjunction degree fell on Uranus (19.18 Pisces) in the chart of William Blake.

This astonishing galaxy of communal degrees pulls together three individualities from three different centuries, who, in a very real sense, meet in the statue on the forecourt of the British Library. Newton of the seventeenth century was the subject of a painting by Blake in the late eighteenth century: both became subjects of a sculpture in the late twentieth century.

In his print *Newton*, Blake emphasises the terrible single vision to which the scientist was subject, and which led to this materialism. The geometric design is being drawn, or constructed, by Newton on a scroll of paper. The curled spiral end of the roll is intended as a symbol of the life-force, of the higher spirituality, meant by Blake to contrast with the rectilinear triangle of the dividers alongside.

However, Newton's intense gaze at the design reveals what Blake regarded as the essential weakness of science – it is concentrated and one-sided. The lines Newton draws are reflected by the concentrated vision of his eye. The colour-print of Newton, which was the inspiration for Paolozzi's giant statue, has rightly been interpreted as a Blakean commentary on the limitations of single vision, and on the knowledge gained by mere intellect.

Blake is condemning the Newtonian science because it creates a world of abstractions and formulae. The effect of this is to turn man into a materialist, to armour mankind in the limitations of the physical world. Perhaps this explains why Paolozzi has armoured his own Newton with marionette joints, as though he were a puppet figure. The great mind of Newton is a prisoner in the material form his intellect has created.

The triangle formed by the pair of dividers is the primal symbol in both the painting and the statue. Newton stares down at a triangle, which is a symbol of the higher ternary, the Trinity, which he is pinning down, into the material earth. The geometric form within the triangle formed by the dividers is a curious one.

One other thing that Newton and Blake had in common was that, while neither was deeply interested in practical astrology, they both studied the art, and both counted among their friends a number of important practitioners. When Newton entered Cambridge University as a student, he elected to study mathematics as he was anxious to test judicial astrology, to which he had been alerted when he read a popular book on the subject. It is a matter of record that, years later, when Halley chided him for his belief in the validity of astrology, Newton replied, 'Evidently, you have not looked into astrology: I have.' Blake was sufficiently interested in the art to take lessons from his friend, the artist–astrologer, John Varley, during the first decades of the eighteenth century. Even before this time he had incorporated into some of his own paintings a number of astrological sigils.

The symbolism of Blake's *Newton* points to something else which Newton and Blake had in common: both were interested in alchemy and alchemical symbolism.[6] It is generally admitted by historians of the period that Newton was deeply interested in practical alchemy, yet it is not sufficiently realised that it is not possible to practise alchemy without recourse to astrology.

Blake had derived the symbolism of the dividers, as an emblem of Trinity, from illustrations to the alchemical writings of the sixteenth-century German mystic Jacob Boehme. For Boehme, the triangle was the symbol *par excellence* of the Higher Spirit. It is portrayed supreme above the circle containing the twelve signs of the zodiac, in one of the engraved frontispieces to Boehme's works (overleaf, left).[7]

This triangle is winged and contains the Hebrew letters of the name of God. In yet another frontispiece (overleaf, right), the triangle forms part of a subtle six-rayed Star of Solomon: its apex is crowned by an eye, and the wings are now visibly the wings of the Holy Spirit, in the form of a dove. What is of immediate interest is that the base of this upper triangle is hidden

behind the celestial globe: one has the impression of a triangle with a curved base. This is precisely the pattern seen through Newton's callipers, for he appears to have drawn a triangle and then placed within it a segment of a circle.

Perhaps Blake had actually intended a reference to this latter Boehme plate, for the triangle of light is topped by an eye. Just so, the single vision of Newton's eye is held down by the callipers – by the geometric design he has just constructed. It is surely no accident that if you place a straight edge on the right-hand arm of the callipers in Blake's print, you discover that the line continues directly up to Newton's eye. It is a perfect symbol of the single vision, in which the eyebeam of light is materialised into a metallic form, pinned into the matter of the earth.

It was in the work of Boehme that astrology was most intimately integrated into alchemy and the literature of Christian initiation. While Blake was not the first to take up a penetrating study of Boehme's symbols,[8] he was however, the most talented of Boehme's eighteenth-century followers, and most of the alchemical symbols that are hidden in his paintings and drawings can usually be traced back to the German mystic. In Paolozzi's *Newton after Blake* we find traces of a continuity of vision through the five centuries of astrology which we study in this present book. The original idea for the figure was derived from a painting of Abijah, in Michelangelo's fresco in the Sistine Chapel: this was transformed by Blake at the end of the eighteenth century – a century of intense interest in both alchemy and astrology. Blake's visionary figure was further ransformed by Paolozzi towards the end of the twentieth century. There is no horoscopic symbolism in the statuary dominating the forecourt of the British Library, yet the figure is as much an example of living astrology as any zodiacal circle. *Newton after Blake* reminds us of the mportance of astrology, and other arcane ideas, during the late eighteenth century – a period which is so often claimed by scholars to mark the decline of astrological studies.

In his excellent survey of eighteenth-century almanacs the modern historian, Bernard Capp, recognised that astrology survived in that century and beyond, but it did so in a crude form, as a sub-cultural activity, cut off from the intellectual mainstream of the period.[9] Astrology had always been the butt of criticism – most usually at the hands of those who had not studied the art. However, in the eighteenth century this kind of criticism reached a peak in a literature which often demanded some knowledge of horoscopy for its critical mordancy to be appreciated.

An example may be seen in a detail of the eighteenth-century illustration by Hogarth to Butler's poem *Hudibras* (figure 5). This engraving depicts the moment when the eponymous hero draws his sword against the crooked old astrologer Sidrophel. On the table, between the two men, is the large quadrate horoscope. In the second house of the figure are three sigils, signalling Saturn, Mars and opposition.

The sigils have been chosen to describe the belligerent relationship between the violent Hudibras (Mars), who is confronting ('opposition') the old man (Saturn), Sidrophel. It is a horoscope of occasion, which may be read in modern times only by those familiar with astrological sigillisation.[10] However, in the eighteenth century almost anyone with a modicum of education would have recognised its significance, just as they would have recognised the significance of the sacred word (the AGLA incised on the blade of the knife) being represented as pointing to the lowest part of the heaven, the IC.[11] The symbolism suggests that the entire engraving must be visualised as being horoscopic. It is part of the irony of the design that the monsters, such as the stuffed crocodile, should occupy the Midheaven of the illustration. The skeleton, symbol of the death forces, marks the eastern side, which should signal the ascendant life-forces. The implication is that the entire image must be read as symbolising a horoscope which is upside-down – that is, as a world in spiritual chaos.

As is Hogarth's wont, the plate is filled with subtle delicacies. For example, the cat is not frightened by the anger of Hudibras, but is watching a mouse, hidden under the tablecloth. A telescope lies partly under the same tablecloth. These are references to the supposition that in Butler's poem Sidrophel represented the conceited astronomer Sir Paul Neal. According to a tale that circulated widely in Butler's day, the unfortunate Neal had claimed that, while gazing through his telescope, he had discovered an elephant on the Moon. However, it turned out that he had a mouse in the instrument.

For all the intelligent interest in astrology, and for all the humour furnished by the critics, there was a decline in astrology during the century. However, the decline in horoscopy was even more serious — so serious, indeed, that one might even go so far as to say there can be no extensive history of the subject for the century. Nor are the reasons for the decline in these arts hard to find. Scholars, scientists and the general reading public became interested in other, more scientific, models of the universe than that offered by astrological traditional views. On the Continent, the papal interdiction against astrology had publicly discouraged the dissemination of the art and, almost inadvertently, supported the new Enlightenment, which favoured a mechanistic view of the universe.[12] In spite of this, astrology continued to be practised in certain areas — especially in England. Although, as we shall see, the names of several astrologers have come down to us from that century, serious horoscopy seems to have become the interest of a handful of more or less competent dilettanti, and, in comparison with the plethora from the previous century, relatively few horoscopes have survived. As the historian, Patrick Curry, has pointed out, in contrast with the heyday of astrology in the previous century, only three new textbooks on astrology were published throughout the entire eighteenth century.[13]

The decline may be traced both to the materialism that was sweeping Britain during the early eighteenth century, and to the change in those years in the apprenticeship system, which underlay many forms of education. In the late medieval period, those who were anxious to learn astrology might have access to the lectures on the subject which were an important part of medical courses in the major universities of the West. Although there were severe social and financial limitations as to who might attend such courses, even the lesser universities usually had official classes in astrology to serve their medical faculties. This no doubt explains why so many of the leading late medieval horoscopists had started out their careers as doctors, or with an interest in medicine. By the mid-seventeenth century, such academic support for the art had been abandoned, and the only hope for direct tuition was for a pupil to attach himself to one of the famous or competent astrologers of the period. This explains why so many contemporary astrologers were so anxious to acknowledge the names of their teachers in their private correspondence and autobiographies. Christopher Heydon had learned astrology from Richard Forster. John Gadbury had studied under Nicholas Fiske. William Lilly had learned astrology from the scholar John Evans and then, in turn, taught Henry Coley. In his youth, John Partridge had taught himself Latin, Greek and Hebrew, but found it easier to learn astrology from Dr Francis Wright.

George Parker, an astrologer from Shipston on Stour, Warwickshire, was sufficiently long-lived to survive through the first half of the eighteenth century, and yet to have studied under a tutor who was well versed in the very best of seventeenth-century astrology. He had been taught the art by the Irish astronomer, Thomas Streete, who had been born in 1621 and who, after the Restoration, lectured at Gresham College, and published his *Astronomia Carolina* in 1661.

Parker was probably the first English astrologer to sell printed blank schemes for the insertion of horoscopes.[14] Born on 9 August 1654 (he had both the Sun and Cauda in the astrologer's degree), Parker outlived his own age: he had been acquainted with John Partridge and had counted Flamsteed among his friends. In his turn, Parker personally taught horoscopy to Edward Thwaites, a noted scholar of Anglo-Saxon and professor of Greek, 'one of the most inspiring teachers which Oxford has ever produced'.[15] Furthermore, Parker unwittingly bridged the tutorial gap caused by social changes when he passed on the horoscopic tradition (if in a somewhat garbled form) by editing for republication Eland's influential *Tutor to Astrology*.

Parker's edited version of this elementary primer of astrology was published in 1704, and appeared in a number of editions in subsequent years.[16] As Parker admitted, this book suffered from having originally been written to serve horary astrology, yet it did offer a newcomer to the art an opportunity to learn the basic rules of horoscopy, including even the difficult art of directing planets to assess future events. The primer contained only two horoscopes: significantly, one (termed an 'experiment') was a horary chart, cast for 7 November 1687. Our main interest in this primer, which was advertised in the United States, is that it offered Americans an opportunity to study practical horoscopy without having direct access to teachers, who were, in that century, few and far between.

As we shall see when we come to study a sample eighteenth-century reading of a chart, the horoscopy of the period was little different from that practised in the more astrologically learned seventeenth century. Eighteenth-century astro-analyses were rich in references to lordships, dignities, terms, Arabian terminologies and fixed-star influences, which were to all but disappear from popular astrology by the twentieth century.

While the terminologies had changed but little, there was a general decay in proficiency. From surviving examples of horoscopy, it is evident that amateurs, lacking in the experience and knowledge common to astrologers of the seventeenth century, were being called upon to pronounce astrological judgements beyond their capabilities. One tragic example of the quality of horoscopy on offer is recorded by the historian, Leventhal, who mentions charts cast for the sailing of two Rhode Island privateers, in 1745. The horary 'horroscope' was cast 'according to the custom of the time', yet it seems that the choice of astrologer had been unfortunate. The latter elected that the vessels should sail on Friday, 24 December 1745. Both vessels were lost.[17] In fact, the astrologer could hardly have selected a more unfortunate time to embark on a voyage: the obvious truth, hidden behind the story, is that the astrologer was not very learned in his art. Given the limited knowledge of the period, he might be forgiven for not knowing that Neptune was in opposition to the Sun, and that Uranus was on Mercury. However, a simple scrutiny of an ephemeris would have revealed that the Moon was in opposition to Jupiter, and that Saturn was in close square to the Sun!

A more learned astrologer might have been familiar with a famous case-history which involved a communal degree on that fatal day. John Gadbury had published a chart for the sailing of Lord Willoughby from the Barbados on 18 July 1666: his fate was much the same as that of the earlier example, for, as Gadbury tersely recorded, 'he was never seen any more'. The planet Jupiter was retrograde in the second house in 28 Pisces. On the day the Rhode Island privateers were advised to sail, their Caput was in exactly the same degree. In each tragedy, the astrological cause of the loss was the same. The degree was dangerously close to the fixed star Scheat, which had a bad reputation for causing shipwreck, and for death by drowning.[18]

If there was one area in which astrology could survive, and even flourish, it was in that which served ordinary people – the almanacs. Providing useful astronomical and meteorological information nominally of importance to agrarian societies, the almanacs were also repositories of both astrology and horoscopy. The popularity of almanacs in the eighteenth century cannot be overstated: for example, Moore's *Vox Stellarum* sold as many as 230,000 copies in 1789. By 1839, its sales peaked at over double that number.[19] Some of the more interesting horoscopes of the eighteenth century are found in almanacs.

The almanacs of that century served as a lifeline for English astrology – and, by extension, for its American counterpart. These almanacs were far from being purely astrological in nature: they were designed to offer simple data relating to the seasons and meteorology, or weather-forecasting, which was of such importance for agrarian communities. In some cases, the data were presented in the form of sophisticated ephemerides, with planetary positions set out for each day. The better almanacs contained information on such phenomena as eclipses and the 'ingresses' marking the beginnings of the four seasons. In such documents – so practical as to inform and entertain both rural and urban communities – horoscopy and astrology lingered on, if only weakly by comparison with the previous century.

As the historian, Leventhal, observed, the almanacs of 1778 reported the complete eclipse of the Sun in 03.04 Cancer, on 24 June 1778, but not one of them used this cosmic event to hazard a prognostication for the outcome of the American Revolutionary War.[20] In fact, the eclipse had fallen sufficiently close to the Mercury in the revolution chart of George III for 1776 to threaten loss to the King, but no astrologer appears to have noticed. Such an oversight could never have happened in the previous century. However, a year or so later, one American astrologer, Roger Rintoul, amused himself by casting a posthumous horoscope of General Joseph Warren.[21] The chart was an obvious forgery in terms of time: though dated 1743, it had been cast long after the death of Warren, who had been killed at Bunker Hill on 17 June 1775. Rintoul may have been a proficient enough astrologer, yet his notes on the astrological cause of Warren's violent death were sheer fantasy.[22] As it was, Warren's natal chart had five planets in Cancer. Of these, the only one unknown to astrologers of the period was Neptune, which was in 7.05 Cancer. In the year of his birth (1741) a lunar eclipse had fallen exactly upon this planet, in 7.00 Cancer. At noon, on the day of his death, the Sun was in the same degree, at 6.41 Cancer.

The early almanacs often contained an 'Anatomy' – technically, the melothesic man, or zodiacal man. This is an image of the human frame marked with the zodiacal signs ruling the respective body parts. The one to the left, on the opposite page, appeared in a number of almanacs published in America during the eighteenth century.[23] The one to the right is from the 1774 edition of an English almanac entitled *Poor Robin*.[24]

Almost all almanacs made some reference to the eclipses for the given year. Some almanac-makers went so far as to cast charts for the more important of these cosmic events. Below, on the opposite page, is the horoscope cast by Henry Season for the lunar eclipse of 30 July 1776, which happened to be the first eclipse following the Declaration of Independence.[25]

♈ The Head and Face.

♓ The Feet.

Almost every almanac contained reference to the seasonal ingresses, and some offered charts or at least the vernal ingress, marking the entry of the Sun into Aries. An example of such a chart is given overleaf, alongside an interesting dissident horoscope. The standard quadrate (left) for the vernal ingress for 1774 was given by Francis Moore.[26] The dissident chart (to the right) was calculated by the astronomer Tycho Wing, who was intent on offering an alternative method of charting, based on the time of the lunation next preceding the vernal ingress.[27]

The important thing about the differences exhibited in these two charts is that they were both used as the basis for predicting coming events over the next three months, or even over the following year. Charts so different must have posited very different futurities.

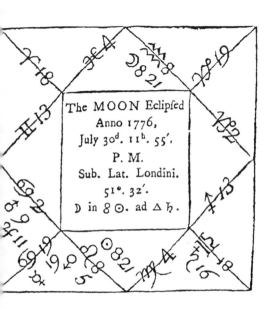

The MOON Eclipſed
Anno 1776,
July 30ᵈ. 11ʰ. 55′.
P. M.
Sub. Lat. Londini.
51°. 32′.
☽ in ☍ ☉. ad △ ♄.

Some almanacs were more imaginative in their inclusions of astrological or prophetic data. For example, for several years Francis Moore – the original Old Moore of later almanac fame – included a quatrain (alongside a translation) from the *Prophéties* of Nostradamus. In most cases, the inclusion of the particular verse was ingenuously explained on the grounds that its prophetic content was to come 'to fulfilment near these times'. There is little evidence that Moore knew much about

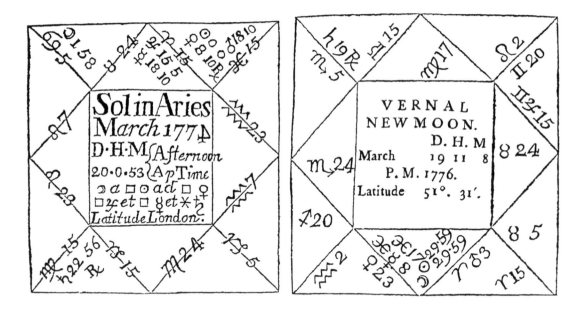

Nostradamus or his methods. Even so, it is interesting that in his almanac for 1776, prior to discussing the 'present Enmity with his Majesty's North American Subjects', Moore should have elected to choose a prophecy of Nostradamus which mentioned *La Terre neufue*, or New Land – a phase which the savant used indiscriminately for North and South America.[28]

Old Moore was not the first to incorporate potted interpretations of Nostradamus into his almanacs. Ever since 1672, when the French doctor, Theophilius Garcencières, published the first complete translation into English of the *Prophéties*, the obscure verses were pillaged by popular writers and astrologers.[29] For example, in 1679 John Gadbury's almanac quoted one of Nostradamus' astrological verses as though it had some contemporary relevance. In the same section, extrapolating from the vernal ingress chart for that year, Gadbury had predicted 'some famous Battail … near at hand Northward, or North-east'. This was the year in which the Duke of Monmouth crushed the Scottish Covenanters at Bothwell Bridge in Strathclyde.[30]

A few almanacs maintained contact with the roots of their art and included horoscopes for individuals – usually, for the recently dead. Thus, in 1775 John Partridge published the horoscope for the recently deceased astrologer and almanac-maker Robert White (opposite page, left). As a further example, in 1793 Henry Andrews (writing under the pseudonym of Francis Moore) published the death chart of Louis XVI (right). The time the guillotine fell is specified as quite literally 1 hour and 38 minutes 'before the Meridian' – that is, at 10:22 AM.[31]

The former chart is inaccurate by modern standards: converted into the modern time system, it was cast for early morning on the 7 June 1693. The block-maker has misread the figures 11, intended for the tenth and fourth house cusps, and rendered these as representing the sigil for Gemini. Furthermore, the latitude is hopelessly out, at 58° North, for White was born near Grantham (which is 52.55° North). Robert White was among those almanac-makers who had never hidden his interest in astrology, and included accurate tables for the positions of notable

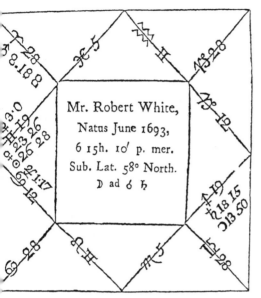

Mr. Robert White,
Natus June 1693,
6 15h. 10' p. mer.
Sub. Lat. 58° North.
☽ ad ☌ ♄

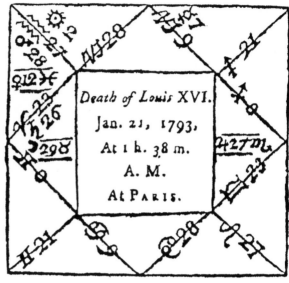

Death of Louis XVI.
Jan. 21, 1793,
At 1 h. 38 m.
A. M.
At Paris.

ixed stars. Like Parker, alongside the standard geocentric tabulations of the planetary positions he offered the heliocentric positions, tabulated at five-day intervals.[32] A detail from a page from White's almanac for 1774 reveals the service offered to astrology by the best of these annuals below). It is hard to conceive that such tabulations of fixed-star positions, though derived from tables designed for astronomers, and given by Right Ascension for conversion to zodiacal positions, would be of value to anyone other than astrologers and seafarers.[33]

In his almanac for 1734, Henry Season had filled a number of pages with a survey of his own personal horoscope, rendered infuriating by his refusal to specify the year or time, on the somewhat specious grounds that this would furnish his enemies and detractors with ammunition.[34] However, the data he offered later in his commentary (in the same

A TABLE of the right Ascensions in Time, Semidurnal Arches, Declinations, and Magnitudes of 30 remarkable fixed Stars, with their Names, and BAYER's Literal References, as they stand in Mr. FLAMSTEED's Catalogue. Exactly rectified to the Beginning of the Year 1772.

The NAMES of STARS.	Bay Ch.	R. Ascen. h. m. s.	Semidiur- Arches. h. m. s.	Declination. d. m. s.	Magn.	
The Southern Star, in Andromeda's Girdle, Mirach.	β	0 56 39	10 6 20	34 12 35 N	2	
The bright one in her left Foot, Alamack.	γ	1 49 54	sets not.	41 12 17 N	2	3
The unformed.Star above the Ram's Head.	α	1 54 10	8 9 13	22 21 24 N	2	
In the Head of Medusa, Algol.	β	2 53 12	sets not.	40 2 37 N	2	3
In Perseus's right Side, Alganib.	α	3 7 56	sets not.	49 1 24 N	2	3
The Middle and brightest of the 7 Stars.	ℵ	3 33 50	8 16 26	23 22 15 N	3	
The Bull's South Eye, Aldebaran.	α	4 22 43	7 28 44	16 1 38 N	1	
In the left Shoulder of Auriga, Capella.	α	4 59 40	sets not.	45 45 37 N	1	
The left Foot of Orion, Rigel.	β	5 3 28	5 20 27	8 29 5 S	1	
The middle Star in his Girdle.	ε	5 24 30	5 56 45	1 22 7 S	2	
In his right Shoulder, Betelgeuse.	α	5 42 42	6 41 2	7 20 52 N	1	
In the great Dog's Mouth, Sirius.	α	6 35 3	4 37 18	16 22 39 S	1	
In the Head of the 1st Twin, Castor and Pollux.	α	7 19 55	9 38 52	32 23 3 N	1	
In the lesser Dog's Thigh, Procyon.	α	7 27 16	6 33 12	5 49 47 N	1	2
In the Head of the 2d Twin, Pollux or Hercules.	β	7 31 14	8 58 42	28 34 38 N	2	

almanac) were evidently designed to permit a practised astrologer to work out the chart in detail: he seems to have been born at about 5:00 PM on 23 January 1693, with four planets in Capricorn.

The original Vincent Wing – the most famous astrologer of his extended family – belongs firmly to the seventeenth century, but his descendants continued the study of astrology through the eighteenth. The memory of the original Vincent Wing as mathematician, astronomer and surveyor persisted in astrological circles for well over a century and a half. Not only had his admirer, John Gadbury, published his natal and death charts shortly after Wing's death in 1668, but the birth chart was published as part of an engraved plate in the magnum opus of Ebenezer Sibly (which we shall examine shortly) at the end of the eighteenth century.[35]

Wing's namesake son, born in 1656, continued the family tradition of compiling and editing almanacs. Vincent Wing III was probably a descendant of the second namesake. He seems to have been born in 1727, and died in 1776: he was a friend of, and collaborated with, the 'professor of astrology', Thomas Wright of Eaton, who worked as an almanac-maker and boarded pupils, whom he taught Latin, Greek and English.[36] Tycho Wing of Pickworth was born in 1696, and became a close friend of the astrologer, Edmund Weaver, of Catthorpe, in Leicestershire.

Independently of Wing's personal fame, the family name persisted well into the nineteenth century in the almanac literature. The historian, Bernard Capp, has suggested that this dynasty of Wings, as leading mathematicians, astrologers, surveyors and almanac-makers, spread these intellectual and practical activities throughout the East Midlands.[37] Capp listed a number from their immediate circle, such as Richard Saunder, Joseph Pepper of Stamford, Thomas Sparrow of Hose, Robert White 'of Bingham', and Edmund Weaver of Frieston. Also from Frieston was the astronomer–astrologer, Henry Andrews (see below), who later compiled Moore's almanac, *Vox Stellarum*. From the same area, but not necessarily connected with the Wings, was William Harvey of Knipton (near Grantham), who compiled almanacs, and Edward Sharpe, also of Grantham, who advertised that he could make medical judgements, either from the patient's urine or from the date of birth. Sharpe was a friend of the most remarkable astrologer of the period, Henry Season. John Worsdale, whose chart of Napoleon we shall examine in Chapter 5, was born at Fulbeck, and seems to have been among the most important astrologers in the Grantham area. Indeed, historians have observed that a large number of astrologers lived in this area during the eighteenth century: it is likely that this dissemination of interest in the art was engendered and encouraged by the Wing family. Among the leading figures were Edmund Weaver and Robert White. Edmund Weaver of Grantham was a physician who advertised his astrological services, and who published the *British Telescope* from 1723 to 1749, the last edition being printed posthumously. Robert White, whose birth chart we examined above, was also from Grantham: he began the publication of *The Coelestial Atlas* in 1749 (he had compiled others in previous years). The *Atlas* proved so successful that it continued well into the nineteenth century – shorn of its horoscopy – under the guidance of W.S.B. Woolhouse, as *White's Coelestial Atlas*. Undoubtedly, this was one of the best almanacs of the nineteenth century, publishing, for instance, the monthly positions for Herschel's Planet, Uranus, and for the asteroids Ceres (called Piazzi's Planet), Vesta, Juno and Pallas.[38]

Henry Andrews, born at Frieston near Grantham in 1744, is said to have begun his astronomical studies and observations at the age of ten, when he would pass the nights sitting with a telescope mounted on a table in the middle of Frieston Green. In 1766, he moved to Royston, at that time the centre of much speculation regarding the newly discovered Templar's Cave, beneath the centre of the town.[39] From about 1789, until his death in 1820, he compiled and edited the immensely successful *Vox Stellarum* – better known as *Old Moore's Almanack* – and for about forty years supplied the astronomical data for the official publication, *The Nautical Almanack*.

Impressive as the list of the Grantham-area practitioners might be, there is every indication that astrology was alive and well in other rural areas in England. The many well-written articles on the art which appeared in the *Conjurer's Magazine* from 1791 onwards implied an established astrology – even an astrological community in London – as well as a receptive audience, informed enough to follow astrological arguments and terminologies. Many of these articles were written (under the pseudonym 'B') by William Gilbert who lived at 11 Devonshire Street and who, besides casting charts, prepared and sold magical talismans. Perhaps more serious in intent was the long-lived William Seed, who advertised himself as 'Professor of Astrology and Mathematics' in his almanacs, which were published under his name until the middle of the nineteenth century. He was clearly an excellent mathematician, but his published charts, while astonishingly accurate, have nothing original in their make-up and can play no part in our history.[40]

In the short-lived astrological and astronomical magazine the *London Correspondent*, one of the contributors, a professional astrologer called James Wright, identified the names of several of those anonymous writers of astrological articles for the *Conjurer's Magazine*. For example, 'W.E.' was William Elder, who had been born in 1739: we shall examine one of his horoscopes shortly. According to Wright, 'H.D.' was John Lambert, who had been born in 1757. It is evident that, even in London itself, there must have been many astrologers of fair repute. Among these, we learn of the gentleman-scholar, Mr Creighton, who, working from Ludgate Hill in the middle of the century, had a great following on account of his skill in astrology.

Of the several astrologers discussed above, Thomas White seems to have been the only eighteenth-century practitioner to introduce something new to horoscopy, even though the relevant chart did not see publication until 1810 (see pages 146–7, below). Another chart he published in the same year, cast for the birth of William Cromwell (overleaf), is among the more historically interesting personal figures of the time. Unlike so many published charts of the period, it is not a copy of an earlier horoscope and, in contrast to the general tenor of seventeenth-century horoscopy, it concentrated almost uniquely on fixed stars.[41]

By the astrological standards of the eighteenth century, the plethora of fixed stars were valid, since an orb as wide as 8 degrees was permitted. Thus, White located Spica (the 'Virgin Spike') on the cusp of the seventh house (15.37 Libra), whereas, in 1789, Spica was in 20.52 Libra.

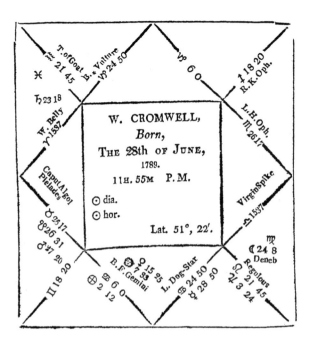

It is likely that anyone intent on exploring this chart will need help with the personalised abbreviations which White employed so liberally. *W. Belly* is the star in the Whale's Belly, and denotes Baten Kaitos, in Cetus. *B.F. Gemini* is the star marking the Back Foot of Gemini, denoting Alhena in Gemini. *L. Dog-Star* is probably 'Lesser Dog Star', or Procyon, the brightest star in Canis Minor. *Regulous* is Regulus, or Cor Leonis, the brightest star in Leo. *L.H. Oph.* is the star in the Left Hand of Ophiuchus, which includes Yed Prior, the δ of the asterism. *R.K. Oph.* is Right Knee of Ophiuchus, the η of the asterism, called Sabik, in Serpentarius. Almost certainly, 'B. * Vulture' is the Body of the Vulture, which is Wega, in the constellation Lyra (in 1789 in 12.21 Capricorn). *T. of Goat* is Tail of Goat, and probably refers to Deneb Algedi, in the fish-tail of Capricornus.

Even today, Ebenezer Sibly of Bristol is held in high esteem as an astrologer by those who have not troubled to examine his charting and have not read his magnum opus. The truth is that most of the fifty-nine personal charts that Sibly published and discussed in *An Illustration*, which first appeared in 1784, were borrowed from earlier astrological sources.[42]

For example, Sibly's chart of the sixteenth-century scholar Erasmus of Rotterdam (which he reproduced in his book) had been lifted, warts and all, from a horoscope reproduced by the Italian astrologer Junctinus two hundred years earlier. A comparison of the two charts (opposite page: Sibly's figure is to the right) reveals their similarity, and Sibly's plagiarist method.[43]

Developments in astronomy had meant that the tabulation of planetary positions had improved enormously since the sixteenth century when Junctinus practised astrology. In spite of this, Sibly seemed prepared to compound the several errors in the chart by not recasting the data to check their accuracy.[44] Thus, in the Junctinus version of the chart, Mercury is erroneously given in 29.18 Libra, when it was, in fact, in 8.9 Scorpio. Since Sibly had not troubled to recast the chart himself, he also gave the position as 29.18 Libra. Needless to say, Sibly copied into his own version of the chart all the other errors in the earlier one.

This irresponsible and desultory pillage of past charts was one of the hallmarks of eighteenth-century horoscopy. The elaborate and delicately engraved charts of the Sibly plates, with their interesting portrait busts in oval horoscopes, cannot obscure this practitioner's innate laziness in his attitude to astrology. The few natal horoscopes that Sibly cast personally were invariably incorrect – not merely in detail, but even in the matter of dates. Sibly was by no means ignorant of the rules of the art, yet he seems to have been a careless astrologer, and this alone

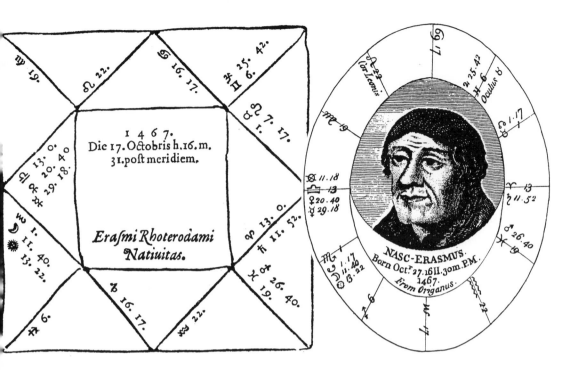

makes it difficult for us to select from his charts useful examples of eighteenth-century horoscopy. It is not at all surprising that one contemporary review dismissed Sibly's book as 'a quack performance' written 'in the very language of Bedlam'.[45]

Aware of these problems, I offer below two wood-block prints from Sibly's book. The first is the chart for the multifaceted genius, Emanuel Swedenborg, the other that of the poet, Thomas Chatterton, who committed suicide at the age of twenty-eight.

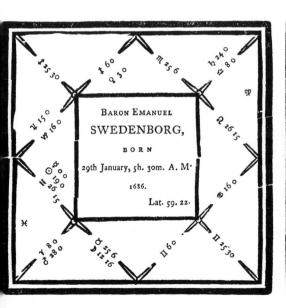

Swedenborg was a polymath genius. The first half of his long life was dedicated to the study of algebra, navigation, astronomy and chemistry. In 1724, he declined the chair of mathematics at the university of Uppsala, on the grounds that it was a mistake for mathematicians to be limited to theory. Many of his discoveries were years ahead of their time – especially his observations in regard to human physiognomy, but he also designed workable models of a submarine and a flying machine (which he probably designed while living in England). In his youth, Swedenborg spent over a year in London learning the English language, during which time he met a number of the great men of the age – some of whose horoscopes have already appeared in this book. For example, he was on intimate terms with Flamsteed, the royal astronomer, who permitted him to inspect the heavens through the newly perfected telescope at Greenwich. He was acquainted with Governor William Penn (see horoscope on page 92) – indeed, Swedenborg's cousin, Gustaf Hesselius, was later to settle in Pennsylvania, and became the first American artist of note.[46] Later, Swedenborg devised a method for determining longitude at sea by observation of the lunar position, desperately awaiting the essential new readings for the lunar positions promised by Flamsteed. In mid-life, Swedenborg began to have strange dreams and experiences, through which he became convinced that he had direct perceptual contact with the spiritual realms. This changed the whole direction of his interests and he began to explore and write about these experiences, penning many striking descriptions of the spiritual world and its inhabitants, among which, he believed, dwelled the earthly dead. Swedenborg died as late as 1772 and, as Sibly observed in his astro-analysis (begun in 1786), the great man had been known personally to many respectable personages still living, and presumably also to Sibly.

Sibly dedicated about 3,500 words to a study of Swedenborg's life and horoscope. In the same text, he printed a letter from the scientist to a correspondent in which was recorded the date of his birth: 'I was born [wrote Swedenborg, according to this record] in Stockholm, in the year of our Lord 1689, Jan. 29.' Surprisingly, on the previous page, Sibly had printed the horoscope (previous page) which gave the year of birth as 1686. Even more surprisingly, the planetary positions in the chart refer to 29 January 1688. Rarely do astrologers exhibit such carelessness.

Most standard reference books, including the excellent biography of Swedenborg by Sigstedt, give the year of birth as 1688. Indeed, Sigstedt is very specific as to the date: he pointed out that, according to the present Gregorian calendar, Swedenborg would have been born on 9 February 1688.[47] However, the old style (Julian) calendar was then in use in Sweden, and this was eleven days behind: he was born on Sunday, 29 January 1688.[48] It is something of a mystery as to how Sibly arrived at a chart based on the correct year, 1688.[49]

We cannot learn a great deal from the astro-reading that Sibly attached to Swedenborg's chart other than that very little had changed in astrology for almost a hundred years. The specialist terms Sibly used, as well as his method of interpretation, belonged to that phase of astrology in vogue among horoscopists during the seventeenth century. Indeed, the general tenor of this analysis suggests the horoscopy of the eighteenth century had added little new to the science.

To highlight Sibly's archaising, I shall print in italics the eight technical terms he used in his astro-readings. The terms so marked are among those discussed in the Glossary (page 249, below).

Sibly argued that because Venus (in Capricorn) demonstrated no *fortitudes* or *dignities*, Swedenborg was indifferent to women. We find no trait in the life of Swedenborg which 'describes his having formed any connection with the softer sex, or his having been at any time stimulated with those unconquerable desires for connubial enjoyments ...'.[50] Sibly seems to have overlooked the fact that Venus (in 30 Sagittarius) was in close trine to Mars (in 28 Aries). This aspect usually stimulates affections and often leads to an early marriage. In essence, however, Sibly was right in his assessment, for Venus, through lack of fortitudes and dignities, was not well integrated into the chart, and was overlaid by the dark planet. Later, Sibly admitted that Swedenborg, like Isaac Newton, had a mind that was not founded on a love of intimacy with the female sex.[51] The *elevation* and *isolation* of the planet Saturn was partly to blame for this, as such a placing invariably compelled the native to lead a single and solitary life. Sibly further linked this isolation with Swedenborg's delight in conversations with spirits – that is, with the realm of the dead, with which he had a unique familiarity.[52]

Jupiter was angular, being located within a few degrees of the ascendant. This, insisted Sibly, denoted good health and uninterrupted prosperity to the native. However, Sibly issued a word of caution: Jupiter has his *fall* in Capricorn, which suggests that Swedenborg will feel occasional indignities from the opposition of persons out of sympathy with with his own opinions and doctrine.

The planet Mercury is in the ascendant, approaching his *own triplicity* in the sign Aquarius. According to Sibly, this Mercury signifies a native of acute and penetrating genius, a sharp and ready wit, with a mind apt for the sciences. When we add to this the fact that Saturn was *Lord of the Ascendant*, in his *exaltation*, in trine to the ascendant, and in trine also to the Sun, then something of the enormous power of Saturn may be appreciated. Sibly puts it more poetically:

Saturn is lord of the ascendant, in his exaltation, and beholding the ascendant with triangular beams, at the same time that the Sun, the prince over the planetary system, beholds Saturn with a trine also, we shall not be surprised to find this native possessed of a most comprehensive and elaborate understanding, fraught with the strongest and sublimest ideas.[53]

Poetic or not, Sibly was being extremely careless. It is true that Saturn was Lord of the Ascendant, in Libra, and in the sign of his exaltation, but he was certainly not in trine to the ascendant. Fortunately, in spite of this astrological carelessness, Sibly's other conclusions still hold water.

Sibly points to the opposition of Saturn and Mars – 'an aspect which operated with uncommon strength and duration' – as one that gave Swedenborg the most enthusiastic flights of imagination, 'exposing him to the censure of the learned, as well as of the illiterate, who charged him with exorcism and madness'. However, Sibly was quick to emphasise that there is not the slightest trace of madness in the chart.[54]

Sibly's study of the horoscope for Chatterton was not so intensive as that for Swedenborg. The early death of the promising young poet by self-administered poison had clearly impressed Sibly, who attributed most of Chatterton's woes to the gathering of the planets and node in the sixth house. No fewer than four planets, Caput and Fortuna (augmented by Pluto, in modern charts) were in the sixth. This coalition

> presages every species of misfortune that can arise from poverty, and from the chicanery of prostituted women; the immediate effect of the baleful rays of Saturn and Venus.

The Moon in the twelfth house was 'receding from a sextile with Jupiter, and forming an opposition with the Sun'. That is to say, the Moon was departing from an early beneficial temperature towards an increased virulence from other malefic rays. Because the Moon was lady of the second house (15 Cancer is on the cusp) she governs his substance (i.e., income), and by virtue of being in the twelfth house, the house of imprisonment and affliction, denotes a frequent want of money. He was saved from a debtor's prison by Jupiter alone, which was in the second house and in his exaltation, and is the 'the means of producing timely and unexpected relief, in pecuniary matters'.

Saturn is in a sign out of all his dignities, and is lord of the eighth house (Capricorn is on the cusp). Sibly read this as indicative of certain ruin, by means of wicked and debauched women, described by Venus, which is conjoined to the worst rays of Saturn. Sibly calculated that Saturn was the anaretic, or 'destroyer of life'. Since 'Venus is in conjunction with Saturn, who rules these evils, and draws them as if it were within the focus of her own orb, it is evident that his death would come by his own hand, under the pressure of despair, heightened by meagre want, through the perfidy of some abandoned female'.[55]

Sibly discusses the fact that Chatterton committed suicide by taking poison, and attributes his self-murder to the conjunction of Saturn and Venus in the same degree of Sagittarius. He confirmed the importance of this conjunction when he calculated that Saturn would have returned to its natal place (and thus to the conjunction) in August 1770, the year of Chatterton's death. In fact, once again, Sibly was wrong. In 1770, Saturn was in Cancer and Leo, and nowhere near Sagittarius. Had he troubled to do progressions for August 1770, the cause of Chatterton's death would have been more evident. The progressed places for that time included the precise conjunction of the Moon with Venus (both in Capricorn), and both opposed by Jupiter, across the horizon angles.

The real source of Chatterton's predilection for poison lay hidden from Sibly, when he first cast the chart. The planet Uranus had been discovered by the time Sibly wrote the book, but, in the five years since its discovery, no astrologer had yet proposed what the significance of the new planet might be. At the birth of Chatterton, Uranus was in 29.33 Aquarius, and within a few degrees of the MC. The planet was very close to the star Fomalhaut, which, in 1752, was in

00.23 Pisces. In modern times – thanks mainly to studies of the influence of Uranus – astrologers have realised that the combination of this planet with the star gives rise to 'wasted talents', addiction to drugs, and suicide.[56]

Sibly may be forgiven for knowing nothing about the influence of Uranus. However, it is hard to forgive him for not inserting the new planet in his charting systems, especially in the later editions of his book, which appeared during his lifetime.

A careful reading of the astrological sections of Sibly's book reveals that, in most essentials, his interpretation of horoscopes was little different from that employed in the sixteenth century. This implies a continuity in English astrology that was lacking in all other European countries, where the practice of astrology seems to have become moribund. One historian has concluded (perhaps just a little rashly) that in the West, for a period of close on two hundred years, from about 1700 until 1890 or thereabouts, astrology was practised only in Great Britain, and was almost completely forgotten on the Continent.[57] One must counter this assertion by pointing out that astrology was also practised widely in the United States during this period, especially during the nineteenth century.

PARTRIDGE AND SWIFT

Throughout most of the eighteenth century, there was one almanac of repute which appeared without fail. An annual version of Partridge's almanac, *Merlinus Liberatus*, had been published for several years before the beginning of the century, but a famous and cruel literary hoax of that period disrupted its continuity. The satirist, Jonathan Swift, who had an interest in astrology which is sometimes evident in his writings, decided to lampoon the almanac-writer, John Partridge, partly in fun and partly in satire.[58]

The Partridge almanacs were no more inelegant in style than any others of the period.[59] However, in 1707 the astrologer George Parker, reacting to certain infelicities in *Merlinus*, suggested that some able and polite pen of the Church of England might care to chastise Partridge, both for his scandalous use of astrology and for his continual denigration of the Church.[60] Jonathan Swift responded to this call.[61] Writing under the pseudonym Isaac Bickerstaff, Swift wrote a pamphlet that contained a number of predictions, included one that Partridge would die on 29 March 1708.[62]

Of course, Partridge did not die. Indeed, he might have been inclined to join in the fun of the occasion, had not Swift published another pamphlet giving a straight-faced account of his death, on the predicted day.[63]

The joke spread, and caused much hilarity, yet it got out of hand for Partridge personally. The bureaucrats at the Company of Stationers (which controlled the sale of almanacs) were taken in by Swift's little joke, and struck Partridge off their lists, immediately applying for the rights to publish the lucrative almanac themselves. This meant that Partridge's livelihood was effectively destroyed. When he did manage to get his act together once again, in 1714, Partridge published his almanac under a new title, *Merlinus Redivivus* – a title which made some capital from the story of his experiences, and one that remained in use for many years, until changed to *Merlinus Liberatus*, with compilation still attributed to 'John Partridge'.[64]

It is evident from this story that Swift's actions had a disastrous impact on Partridge, which leads us to question whether this interaction was reflected in their personal charts. I have not been able to ascertain the exact birth time of Swift, but he was born on 30 November 1667, in Dublin: for want of a time, I have cast a midday figure. John Partridge was born on 18 January 1644, at 8:27 PM, in East Sheen. As we might expect, the pair had a communal degree. Swift's Mercury was on the Mars in Partridge's chart.

Mercury in chart of Swift:	07.44 Capricorn
Mars in chart of Partridge:	07.09 Capricorn

There could be few more unequivocal examples of astrology at work than in this pen-portrait of literature (Mercury) affecting the work (Mars) of another individual. Below, is a modern nativity of Swift, alongside an eighteenth-century version of Partridge's chart.[65]

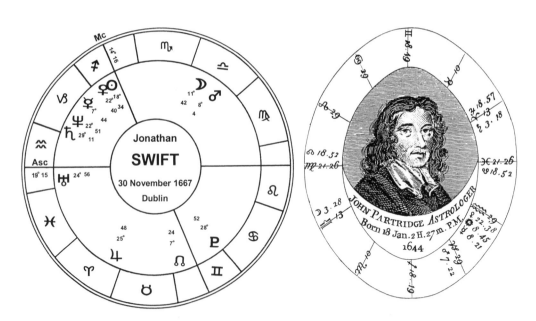

The story of Swift's over-savage treatment of Partridge offers its own commentary on the decline of astrology in the eighteenth century. Previously, almanac-makers and astrologers had frequently attacked one another – especially during the seventeenth century, and more especially during the periods before, during and shortly after the Civil War – yet no amateur astrologer had previously entered the fray. Swift felt that almanac-makers, who were critical of the Church of England, were fair game for his vitriolic pen.

In fact, according to one contemporary – as it happens, a critic of astrology – it had been Part-ridge who had helped rehabilitate the reputation of the art in the last years of the seventeenth century. In his book *Mene Tekel*, Partridge had predicted the end of James II.[66] Of course, it was legally impossible for him to mention the King by name, so he wrote of a 'man of 55 years of age', who 'hath Leo Ascending', and revealed from the chart of this man the series of directions that would lead to his end. In 1688, when the prophecy was made, James was fifty-five years old: his horoscope showed not only Leo on the ascendant, but Moon and Mars rising in this sign. Furthermore, the list of difficult directions given by Partridge corresponds to those found in the King's chart. As a critic of 1699 admitted, this successful prediction in '*Mene-Tekel* not only got the Author a great Name, but patcht up the decayed Credit of Astrology among the Populace . . .'.[67]

In 1732, Benjamin Franklin – as always impelled by his immense sense of fun – successfully repeated Swift's mock death, by predicting, in his own almanac, the demise of the almanac-maker, Titan Leeds. The joke played on for just over eight years.[68]

SOME HOROSCOPES FOR THE FRENCH REVOLUTION

The guillotine was made ready – we cannot say 'invented' – just in time to be of service to the more extreme of the French Revolutionaries. On 3 June 1791, Lepelletier de Saint-Fargeau persuaded the French Assembly to vote that all criminals condemned to death should die by decapitation. Shortly afterwards, each of the major cities in France was furnished with a suitable machine, named after its supposed inventor, Guillotine.[69]

The date is not without significance. On that Friday in June 1791, the planet Mars was in 23.32 Taurus. This means that it was in the same degree as the fixed star Algol, infamous for its violence, and for bringing about death by strangulation or decapitation.

Mars on 3 June 1791:	23.32 Taurus
Position of Algol in 1791:	23.16 Taurus

At about the same time as this new infernal machine came into infamous use, Sibly observed that when Algol is in the same degree as that planet, it 'shews danger of sudden death'.[70]

Virtually all the images of the constellation Perseus (where Algol is located) are in the form of the warrior, holding the head of the Gorgon Medusa, whom he had just decapitated. On the whole, these images of Perseus are grisly things, yet there is a certain graphic beauty about the portrayal overleaf, which emphasises that Perseus rescued the chained damsel, Andromeda.[71] The demonic head held in the left hand of Perseus reminds us that the name Algol is itself derived from the Arabic, *Al Ghoul*, meaning, 'the demon'.

In the 1790s, violence and murder were everywhere perpetrated in the streets of Paris, as the bloodletting of the French Revolution continued unabated. A large number of horoscopes cast for individuals who died on the guillotine have survived, but in most cases these were either cast by English astrologers shortly after the natives' deaths, or were computed and published – especially by French astrologers – during the twentieth century.[72]

Towards the end of the eighteenth century, Ebenezer Sibly drew up and published an astonishing communal horoscope of Marie Antoinette and her husband, Louis XVI: this is reproduced on the opposite page. As we shall see, this was not the first horoscope of the doomed couple, nor was it to be the last: we might confidently describe the two horoscopes of this unfortunate pair as the most famous of all eighteenth-century personal charts to appear in popular books on astrology.[73] Only one other chart in Sibly's book, which is not, however, a personal horoscope, became just as famous: this was the horary figure he erected in connection with the American Declaration of Independence, in 1776 (reproduced in part on page 150).[74]

The plate opposite displays the busts of Louis and Marie Antoinette staring at each other from individual oval horoscopes. Below the portraits, two further oval charts depict grisly details of their deaths. The oval chart below the horoscope of Louis shows the stern walls of the Tuileries, overlooking La Place de la Révolution, where both Louis and Antoinette were decapitated. The other chart depicts the guillotine, under which Antoinette herself lies face down, awaiting the fall of the blade. The four ovals are pinned together by a quadrate chart, which is the horoscope for a happier moment, when Louis was crowned in 1775.

The five charts in Sibly's plate were delicately engraved and do not reproduce easily. Accordingly, I have prepared a copy of the two birth charts (on page 144) in a form that is easier to read.

Although it is of little significance for our own study, the birth times used by Sibly for the two birth charts were incorrect. Marie Antoinette was born on 2 November 1755, in Vienna, Austria, at an official time of 7:30 AM[75] Her birth occurred on the day of the terrible earthquake which virtually destroyed Lisbon.[76] Louis was born on 23 August 1754, in Versailles, at what I estimate to be 6:14 AM.[77] As is usually the case with people destined to

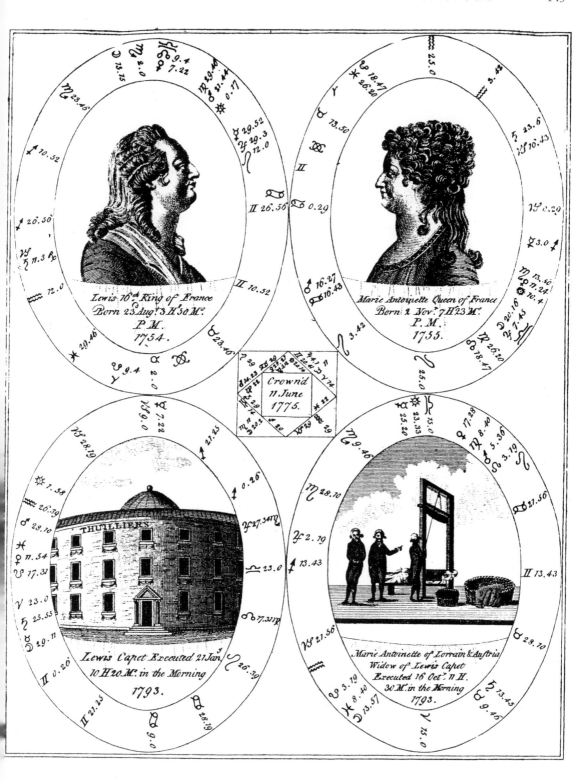

Lewis 16th King of France
Born 23 Aug.t 3 H.r 30 M.s
P. M.
1754.

Marie Antoinette Queen of France
Born 2 Nov.r 7 H 23 M.s
P. M.
1755.

Crown'd
11 June
1775.

Lewis Capet Executed 21 Jan.y
10 H 20 M.s in the Morning
1793.

Marie Antoinette of Lorrain & Austria
Widow of Lewis Capet
Executed 16 Oct.r 11 H.
30 M. in the Morning
1793.

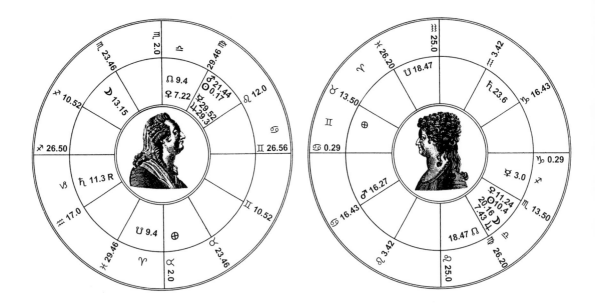

play an important role in society or history, both births were linked with eclipses. The secret of the two charts is linked with their related eclipse degrees.

In the case of Antoinette, in the year of her birth a lunar eclipse fell on her Jupiter:

> Lunar eclipse of 28 March 1755:   06.57 Libra
> Jupiter in chart of Antoinette: 07.44 Libra

By a strange coincidence, it was this same degree that bound together Marie Antoinette and Louis XVI in life. Furthermore, it was also precisely the same degree that influenced their deaths.

> Jupiter in chart of Antoinette: 07:44 Libra
> Venus in chart of Louis XVI: 06.57 Libra
> Solar eclipse of 30 September 1792:   07.44 Aries/Libra

The eclipse that marked the coming of Louis was intimately connected with these degrees. This was the lunar that fell on 1 October 1755, just over a month after his birth:

> Lunar eclipse of 1 October 1754:   08.06 Aries
> Cauda in chart of Louis XVI: 09.4 Aries

THE SIGIL FOR URANUS

The astrologers of the eighteenth century do not appear to have introduced any strikingly new horoscopic techniques, and the majority of the charts that were used to adorn books published on the subject of astrology were usually borrowed from earlier sources.

The only thing that might exercise a historian in relation to the horoscopy of the eighteenth century is the reaction of astrologers to the discovery of the so-called 'new' planet Uranus, in 1781. The English astrologer John Corfield, whose charting we shall examine in Chapter 5, wrote in strong terms of Uranus – which he called the 'Georgian', after its earliest name, *Sidus Georgium*:

> I shall observe that the *Georgian, is a violent star!* ... that stamps the person with an *eccentricity* that renders him an object of pity to the refined, and of ridicule to the vulgar mind.... whatever he produces or signifies, is of a *strange, romantic,* and *unexpected* kind.[78]

Corfield's recognition of the nature of Uranus may have been pre-empted by another astrologer. The *Conjuror's Magazine*, first published in 1781, is said to have been the first periodical of its kind to appear in Europe and America, though the early numbers were concerned essentially with parlour magic, with astrology as a secondary interest. As the astrological content proved more and more popular, the subject matter was increased and, during 1793, the publication changed its title to the *Astrologer's Magazine*.

Here, we shall examine two horoscopes from the earlier incarnation of the magazine. One is for the birth Louis XVI, the other for his death in 1793. The first appeared in the January 1793 edition of what was then still the *Conjuror's Magazine*, the second was rushed out for the February edition. By the standards of the day the latter article was an astrological scoop: the King had been beheaded only twenty-nine days earlier. As we have seen, even the opportunist almanac-maker 'Old Moore' was not able to rush out a version of the chart until 1794. The commentary to the scoop was written by the English astrologer, William Elder.[79]

Louis was beheaded at 10:20 AM in Paris, on 21 January 1793.[80] By February of that year, the death chart had been published (below right), but with a time that was obviously

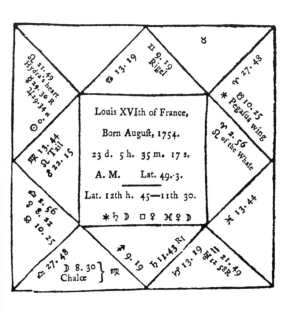
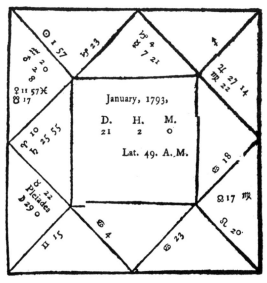

incorrect.[81] The chart was cast and set typographically in such a hurry that it contains several inaccuracies. For example, in the third house, the position of the Moon is given as being in 8.30 Virgo, whereas at the time of Louis birth the Moon was certainly in Scorpio.

Under normal circumstances, one might legitimately reject the chart as unworthy of serious attention. However, it does have a curious historical merit: for all its inadequacies, this crude horoscope is probably the earliest published chart to incorporate the sigil for the planet Uranus, which had been discovered in 1781.

At that time, the new planet was still called Sidus Georgium, the 'Star of George', after the reigning monarch. It is quite astonishing how quickly the sigil for the planet appeared, based not on the name officially given to it, but on the H of its discoverer, Herschel.

In the horoscope, the planet was recorded as being retrograde in 12.58 Aquarius. In fact, Uranus had been in 9.44 Aquarius during August 1754. This inaccuracy need not concern us unduly, however, as almost every planetary position given in the chart is incorrect by a degree or more – the two exceptions being Saturn (32 minutes in error) and Jupiter (29 minutes in error). Even so, the chart is worthy of consideration as being among the earliest, if not actually *the* earliest surviving horoscope, to incorporate the Uranian sigil.

Strangely enough, the sigil for Uranus is missing in the related death chart for Louis XVI (page 145, right). Perhaps, as the historian, Patrick Curry, has suggested, it was the haste to scoop the event that led to the several errors in the chart.[82] My guess is that the errors were introduced by the compositor, and that the astrologer who had erected the chart was given no opportunity to check it prior to printing.[83] The chart seems to have been cast for about 10:20 AM on 21 January, and may therefore be compared easily with the chart in Sibly's engraving, on page 143.

THOMAS WHITE'S HOROSCOPE OF LOUIS XVI

In retrospect, it is difficult for us to see what it was that the authorities found objectionable in the astrological writings of the English scholar Thomas White.[84] His persecution appears to have been linked with the publication of his remarkable book on the subject, the title of which is often abbreviated to *Celestial Intelligencer*.[85] Perhaps the authorities were uneasy because White appeared to be breaking the law by publishing prophecies – or, as the law put it, by *pretending* to predict the future (prediction not being possible in the eyes of the law). At all events, the appearance of the book certainly led to his arrest, in 1813. His persecution was among the first of what was to be a long line of official persecutions of astrologers both in the United Kingdom and in the United States, where similar laws prevailed.[86]

On the face of it, the *Celestial Intelligencer* was a scholarly affair. It contained an account of calculating and directing nativities according both to the Ptolemaic and Argolian systems, and included charts and analyses of Louis XVI and Napoleon Bonaparte. Later, I shall deal with the latter in some depth, for it offers an example of just how wrong an astrologer can be when making predictions amid the turmoil of contemporary fears. The former chart, that of the French King, is given right.[87]

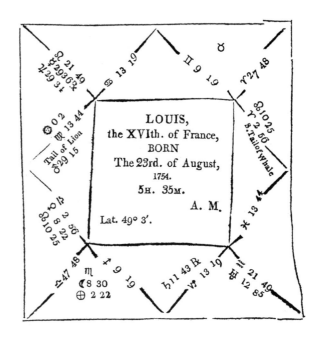

It will be seen at a glance that this is a copy of the 1793 figure we examined on page 145, with the omission of certain fixed stars and the addition of others. As we have seen already, the 'new' planet Uranus has been included but, in this later chart, the typographer has made an error, marking the position as an impossible 12.85 Aquarius.

One of the astonishing things about this appearance of Uranus (which seems to have been forced upon White by the source from which he copied) is that, unaccountably, he appears to have had some intimation of the violent nature of the planet. This is surprising, for, in the early decades of the nineteenth century, the influence of the planet was still a mystery to most astrologers. His recognition of its destructive power is set out in the tabulation of directions that he drew up for the chart of Louis XVI. White emphasised the role of the opposition of Uranus to the ascendant, which, according to his chart, would occur in the last year of the King's life.[88] One wonders from which source White had learned that Uranus was an evil or destructive planet. The English astrologer, John Corfield, was almost certainly the first practitioner to publish an article on the dramatic nature of Uranus, in his short-lived magazine, *Urania*. However, this article did not appear until 1814, by which time White had already made clear his own views about the planet in the reading of Louis XVI's chart.

In addition to leading us into interesting questions about the nature of Uranus, White's chart of the King (above) offers us an insight into how astrological symbols may be badly transmitted. In the 1793 horoscope on page 145, the astrologer had marked the position of a fixed star in regard to the cusp of the eighth house. He had recorded it with the sigil Caput (Head) ☊ which meant that the star referred to in the chart was that called the Head of the celestial Whale, better known in Latin as Menkar. The position of this star is represented in the drawing of the asterism, right.

To appreciate the problem attached to the star we must recognise that the arc of the zodiac, measured from the tip of the nose of the sea-monster to the furthest tip of its tail, is almost 56 degrees. The nose is about half-way into Taurus, while the tail is about half-way into Pisces. Now, the only astrologically important star in the head of the constellation of the Whale (Cetus) is Menkar, which is an orange star, located on the jaw of the figure. As this was in Taurus, it could not be anywhere near the cusp of the seventh as the horoscope of 1793 had indicated. We are therefore compelled to assume that the sigil for Caput ♌ should have been the other way up ♉ to represent Cauda (the Tail). This would have meant that the star referred to in the chart was Difda. During 1754, this star was in 29.09 Pisces and close to the eighth-house cusp.

Thomas White was learned enough to recognise the error in the chart from which he copied. In his version of the figure, he dispensed with the sigil, offering instead the English variant for Difda (which White would have known in the variants Diphda, or Deneb Kaitos) as *Southern Tail of Whale*. This star was located towards the other end of the Cetus arc, almost two signs away from it, in Pisces (see drawing of Cetus, above). The identity of the star was of profound importance for White. In his directions for the chart, he saw the evil power of Difda (which causes self-destruction, disgrace and misfortune) as one of the contributory forces in the King's dishonourable death.[90]

However, notwithstanding the considerable scholarship that underpinned his interest in astrology, Thomas White was persecuted by the authorities. In 1813, a few months after publication of the *Celestial Intelligencer*, White was arrested on the Isle of Wight, under the terms of the relict of the old witchcraft law, the Vagrancy Act, and imprisoned. He is said to have died in Winchester gaol during the following year.

AN EARLY CHART FOR AMERICAN INDEPENDENCE

Earlier, I remarked on how inaccurate were many of the charts in Sibly's book, *An Illustration*. The stark truth is that, from among the fifty-nine included in Sibly's book, the most accurate personal horoscope is the one cast for the birth of King George III (see opposite). However, it is significant that this figure was not calculated by Sibly personally but by the mathematician–astrologer, Charles Brent.[91] Sibly's astro-analysis of this chart is in the sycophantic mode from which the Wiltshire astrologer, Henry Season, prayed King George might be preserved – that 'bane of princes, fawning flattery'.[92]

For all that, the analysis does introduce something of real interest. Aware that the loss of the American colonies had been a severe personal blow to the King, Sibly suggested that any astrologer might usefully contemplate his radical figure alongside the revolution figure for the age of thirty-eight (that is, for 1776), and the schema for 'the scheme of the American æra of independence'.[93] He concludes, 'I am bold to say, that no one will be at a loss to account for those unhappy events, which have seldom been attributed to the right cause'.

As we have seen, Sibly did provide a chart of sorts for the time of American Independence, but this seems to have been a horary chart – a response to a question posed by Sibly personally.

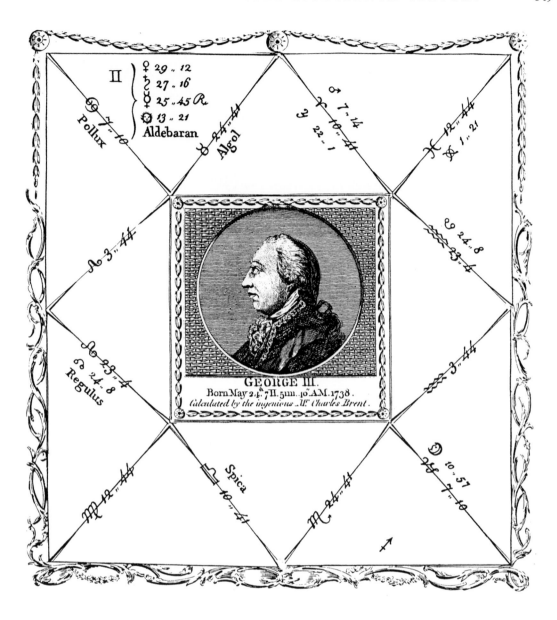

GEORGE III.
Born May 24.ʰ 7ᴵᴵ. 5ᵐ. 10ˢ. A.M. 1738.
Calculated by the ingenious Mr. Charles Brent.

This engraved horoscope has been widely discussed by modern astrologers, but not along the lines suggested by Sibly himself.[94] Sibly had suggested that other astrologers might care to compare the revolution with 'the scheme of the American æra of independence'.[95] This latter chart, held by a trumpeting angel, is reproduced overleaf. I have juxtaposed it with the revolution chart for the King's thirty-eighth year so that the pair may be studied in the manner suggested by Sibly.

As Sibly intimated, the loss to George III (and hence to Great Britain) is immediately evident. In the revolution chart, George's Saturn is exactly on the cusp of the second house (the house of possession), in 14.41 Libra.[96] This Saturn lies exactly upon the Saturn in the horary chart for the United States, which was in 14.50 Libra.

VARLEY'S CHART OF WILLIAM BLAKE

If there is one late eighteenth-century chart that most learned astrologers would like to see, it is the one cast by the artist–astrologer, John Varley, as his London house burned down. The chart itself has not been preserved and it has not been possible for historians to reconstruct it: indeed, Varley does not appear even to have recorded the time at which the catastrophe occurred. We know about the conflagration only because Varley's biographer, Alfred T. Story, used it as a dramatic backdrop to illustrate just how dedicated Varley was to astrology.[97] At the time of the fire, Varley did not seem overly concerned about the loss of his property, which was being consumed by the flames. He was more fascinated by the recognition that the catastrophe marked a solution to an astrological problem that had vexed him for a long time. This problem concerned the nature of the newly discovered planet Uranus.

Uranus had been discovered by William Herschel in 1781. Although some astronomers had wanted to name the new planet after Herschel himself, he elected to name it Sidus Georgium, 'The Georgian Star', after the reigning monarch and fellow-Hanoverian, George III. Because the planet was new to astrology, no one who practised the art could be sure what influence it would exert on personal horoscopes. However, since its discovery was seen by some astrologers as heralding the troubled era of the French Revolution and the terrible Napoleonic Wars, they concluded that whatever influence it did exude, this would probably be violent or dramatic in its effects.

John Varley, by then well known as a water-colour painter, was also a keen astrologer. Indeed, as one of his acquaintances, the picture-dealer, William Vokins, declared, astrology was a veritable 'mania' with Varley.

Every morning, as soon as he rose, and before he did anything else, he used to work out transits and positions for the day, or what astrologists designate 'secondary directions and transits'. Thus he would work up his own horoscope for the day.[98]

Varley seems to have put a great deal of his spare time into the study of Sidus Georgium in an effort to discover the nature of its influence. One morning he realised from his calculations that the planet would shortly be exerting a particularly strong influence on his own horoscope. He concluded that if this were the case, then he should be able to see at first hand the nature of the influence exerted by the new planet. With this in mind, he calculated the transit of the planet against his own horoscope so that he might be prepared for whatever transpired in his life. While thus engaged, Varley discussed the mysterious planet with his son, Albert, remarking, '... something very serious [is] going to happen to me to-day so many minutes before twelve o'clock, but whether the danger is to me personally or to my property I cannot tell'.[99]

At that time, Varley and his family lived at Bayswater Hill in London and his painting studio was adjacent to the house. So anxious was Varley to study the effect of this transit, he cancelled a business appointment for that morning and, to avoid tempting fate, stayed at home.

> As the hour of twelve approached he became greatly agitated, and walked up and down his studio unable to settle to anything. A few minutes before the hour he said to his son, 'I'm feeling all right; I do not think anything is going to happen to me personally; it must be my property that is threatened.'[100]

At the calculated moment there was a loud cry outside. Varley and his son ran from the studio, to discover that their house was on fire. 'He was so delighted,' said Albert later, 'he was so delighted at having discovered what the astrological effect of Uranus was.' Immediately on seeing the flames – seemingly insensible to the fact that, since the property was uninsured he had lost everything material in his life – Varley sat down to write an account of his discovery. He regarded his losses as a small matter compared with his discovery of the new planet's potentiality.

Varley is still remembered as an influential artist by art historians, even by those who have no knowledge of his mania for astrology. Not only was he a fine water-colourist, but he also exerted a very strong artistic influence on certain of his contemporaries. Undoubtedly, his most remarkable friend was the fellow-Londoner, the mystic painter–poet, William Blake. Varley was the person who most actively encouraged Blake to experiment with drawing psychic figures, which Blake claimed to see clairvoyantly.[101]

One undeniable contribution that Varley made to horoscopy was the chart he cast for Blake early in the nineteenth century (overleaf). This was reproduced in a short-lived astrological magazine, two years before Blake died.[102]

The chart is remarkable more for what it misses out than for what it includes.[103] We know from surviving examples of Varley's horoscopes that he usually included the lunar nodes (Caput and Cauda), which makes it all the more surprising that these are not recorded on the Blake chart. This is a serious omission for the lunar nodes were intensely powerful, and reflected Blake's own interest in lunar phenomena. A modern computerised version of the chart reveals Caput in 7.19 Leo. Its intensity in the life of Blake is reflected in its proximity to the ascendant.

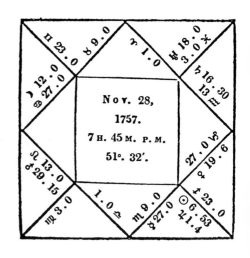

Another omission in the chart may not be blamed on either Varley or the typographer. This omission is the planet Neptune, which was not discovered telescopically until 1846. In this particular chart, the position of Neptune proves to have been of primal importance because it was in opposition to Saturn:

Neptune in chart of William Blake: 15.20 Leo
Saturn in chart of William Blake: 16.49 Aquarius

In fact, it is the Neptune placing which, perhaps more than any other single factor in the chart, explains Blake's continual penury. Neptune was exactly on the cusp of his second house. The chaotic and confused energies of Neptune, which intensify Blake's spirituality, tend to bring confusion into the second house, which rules money and income. It is perhaps Neptune (then, of course, an invisible influence) that explains why a man of Blake's astonishing genius could not earn a satisfactory living as a painter or poet.

One cannot examine Blake's horoscope in any depth without realising the extent to which he was influenced by the Moon – the planetary ruler of imagination.[104] Blake's Moon in Cancer (that is, the Moon in its own sign), and the proximity of Caput to the ascendant, made him particularly sensitive to lunar fluctuations. As we have seen, among the most powerful of such fluctuations are eclipses. Not only did Blake paint and draw eclipses – recognising their emotional impact in works of art – but his personal life was dominated by them. Indeed, it is possible to show a relationship between eclipses and the majority of the main events in the life of William Blake.

As we have seen, eclipses only influence events in the life of individuals when the degree upon which they fall corresponds to an occupied degree in the natal horoscope.[105] In 1819, the year in which Blake met John Varley, a solar eclipse fell exactly upon the degree marking Blake's Midheaven:

Solar eclipse of 25 March 1819:   04.30 Aries
Midheaven in Blake's chart: 04.22 Aries

This eclipse seems to have had a galvanising effect on Blake's life. In that year he had been introduced to John Varley by the artist John Linnell and, for the first time in his life, he found himself surrounded by friends, many of whom were interested in painting and poetry. In his final year (1827), a solar eclipse fell exactly upon his own Sun:

Solar eclipse of 29 November 1826:   06.46 Sagittarius
Sun in Blake's chart: 06.52 Sagittarius

Blake's graphic interest in the Moon and in eclipses was well developed long before he met Varley. So deeply imbued with eclipse-lore are some of his pictures that it is quite impossible fully to understand their meaning without reference to astrology.[106]

On the whole, astrology in the eighteenth century seems to have been in the hands of learned amateurs and specialists and, in the words of Henry Season, remained 'too noble an Art to be slightly studied' (see the quotation at the head of this chapter). Not for one moment does this imply that the century was not beset by the usual superficiality and charlatanism. However, it does suggest that, in England at least, horoscopy was saved for the future by members of the emergent middle-class intelligentsia, some of whom were sufficiently unencumbered financially to study the art in an amateur way, rather than to find themselves dependent upon its practice to raise an income.

We may be sure that by virtue of its very nature, as a servitor of the populace a superficial form of astrology continued its usual hidden way, flourishing mainly in rural areas and villages. Among these poverty-stricken classes, where leisure time was at a premium, people were served by local wisemen, few of whom appear to have known much about genuine astrology, and who

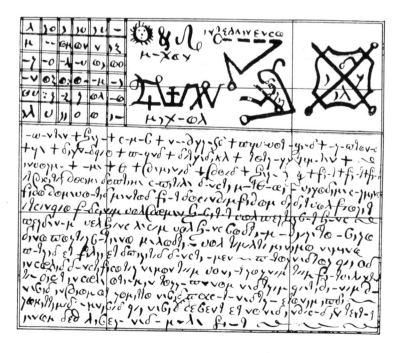

seemed content to handle symbols without fully appreciating their meaning or power. In May 1825, there came to light a relic of this type when a barn at West Bradford, near Clitheroe, was demolished. Hidden among the beams, and intended to work as a magical charm, was a folded sheet of paper containing a curious pseudo Graeco-Latin commentary on the abjuration mentioned in Matthew 17:20, along with a number of astrological sigils.[107]

At the top of this charm was a magical square for the Sun, consisting of a rectangle divided into thirty-six small squares, each apportioned a number. Whichever direction, vertical or horizontal, the numbers are added, one always obtains 111, which was one of the magical numbers of the Sun. Alongside the magic square were a few astrological sigils, including that for Michael, the planetary ruler of the Sun. While we are certainly not dealing here with horoscopy, the charm was nonetheless firmly rooted in the medieval astrological tradition, and is a good example of the kind of debased astrology in use in the lower levels of society. As the archaeologist, Ralph Merrifield, has pointed out, the writing of such charms was probably Sunday work for wisemen, who would be otherwise employed during the rest of the week.[108] The sigillic tradition set down with such clarity in the top register of the charm is evocative of the eighteenth century, yet the forms used may be traced back to a book written by Agrippa, published in the first half of the sixteenth century.[109] The curious sigil in the lower part of the register was a version of what Agrippa had called the 'Daemonii Solis', the Daemon of the Sun. An attempt has been made to write the Latin name of this Daemon, Sorath, within the sigil half in Roman, half in Hebrew characters.[110] Much of the power of this sigil is derived from its associate number, which was 666. The number identified Sorath with the Beast of the biblical Revelation.[111] This kind of charm wisdom was extremely common in the eighteenth century: at best, it required merely a superficial knowledge of the art, and an ability to copy.

The charm was clearly intended to preserve a barn from the incursion of evil spirits and other dangers. One wonders if the only difference between this crude charm and the elaborate foundation chart cast about a hundred years earlier by the astrologer, Samuel Jeake, who wished to ensure that his warehouse would be protected, was merely one of sophistication.

CHAPTER 5

The Nineteenth Century

The work of Ptolemy is the only standard we possess, and has served as a foundation for every other. Some speak of it with much veneration, though very few comprehend its meaning . . . .

James Wilson, *A Complete Dictionary of Astrology* (1819), p. xxvi

A mysterious bronze horoscope has been on public view for well over a hundred years, on the pedestal of a statue on Capitol Hill, in Washington, DC. The horoscope forms part of the decorative symbolism of a sculptural group, and is probably the only nineteenth-century horoscope on public display in the United States of America (figure 6).

This bronze cartouche was made by the American sculptor John Quincy Adams Ward in 1887. It is part of the decorative surrounds on the pedestal supporting the statue of the assassinated president, James A. Garfield, which is located on a traffic island to the south-west of the Capitol building. Disappointingly, the horoscope represents neither the birth chart nor the death chart of Garfield himself: indeed, research has shown that the chart does not relate to any event in the life of Garfield. Rather, it is an integral part of the extensive Masonic symbolism around the plinth of the statue, and represents one of the deeper mysteries of the architecture of the capital city.[1] If nothing else, this astrological cartouche reminds us that Garfield was an active Mason.

The assassination of Garfield, in 1881, took place in the ladies' waiting room of the crowded railway station of the Baltimore and Potomac Railroad, in Washington DC. At the moment when the crazed Charles Guiteau discharged the first of his shots at the President, there was a most extraordinary event in the heavens. No fewer than six planets were in the sign Taurus.[2]

The gathering of so many planets in a single sign is a rare phenomenon, and the coming of such a *stellium* usually stimulates a great deal of interest among astrologers. Almanacs and ephemerides published shortly before the assassination had informed their readers that the last equivalent *stellium* in Taurus had occurred on 12 May 1146, when there had been six planets in the sign.

James Abram Garfield had been born in a log cabin in Ohio, at 2:25 AM, on 19 November 1831.[3] The chart for his birth is given overleaf.[4] Alongside is that for his assassin, Guiteau.[5] Garfield's chart was drawn up by the brilliant English astrologer, Alfred J. Pearce, and published

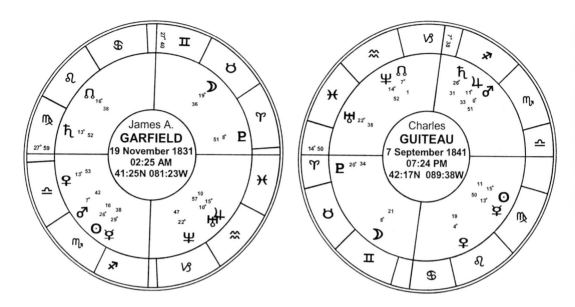

in the English astrological magazine, *Urania*.[6] Although Pearce cast this descriptive chart before Garfield became President, there is little doubt that he foresaw Garfield's assassination.

One of Pearce's specialities was the lore of eclipses, and he cannot fail to have been aware that the solar eclipse of 21 November 1881 would fall directly on Garfield's Mercury:

Mercury in Garfield's chart:	29.37 Scorpio
Solar eclipse of 21 November 1881:	29.33 Scorpio

Pearce had predicted the deaths of several rulers in his past works, and it is something of a puzzle why he did not also promulgate the assassination of Garfield.[7]

Garfield's horoscope is a strangely powerful one. There are a number of fixed stars operative within the chart.[8] Of these, the most dangerous is Menkalinan, which, in the astrological tradition, virtually guarantees a violent death. In 1831 Menkalinan was in the same degree as Garfield's Midheaven.[9]

Menkalinan in 1831:	27.33 Gemini
Garfield's Midheaven:	27.39 Gemini

Our own interest lies in the relationship between the chart of Garfield and that of his assassin. The first astrologer to point to a strain of madness in the chart of Guiteau was A.G. Trent, in 1893.[10] As we may see from Guiteau's chart, his Mercury (very close to his Sun) lay on the Saturn of Garfield's chart:

Mercury in chart of Guiteau:	13.50 Virgo
Saturn in chart of Garfield:	13.52 Virgo

Tragically, a similar communality, between the killer and his victim, was to be played out several times in the following century. The murderer of each assassinated president of the United States, during the twentieth century, was related to his victim by a similar communality of degrees. Meanwhile, in the nineteenth century, an equally striking communality had existed in the earlier assassination of Abraham Lincoln.

On 14 April 1809, there was a powerful solar eclipse. It was of a remarkably long duration, extending for over 4½ minutes – burning, as it were, a spiritual mark into 25 degrees of Aries. Later astrologers, familiar with the lore of eclipses, would recognise this as an influential degree for a number of reasons. On Sunday, 12 February 1809, two months before that solar eclipse, a child was born, in a rough log cabin, hastily built on a remote farmstead in western Kentucky – the first son of Nancy Lincoln. He would not be the first president of the United States to be born in a log cabin, but he would be the first to be assassinated. His birth, and his death, would be linked with the solar eclipse of April. At the moment of the child's birth, the planet Mars fell within 1 degree of arc of that eclipse:

Mars in Abraham Lincoln's chart:	25.26 Libra
Solar eclipse of 14 April 1809:	24.26 Aries/Libra

The degree would haunt Abraham Lincoln throughout his life, yet, for those unfamiliar with astrological lore, it was not the eclipse that was prescient, but the date on which it would fall. On the day that Lincoln was assassinated, fifty-six years later, the planet Mercury was in the same degree as the eclipse and Mars:

Solar eclipse of 14 April 1809:	24.26 Aries/Libra
Position of Sun on 14 April 1865:	25.10 Aries
Mars in Abraham Lincoln's chart:	25.26 Libra

On the next page is the chart of Abraham Lincoln.[11] Alongside is the chart of his assassin, Booth.[12] We need not look far to see what, in this case, bound together the killer and the killed.

On the surface, the story of the assassination is a simple one. President Abraham Lincoln and his wife Mary Todd Lincoln were sharing a box in Ford's Theater, Washington, DC, with Lieutenant Colonel Henry Reed Rathbone and his beautiful young fiancée, Clara Hamilton Harris. John Wilkes Booth, a Confederate sympathiser and one of the most famous actors of his day, forced his way into the box, and shot Lincoln with his derringer in the back of the head.[13] Rathbone sprang to the defence of the President, in consequence of which Booth savagely slashed at him with a knife. Rathbone held up his arms to defend his face, and blood began to spurt from a bad wound. Without further hesitation, Booth jumped from the presidential box, on to the stage.

He was an agile man and famous for his dramatic stage leaps, yet on this murderous occasion he had an accident. While in the air, 'twixt box and stage, Booth's spur caught in the Treasury

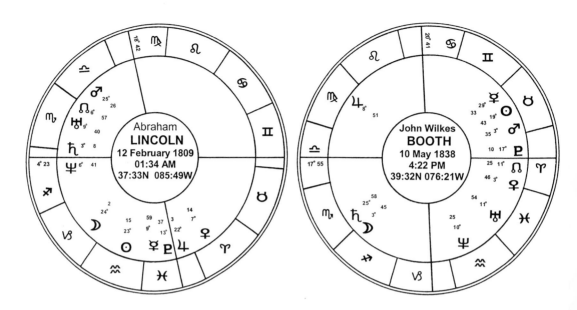

Guard flag, draped alongside the box.[14] Thrown off balance, he landed badly and broke the lower part of his fibula, just above the ankle. Undoubtedly, this accident eventually impeded his escape, and contributed to his capture a few days later. An astrologer might be amused by the accident, for in Booth's chart, the planetary ruler of accidents, Uranus was in Pisces, the sign of the zodiac that rules the feet.

When the astrologer, Luke D. Broughton, first predicted the death of Abraham Lincoln he did so in very general terms. Perhaps he was fearful of falling foul of the police, who were periodically given to arresting astrologers on the unreasonable grounds that all astrology was, by definition, fraudulent. In an article written in 1864, Broughton had warned of the danger of assassination in the coming months.[15] In a column written for future events, that were to unfold in April 1865, he predicted that some noted general, or person in high office, would die, or be removed, on about the 17th or 18th of the month.[16]

Broughton had been among the first astrologers to publish Lincoln's horoscope, in 1860. The chart, with an inset portrait, was emblazoned on the front of his monthly astrological magazine, printed in Philadelphia (see opposite).[17] In a later edition of the same year, Broughton predicted an evil that would befall Lincoln: '... it would be one of the worst things that could have happened to the United States ....'[18] In 1864, in an article written during the presidential campaign (which he foresaw Lincoln winning), Broughton wrote that 'shortly after the election is over' Lincoln should be 'especially on his guard against attempts to take his life; by such as fire arms, and infernal machines'.[19]

In order to make these remarkable predictions, Broughton seems to have been using the traditional techniques of progressions and transits, which reveal quite clearly the death of Lincoln.[20] Even so, it is remarkable that Broughton succeeded in making this prediction, as Lincoln's death was intimately involved with Pluto, a planet still unknown to astrologers. In his own astrological account of the event, Broughton wrote of Lincoln:

it was next to impossible for him to have died a natural death ... the Sun and Moon were ... afflicted by the evil planet Saturn, and Mars and Herschel (i.e., Uranus), both in the eleventh house, denoting him being surrounded by secret enemies and false friends.[21]

The truth is that the Mars of the radical chart was in trine to the Sun, so the real problem must have been the angular Saturn (in fact, as we may see, the angular Saturn–Uranus). It was only in the directed chart for 14 April 1865 that Mars and the Sun progressed to opposition.

Lincoln's personal chart had been published long before the assassination. At the time of his inauguration, Lincoln was the most famous person in America, and it was inevitable that professional astrologers should take note of his birth chart. John Wilkes Booth was well known as an actor, yet, if his horoscope had been cast before 1865, then it was in private, and has yet to come to the eyes of historians. Although the chart for his more famous actor brother, Edwin Booth, had been published, that of John Wilkes himself remained unknown until his terrible deed made him the quarry of popular journalists.[22]

The chart helps explain something about John Wilkes Booth that nothing else explains – his almost magnetic and charming personality, concerning which a large number of his contemporaries comment. The proposed birth-time places the magnetic Pluto exactly upon the cusp of the seventh, explaining his powerful attraction for women – an attraction fronted by the ease and charm of the ascendant Libra. The Midheaven, that great indicator of career and reputation, was in the same degree as the fixed star Pollux.

Position of Pollux in 1838:   21.00 Cancer
Midheaven in chart of Booth: 20.41 Cancer

The star brings great honours that end in disgrace and ruin. In proximity to both the Moon (ruler of Cancer) and Saturn (ruler of tenth house), Pollux brings violent death, with danger to either the eyes or the head.

The truth about Booth's chart is that the most terrible violence was well hidden – as indeed it had been well hidden during his successful life as an actor. It was only in the unfolding of this chart, through progressions, that the full violence implicit within the configuration of planets becomes evident. On 14 April 1865, when he shot Lincoln, his progressed chart was dominated by the conjunction of Mars and Mercury. This powerful conjunction was reduced to one of terrible violence by virtue of the fact that it fell upon the most evil fixed star in the heavens – Algol, in the head of Medusa. In 1865, Algol was in 24.17 Taurus.

Mercury in progressed chart of Booth:	23.41 Taurus
Mars in progressed chart of Booth:	23.21 Taurus
Position of Algol in 1865:	24.17 Taurus

As we have learned already, the violent death associated with Algol usually involves decapitation, or disfigurement of the face. Booth was shot in the head, in a barn on Garrett's farm, near Bowling Green, on 26 April 1865.

Naturally, our own interest in the chart rests on how it relates to that of his victim. We see at a glance that Booth's Moon is exactly on Lincoln's Saturn:

Moon in chart of Booth:	03.45 Sagittarius
Saturn in chart of Lincoln:	03.08 Sagittarius

In an article on Booth, written in that year, the *Chicago Post* sought for a poetic way of expressing the famous actor's fate, and came up with the happy phrase, 'the star of his destiny having set in blood'.[23] In truth, unbeknownst to the journalist who wrote these words, they were no mere poetic effusion. In fact, the idea of a star of fortune seems to have followed Booth through his life. In his youth, in the woods of Cockeysville (near his school), he had encountered a gipsy chiromante, who had told him (among other things) that he would die young, and come to a bad end. He was, the prescient palmist insisted, born under an unlucky star.[24] The theatre posters would later bill him as *A Star of the First Magnitude*, yet it was the gipsy who had the last laugh, even though the star under which Booth had been born was of second magnitude only.[25]

As we have seen, Booth's lunar node, Caput, had been in 11.25 Aries. In 1838, the year of Booth's birth, the star Alpheratz had been in 12.02 Aries. Since Caput and Alpheratz were within the same degree of arc, the powerful star threw its influence into the life of Booth, through this degree. As the specialist in star lore, Richard H. Allen, insists, the star 'portended honor and riches to all born under is influence'.[26]

There was, however, one fixed star in the chart of John Wilkes Booth which did not augur quite so well: within this context, we might call it the chiromante's star. In 1838, the fixed star Armus was in 10.28 Aquarius, on Booth's Neptune.[27]

Star Armus in 1838:	10.28 Aquarius
Neptune in Booth's chart:	10.25 Aquarius

rmus has a reputation for indicating mental instability. It bestows a troublesome nature, and namelessness. By a curious coincidence, this star happened to be operative in the chart of a later ssassin, Lee Harvey Oswald, who killed John F. Kennedy.[28]

Just as Lincoln's death had been signalled by an eclipse, so was the death of John Wilkes ooth. On 25 April 1865, the day before Booth was shot, there was a solar eclipse, in 5.21 aurus. It was a total eclipse, which lasted for well over 5 minutes. John Wilkes Booth did not ave a planet in this degree. However, he did have Mars in 03.19 Taurus, within 2 degrees of he eclipse. Under normal circumstances, an astrologer would be inclined to dismiss the onnection as being too wide of orb for it to be regarded as 'communal'. Yet, the fact is that this egree of Taurus had a profound meaning in itself. It lay on the same degree as Lincoln's Cauda, 1 the progressed chart for the moment of the President's death.

Mars in Booth's horoscope:	03.35 Taurus
Cauda in Lincoln's death chart:	03.58 Taurus

At the moment Booth fired his shot, the heavens reflected the deed with an astounding ommunal degree. In the horoscope of Abraham Lincoln, the planet Mars was in opposition to ne Sun at the moment of the assassination:

Mars in Lincoln's horoscope:	25.26 Libra
Position of Sun at killing:	25.10 Aries

Vhen Lincoln died, at 7:22 AM, on the following morning, the opposition between the two as even more precise. During his death throes, the Sun had passed the *exact* opposition, and at ne moment of his death had moved to 25.32 Aries.

Even more extraordinary was the relationship which the Sun held with an eclipse at the noment of the assassination. As we have seen, on 14 April 1809, just over two months after incoln was born, a solar eclipse fell in 24.26 Aries. That is to say, it fell within a degree of the osition held by the Sun at the moment of the assassination:

Eclipse of 14 April 1809:	24.26 Aries
Sun at assassination of Lincoln:	25.10 Aries

Just as it has proved possible to trace a succession of astrologers in Britain across the expanse f the seventeenth century, so it proves possible to trace a similar succession in the history of merican astrology, from the nineteenth to the twentieth centuries. Luke Broughton had arned the art from his own father, who lived in Leeds (England), and was born in the first years f the nineteenth century. In his turn, Broughton introduced a European astrology into the Inited States when he settled in Philadelphia in 1854, at the age of twenty-six. His most uccessful pupil was 'Professor' Chaney, who met Broughton in 1866 and who made every effort to Americanise astrology. In Chaney's autobiographical primer on astrology – or what he pointedly called *American Urania* – we learn that he had many students.[29] Among these Chaney mentions John W. Beckmann, who was not only a student but was, as Chaney readily admits, prepared to loan Chaney money to publish his magnum opus.

The late nineteenth-century astrologer, the Bostonian Evangeline Adams, first studied the art under the guidance of the homoeopathist, Dr J. Heber Smith, Professor of Materia Medica at Boston University.[30] Also in Boston lived the 'professor of Astrology', Dr Lister, whom the English astrologer Christopher Cooke visited in 1859 during a trip to the United States.[31] Lister had learned the art from the father of Luke Broughton, in Leeds, and admitted to being very partial to the writings of Zadkiel (see pages 176–8). Cooke was astonished to observe that Lister had affixed a brass plate to his door announcing the nature of his profession – no astrologer would dare to have such a blazon in England, for fear of the law. Later, while visiting Chicago, Christopher Cooke took tea with a 'practical' astrologer – also from England – who announced his profession to all and sundry by means of a star, raised over his cottage. Cooke was astonished to find that the man did his calculations by means of 'that slovenly substitute for mental calculations', the planisphere.[32] Such tantalising autobiographical details as these indicate that there was a living tradition of astrology in the United States, concerning which little is presently known.

Alongside the innovators and the scholarship of the earnest researchers, there was the eternal undercurrent of venality and commercialism which has characterised the lower reaches of astrology in all ages. Prefabricated material, described as 'horoscopes', has been traced back to the dubious activities of the American astrologer C.W. Roback, of Boston, Massachusetts (right). Roback had thousands of identical horoscope-sheets printed for distribution to punters: these were the prototype of the prefabricated charts which Alan Leo would find so lucrative over fifty years later in England.[33] With the aid of these sheets, Roback could cast a chart and bundle together a number of pre-printed sheets dealing with the appropriate planets in signs and houses along with a general reading for the ascendant, and sell these as a 'genuine' horoscope.

Charles W. Roback was among the more colourful of the charlatans who travelled the United States during the mid-nineteenth century. He claimed to have been born in Sweden, and to have emigrated to the United States in 1844. Unfortunately, almost everything he claims about himself, his life and his achievements is deeply suspect. His real name was Carl Johan Nilsson Fallenius, and it is noteworthy that one reliable modern Swedish source has described him as an 'impostor and quack doctor'.[34] There seems to be not a shred of evidence that one of Roback's ancestors took part in the famous Norse expedition that set out, 'a thousand years before the birth of Columbus', to North America.[35] Nor could there possibly be any truth in his assertion that he had purchased, in Egypt, a number of papyri that contained the horoscopes of several Ptolemaic kings, and that the 'system of calculation employed in casting them' proved useful to him in many instances.[36]

Whether or not there is any truth in his claim that, during his first nine years in the States, he personally cast 38,000 nativities is anyone's guess, but this would have been a record-breaking achievement for any astrologer in pre-computer days.[37] Certainly, there is no way he could have submitted so many charts to serious scrutiny. Indeed, for all the grandiloquent titles he claimed for himself, there is no evidence from his book on the subject that he knew much about astrology. It is revealing that the handful of famous charts he reproduced in his published work were lifted from those in Ebenezer Sibly's classic work, *An Illustra-tion*.[38] Even in this easy theft, Roback per-pretrated an amazing incompetence, for he managed to get the birth of Henry VIII wrong by a century and a half (see chart on the right)!

The archaising portrait, which serves as frontispiece to Roback's book on astrology, is clearly intended to give the impression that it represents the astrologer himself. However, Roback had simply taken the image from elsewhere. The original was a frontispiece portrait of the famous English astrologer, John Gadbury; Roback had merely covered Gadbury's name with his own flourish of a signature.[39]

One distinctive feature of nineteenth-century astrology was the bifurcation between the traditional, complex astrology and a more simple form, designed to cater for amateurs or to attract non-specialists as clients. The popularisation of astrology – which certainly involved a demolition of some of the finer elements of the art – began in the nineteenth century, and was largely responsible for the enormous popularity of astrology during the twentieth century. The bifurcation meant that there came into existence, during the nineteenth century, two distinct streams of astrology. On the one hand (as in former centuries), learned astrologers, familiar with the complexity of the art, continued to pursue their interest in traditional astrology, and to publish analyses well beyond the comprehension of the general public. Good brief examples of the more complex astro-readings of the period are those published by the English astrologers, George Wilde and J. Dodson.[40] Their charts and readings for Marie Antoinette, Samuel Taylor Coleridge, Humphry Davy, Frederick the Great and George Washington are astonishingly succinct and accurate, but expressed in a terminology well beyond the comprehension of the non-specialist. On the other hand, Broughton's analyses, written in simple language, and devoid of the usual technical terms, are evidently intended for a mass audience and are typical of the kind of astrology which became popular in the following century.

In view of this, if we wish to study the astrology of the nineteenth century, we should do so by means of a comparison. We can do no better than study the brief analysis by Luke Broughton of the horoscope for Lincoln, published in Philadelphia on 1 September 1860.[41] We may then compare this with the reading for the assassination of the Russian Tsar, Alexander II, on 13 March 1881, published by Alfred John Pearce.[42]

Unlike most of the other astro-readings we have examined so far, the Broughton analysis of Lincoln's chart is simplicity itself, and ideally representative of the popular stream of horoscopy that emerged in the nineteenth century. In keeping with the wish to provide articles for his popular astrological magazine, Broughton went to great lengths to avoid all technical terms.

Broughton tells his readers that Saturn in Sagittarius describes a person who is raw-boned, and rather dark in complexion. The personality is careful but choleric, and will not bear an affront: he is a lover of his friends, and merciful to his enemies. The Moon is in good aspect to Jupiter (Broughton avoids even the word 'sextile'), which causes the native to be good-natured, benevolent in disposition and sociable. It will also cause him to be of sound judgement and of a practical turn of mind. Mercury has no aspect to the Moon. This leads Broughton to foresee that Lincoln would never become noted for his learning or scholarship. However, since Mercury is in good aspect to Uranus (it is in trine), this will induce him to be of an original turn of mind, and cause him to think and act for himself and to spurn fashions or the rules of etiquette. This same benefic aspect, which induces originality of thought, will also induce him to appear blunt or abrupt in his comportment: he will have 'a comical way of expressing himself'.

The reading is interesting, not merely because Broughton picks out the salient personality of Lincoln, but also because it survives as a reading published prior to Lincoln being elected president. When he wrote this astro-analysis, Broughton was firmly convinced that Lincoln would not be elected. He appears to have come to this conclusion because he wrongly interpreted the bad aspects looming in the chart, and assumed that they related to Lincoln's personal life. However, had he read these aspects more carefully, and with a deeper awareness of political trends, then he would have foreseen that the entire period of the presidency would be dominated and overshadowed by fairly awful aspects that were reflected in the dark days of the Civil War, and in the difficult political decisions which Lincoln was compelled to make.

In the reading, Broughton listed the opening phase of these transits. He saw that the planet Saturn would shortly square its radical place, in opposition to Mercury. This was quite true, and Broughton's notes indicate that he was using transits, rather than progressions, in regard to his study of the future. In fact, the transits in Lincoln's chart for the next couple of years were absolutely dreadful. By 5 September 1861, a total of six planets would be gathered together, in loose conjunction, in the first half of Virgo, throwing some very unhelpful oppositions to planets in his radical chart.[43] During October 1861, that most feared of conjunctions in traditional astrology – Saturn and Jupiter – was operating in 18.14 Virgo, directly on Lincoln's Midheaven. When, at last, Saturn moved out of Virgo, it entered directly into opposition to Lincoln's radical Neptune. Rarely does one see such unfortunate series of transits in a personal chart. It is curious that Broughton did not expand on the series of transits which would trouble Lincoln after 1 September 1860.

Pearce's commentary on the chart of Tsar Alexander II offers an illuminating contrast with Broughton's simplicitic treatment of Lincoln. The analysis is written in a form that is immediately comprehensible only to astrologers.[44] I can do no better than quote from Pearce, at some length, underlining those few technical words which require some commentary in the Glossary.

Tsar Alexander II. was born at 10h a.m., on the 29th of April, 1818, at Moscow, Leo 4° 42′ ascending. The Sun (<u>hyleg</u>) was in the tenth house in Taurus 8° 21′, in <u>mundane</u> semi-quartile aspect with both Mars and Saturn (the latter planet being ruler of the eighth, the house of death), and the <u>mundane parallel</u> of Saturn. The Moon was afflicted by the sesquiquadrate of Mars, the mundane parallel of Uranus, and was in opposition to the martial star Regulus. The *Asselli* were very near the ascending degree, which had the sesquiquadrate aspect of Uranus. The primary directions of Sun <u>rapt parallel</u> Mars 63° 12′ = July, 1881. As Zadkiel I. and the author have observed and maintained (for years previous to 1881) all <u>directional parallels</u> operate, as a rule, several weeks before they are exactly due. Moreover, if the Sun's semi-diameter 0° 16′ be subtracted from the arc of 63° 12′, we have 62° 56′ = March, 1881, as the arc of first contact of the Sun's limb with the parallel of Mars (the direction being computed to the Sun's centre) and the Tsar was cruelly assassinated on the 13th of March, 1881, by the explosion of a bomb thrown at his feet by the assassin .... It was the train of five evil directions (62° 20′ to 63° 52′) which led the author to foretell that: 'The Tsar of Russia will be in some personal danger about the 6th of March, 1881,' and to say that 'He will do well to prepare for the dread summons.'[45]

A comparison of the two astro-readings for Lincoln and the Tsar reveals the chasm that now divided the astrologies of the nineteenth century, a chasm that had nothing to do with the abilities of the astrologers. Both Broughton and Pearce were, in their own distinctive ways, learned in the art, and excellent at predicting the future from charts. After all, Broughton had predicted, from his own horoscope, that he would die on 22 September 1899: it was not a serious reflection on his horoscopic abilities that he survived for a further day.[46] The chasm was related to the attitudes of the astrologers concerned as much as to the demands being made upon them by their clientele. It is a chasm that would grow wider and wider in the coming century.

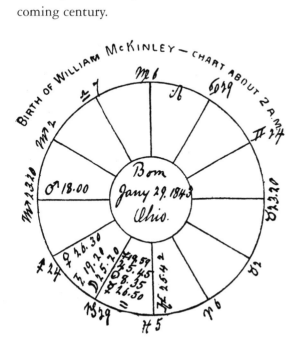

During the latter half of the nineteenth century, personal horoscopes of political leaders, or political hopefuls, began to appear in newspapers in the United States of America. Perhaps the earliest was that of Lincoln, published in the *Boston Sunday Herald* by Professor Lister, concerning which Broughton had complained.[47]

A later example, left, is the horoscope for the birth of William McKinley, cast in 1896 by Luke Broughton, wrongly billed in the newspaper as John J. Broughton. The chart is from an article on the presidential elections in the *Baltimore American*, which, following Broughton's reading, announced that McKinley would become the next President of the United States.[48]

One surprising book title, which appeared at the end of the nineteenth century, might lead the unwary to conclude that a system of heliocentric astrology had been introduced into the United States at that time. However, the title of the work, *Heliocentric Astrology or Essentials of Astronomy and Solar Mentality*, proves to be something of a confidence trick.[49] The work had little or nothing

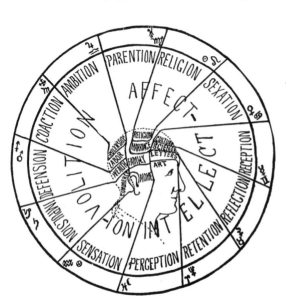

to do with heliocentric astrology, and certainly did not contain a heliocentric horoscope. However, of immediate interest are a number of astrological sigils that appear in a crude and near-incomprehensible diagram (right).[50]

In the outer band, we see the standard zodiacal symbols, alongside a number of planetary sigils which are rather surprising. At the top left we see the symbol for Libra, alongside Jupiter. The author, Vedra, had argued that Jupiter (rather than Venus) is the legitimate ruler of this sign. As we follow the circle, widdershins, we find that Scorpio is governed by the asteroids (for which Vedra offered a new sigil ✠), Sagittarius is governed by Mars, Aquarius by the Earth, Neptune by the Moon, Aries by Neptune. The associated ruler of Taurus is something of a puzzle: Vedra presents a sigil that closely resembles that of Ceres (one of the asteroids that rules the opposite sign, Scorpio). However, in the text itself, Vedra writes:

> In planetary sympathy, Taurus has no direct respondent. Its energies are centralizing and recipient from the true Solar pole, one of the Pleiades, and by response the energy of Venus.[51]

One might be tempted to ignore this type of astrology, were it not for one idea – seemingly as outlandish as that proposed by Vedra – which cropped up in the intuitional astrology of the clairvoyant, Alice Bailey, in the early decades of the twentieth century. Bailey insisted that cosmic forces flow into the solar system by way of three channels – the star Sirius, the asterism of the Pleiades, and the Great Bear.[52]

The extraordinary fact is that Vedra's imaginative incursion into heliocentric astrology seems to have been representative of a way of thinking that had seized whole groups of astrologers. This was particularly true of those who had become involved with the Theosophy of Madame Blavatsky, and with the various splinter groups that fell away from Theosophy in the following century. Among these were several astrological systems intimately related to Theosophy itself, which was most directly represented by Alan Leo's horoscopy (see below). Anthroposophy, which splintered from Theosophy under the direction of Rudolf Steiner, encouraged the Astrosophy of Elizabeth Vreede and Willi Sucher. Later came the modern Rosicrucianism of Max Heindel (whose ideas were largely borrowed from the writings of Rudolf Steiner), and the Intuitional Astrology of Alice Bailey, which had a profound influence on American astrology by way of the writings of Dane Rudhyar. Each of these esoteric systems had roots in the nineteenth century, and each became associated with a horoscopy that was highly distinctive. We shall discuss sample horoscopes later.

The earliest of these esoteric groups was that formally instituted in 1875 under the name of Theosophy by the Russian émigrée, Helena Petrovna Blavatsky. One consequence of the introduction of Theosophy into America and England was the systematic popularising of astrology by the Theosophists Alan Leo and his wife Bessie. The beginning of this popularisation – itself lamented by many serious occultists – belongs to the history of late nineteenth-century astrology, and provided an impetus that has not yet come to an end.

One distinctive horoscopic form was designed against the background of Theosophical symbolism. This was built up from symbolical forms that had become popular in theosophical circles during the last decades of the nineteenth century, incorporating the Ouroboros serpent (tail in mouth), an encircled swastika, and the interlocking triangles of the Seal of Solomon (overleaf).[53] This particular figure is the chart of the paraplegic Fannie W. Tunison, who had been born at Sag Harbor, Long Island, and who had learned to paint, sew, embroider and write with her tongue.[54]

The following studies of representative nineteenth-century horoscopes include a few of the forms invented by followers of Theosophy. Had space permitted, I would have dealt with a much

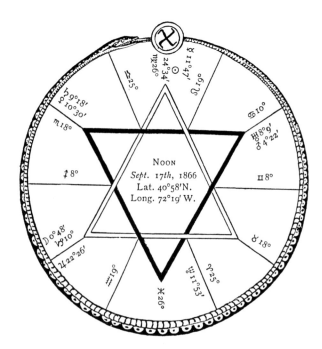

NOON

Sept. 17th, 1866
Lat. 40°58′N.
Long. 72°19′W.

wider range of personal horoscopes, for in this way certain facets of nineteenth-century astrology could have been explored more fully. Here I mention only the more notable examples.

The chart of Joseph Smith, the founder of the Mormon religion, is of great interest, not only because of its intrinsic qualities but also because it offers a nexus for the study of communal degrees. It has proved possible to cast the charts of thirty-six of his forty-eight wives: of these, all but two had at least one degree in common with Smith's chart.[55] Smith was born in Sharon, Vermont, at about 9:17 AM, on 23 December 1805, with six placings in Capricorn.[56] The birth was marked by the lunar eclipse of 30 June 1806 (8.13 Capricorn), which fell across his natal Caput. At the moment of his murder, on 27 June 1844, the progressed Moon was in 23.55 Gemini, and was thus in the same degree as the solar eclipse preceding his death.[57]

The chart of King Umberto I of Italy is also of considerable interest, mainly because of the astrological factors around his assassination. He was born on 14 March 1844, in Turin, rectified to 09:52 AM: this chart is of interest to us because of the classical nature of the progressed chart at the moment of his assassination. The primal astrological source is Sepharial's chart.[58] Umberto's assassination, at the hands of Gaetano Bresci, occurred at 8:20 PM on 29 July 1900 at Monza. Progressions for this time reveal a classical pattern. Mars was exactly on Cauda, Saturn on the descendant, while the conjunct Neptune and Moon hung over the cusp of the eighth house. The progressed Pluto was still conjunct with the progressed MC. His assassin, Gaetano Bresci, was born on 10 November 1869 in Coiano, Prato.[59] Fairly typical of this mortal relationship, Bresci's Saturn (16.01 Sagittarius) and Mars (16.49 Sagittarius) were on Umberto's descendant (16.07 Sagittarius).

An especially fascinating chart is that of the Russian, Grigory Efimovich Rasputin, who was born in the village of Pokrovskoe, in the Siberian expanse beyond the banks of the Tura river, in the province of Tobol, on 10 January 1869 (Old Style).[60] One might have expected the chart for such a dramatic personage to be charged with some truly outstanding evil, but this is not the case: rather, it is a *difficult* chart, its tensions reflected in five strong square aspects. There are several powerful fixed stars. Facies ensures a violent death, while Castra gives a violent and destructive personality. The rectified time of 10:08 AM gives a revealing progressed chart for Rasputin's murder, which took place in the Iusupov Palace, St Petersburg, at about 3:30 AM on 30 December 1916. The progressed Uranus (13.22 Cancer) was on the Midheaven, progressed Mars was conjunct with Caput, Jupiter with Neptune, both of which were close to setting on the descendant. Progressed Mars (16.42 Leo) was on the radical Caput, while progressed Moon (01.35 Pisces) was almost opposite the radical Mars, reminding us that after being poisoned and shot, Rasputin was finally drowned. Rasputin's chart offers an instructive comparison with those of his known murderers. Among these was Prince Feliks Feliksovich Iusupov, who was born in St Petersburg on 23 March 1887.[61] Iusupov's Mars (09.50 Aries) was on Rasputin's Jupiter (09.11 Aries); his Saturn (15.36 Cancer) was on Rasputin's Uranus (14.37 Cancer).

The chart of Ferdinand Maximilian Joseph, who was to become Emperor of Mexico, is almost classical in terms of eclipses and fixed stars. He was born in Vienna, on 6 July 1832 at 3:28 AM, a few hours before his probable father, the Duke of Reichstadt, died (as the sun rose above Schönbrunn Palace).[62] The first solar eclipse (04.27 Leo) to follow this birth fell exactly on Maximilian's Caput (04.28 Leo). Maximilian was lifted to high estate by Alpheratz (11.57 Aries) on his Mercury (11.44 Aries), which elevated him to the role of Emperor, and aligned him to the ordinary people of Mexico. It was Praesaepe (04.53 Leo) on his Caput (04.28 Leo) that ensured a violent death. Maximilian's execution took place shortly after 7:15 AM, on 19 June 1867, on the Hill of the Bells outside Queretaro, Mexico. The progressions for the proposed moment of birth give Pluto (11.35 Aries) less than 2 degrees from the Midheaven, with progressed Sun (17.20 Leo) opposite progressed Uranus (16.32 Aquarius), and in opposition to the radical Uranus. The progressed Moon (00.18 Aquarius) was within 2 degrees of the progressed Cauda. Progressed Saturn (14.26 Virgo) was conjunct with progressed Mercury (14.34 Virgo).

The distinctive chart of the American writer Jack London, the son of the astrologer Chaney (see page 181) and Flora Wellman, deserves some attention.[63] The troubled fourth-house cusp in this chart is typical of those who have an unfortunate beginning. Uranus within a degree of the cusp and with Venus in opposition is an unpleasant combination at the best of times, but in this case Uranus was on the cusp, along with the star Algenubi, which ensures a brutish beginning, along with the power of expression.

THE STRANGE DEATH OF NAPOLEON BONAPARTE

Just as the horoscopy of the last decade of the eighteenth century was dominated by the lives and destinies of the French royal family, so the first decades of the next century were dominated by the life and destiny of Napoleon.

Several of the horoscopes for Napoleon are fascinating in themselves, as attempts to chart genius. However, I shall restrict my study to those charts that led the astrologers concerned to predict the time of his death. My interest in his end stems from a recent medical reassessment of the manner in which Napoleon died, on the island of St Helena, in 1824. This reappraisal of his death (which we shall examine shortly) reveals at least two of these early charts in a more favourable light than they were previously viewed. The new understanding of how Napoleon died enables us to see that these two charts were predictively accurate.

Unfortunately, there is considerable dispute as to the precise birth time of the future Emperor: each of the astrologers whose charts we shall examine below had access to a different time of birth. At least one astrologer was convinced that the time 9:45 AM had been confirmed by Napoleon himself, to an eminent astronomer in Corsica.[64] According to the modern historian Vincent Cronin, Napoleon's mother insisted on going to the cathedral at Ajaccio for high mass even though the birth was imminent.[65] Shortly after mass had begun, she experienced the first signs of labour. Helped by Geltruda Paravicini back to her house (a minute's walk away), she had no time to reach her bedroom. The child was born shortly before noon. This birth time is reflected in the charts published by the English astrologer John Corfield, both of which we shall examine below.[66] This birth time may be precise, and soundly founded on available contemporary literature, yet the fact remains that the times given in the ten charts known to us vary by as much as twelve hours.

A large number of horoscopes for Napoleon appeared during the first decades of the nineteenth century, and most of the analyses predicted for the Emperor a violent death.[67] I shall examine in detail only two of these, both of which have proved astonishing in their predictive accuracy.

The most decorative of the charts for the Emperor was that cast by the Lincoln astrologer, John Worsdale, in 1807 (see page opposite). Worsdale recorded the birth at 9:51:40 PM, at latitude 41° 40′ North, 9° East.[68] Typical of his method, Worsdale applied the rules of Ptolemy to the chart, and concluded, 'The sun is ... conjoined with a violent fixed star [Cor Leonis], and the moon is afflicted by the opposition of Saturn, so that the whole position, duly considered, forebodes a *violent death*.' Worsdale opined that 'Death will happen by slaughter ...' in an end that *'is violent beyond all question.'*[69]

For an appreciation of Worsdale's analysis of Napoleon, we must glance at some of the views of Thomas Oxley.[70] This nineteenth-century mathematician–astrologer was one of the first to recognise the genius of Worsdale's astro-analysis, even if he did not agree with the latter's view of the Emperor's immorality. Oxley emphasised that Worsdale had *wrongly* predicted a violent death for the Emperor.[71]

Oxley was staunchly pro-Napoleon and had been distressed by the criticisms levelled by Worsdale at his hero and his entourage. Even so, the principal directions in Napoleon's nativity, which Oxley published, were remarkably similar to those provided by Worsdale. The major difference was that Oxley traced Napoleon's death to the progressed Sun reaching semi-quadrate to its natal position, which occurred at fifty-six years and five months. Oxley had the

benefit of hindsight, for by the time he published his book, Napoleon had been dead for nine years.

Modern research has shown that Napoleon was murdered by the systematic administration of poison in his food. In the light of this knowledge, Napoleon's gradual deterioration during the last years of his life may be seen even more clearly in the directions given by Oxley. Napoleon did not die merely because of the semi-square of the Sun to its radical place, but because of a build-up of difficult directions which began even before the battle of Waterloo. These directions were of so serious a nature that even Oxley recognised them as premising 'great danger of Death' to his hero.[72]

Two other charts are of interest to our study, even though both are versions of a single original. Both charts are of poor print quality, and are unlikely to reproduce well. Accordingly, I have cast a modern version (below, left), retaining the placings given in the original. The original chart is reproduced alongside.[73]

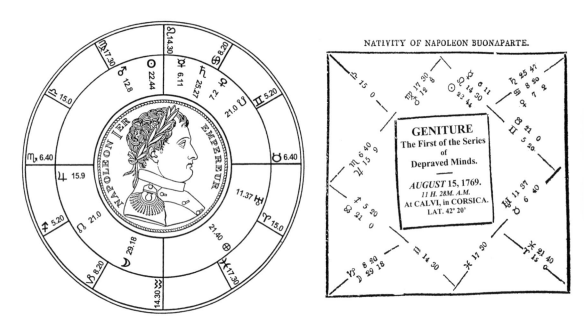

The original chart (right) was cast by the English astrologer John Corfield.[74] It had appeared in an article in the monthly magazine which Corfield both funded and edited, and which was published in June 1814, but which seems to have been discontinued after only one month.[75]

It is the reading attached to the former chart which we find the most astonishing, and the most relevant to modern discoveries about the true nature of Napoleon's death. Corfield, while admitting that the prediction of the quality of death is a difficult subject to deal with astrologically, tells us that he knows from his own experiments that Georgium Sidus (Uranus) is a great malefic. However, since in the chart of Napoleon Uranus is opposed by Jupiter, he doubts that it will be sufficiently malevolent to occasion a violent death:

> What he [Uranus] contributes however will be very remote, and exceedingly obscure; and as he is as well as the Luminary of the time in fixed and violent signs, I conclude that his Influence may tend to accelerate the end of the native by unfair means . . . . I will venture to predict . . . that there will be no external marks of violence about his person after death, and that tho' by some means prescribed either by accident or design, his death may be hastened, yet, to all intents and purposes, it will be deemed a natural one![76]

Few prophecies of so complex a subject as a future murder have been as accurate as this one.

Recent forensic and toxicological research has shown that Napoleon died of poisoning, and that the last years of his life were ruined by the ill-health consequent on the systematic administration of arsenic. This administration had been so subtle as to be unobserved by his doctors, and resulted in a death which was 'deemed a natural one' by those who attended his last days.

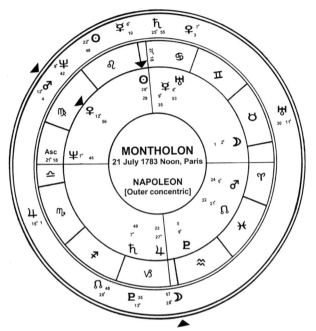

Modern historians and toxicologists have identified this poison, and thereby pointed to the identify of the person in Napoleon's trusted entourage who dispensed it.[77] The man was the aristocrat Charles-Tristan, Count of Montholon, who acted as the Emperor's aide-de-camp, fighting at his side at Waterloo, and tending him in exile on the island of St Helena. The truth is that Montholon was a secret agent for the Bourbons and for years had been actively involved in planning and executing Napoleon's demise.[78]

As I have mentioned more than once, in the case of murder or assassination it is usual for the two people involved (the victim and the perpetrator) to have in common at least one single degree in their respective horoscopes. Napoleon and Montholon were no exceptions to this astrological rule. In this particular case, an astrological contact would be required that would serve to induce Napoleon to form a close friendship with his murderer – a friendship that would disguise the true intentions of the assassin. The chart of Montholon offers precisely such a contact.[79] The horoscope of the murderer is given below: in the outer concentric is a modern version of Napoleon's chart, to facilitate comparison. The revealing communality was effective through the fact that Napoleon's Mars was in the same degree as Montholon's Venus:

Mars in chart of Napoleon:	12.04 Virgo
Venus in chart of Montholon:	12.56 Virgo

A more precise tension between the Emperor and his murderer is found in the following communalities:

Moon in chart of Napoleon:	28.57 Capricorn
Sun in chart of Montholon:	28.29 Cancer

However, there is also a further contact. The planet Neptune, which deals with deception, and with poisons, is very close to this conjunction. In the chart of Napoleon, Neptune was in 08.42 Virgo. The killing planet in the chart of Montholon was Uranus, in conjunction with Mercury. This conjunction, with the wider orb permitted of conjunctions, was on the planet Venus in the chart of Napoleon.

Uranus in chart of Montholon:	08.53 Cancer
Mercury in chart of Montholon:	09.35 Cancer
Venus in chart of Napoleon:	07.03 Cancer

It has taken almost two centuries for the true nature of Napoleon's death to become known to historians. Appraised of the method of death, we are now in a position to see just how accurately it had been predicted by John Corfield while Napoleon was still alive. In 1814, Corfield had written of Napleon's end, '. . . either by accident or design, his death may be hastened, yet, to all intents and purposes, it will be deemed a natural one!'

TWO DISASTERS

One of the delights of studying the history of horoscopy is the occasional glance the researcher is offered of an astrologer at work, in connection with dramatic contemporary events. A particularly tragic occurrence was noted by the nineteenth-century English astrologer, Abraham Beresford, regarding an emigrant ship that sailed in 1848, from Liverpool, destined for the United States. The vessel was lost off the north coast of Wales. Beresford's manuscript note (below) set out the essence of the tragedy: unfortunately, any horoscope he cast for either the departure or the sinking must have been made on a separate sheet, and is now lost.[80] His note read:

[Emigrant ship "Ocean Monarch" left L'Pool Aug. 24th at 8 H.AM. & at 12 at Noon was on Fire & lost (Abergilly Bay') about 170 lives lost!][81]

The *Ocean Monarch* was an American vessel, bound for Boston, with 400 people on board. Six miles off Great Orme's head, Caernarvonshire (North Wales) she caught fire. Within a few hours, she was burned utterly to the water's edge, and 178 people perished. As it happened, the Brazilian steam-frigate *Alfonzo* was out on trials in the neighbourhood, with the Prince and Princess de Joinville and the Duke and Duchess d'Aumale on board. These aristocrats witnessed the burning of the *Ocean Monarch*, and helped rescue some of her passengers. The *Alfonzo* and the yacht, *Queen of the Ocean*, saved 156 of the drowning passengers, and a further 62 escaped by other means.[82]

The astrology of the event reveals the cosmic nature of the tragedy. At 8:00 AM, when the vessel left Liverpool, Saturn was on Cauda, and Neptune was opposite the Sun:

Saturn on 24 August 1848:	23.28 Pisces
Cauda on 24 August 1848:	22.24 Pisces
Neptune on 24 August 1848:	01.11 Pisces
Sun on 24 August 1848:	01.14 Virgo

Typical of a sea disaster, it is the watery Neptune, in opposition to the fiery Sun, which seems to have signalled the catastrophe. At this particular time, the planet Neptune was exactly on the powerful fixed star Sadalmelik, the alpha of Aquarius.

Neptune on 24 August 1848:	01.11 Pisces
Sadalmelik in 1848:	01.14 Pisces

Sadalmelik has a reputation for bringing about 'sudden destruction'.[83]

The astrological story of the disaster is noted, briefly, in Beresford's almanac. Any charts he cast for the event have not survived. Because of this lack of documentation, we do not have his notes on the effects of the total lunar eclipse, which fell on 13 September 1848. However, just as he had written an account of the disaster in the margin of the almanac, so he has scrawled a line alongside the notation for the eclipse, which was marked as being visible in England.[84] One presumes that he recognised the connection between the disaster and the eclipse. The diagram overleaf (left) is from a contemporary ephemeris, and depicts the appearance of the eclipse at Greenwich, whence it would be total at 6:18:48 AM.[85] To the right is a horoscope for this moment.

This eclipse fell on 20.33 Pisces. As a glance at the chart overleaf reveals, more than the Sun and Moon are involved in this watery Pisces. The axis line of the eclipse runs through Saturn (21.59 Pisces), Cauda (21.20 Pisces) and, of course, through the Moon in that sign. Neptune has just entered Pisces.

Beresford's reading, with his note of the imminent eclipse, reminds one of an astrological analysis of the Tay Bridge (Scotland) railway catastrophe, of 28 December 1878. On that date, as a passenger train was passing over the bridge, it collapsed, and nearly a hundred lives were lost. The disaster occurred at 7:15 PM, a few minutes after a lunar eclipse, in 6.42 Cancer.[86] The eclipse, recorded in advance in an almanac horoscope would have been visible in the east to those on the doomed train.

The astrology behind this disaster is fascinating. Although Zadkiel had failed to mention the eclipse in his almanac for 1878, he had predicted 'a catastrophe on a northern railway' for December of that year. Furthermore, in one of the six vignette hieroglyphics for the year, Zadkiel

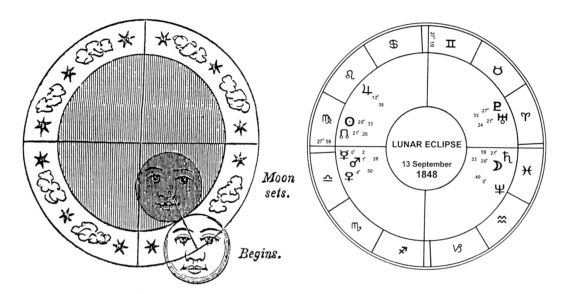

had associated the sign Pisces with the image of a broken stone bridge: the Tay Bridge had been constructed from steel.[87]

SOME CHARTS OF ZADKIEL

A little earlier, I wrote of the bifurcation that characterised nineteenth-century horoscopy and pointed to the American astrologer, Luke Broughton, as a good example of the popularising camp. Among the best examples of leading astrologers in the other camp – that is, in the one dedicated to a study of the arcane technicalities in astrology – was the English horoscopist, Richard James Morrison. Morrison worked under the pseudonym 'Zadkiel', and issued most of his striking prophecies by way of almanacs, published under this name.

Born in 1795, Morrison had been friendly with the astrologer R.C. Smith (the first 'Raphael' of almanac fame), and, from about 1824, had briefly been a member of the mysterious group, The Mercurii.[88] No doubt learning the art from Smith, Morrison appears to have become a professional astrologer in 1830. Four years later, he moved to Cheltenham, and later still settled in the village of Painswick, where he constructed the nineteen issues of his astrological magazine, the *Horoscope*.[89] During the mid-century, the solicitor Christopher Cooke wrote to him, requesting a personal reading and enquiring about horary charts. The two men eventually met in 1852, and became firm friends. Cooke is remembered by historians as the solicitor who advised Zadkiel on the defence of the astrologer–bookseller, Francis D. Copestick of Bath, when the latter was prosecuted in 1851 for practising astrology.[90]

In later years, Cooke wrote a number of entertaining books on astrology and related subjects. In his best known, *Curiosities*, he wrote of his involvement with the Copestick case, his trip to the United States as a fellow-passenger with the diminutive Tom Thumb, and about various astrological encounters in both England and the States, some of which we have already noted.[91]

Zadkiel was especially adept at using eclipses as the basis for predicting mundane events. In his ephemeris for 1865, he predicted the end of the American Civil War from the eclipse of the Moon in 21.23 Libra, which had been visible in Washington, DC, on 11 April 1865.[92] In the same almanac, he also foretold the death of Lord Palmerston from the solar eclipse, in 26.18 Libra, which occurred on 19 October of the same year.[93] This eclipse was less than a degree from Palmerston's natal Sun, and the elderly politician died on the day immediately prior to the eclipse.

Zadkiel had a habit of publishing non-pictorial horoscopes – a method that was adopted by several other Victorian astrologers. The example below is the chart of Wellington, which offers an interesting comparison with the horoscope of Napoleon.[94]

NATIVITY OF THE DUKE OF WELLINGTON.
Planets' Place at Birth, Midnight, May 1st, 1769

☉	☽	♅	♄	♃	♂	♀	☿
♉	♓	♉	♋	♍	♋	♊	♈
11° 48′	16° 0′	7° 36′	13° 17′	19° 7℞.	7° 10′	19° 18′	23° 17′

I cannot pass by this reference to the most influential astrologer of the nineteenth century without giving an example of his personal horoscope. Below, is a pencil sketch of his chart, from a page of an almanac published in 1844.[95] The drawing is based on that made by Christopher Cooke, in the copy of one of his books, now in the possession of the British

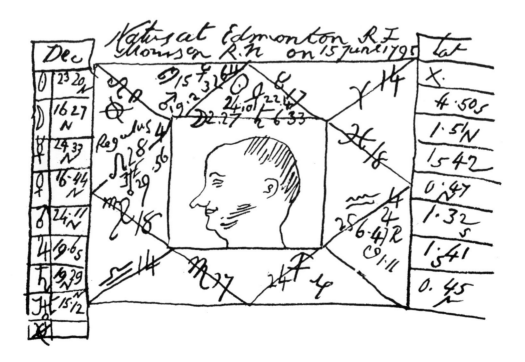

Library.[96] From the notes attached to the original, we learn that Zadkiel was born on 15 June 1795, at 09:45 AM. The chart is interesting in that it offers an early example of how the presence of a star (in this case Regulus) is not merely indicated in the chart, but has its position specified.[98]

The British Library copy of the work in which the original manuscript horoscope is to be found also contains copious notes and several manuscript horoscopes. Among these are the charts for the Prince Consort and Queen Victoria, 'rectified by marriage' on 10 February 1840, and by the death of the former, on 14 December 1861.

CHANEY'S ABBREVIATED CHART

The American astrologers of the nineteenth century never seemed reticent in publishing their own horoscopes. Luke Broughton had reproduced his personal horoscope, cast for 20 April 1828, in Leeds (England) at 10:00 AM.[99] I reproduce this, below, alongside a wood-engraved portrait, which appeared in the same work.

Broughton was probably not the first astrologer to publish his full personal horoscope in America, but I suspect that he was the first to publish his own chart, along with a portrait of himself.[100]

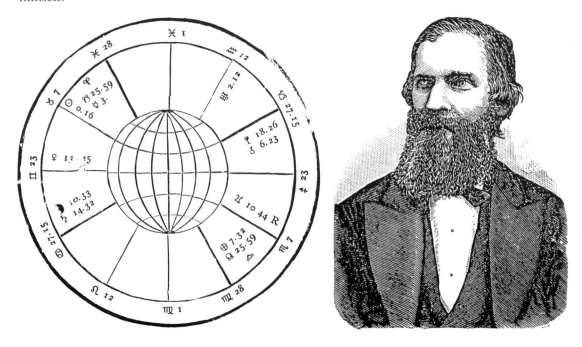

In 1872, William Henry Chaney, the best-known of Broughton's astrology pupils, published his own chart as a sort of lead-in to his dictionary of astrological definitions.[101] Presumably, the typographers at the jobbing printers of E.M. Waite, of Salem, Oregon, had no access to sophisticated astrological sorts, for the chart was published without sigils. This shortage seems to have created a first in horoscopy: one printed with abbreviations in place of sigils.

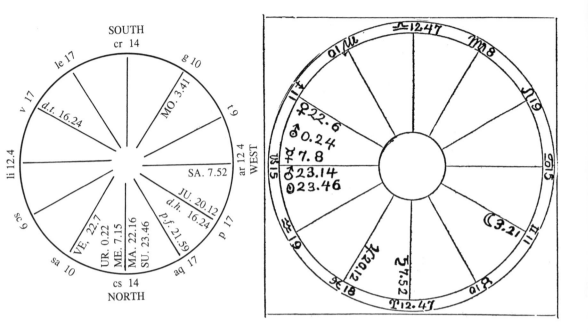

The resultant chart may be seen as an interesting preview of the type of alphabetical abbreviations that would be adopted in 1975 by an international consortium of astrologers.[102] I reproduce the horoscope (above left) alongside a later sigillised version of a similar chart, published by Chaney around 1890.[103] In the left-hand figure, the lower-case abbreviations for the signs are self-evident. The only troublesome abbreviation is **cs** for Capricorn: presumably this a typographical error for either **ca** or **cp**.

Like many Americans of his generation, 'Professor' W.H. Chaney seems to have been proud of his humble origins. Below his chart, he printed an announcement that he had been 'Born in a log cabin, in the forest, but now town of Chesterville, Franklin county, Maine, Jan. 13th, at 11:30 PM, 1821'.

The book on astrology which Chaney wrote towards the end of his life, at the age of seventy, is a gem of the American genre and a classic astrological tutorial. His *American Urania* (to give the short title) was begun in St Louis, Missouri, in 1890.[104] As Chaney could not afford to publish an entire book, he borrowed money from two students and published it in part works, with the notion of having the complete sets bound together to form a single volume. Altogether, there were eight parts, published at 25 cents each, along with a series of tables, which were printed separately.

Since its eighteenth-century heyday, the American almanac tradition has encouraged a humorous and irreverent approach to the world, and Chaney has succeeded in incorporating both these refreshing attitudes into his *American Urania*. In the guise of analysing his own horoscope, Chaney examines the rules of astrology. The result is one of the funniest nineteenth-century works on astrology, which breathes the essence of contemporary life – as, for example, in his account of his spell in prison, in New York City.

In 1867, when I first began the practice of astrology, while living with my preceptor, Dr. Broughton, at 814 Broadway, we displeased 'Boss' Tweed, then mayor of the city, and forthwith he had us sent to Ludlow-street Jail, where I remained, *without a trial*, for twenty-eight weeks and was then *honorably librated*.

However, the laws of retribution did not slumber, for, as Chaney recorded, with some satisfaction,

'Boss' Tweed died in that same Ludlow-Street Jail where he had Dr. Broughton and myself confined for the awful crime of being ASTROLOGERS![105]

Chaney is right to describe his work as 'the first of the kind ever published in America'.[106] Since his teacher, Luke Broughton, was English-born, it is reasonable to describe Chaney as the first truly American astrologer to write a textbook on the subject: certainly, he was the first astrologer to write about the subject in a vociferous and racy American style. The impulse to include the words *American Urania* in the title of his primer is relevant not only to his style, but also to his attitudes – he is prepared to write scathingly of the achievements of the pair whom he calls the 'Raphael Robbers' – the English astrologers, Raphael and Alfred J. Pearce – and to be scathing too about certain members of the English royal family.[107]

Chaney seems to have had an innate dislike of the English, and often poured scorn on many astrological traditions as though these were solely the product of English culture. For example, in admitting that he had never been able to distinguish between the two halves of Sagittarius (one half being traditionally 'humane', the other 'bestial', as befits the image of a horse–man), he recommends his students to disregard such distinctions:

They may do well enough for conservative England, but Young America cares more for truth than for doubtful fossils of antiquity, or the prestige of the inherited titles from a corrupt and enervated aristocracy.[108]

From his self-analysis, we learn that he has found it expedient to disregard retrograde motion, that he omits 'the triple myths' of Caput, Cauda and Fortuna, along with the tradition that Mercury combust the Sun meant that the person so born would have a feeble intellect. After all, as he pointed out, the Revd Henry Ward Beecher and Thomas Edison, 'the great American Inventor', had such combustion in their charts, and they might scarcely be condemned as having poor or enfeebled intellects.[109] Along with these traditions, Chaney also saw fit to dump the old fossil doctrine of the quincunx – though he admitted that even Alfred J. Pearce had had the good sense to reject its barbarous name, and call it '150 degrees'.[110]

His forthright Americanism extended beyond the text into useful tabulations. Tables of houses for New York were readily available in ephemerides of the time, but Chaney thought fit to introduce tables designed for such places as Alaska, Chicago, Huntsville, Jackson and San Francisco.

Chaney died in 1903 – just about old enough to realise that the child he had deserted might become more famous than himself. In that same year, his son John Griffith Chaney (who lived and wrote under the name of Jack London), published his immensely successful novel, *The Call of the Wild*. The son had been conceived during Chaney's short-lived marriage to Flora Wellman, which was celebrated in July 1874, and which had lasted almost a year.[111]

THE CHART OF SHELLEY

Alan Leo's associate, the Welsh clairvoyant Charubel, was responsible for the introduction into modern astrology of a method of horoscopic reading relating to single degrees. Charubel, and the late Victorian school of astrologers around him, appears to have believed that the medieval astrologer John Angelus (whose work we have already discussed) had arrived at his degree readings by clairvoyant means. This is certainly not the case. The readings, and the quaint pictorial equivalents (which were highly popular in medieval art and astrology – see pages 55–7), almost certainly came into medieval astrology by way of a late Egyptian stream of the art.[112] Most certainly, they had nothing to do with clairvoyancy, in the modern sense of the word.

In contrast, Charubel's approach was entirely clairvoyant. By psychic means, Charubel determined a reading, or significance, for each of the 360 degrees of the zodiac, and published these readings in 1898.[113] The same title by Charubel contained a series of translations, by Sepharial, of similar series of degree symbols, originally constructed by La Volasfera.[114]

It is difficult to justify the use of Charubel's degree symbols in horoscopic interpretation. One serious objection is that it is not always easy to determine, beyond doubt, the precise degrees in respect of the four angles. A good example of these difficulties may be studied in the preface to the second edition of Charubel's work on degree symbols. The astrologer pointed to one quite astonishing example of a relevant degree symbol: he tells us that Shelley was born when 27 degrees of Sagittarius rose on the eastern horizon.[115] He seizes on this as evidence for the relevance of this degree in his series, the reading for which was

> a beautiful star the colour and size of the planet Venus, situate about 50° from the midheaven, it shines brighter and brighter, then it suddenly disappears. A mighty genius, poet, painter or musician, promises great things, but dies before middle life.[116]

Immediately after making this claim, Charubel refers the reader to an article by Sepharial on the horoscope of Shelley, which leads one to suspect that the degree reading was dependent upon this article, rather than upon anything psychic. This becomes even more likely further on in the text, where the corresponding reading, for the supposed 28 degrees ascendant, at Shelley's death by drowning, is equated to the symbol reading, 'death through violent means, an accident'. As a matter of fact, since no one witnessed the sinking of the *Ariel* on the waters of the bay of Spezia, it is clear that no one can say precisely what the ascendant degree would have been on that tragic occasion.[117]

The exact cause of the accident on the evening of 8 July 1822 is not known, but a storm had blown up at about 6:30 PM while the *Ariel* was still some 10 miles out at sea. A chart published in *Modern Astrology* purported to be for this time.[118] However, the condition of the

Terminus Vitæ.—Percy Bysshe Shelley.

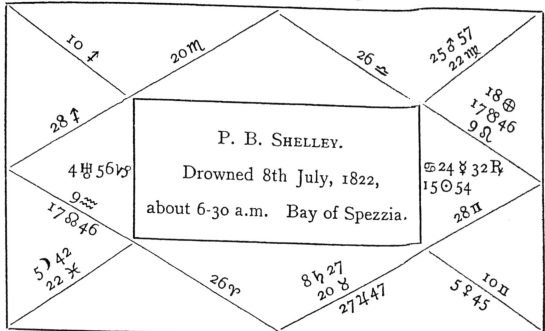

recovered craft, and the later confession of a dying seaman named Sarsanna, suggested that the *Ariel* had been run down by Greek sailors, intent on robbery. If this is the case, then Shelley was murdered. That it was almost certainly murder was signalled by a solar eclipse, which fell on Shelley's natal Pluto:

Solar eclipse of 16 August 1822:	23.26 Aquarius/Leo
Pluto in chart of Shelley:	22.36 Aquarius

As a matter of fact, the data on which Sepharial based his chart for the birth of Shelley have since been proved inaccurate. Family letters, discovered some years after Sepharial wrote, leave no doubt that Shelley was born in the late hours of the evening: his ascendant degree was actually 20 Taurus.[119] Thus, while Shelley's chart is certainly among the most fascinating of the period, Charubel's degree reading for Shelley's figure has no relevance whatsoever to the poet, or his achievements.

As we saw when we examined the system attributed to Johann Angelus, degree symbolism is sometimes extended to cover one or two contiguous degrees. Thus, for example, there is an arc called the 'astrologer's degree' or 'arc', which covers the arcs from 25 to 29 degrees of Leo, and

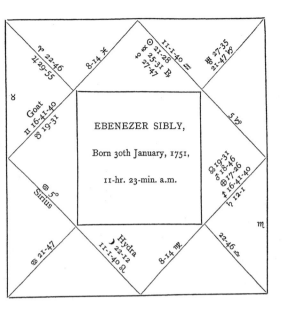

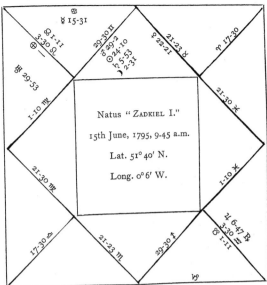

the opposite arc of Aquarius. When a degree in these arcs is occupied by a planet, a nodal point or an angle, then it is said to confer on the native an interest in astrology. Above, I give two birth charts of well-known astrologers, Ebenezer Sibly and Zadkiel.[120] In Sibly's chart, both Mercury and Venus are in the arc, in Aquarius. In Zadkiel's chart, Uranus was in the arc, in 29.63 Leo.

BAILEY AND THE PRENATAL EPOCH

The Prenatal Epoch is the name given to a certain moment which is linked loosely with the approximate beginning of gestation, in the womb. It is not the precise moment of conception, impregnation or fertilisation. In astrological terms, it is the time, near the possible time of gestation, when the ascendant degree and the position of the Moon are interchangeable with the ascendant and degree occupied by the Moon, at the time of the later birth (or, when they were in their respective opposite points). Various refinements of this general definition involve consideration of whether the Moon is above or below the Earth, and whether it is decreasing or increasing in light. Fortunately, there is no need here to delve into all the laws governing the epoch: it is sufficient that we examine an epoch chart, cast by the greatest exponent of Prenatal astrology, E.H. Bailey.

According to his own account, Bailey had begun researching the Prenatal Epoch in 1895. In the winter of 1898, he began collecting together birth and death data, with a view to investigating the matter more closely. Having established a bank of 250 horoscopes, he subjected them to analysis, and came to the conclusion that the theory of the epoch, as outlined by Sepharial some years earlier, was essentially correct. Bailey became so proficient in the handling of the epoch that he later used it as an aid in the rectification of charts.

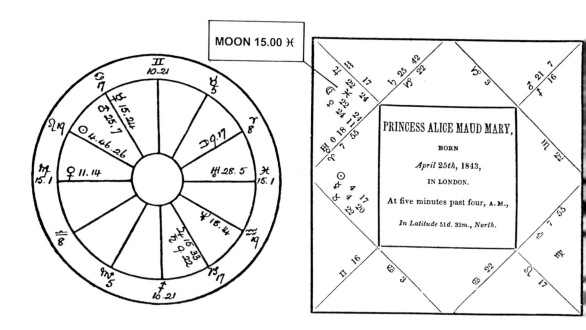

Above (left), is the epoch chart cast by Bailey for Princess Alice, the daughter of Queen Victoria, who had been born at 4:05 AM, in London, on 25 April 1843.[121] A chart for this birth, cast by the English astrologer William Seed, is given alongside Bailey's epoch chart.[122] A comparison of these two charts might initially suggest that Bailey's chart is incorrect, for the Moon in Seed's chart is given as 22.24 Pisces, when, in fact, it was in 15.00 Pisces. I have inserted the correct placing in bold, alongside the chart. The discrepancy reflects well on Bailey, who had obviously gone to the trouble of casting his own chart for the birth of the Princess, rather than relying on that cast by Seed.[123]

A comparison of the two charts enables us to grasp the principle of the Prenatal Epoch. The natal Moon is 15.00 Pisces, while the epochal ascendant is 15.01 Virgo. The epochal Moon is 9.17 Aries, while the natal ascendant is in 8.45 Aries. Only a slight adjustment to the ascendant of the natal chart pulls the two charts into the precise relationship required by the rules of the Prenatal Epoch.

According to Bailey, the epoch was on 28 July 1842, at 8:13:15 AM. He had selected this particular chart in order to illustrate his method of computing directions from an epochal horoscope. In this case, he was intent on computing directions for the year in which Alice's father, Prince Albert, died, on 25 September 1861. The progressed chart for this date shows that, by that date, the MC has moved to 27.49. This meant that it was now in square aspect to the epochal Uranus. At the same time, the progressed ascendant (28.18 Virgo) was directly opposite the epochal Uranus. These aspects would be sufficient to ensure a great shock in the life of Princess Alice. If Bailey had consulted the list of eclipses for the year of Albert's death, then he would have observed that the solar eclipse of 8 July fell on the epochal Mercury in Alice's chart, and was therefore in opposition to the epochal Jupiter.

Solar eclipse of 8 July 1861:	15.50 Cancer
Mercury in epoch chart of Alice:	15.24 Cancer
Jupiter in epoch chart of Alice:	15.33 Capricorn

All these factors – the progressed aspects, and the effect of the solar eclipse on the epochal chart – would have been sufficient to signal the death of a father.

Eclipses are not used in modern horoscopy as widely as in former times, but this does not reduce their utility. The American astrologer, Edward Johndro, rightly observed that 'no horoscope is complete till it has been overlaid by the near-term eclipses preceding and following the birthdate'.[124]

PLUTO AND CHARLES NICOULLAUD

It is a strange historical fact that the planet Pluto was intuited, recognised and named over thirty years before it was discovered by scientists, in 1930. The existence of Pluto was identified by the French astrologer, Charles Nicoullaud, a short while before 1897. In an influential work published in that year, he had announced, 'A planet beyond Neptune exists [and] is called Pluto'.[125] How Nicoullaud became privy to this knowledge remains a mystery. However, the end of the nineteenth century was rich in clairvoyant claims relating to the existence of imaginary and hypothetical planets, some of which have entered into practical modern astrology.

A good example of a horoscope by Nicoullaud is given below.[126] The one to the left was cast for the former President of the French Republic, Marie-François Sadi Carnot, who had been born at Limoges on 11 August 1837. Mainly because of the notoriety of his assassination, in 1894, several versions of his horoscope and death chart have survived. The natus given by

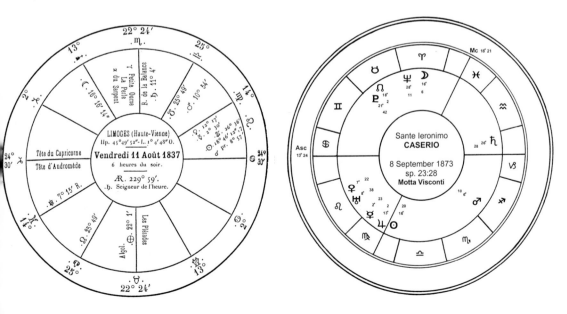

Nicoullaud (above) is cast for a birth time of 6:00 PM.[127] The chart to the right is that of the Italian anarchist Caserio, who assassinated Carnot at 9:30 PM on 24 June 1894, in Lyons.[128] Sante Ieronimo Caserio was born at Motta Visconti, near Milan, on 8 September 1873, at a speculative time of 11:28 PM.[129]

As may be seen from these charts, Nicoullaud incorporated the sigil for Uranus into the nativity, and sigils for both Uranus and Neptune into the revolution chart. However, there seems to be no symbol for the planet Pluto, which, with such inexplicable prescience, he had named. It is reasonable to presume that Nicoullaud had no idea as to where in the zodiac his new planet was actually located.

The horoscopes above are of interest to us for matters that have nothing to do with Pluto. In the birth chart is the curious sigil **♂pr.** In the revolution chart is the curious sigil **☍pr.** With these sigils, Nicoullaud is reverting to a version of a Ptolemaic idea relating to eclipses. Ptolemy had insisted that the eclipse most nearly related to the time of birth was a relevant influence in the chart of the native. Nicoullaud seems to have extended this idea to 'symbolic eclipses', which are the conjunction and opposition of the Sun and Moon. In the birth chart, he is merely recording that the previous conjunction of the two luminaries had fallen in 8.77 Leo.[130] In the revolution chart for 1893, he is recording that the nearest opposition between the two fell in 5.54 Aquarius.

We have already encountered the notion of there being communalities of degrees in the compared charts of killers and the killed: usually, the assassin and the assassinated have at least one zodiacal degree in common. The horoscopes of Carnot and Caserio were no exception to the general rule: if we compare the two charts, we discover that, in each horoscope, Mercury is in precisely the same degree:

Mercury in chart of Carnot:	02.29 Virgo
Mercury in chart of Caserio:	02.23 Virgo

By a most curious coincidence, just over two months before the assassination, on 6 April 1894, a solar eclipse (16.20 Aries) fell on the radical Pluto (16.48 Aries) in Carnot's horoscope. This was the degree in which the Moon of Caserio's chart was placed (16.37 Aries).

In this comparison of charts, we are alerted to a truth promulgated almost two thousand years ago by Ptolemy – that an eclipse degree related to a time of birth is an operative factor in a chart. In the chart of Caserio, the destructive Uranus is in 08.37 Leo. This is precisely the degree marked by the solar–lunar conjunction, marked as *pr. 8.57 Leo*, in Carnot's horoscope.

During the first two decades of the twentieth century, at least two English astrologers (both perhaps standing on Nicoullaud's shoulders) not only mentioned Pluto, but gave every indication that they were using it in the horoscopes they cast. I shall discuss the knowledge of the English astrologer, Isabelle M. Pagan, at a more appropriate point. Meanwhile, I should record that Sepharial, in one of his works, published in 1918, discussed the still-unknown Pluto as a harbinger of war:

Figure 1. The bull-headed Moloch, with a radiant sun set against zodiacal Gemini: painted in England, c. 1893, by the American artist, John Singer Sargent, for the arched entrance to the upper library in Boston Public Library, Massachusetts.

Figure 2. Portrait of the Elizabethan, Sir Christopher Hatton, painted within the zodiacal and planetary concentrics marking his personal revolutional horoscope for 12 December 1581, which marked the beginning of his forty-second year. *(Reproduced with the kind permission of the Northampton Museum and Art Gallery)*

Figure 3. Woodcut plate of a volvelle depicting the northern constellations, from a work by the Scottish astrologer, Jacques Bassantin, *Astronomique discourse* (1562). The pointer *Auge Comuni*, or 'the communal Auge' (mentioned in the text of this work) is marked by an arrow, on the circumference of the figure.

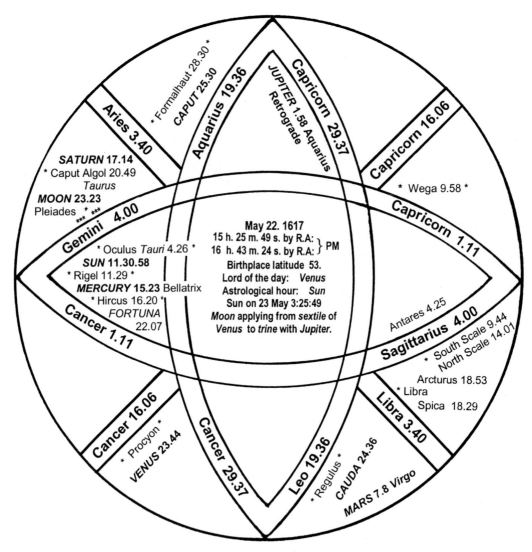

Figure 4. A modern representation of the natal chart of the antiquary, astrologer and collector, Elias Ashmole, cast for 22 May 1617. The original horoscope is in the Bodleian Library, Oxford.

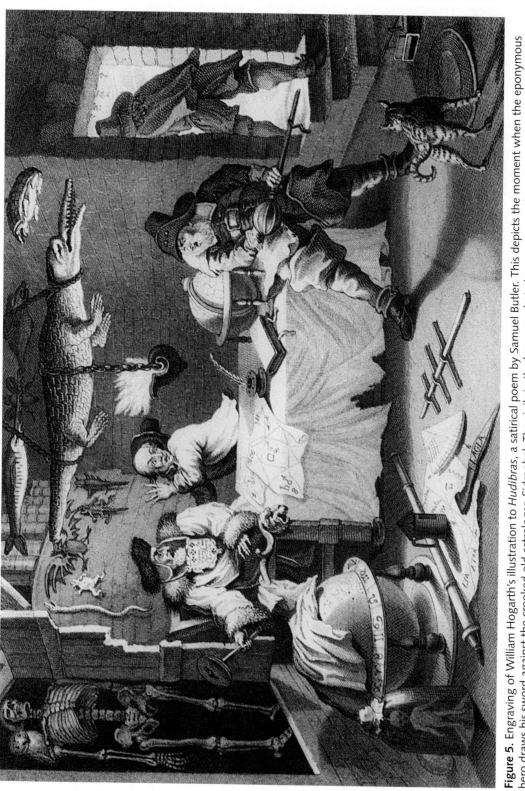

Figure 5. Engraving of William Hogarth's illustration to *Hudibras*, a satirical poem by Samuel Butler. This depicts the moment when the eponymous hero draws his sword against the crooked old astrologer, Sidrophel. The sigils in the large quadrate horoscope, on the table, are intended to symbolise the human tensions within the image.

Figure 6. A bronze horoscope in the form of concentric planetary orbs, centred on the Earth, with the planets represented within the orbs as globules. The cartouche on the statue to the assassinated President, James Abram Garfield, was sculpted by John Quincy Adams Ward, in 1887, and is located to the south-west of the Capitol Building, in Washington, DC.

BRACKEN HOUSE

Figure 7. The zodiacal clock, some two metres in diameter, on the façade of Bracken House, the former offices of the *Financial Times*, in Cannon Street, London. Designed by Thwaites and Reed, in 1959, the solarised face at the centre of the zodiacal circle is intended as a portrait of Sir Winston Churchill.

Figure 8. Albert Einstein, sculpted by Robert Berks, and located to the south of the National Academy of Sciences, Washington, DC. The statue is seated on an elaborate image of the stars, set in a marble plinth, 28 feet in diameter. The arrangement of stars, planets and asteroids is in the form of a huge horoscope, cast for noon on 22 April 1979, the moment of the Memorial's dedication.

This, when discovered, will prove to be an extra-Neptunian planet of great dimensions but small density. It may be called Pluto, Lord of the Pit, Lord of Destruction, etc., according to the fancy of astrologers; but its functions will be those of Mars on a grand scale, and its place at the date 1914 will link it directly with the indications of the Great War.[131]

ALAN LEO'S PREFABRICATED CHARTS

Alan Leo was the legally adopted name of W.F. Allen.[132] According to a chart which Leo cast personally, he was born in London on 7 August 1860, at 5:49 PM.[133] This horoscope, with four placings in Leo (see page 189), explains the reason for his adopted name. The long list of his published books is silent testimony to his popularity, even though, in the opinion of some purists, he is not deserving of the fame ascribed to him, and was at times a careless astrologer.

Leo claims to have learned the rudiments of astrology from a Dr Richardson, an astro-herbalist who lived in Manchester.[134] The younger, but far more proficient astrologer, Walter Richard Old (who was to write a number of astrological books under the name of Sepharial), introduced Leo to Theosophy, and he became a member of the Theosophical Society in 1890. In so far as Leo had a profession prior to his entering this heady circle, it was as a salesman, and almost immediately he grasped the commercial potential of a Society that was already spreading throughout the globe, with roots in India to the East, and in the United States to the West. Unlike the bright and intellectual individuals who had found their way to Theosophy at that time, Leo was neither widely read nor particularly learned: even his wife reported that he read very few of the books she placed before him, and those he did look through, he read only superficially.[135] In effect, it is more as a salesman than as a proficient astrologer that Alan Leo should be remembered in the history of horoscopy.

Alan Leo was the first astrologer to commercialise astrology on a massive scale. He set up an office – the heart of his Modern Astrology Publishing Company, which (Leo claimed) had sub-offices in Paris and New York – to deal with the thousands of requests he received for horoscopes. He was the first English astrologer to devise a system of satisfying these demands, with what have since been called 'prefabricated horoscopes'. These were preprinted readings of salient planetary and nodal positions (such as Moon in Aries, Moon in Taurus, etc.), which were bundled together, and sent out as constituting a reading of a chart. Each prefabricated reading consisted of print-outs of readings for at least nine planets in respective signs, with four readings for the angles. No reputable astrologer would have treated the art in such a way – each chart is a unique thing, and must be handled accordingly. There can be no such thing as a valid mass-astrology.

One early member of the substantial staff of the Modern Astrological Publishing Company had been the astrologer E.H. Bailey, whose Prenatal Epoch we examined above. Bailey rapidly grew to detest both Leo and his methods, and he later struck out as a professional astrologer in his own right.[136] Bailey was by no means the only critical worker in the office – on one occasion, during 1903, Leo's entire staff, demoralised by his prostitution of the art, walked out in protest

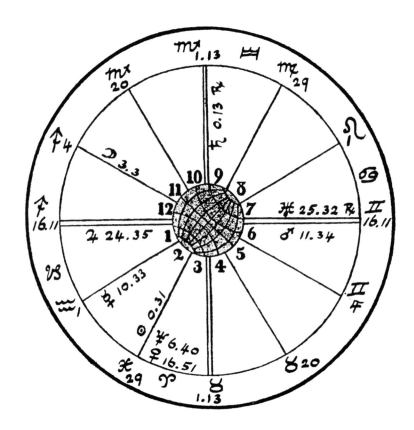

at his methods. With typical pseudo high-mindedness (and, as it happened, lack of astrological insight), Leo blamed the cosmos, attributing the strike to the transits of Neptune and Mercury in opposition to the Sun in his own chart – an astrological invention.[137]

More destructive of future horoscopy, Leo was prepared to change the traditional basis of astrology in order to make the practice more acceptable to non-specialists. For pecuniary reasons, Leo published a large number of books under his own name, not all of which were written by him. In some cases, this method backfired. Among Alan Leo's astrological manuals was *A Thousand and One Notable Nativities*, which must be one of the most confused, slipshod and inaccurate compilations of horoscopes ever printed. Although most of the material for the work had appeard previously in *Modern Astrology* (of which Leo was editor), the book itself was compiled by one of his numerous assistants, H.S. Green. Its reputation (such as it is) rests on the sheer number of horoscopes, rather than on any merit in either the organisation of the material or the accuracy of the data. The only horoscope (as opposed to tabulated data) in the book is the chart for the Swedish explorer, Sven Hedin, which served as frontispiece (above). The chart is reasonably accurate so far as planetary positions are concerned (though this is certainly not true of many of the other horoscopes listed in the book).[138] The most disturbing element is not the chart itself, but the fact that, in a book of this kind, Leo did not trouble to offer a time, place or date of birth, nor even a source for the horoscope.[139]

PHOTO-HOROSCOPES

By 1893, a number of technical developments in printing permitted the reproduction of reasonable quality letter-press photographs in books, magazines and newspapers. Alan Leo and his co-workers in the office of *Modern Astrology* took advantage of this, and published the first horoscopes incorporating photographic likenesses of natives at the centres of the charts. They called these 'photo-horoscopes'. The earliest of such published charts were confined to astrologers – presumably because those working in the office of *Modern Astrology* had access to photographs of themselves and their associations, to supply to the block-makers serving their printers. The first to be printed in *Modern Astrology* was that of the astrologer Aphorel, the second was of Alan Leo (below), and the third the chart of Sepharial.[140] The method of portrayal was adopted in a number of almanacs, and within a few years had become justifiably popular, especially in ephemerides and magazines. We shall study some of these in the next chapter.

EVANGELINE ADAMS AND THE FIRE OF 1899

During the first part of the twentieth century, Evangeline Adams was probably the most famous of all American astrologers. Her amusing and informative autobiography reveals her as the most outstanding horoscopist of the day.[141] However, what many astrologers regard as her most famous and influential chart was cast at the very end of the nineteenth century.

In 1899, Adams was already thirty-two years old and well known as a practitioner in Boston when she decided to move permanently to New York City. In mid-March, she took rooms in the Windsor Hotel and, out of interest, cast the horoscope for Warren Leland, the hotel manager. She was astonished to see that he was 'under one of the worse possible combinations of planets'.[142] From a study of transits and progressions, she saw that he was due for a terrible shock on the following day. After enquiring about his previous experiences during similar cycles, she rapidly came to the conclusion that there would be a fire in the hotel. She was right. The fire broke out on the morning of the following day, 17 March 1899, in consequence of which many people died. Leland lost several members of his family in the conflagration, including his daughter Helen. The shock proved too much for him, and he died a few weeks later.

Immediately after the fire had been put out, Leland told all who would listen about Evangeline Adams' prediction, made on the previous evening. Naturally, this information was taken up by the press, and her first astrological reading in New York was bruited as headline news. Writing about the event later, she described the unfortunate horoscope as 'a grim success', since it established her fame in the city as an astrologer.[143]

The chart of Warren Leland – almost certainly based on the chart cast by Adams – is given below, from an article by Sepharial.[144]

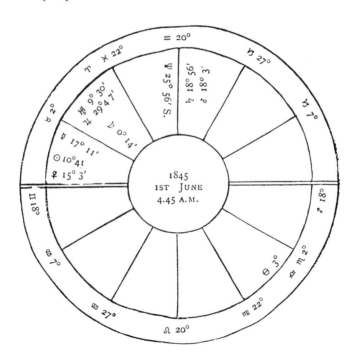

1845
1ST JUNE
4.45 A.M.

In her autobiography, Adams recorded the precise time when she had cast the fateful chart, suggesting that later astrologers would be interested in the transits. From the chart itself one would be inclined to see the most violent point as being the conjunction of Mars and Saturn in Aquarius, just within orb of Neptune, and within a degree or so of the Midheaven. This conjunction was rendered all the more dire in that Mars fell on the destructive fixed star Castra (in 1845, the star was in 18.06 Aquarius).

In the progressed chart Mercury and Venus were in platic conjunction (21.02 Leo) and directly opposite the radical MC, thus sparking off the dangerous combination gathered around his angle in the natal chart. In the transit chart for the day of the fire (at 6:00 AM) the Moon was in direct opposition to Uranus, and within 2 degrees of the radical Sun.

One sigil in this chart catches our attention. In the fifth house is a sigil that resembles the Greek letter theta, θ. This was almost certainly drawn into the chart by Sepharial, for it represented the hypothetical planet Lilith, which he believed to be an invisible dark Moon, circling the Earth.

HOROSCOPES FOR THE UNITED STATES OF AMERICA

The nineteenth-century American astrologer John Hazelrigg was one of the first to study in depth the cycles of the so-called 'new' planet, Uranus.[145] We are fortunate that one of these intensive studies relates to a horoscope for the beginnings of the United States of America – literally, a chart cast for the birth of the nation.

As we have already seen, many charts have been erected for the inception of the United States, the majority of them constructed around supposed, or claimed, times for the Declaration of Independence. Indeed, over forty such American charts are now on record.[146] What makes Hazelrigg's version particularly impressive is the extent to which he revealed how certain latent elements in the chart related to significant events in American history.

The national chart cast by Hazelrigg (overleaf, left) was based on a time recorded in the *Journal of Congress* for 4 July 1776.[147] According to this version of events, the Declaration of Independence, made in Philadelphia, was announced at 12:20 PM.

Hazelrigg cast the chart shortly before 1917. Previously, at the very end of the nineteenth century, he had published a slightly different version of the horoscope.[148] This chart (overleaf, right), cast for Philadelphia, on 4 July 1776, at 12:15 PM, differed from the later one by only 5 minutes.

The second chart is the more important one from a historical point of view. The really distinctive thing about this second national horoscope is that Hazelrigg felt free to insert on the chart the name of the fixed star, which he had indicated in the earlier chart by means of the Greek letter *alpha*. Just below the position of Uranus (given as 8.51 Gemini), Hazelrigg indicated the presence of the star Aldebaran.[149] By inserting this star in the chart, Hazelrigg was making public a highly significant point about the national horoscope of the United States. He was able to demonstrate, from forces latent within the chart, a cycle of warfare that he saw

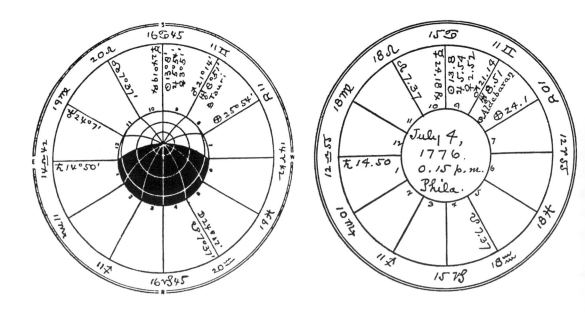

had influenced American history, and which he foresaw would continue to influence it. This cycle was linked with the planet Uranus, and its dangerous proximity to Aldebaran. Hazelrigg wrote:

> for our purpose it will be needful only to direct the attention of the reader to the position of Uranus [♅] in the ninth degree of Gemini [♊] ... in close proximity to Aldebaran (*a* Tauri), a fixed star of the first magnitude, of a fiery, martial nature, at that time in 6° 42′ Gemini.[150]

Hazelrigg was deeply interested in the theory of cycles.[151] This permitted him to recognise the awesome power behind the combined influence of the deadly Uranus and the fiery Aldebaran. Within a few years of its discovery in 1781, the planet Uranus had revealed itself to astrologers as a destructive power, linked with wars and revolutions. Indeed many historians of astrology had been tempted to see even the specific time-frame, when the planet was discovered, as a revelation of the new revolutionary impetus in world history. The year 1781 stood between the two major revolutions which engulfed Europe and America at the end of the century – the bloody American War of Independence, and the fratricidal French Revolution.

Aldebaran is the brightest star in the constellation Taurus (opposite; I have marked its position with a dart).[152] Set in the right eye of the cosmic Bull, its proximity to the horns of the fierce creature goes a long way towards explaining its traditional association with threatening power and headstrong violence. Ever since Ptolemy had interpreted the star as representing a second Mars in the skies, its reputation for bringing about violent death, military endeavours quarrels and disgrace had become formidable among astrologers.[153]

In the national chart, the star and planet were close to each other, even though they were not exactly in the same degree:

Position of Aldebaran in 1776:   6.42 Gemini
Position of Uranus on 4 July 1776:   8.55 Gemini

It is evident that Hazelrigg was prepared to allow a much wider orb (in this case, 2 degrees 16 minutes), in which the influence of Aldebaran could commingle with that of the planet.

Hazelrigg wisely recognised that when the planet and the star were in such close proximity in a chart, then the degrees they occupied would mark dire consequences in the unfolding of history. The Geminian arc in the chart would act as a nexus, or nodal point, which, whenever tripped by other baleful planetary influences, would threaten war, discord or some catastrophe. Hazelrigg knew that it was not possible to separate the fiery and military star from the dramatic and explosive Uranus. This combination enabled him to trace a number of baleful events in the

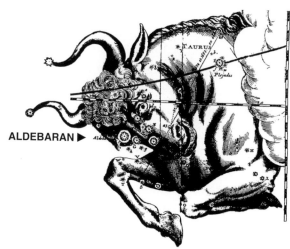

ALDEBARAN ▶

history of the United States to the specific area of Gemini dominated by the pair. Among these events was the commencement of the terrible Civil War which almost destroyed the new country.

Hazelrigg pointed out that Uranus, after its long circuit of the zodiac, would re-enter Gemini in June 1858. Then it would begin to edge its way back to the same degree it had occupied in 1776, at the birth of the new nation. He recognised that this progression would stimulate warlike influences that would lead up to the Civil War. According to Hazelrigg, the first decisive measure of secession was when South Carolina declared its independence, on 20 December 1860: on that day (he insisted) Uranus had arrived at the same degree of Gemini it had occupied at the Declaration of Independence.

As a matter of fact, although Hazelrigg was correct in his approach to astrological prediction based on the cycles of Uranus), he appears to have made an error in this particular set of calculations. No doubt the tabulations of positions available to him were inaccurate.[154] In December 1860, Uranus had been in retrograde movement, and was *not* in the degree he specified. In fact, Uranus did not return to the same degree it had held in the chart for the United States until the evening of 1 April 1861. Of course, in terms of Hazelrigg's theory, this was an even more pertinent date.

The great circuit of Uranus in the heavens takes approximately eighty-four years. In this case, the complete circuit – between 4 July 1776, when the nation found a new unity, and 1 April 1861, when the nation found itself under threat of losing that unity – had taken just under 84 years and 10 months. Within a few days of the planet returning to its original degree in the chart of American Independence, the Civil War broke out.

On 4 March 1861, Lincoln delivered his Inaugural Address. On 8 April, he began to send supply ships to Fort Sumter. The Confederates interpreted this as a preparation for hostilities. The confederate batteries opened fire at 4:30 AM on 12 April 1861.[155] On that morning Uranus was in 9.20 Gemini – that is to say, it was within only 25 minutes of the position it had held at the moment of the Declaration, in July 1776.

Just as Hazelrigg was able to demonstrate convincingly how the fiery torch of Uranus had been linked with warfare in the past, so he was able to predict, with fair accuracy, how that same torch would be linked with warfare in the future. By virtue of his study of the interplay of Uranus in Gemini, in relation to Aldebaran, he was able to predict, decades in advance, when the United States would become involved in another war. In relation to the national chart we have just studied, Hazelrigg specified the years beginning in 1942, and culminating in October 1943.[156] Given that he was writing over fifty years before the events occurred, his predictions of American involvement in Pearl Harbor and in the Second World War are astounding. The Japanese attack on Pearl Harbor, which brought the United States into the war, occurred on 7 December 1941 – only six months earlier than the time predicted by Hazelrigg. Elsewhere, Hazelrigg and Broughton had predicted a major conflict, beginning in 1940.[157]

Although Hazelrigg made these predictions during the last years of the nineteenth century he lived just long enough to experience the outbreak of the Second World War, which was to see his prediction come true.

Earlier, we compared two charts of nineteenth-century leaders who had been assassinated – those of Abraham Lincoln and Tsar Alexander II. From the two sample astro-readings, we were forced to conclude that there was a wide chasm between the astrologies practised in the nineteenth century. It is likely that this chasm reflected growing literacy in Britain and the United States: the classes that previously had been illiterate formed a new readership for an art that had, until now, been the preserve of the learned and the specialist. There was no hope that the majority of these readers could be lifted to the levels where the intricacies of the art could be appreciated, so a low-brow astrology was developed to serve their needs. The chasm that had been created by commercialism was later serviced by newspapers.

This chasm would not be bridged in the coming century. Indeed, as the popular form of astrology began to flourish, to serve the masses, and a more technical astrology was developed to serve specialists, the gap was to grow wider. As is the way of things, the popular form was dumbed down, to a point where it could no longer properly be called astrology. The specialist form became even more complex and convoluted, to a point where certain forms could be understood only by specialists. The first stages of this separation of astrological cultures, which became the hallmark of the twentieth-century astrologies, may be traced to certain trends in nineteenth-century horoscopy.

CHAPTER 6

The Twentieth Century

One occasionally meets the student who eagerly follows up every new method suggested in the hope that at last he will find the solution to all his problems, not realizing that most of these problems spring from an imperfect acquaintance with the ordinary basic processes of astrology. There would be far less dissatisfaction with existing methods if students took the trouble to master them thoroughly before turning their attentions further afield!

Ronald C. Davison, *Astrology: The Astrologers' Quarterly* (1962), Vol. 36, No. 3, p. 78

In 1959, an elaborate zodiacal clock, some 2 metres in diameter, was installed on the façade of Bracken House, the former offices of the *Financial Times*, in Cannon Street, London. It is a beautiful mechanism, with an intriguing symbolic face (figure 7). However, few people who have glanced at this clock have grasped the astrological mystery hidden behind its design.

The entire zodiacal circle of gilded zodiacal images revolves slowly around a massive sunburst. The clock is designed to tell the hours and minutes of the day, and to point the degrees occupied by the Sun during the course of the year. Perhaps the most surprising feature of this time-piece is that in many respects it suggests the idea of a horoscope. In the centre of the sunburst is a face which on casual inspection seems to be a traditional personification of the solar deity. However, on closer examination this turns out to be a portrayal of the great statesman Sir Winston Churchill, his face centred to the zodiac in the manner of the astro-portraits that had become so popular in astrological magazines. It would be delightful if we could surmise from this that the zodiacal clock is somehow a personal horoscope, but unfortunately this is not the case. However, the instrument *does* contain horoscopic material relating to Sir Winston Churchill.

It is true that Lord Bracken, who commissioned Thwaites and Reed to design this clock, was a friend of Churchill, and it is quite possible that the face was intended to celebrate the friendship between the two men. However, there are several other details on the clock face which suggest a hidden content.

First, we should consider the form of the elaborate pointer at the top of the clock, overlying the moving zodiac, which indicates the month. The pointer itself ♈ is in the form of the sigil for Aries. It is true that the so-called zero-point of Aries marks the vernal equinox,

the beginning of spring, yet there is nothing within the clock which is intended to giv
pre-eminence to any particular time, season or month. It is only when we examine other curiou
elements in the clock design that the importance of this sigil for Aries becomes clear.

The sunburst around the portrait of Churchill is both dramati
and interesting. As we scrutinise it, we discover that it is actually
double sunburst. The inner, which encloses the portrait itself
consists of twenty-eight pointed radiants. This is a lunar numbe
and is the approximate number of days taken by the Moon to circl
the Earth. In astrology, it is rightly termed a lunar number. I
contrast, the outer sunburst is clearly solar. Not only is it painted i
celestial gold, like the zodiacal creatures in the contiguous imagery
but it consists of forty-eight radiants. The number 48 is divisibl
by 12 (12 × 4), which is the number of signs transited by the Sun in the course of a year. It i
also the number of months in a year. Since each month is divided into 4 weeks, we may describ
the number 48 as a solar number. This number is entirely symbolic, for we all know that ther
are 52 weeks in a year. The numbers 28 and 48 are *symbolic* of a solar–lunar relationship.

In their most simple numerology, the Bracken House sunbursts point to a relationshi
between the Sun and the Moon. It is a numerology echoed in other elements of the design
When we examine the central part of the clock in the light of this solar–lunar imagery, w
realise that it was intended to convey more than merely the likeness of Churchill, in the guise o
a pagan Sun-god: it was designed to suggest a solar eclipse, when the dark face of the Moo
passes exactly in front of the radiant Sun
itself.

On 8 April 1959 – the year the
zodiacal clock was erected – a solar
eclipse fell in 17.33 Aries. This was
directly opposite Mars in the horoscope
of Winston Churchill. To the right is
Churchill's chart, cast for 30 November
1874, at Woodstock, England, at 1:30
AM.[1] In an astrological appreciation of
Churchill published shortly after his
death, Ronald C. Davison attributed
Churchill's enormous popularity to the
sextile aspect between Jupiter and
Venus.[2] It is true that the Sun and
Saturn were in sextile and that Venus
was in trine wih Caput, and less power-

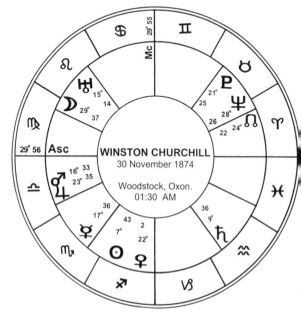

WINSTON CHURCHILL
30 November 1874

Woodstock, Oxon.
01:30 AM

fully so with the Moon, but it is the Jupiter–Cauda contact which seems to reflect in his own
destiny, and in the destiny of the country he led to victory.

Cauda in chart of Churchill: 24.22 Libra

Jupiter in chart of Churchill: 23.35 Libra

This is an extraordinarily powerful placing for a politician, and it was one which helped Churchill win the Second World War. His Caput (supported by the diametric conjunction of Cauda with Jupiter) was in 24.22 Aries, and thus within a degree of Hitler's Mercury, in 25.41 Aries (Hitler's chart is given on page 220). The two world leaders were pulled together by most powerful communality.

On 16 October 1940, a lunar eclipse fell in 22.42 Aries – opposite the Jupiter–Cauda conjunction in Churchill's chart, and within an operative degree of the Caput–Mercury of the combined charts of Churchill and Hitler.

As seems to be natural with the birth of great men and women, Churchill was born with an eclipse marking his chart. However, this was no ordinary eclipse. In 1874, the year of Churchill's birth, a solar eclipse fell on exactly the same degree axis as that of 1959. This means the solar eclipse fell exactly on Mars in the natal chart of Churchill.

Solar eclipse of 10 October 1874:   16.59 Libra

Mars in chart of Churchill: 16.33 Libra

The fact of this birth eclipse is astonishing in itself. However, when it is related to the life of Winston Churchill, it becomes even more astonishing. If we were to ask ourselves which year, in Churchill's long life, marked his supreme genius, then we would have to point to 1940. It was in this year that he came to power, with the resignation of the appeaser, Neville Chamberlain, and it was in this year that his extraordinary speeches began to galvanise and sustain the British people as they faced Nazi tyranny. Of this period, Churchill (who had both Moon and Uranus in Leo) wrote, 'It was the nation that had the lion's heart. I had the luck to be called upon to give the roar.'[3] He began this leonine role on 10 May 1940.

It was in this year (and, incidentally, *only* in this year, during his lifetime) that another solar eclipse fell in this same degree. On 7 April 1940, there was a solar eclipse in 17.52 Aries. Just over a month after the solar eclipse, Winston Churchill found himself in a position to begin what he later called his 'walk with destiny'.

There are secrets in the Bracken House zodiacal clock that few people have even suspected: the most remarkable of the secrets are linked with the mechanisms of the eclipses, which relate to the cycles of Earth, Sun and Moon, evinced in the numerology of the clock. As we have seen, the theory of the way in which eclipses interpenetrate the horoscope is as old as horoscopy itself: when Ptolemy wrote about this interpenetration, in the second century of our era, it was already an ancient idea. However, the theory of cyclical relationships between lunar and solar rhythms found an astrological setting as late as 1925, with the publication of *The Vision*, by the Irish poet William Butler Yeats.[4]

Yeats seems to have studied esoteric astrology more deeply than most other literary figures; at all events, he was among the first to incorporate arcane astrological concepts into his writings. Yeats was interested in many psychic and cosmic truths, but he was especially fascinated by the cycle of 28. A few of the ideas relating to this cycle, which were probably encouraged by his reading in Theosophy, actually entered into the mainstream of twentieth-century astrology. However, Yeats appears to have been more interested in astrology than in horoscopy and, if we seek a twentieth-century literary view on personal horoscopes, then we can do no better than turn to the writings of the American, Henry Miller, who was an amateur astrologer.[5]

Few people go to the trouble of chalking on the walls of their home a giant copy of their natal horoscope. However, this is precisely what Miller did in his Parisian studio at Villa Seurat during the years leading up to the Second World War.[6] Miller was one of the few non-professional astrologers who recognised the immense power of the horoscope – 'the constellated mysterium', as he called it – in its personal extension of space and time.[7] Perhaps this is why he introduced into his writings so many references – some of them obscure and esoteric – to horoscopy.[8]

Miller's account of his studio decoration appeared in the final section of his *Big Sur and the Oranges of Hieronymus Bosch*. The section dealt with the eccentric French astrologer, Conrad Moricand, who, having lost all his possessions, had become dependent on the kindness of strangers and friends. The astrologer was no literary invention of Miller – before his fall Moricand had written a book on astrology, and had gained some fame in France as a horoscopist.[9] He was, as Miller described him, an incurable dandy, living the life of a beggar, 'a sad wizard who in moments of desperation would endeavour to extract a tiny ray of promise from his star Regulus'.[10]

In *Big Sur* we learn that in the early days of their relationship Moricand had presented Miller with a personal birth chart, correcting that cast by Miller himself: apparently, this latter had been twelve hours in error. According to Moricand, the chart should have been cast for about noon. As a result of Moricand's interjection, the time most widely used for Miller's horoscope is 12:17 PM – as in the chart opposite, which includes a fixed star and the four chief asteroids.[11]

Miller was interested in more than merely modern horoscopy – he had the genuine astrologer's wish to study the charts of the great men and women of history. In a letter to the astrologer, Sydney Omarr, Miller confessed that what he would dearly love to see were the charts for Milarepa, Gautama the Buddha, Gilles de Rais, Francis of Assisi, Ramakrishna, Krishnamurti and Joan of Arc.[12] The last two are puzzles, as versions of their charts have been available for years.[13]

Miller and his wife formed a close friendship with Moricand. During 1947, learning that the astrologer was living in penury in Switzerland, they somehow raised the money to pay for a one-way trip to the United States. For some months, Moricand lived in a small room in the Millers' house in Big Sur, California. Inevitably, difficulties arose, and eventually Moricand went back to Europe, where he died in a Swiss retreat for the aged, in Paris – an institution founded by his own parents. He died on 31 August 1954.

'I was born under a lucky star,' Miller was fond of saying. Perhaps he intended a sly reference to the Star of the Three Kings, for he had come into the world on the day after Christmas, 1891, in Manhattan.[14] His joking words were more serious than he intended, for his horoscope reveals that he *had* been born under the influence of a very powerful fortunate star. On the day of his birth, the star Alphecca had been within a degree of his Mars, which was, in turn, within a degree of his Moon. In the astrological tradition, the brilliant white Alphecca was renowned for bestowing 'honour, dignity and poetical and artistic ability'.[15]

Moon in chart of Miller:	12.41 Scorpio
Mars in chart of Miller:	11.05 Scorpio
Alphecca in 1891:	10.46 Scorpio

Alphecca was Miller's 'lucky star'. The secret behind Miller's horoscope rested in this triple conjunction-degree of Mars, Moon and star, rather than on his three planets in Capricorn – the sign which seemed always to obsess him, in his literature, if not in his life. The interesting fact is that Miller shared this same degree with his astrologer-mentor, Conrad Moricand, whose birth data Miller had usefully preserved for posterity.[16] Moricand's Moon was in 12.14 Scorpio.

Big Sur seems to be the first work of English literature in which esoteric astrology is discussed outside a specialist astrological context, and in which horoscopes are discussed in a meaningful way. In *Big Sur*, Miller left the finest and most precise description of the Capricornian in the English language.[17] Miller's choice of Capricorn as a subject for his prose was determined by the fact that technically he himself was Sun-in-Capricornian – as was Moricand. Both the astrologer and the author knew that this was merely fragmentary astrology – that no one is merely an astrological type by virtue of their Sun position. In fact, as his chart reveals, Henry Miller was a Capricornian in the skin of a Scorpion, as indeed was his astrologer-companion, Moricand.[18]

In his description of the Capricornian nature, Miller hinted at his esoteric reading. He described this zodiacal type as having a 'phantasmagorical' memory, arguing that the Capricornian has the power to transcend the usual limitations of ordinary memory: under certain circumstances, they can remember not only their personal tribulations, but their pre-human and sub-human ones. They can slither back into the primordial slime, like eels slipping through the mud.[19]

In this apt description of one facet of the Capricornian nature, Miller was drawing on his wide reading in esoteric literature. The Russian theosophist and esotericist H.P. Blavatsky had pointed to the origins of the Capricorn as a crocodile, or *makara*.[20] The curl in the sigil for the sign ♑ was a relic of the tail of the Babylonian image of Capricorn, which was a goat–fish. The curl in the sigil is a relic of the fish half of the creature, and represents the fear innate in the Capricornian that he or she would slip back into the primordial slime, or back into the sea, by the weight of their tail. The fissiparous bipolarity of the Capricornian is actually one of the astrological themes of *Big Sur*.

I am not suggesting that Miller had necessarily read Blavatsky (though there is every indication that he had), nor, indeed, that he was familiar with the near-esoteric literature that dealt with the nature of Capricorn.[21] By the time Miller wrote *Big Sur*, this kind of esoteric lore was readily available in a number of derivative works designed for those interested in this kind of astrology.[22]

In fact, Miller went beyond ordinary astrology. Not only was he fortunate in having the near-mystic Moricand as a teacher, but he also had as a correspondent the learned American astrologer, Dane Rudhyar. The latter had drunk deeply of the esoteric writings of Alice Bailey, and, to judge from his books, he was schooled in many esoteric trends of the early twentieth century.[23] The very notion of a popular esotericism seems like a contradiction in terms, yet during the twentieth century certain strands of esoteric thought were (albeit in a misunderstood form) popularised.

It has been a tendency of historians of astrology to ascribe the proliferation of different forms of horoscopes, which has characterised astrology's development during the twentieth century, to computerisation. However, the fact is that much of this proliferation took place before computer-astrology became available. The fissiparous forms of astrology, and the search for new forms of astrology and related horoscopes which marked the first half of the twentieth century, appear to have their roots in the esoteric lore, promulgated by such arcane schools as Theosophy, Anthroposophy and Rosicrucianism. It is in the context of this impulse that almost all modern schools of astrology must be understood. Shortly, we shall examine some sample horoscopes derived from these spiritual impulses.

The extraordinary development of an interest in astrology in the twentieth century has had a curious effect on horoscopy. For reasons that are not altogether clear, a large number of astrologers (especially in the United States) have thought fit to pay attention to new theories, and develop these into unique systems of interpretation, sometimes at the expense of troubling to study traditional astrology. The conjuring of new systems appears to be a result of a certain restlessness of soul which has typified the twentieth century. One consequence is that there are now more 'astrologies' available and in use than at any other point in history. Modern methods of charting include sidereal horoscopes, conception horoscopes, pre-natal charts, asteroid charts, even horoscopes involving hypothetical planets. In addition, there are charting methods derived from the extraordinary advances in modern astrology made by a number of learned practitioners: these methods include the harmonics of John Addey, the astrocartography of Jim Lewis, the heliocentric charting of Vreede and Sucher, and so on. The list is seemingly endless, and is certainly confusing. Fortunately, we do not have to study every single astrology developed in the twentieth century, though, shortly, we shall examine each of those I have just listed.

The fact that, by the beginning of the twentieth century, Alan Leo's popularising works were being translated and published in France is an indication that there were signs of a revival of astrology in that country, after a silence of almost two centuries. It is in the French astrology of the twentieth century that the reforms, proposed in the seventeenth century by Morin, become most clearly evident.[24]

The twentieth-century French astrologer, Eudes Picard, experimented with (actually resurrected, from ancient horary astrology) what have been called *derived domifications*.[25] Picard proposed that any house in a chart may be regarded as having the potential to form the initiating house for a superimposed duodenary cycle: thus the fifth house of the radical figure could be regarded as being the first house, which would mean that the radical six would become the second house, and so on. As Picard pointed out, this method offers no fewer than 144 houses for each chart.

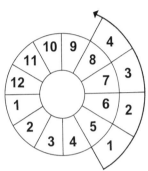

At the same time, another French astrologer, Jean-Pierre Nicola, experimented with relating the so-called solar types of astrology to the psychological types proposed by the Russian physiologist, Ivan Petrovich Pavlov. These types were distinguished according to the mobility or inhibition of the nervous system. The astrological conclusions to be drawn from this interesting exercise need not concern us here; however, what is of interest is the collection of nativities included in his primary work on the subject. Nicola did not publish example horoscopes in this work, but he did collect over a hundred sets of data (usually without times) for as many well-known personalities. This list reflected his own interest in art and music, and ranged from Francisco de Goya and Maurice de Vlaminck to Salvadore Dali, from Ludwig van Beethoven and Niccolò Paganini to Louis Armstrong.[26]

The revival of astrology in France, during the early decades of the century, had been spearheaded by Paul Choisnard. Like many important French astrologers of the day, Choisnard had a profession and was therefore not dependent on astrology for his living. Choisnard wrote several books under the name Paul Flambart, and he is often claimed to be the first astrologer to make extensive use of statistical analysis. To some extent, the leading astrologers of the day were all indebted to the work of Choisnard: these include Henri Gouchon, Alexandre Volguine and Michel Gauquelin. Indeed, Gauquelin was less inward-looking than the majority of French astrologers, for he left sweeping criticisms of the methods not only of Choisnard, but also of the German, Karl Ernst Krafft, and of the American astrologer Donald A. Bradley.[27] Even so, the useful tabulation of birth data (over 5,500 examples) in his study of professions relates mainly to Frenchmen.

Gauquelin and his wife, Françoise Schneider, claim to have collected over fifty thousand sets of data, and subjected these to statistical analysis. The groups had been divided (perhaps questionably, in the eyes of some critics) into professions, and the distribution of the associated planet studied for presentation in a graphic form. We shall examine a sample configuration, related to the acting profession, later.

Although the statistical methods adopted by Choisnard are not beyond valid criticism, their findings have influenced a whole generation of European astrologers, including André Barbault and his distinctive re-evaluation of old horoscopes.[28] One of Barbault's contributions to horoscopy has been his provision of a number of sourced horoscopes of important personalities in French history. Thus, his chart data for Charles VII were derived from Anselme's history of the royal house of France.[29] The chart of the seventeenth-century French statesman, Jean-Baptiste Colbert, was from the version cast by the astrologer, Ismael Boulliau, while that of Richelieu was copied from the version published by Morin himself.[30]

As we have seen, during the late nineteenth century personal horoscopes of political leaders, or political hopefuls, began to appear in newspapers in the United States of America. However, whatever their quality, such horoscopes were cast for individuals and were almost always accompanied by articles written by reputable astrologers. The Sun-sign literature, which began to appear in the English press (later to invade the Continent and the United States), was a result of newspaper editors seeking to develop articles on astrology that would appear comprehensive enough to serve everyone, regardless of the hour, day or year of birth – a sort of non-astrology masquerading under the name 'astrology'. This type of Sun-sign literature has become so popular under various disguises, such as 'Fun with the Stars' or 'Your Personal Future' that there seems little point now in insisting that such offerings have nothing whatsoever to do with astrology, and even less with horoscopy.

Undoubtedly, the most powerful influence on twentieth-century astrology was the introduction of computerised systems, in the early 1970s. While the introduction of computers did change forever the nature of astrology, the urge towards a 'mass' astrology was noticeable almost a century before computers went into action. As we have seen, Alan Leo had dealt with mass-produced charts of a kind. Unfortunately, theirs was a type of horoscopy – repugnant to professional astrologers – that dominated the twentieth century. It is a form of horoscopy that has been rendered more sophisticated and alluring (though none the less repugnant) by the introduction of astro-computing.

The initial application of computers to astrology was directed towards providing accurate ephemerides, and computerisation of ephemerides was introduced in the late 1970s. It is likely that the American astrologer, Neil F. Michelsen, whose work on cosmic co-ordinates is still widely used by astrologers, was among the first astrologers to set up a computer data system to calculate horoscopes.[31]

Within a few years, modern astro-computing systems enabled astrologers to cast charts according to virtually all the known methods evolved since the fifteenth century. Nowadays it is possible to cast a chart for almost any house system, and according to a wide variety of zodiacal systems: it is possible to include a wide range of asteroids, hypothetical planets and nodal points, without knowing anything at all about the cosmic realities behind this kind of astrology – even, indeed, without knowing anything about astrology, or how to read the charts engendered in this way.

Computerisation, by offering reliable methods of casting and a wide variety of different statistical methods, has also encouraged astrologers to search for new methods of charting and interpreting. This has not altogether been for the good, for many of those who explore in this way have not troubled to study the traditional forms in sufficient depth, as the much-needed sound basis for such research. The situation reminds one of Martin Luther's comments about the explorations of Copernicus, which came to light even before the latter had published his ground-breaking work on the heliocentric system. 'So it goes, now,' remarked Luther, perceptively, 'Whoever wants to be clever ... must do something of his own.'[32] Computers have permitted almost anyone, with even a small knowledge of astrology, to 'do something of his own'.

As with the anthologies of methods described in earlier centuries, the following selection of representative twentieth-century charts is by no means complete. Indeed, so varied and so complex in nature are some of the horoscopic methods developed during the twentieth century that one would be hard put to provide even a synopsis of these in the available space.

Among the distinguished forms of horoscopy I have been unable to deal with here, but which deserve passing mention, are those connected with the following researches: the planet Vulcan (be it real or hypothetical) as studied by L.H. Weston;[33] the helio charting that combines heliocentric and geocentric positions, developed by the American astrologer, Patrick Davis, in the 1980s;[34] the complex horoscopy incorporating the asteroids, exemplified by the work of the American astrologer, Eleanor Bach;[35] the 'Life Clock' of the Swiss astrologer, Bruno Huber, developed in collaboration with his German wife, Louise Huber, both of whom were enthused by the psychosynthesis of the Italian psychologist Roberto Assagioli;[36] the combination of solar and lunar revolution charting (the Cycles of Destiny), which may be subjected to progressions, formulated by the English astrologer Ronald C. Davison;[37] the approach to horoscopic mid-points developed by the English astrologers, Michael Harding and Charles Harvey;[38] the horoscopic 'shapings', or distribution patterns of planets in charts, classified by Marc Edmund Jones.[39] Indeed, to be historically objective, one should also include such discontinued methods as the cycle-charts of William J. Tucker, which incorporated what this astrologer called planetary curves, and pulse-cycles, along with a liberal use of fixed stars.[40]

Had space permitted, I would have wished to emphasise the role of sidereal horoscopy in the twentieth century. For example, I would have liked to record the charting related to the sidereal zodiac, which was developed in the last three decades of the century by Robert Powell and which has had an influence on both modern astrosophy (see pages 225–30, below) and biodynamic farming, which is regulated by the sidereal positions of the Moon.[41] I would also have liked to examine in some detail the implications of what was called, in 1969, the first selenocentric horoscope, timed for the first human footstep on the Moon, and cast by Edgar

Maedlow of Berlin.[42] Above all, I would have liked to deal at length with the horoscopic potential of the study of capillary dynamic patterns. This research work has been conducted mainly in Switzerland and is concerned with studying the effects of eclipses (lunar, solar and planetary) on liquids. The planetary effects are studied on patterns left by the capillary action of saps on litmus paper, the images of which exhibit far greater variation at the time of eclipse than at other times. The scientist, L. Kolisko, has tended to concentrate on solar and lunar eclipses.[43] However, some of her co-workers and students have focused their studies on the conjunctions of Mercury with the Sun.

Although Agnes Fyfe did not publish actual horoscopes in her studies of capillary dynamics, she did incorporate diagrams which were essentially fragments of sidereal charts. For example, her interpretation of the conjunction of Mercury with the Sun, which occurred on 24 November 1959, was represented by her as a constellational diagram, but it could just as well have been represented in standard horoscopic form.[44] Below (left) I give a copy (in translation from the German) of her own sidereal fragment depicting the conjunction, centred on the zig-zag retrograde looping of Mercury, alongside a standard chart for the identical event.[45]

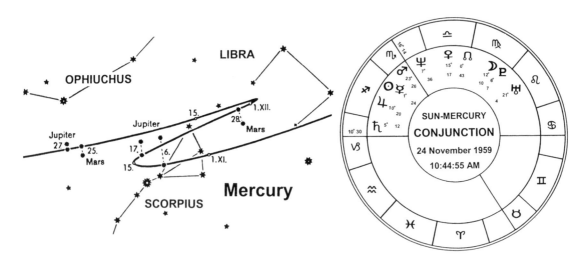

Fyfe's purpose in recording this conjunction was to study its effects on mistletoe sap patterns, which change dramatically during the moment of conjunction. These sap changes are rightly regarded as scientific evidence that liquids (which, of course, predominate in the physical body of man) are subject to specific cosmic mutations. Opposite, is a copy of the capillary patterns left by a solution of *Helleborus foetidus* (50 per cent) with a gold reagent (1 per cent) at different times before, during and after the conjunction. The central two blocks illustrate the patterns at the time of conjunction. Clearly, it is high time that these well-documented experiments be subjected to horoscopic analysis, for no eclipse can stand alone from the planetary and stellar pattern against which it occurs.

Important as the above methods are to the history of horoscopy, I have to admit that they are merely the tip of an astrological iceberg. A full list would, of course, include references to

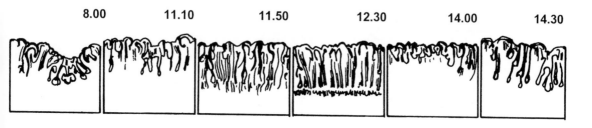

elegant or appropriate methods of charting, along the lines of those we studied for earlier centuries.[46]

THE COMING OF PLUTO

Pluto was the first planet to be discovered by means of photography – as a result of the systematic attempts made by astronomers to discover why Uranus was subject to perturbations. As early as 1928, astronomers were aware that Pluto existed, but it was not until 11 February 1930 that it was actually discovered.[47] The American astronomer Clyde Tombaugh was the first to see its image, while searching a series of photographic plates, taken in the previous month, at the Lowell Observatory, in Arizona. Remarkably, as we have already noted, the planet was named Pluto by astrologers almost two decades before it was actually discovered.

The earliest published horoscopes that I have been able to find with the new planet Pluto clearly marked are those cast for a reigning and future king of England. The charts were published in a contiguous series by the astrologer Raphael in a series of astro-pictures which appeared in 1932 and 1933.[48] The two charts are reproduced overleaf: the one for the reigning king, George V, is to the left; that for his son, then Duke of York, is to the right. According to Raphael, George V was born in London on 3 June 1865 at 1:18 AM. The chart reveals the planet Jupiter close to the Midheaven – a placing which Raphael read as a sign of kingship. The fact that Neptune is rising, a few degrees below the eastern horizon, explains why George V should have gained the popular title of 'the Sea King'.

The Duke had been born in London on 14 December 1895, at 3:05 AM. The short analysis that followed the old-fashioned quadrated chart was astonishing. In 1933, when Raphael published the horoscope, there was little anticipation that George, then second in line to the British throne, would shortly become King. However, in his brief reading of the chart, Raphael made it quite clear that the Duke of York would become King: the meridian position of Jupiter (like that of his father) points to his future position. Raphael (aware of the disastrous chart of Edward VIII) wrote, with intentional double entendre, of the Midheaven Jupiter in the Duke's chart:

It is this ... position of Jupiter that has been the sign that in a world of toppling thrones, the monarchy of England shall yet stand.... Within the next eighteen months, the Duke will see his home life disturbed, and he is likely to suffer bereavement.

Thus, in a few lines Raphael mapped out the future course of history. Less than four years after the horoscope was published, George V died, in 1936, and his popular son, Edward, became King. However, he abdicated on 11 December of the same year, in the face of Establishment opposition to his proposed marriage to a divorced commoner, the American socialite, Bessie Wallis Simpson. On the abdication of his brother, George, the Duke of York, ascended the throne as George VI. He and his wife, the former Lady Elizabeth Bowes-Lyon, gained the hearts of their subjects by remaining in London during the terrible blitzkrieg of the Second World War, living in the centre of the city, in the bomb-damaged Buckingham Palace, making many encouraging radio broadcasts to hearten Londoners.

What renders these two royal horoscopes of historic importance has little to do with the personalities or attainments of the two natives. As I have intimated, the value of the charts is found in the fact that they are among the earliest published horoscopes to contain sigils for Pluto. So new was this sigil to astrology that, in the earlier chart, Raphael felt constrained to explain it, by writing alongside the name of the planet (below, left). Raphael seemed to be satisfied that this concession to his readers was sufficient. In the following year, when Raphael published the chart of the future King, he included the sigil without comment (below, right).

The form used for the new planet is of great interest, and points to one of the great mysteries of twentieth-century astrology. It is evident that this early version of Pluto was intended to suggest a connection with Mars – the more advanced astrologers of the time had recognised

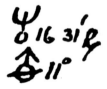

Pluto as what they called a 'higher octave' of Mars.[49] Indeed, the most remarkable thing about this recognition is that it had occurred long before astronomers even discovered the new planet.

In 1911, the English astrologer, Isabelle M. Pagan, almost certainly following the indications of Nicoullaud (page 185, above), had quietly announced that the new ruler of the zodiacal sign Scorpio was Pluto.[50] The new planet was therefore being evoked as a replacement for the traditional ruler, Mars – sometimes called the negative side of Mars, and distinguished from the positive side, which had rule over Aries.

Although she did not elaborate on this remarkable adjustment to traditional astrology, Pagan not only published the name of the ruler of Scorpio as Pluto, but also put on record its new sigil – an inverted Mars: ♀. The historic line in which she makes this remarkable semi-prophecy is reproduced below, from the first edition (1911) of her work:

Ruler : **PLUTO** ♀ (Traditionally the *Negative side of Mars*).

Only two years after he had begun to use the new sigil for Pluto, Raphael dedicated an entire page in his ephemeris to the new planet, for which he gave the sigil ♂. There may have been some significance in the location he chose for this short treatise on Pluto: he placed it opposite the astro-picture of the newly elected President of the United States, Franklin D. Roosevelt, in the analysis of which he predicted that America would be drawn into 'a distant war' (see page 214).[51] Concerning Pluto, he wrote:

We must confess to a very marked prejudice against 'Pluto', and because he invariably comes up associated with underworld activities and curious affairs of violence. Just a few instances:

At the time of the Great War in 1914 Pluto was on the Summer Solstice (0° ♋), conjunct of Saturn.

He was probably in the middle of the sign Gemini during 1665 and 1666, and this sign is the ruling one of London, those years being the dates of the Plague and the Fire of London. The Lindbergh baby, so tragically kidnapped and murdered, was born with Pluto on the Meridian, square of the Ascendant.

Pluto may have another side.

For hundreds of years our human evolution appears to have progressed very slowly. Then came the discovery of *Uranus*, swiftly followed by the marvels of science and speeding-up of human life under the impetus of *Steam* and *Electricity*.

Then came Neptune, bringing *Oil, Aviation, Conquest of the Air*, and the *Etheric waves ....*

And now in Pluto we see an augury of further wonders about to befall we human children, in that dim, distant Star, which set afar, heralds the unknown spheres.

The dual nature of Pluto had been recognised almost from the time it was discovered. On the one hand, Pluto had rule over the Mysteries schools and hence over the acquisition of arcane knowledge.[52] On the other hand, Pluto had rule over the dark violence of organised crime in the criminal underworld. It would take several more years before the deeper connection behind the dark and mysterious planet was fully recognised: well over a decade would elapse before its baneful rulership over the hidden realm of the atom was grasped by astrologers.

THE COMING OF NEWSPAPER 'ASTROLOGY'

The first mass horoscopes to appear in the popular press, during the 1930s, were a direct consequence of an editorial misunderstanding. A day or so after the birth of Princess Margaret, in August 1930, the astrologer Richard Harold Naylor was commissioned by the *Sunday Express* to cast her horoscope (below) and write an article about it.[53]

The rising Uranus, in opposition to a Venus close to the seventh cusp, indicated that Margaret would have difficulties with the opposite sex, and would have at least two marriages.

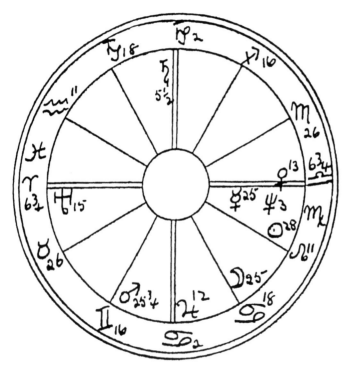

However, Naylor elected not to deal openly with this aspect of the horoscope; rather, he described her merely as 'essentially a woman of the New Age'.

Naylor's somewhat superficial approach to horoscopy in this article proved so popular with the readership that he was asked to write more articles, the first of which appeared on 5 October 1930. Of course, it was one thing to cast a horoscope for a given nativity, but quite another thing to provide predictions for a mass audience. Naylor attempted to get around the problem by producing brief readings based on daily transits, for each day of October. Whatever the readers made of this pseudo-astrology, they could not fail to be astonished by two lines in the article, in which Naylor predicted that British aircraft would be in danger for six days following 8 October.

On the very day this article appeared, the British airship *R–101*, *en route* to India, crashed in Beauvais.[54] The astrological background to the story is told more fully below, but it is worth recording here that, on 5 October, the Sun had been in *exact* parallel to, as well as in close opposition to, Uranus. There may be little doubt that it was the opposition of 7 October, combined with the opposition of Sun and Moon on the following day, that persuaded Naylor to choose 8 October as the beginning of the danger period. It is possible that he had overlooked the powerful parallel between Sun and Uranus which occurred on the day of the accident.

Although he had been wrong by a matter of three days, the prediction ensured Naylor's reputation. Until his death in 1950, he continued to write articles for newspapers and magazines, many of which contained predictions of a sort.[55] However, try as he would, Naylor never made a prediction with quite the same dramatic élan as he had achieved with the *R–101* prophecy.

Inevitably, rival newspapers began to employ astrologers to write articles. As part of this service, the English astrologer William J. Tucker established an office to provide a personal horoscope service for readers of the *Sunday Dispatch*.[56] As demand was anticipated to be in the region of 5,000 horoscopes per week, a vast amount of organisation was required, and a large number of individuals had to be trained to calculate natal charts. Tucker succeeded in catering for this level of demand.

With equal inevitability, newspaper astrology began to move away from its valid remit – the study of individual charts – to a treatment of mass nativities, with which astrology is not able to cope. By the late 1930s, a number of English newspapers began to publish daily guides, based on the notion of Sun-sign astrology, which is little more than a figment of journalistic imagination. So far removed is modern popular newspaper horoscopy from the genuine thing that editors – in Britain at least – avoid using the word 'astrology' in reference to their articles, for fear of breaching the law covering advertising. Astrology of this kind has degenerated into little more than 'Fun with the Stars'.

The role of the *R–101* crash in the introduction of this pseudo-horoscopy of 'Fun with the Stars' was an important one. However, the crash was more deeply involved with astrological factors than is generally realised.

The *R–101* left Cardington at 6:36 PM on 4 October 1930, on its flight to India. On board were 16 passengers, the same number of officials, and a crew of 42. Among these was the Air Minister, Brigadier-General Lord Thompson, who had bullied officialdom into arranging the flight, when the majority of those in charge of the venture believed that the ship was incapable of making it safely. The flight was of special interest to Thompson, for he had been born in India, at Nasik in Maharashtra.

At 2:08 AM, after a rough few hours, the *R–101* slid into a hillside near Beauvais, in France, coming to rest quite gently. Almost immediately, the craft was engulfed in a vast sheet of flame as the hydrogen caught fire. There were only six survivors. Lord Thompson perished in the flames.[57]

Now it was well known among astrologers that two days after the beginning of the flight there would be a lunar eclipse, which would fall in 13.52 Aries. What few astrologers knew was that this would fall within a few degrees of the Caput in the chart of Lord Thompson, who had been born on 13 April 1875 (overleaf). Only a few astrologers were aware that the previous lunar eclipse, of 9 May 1930, had already sealed Lord Thompson's fate. This eclipse had fallen in the same axis as his Sun:[58]

Lunar eclipse of 13 April 1930:	22.40 Aries/Libra
Sun in chart of Lord Thompson:	22.58 Aries

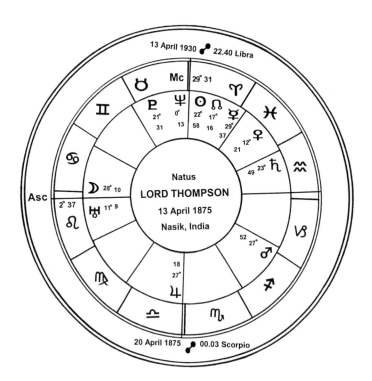

In the above chart, I have marked alongside the outer periphery two significant lunar eclipses, which had an influence on Thompson's life and death. The first, which was the eclipse immediately following his birth, was the lunar that fell opposite his Neptune:

Lunar eclipse of 20 April 1875:	00.03 Scorpio/Taurus
Neptune in chart of Thompson:	00.13 Taurus

The second was the lunar of 9 May 1930 (mentioned above). As we have seen, on 7 October, two days after the crash, the lunar eclipse fell in 13.52 Aries. This means that it also fell directly on Uranus at the time of the crash.

Lunar eclipse of 7 October 1930:	13.52 Aries
Uranus on 5 October 1930:	13.28 Aries

GAUQUELIN'S ACTORS

Shortly before the 1950s the French astrologer Gauquelin (later aided by his wife, Françoise Schneider) began to amass over fifty thousand sets of birth data and, as mentioned earlier, subjected these to statistical analysis. The charts had been divided into professions, and the distribution of associated planet representation in a unique graphic form. A good example is the graphic analysis constructed from the position of Jupiter, in the charts of 500 actors and actresses (below).[59] The dominant Jupiter was statistically emphatic near the MC (here noted as culmination), and, to lesser extent, in the descendant (here marked sunset). Traditionally, Jupiter has always been seen as the planet of professional acting, and it is not surprising to find it placed in the house that is traditionally associated with ambition and social achievement.

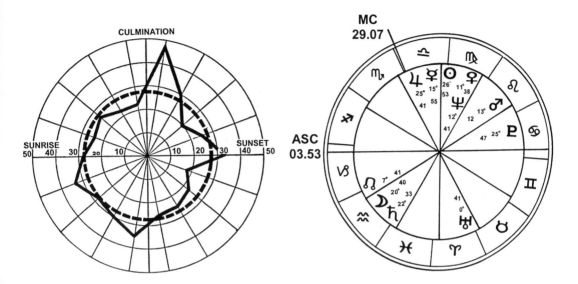

Alongside the diagram, I have reproduced a sample chart of the actress Sophia Loren, who was born on 20 September 1934, at 2:04 PM.[60] In her chart, Jupiter is in the tenth house, a few degrees from the MC – a classical 'actor' placing, as reference to the Gauquelin diagram shows. Noticeable in this remarkable chart is the conjunction between Neptune and Venus – a combination which often gives an alluring physical beauty.

While traditional teachings suggest that an angle should mark the centre of the most powerful influence in a chart, Gauquelin's research has indicated that the arc (or orb) of influence is not centred *exactly* upon the angle. Rather, it is more powerful some 3 to 4 degrees in the clockwise direction (as, indeed, in the chart of Sophia Loren). Gauquelin's discovery was not entirely new. It is interesting to observe that the medieval astrologer, Guido Bonatti, allowed a wide orb for the ascendant influence, and that this orb was not centred on the angle, but askew, at 3 degrees – though in a widdershins direction.

One major objection to Gauquelin's method is the reliance upon official birth certificates to determine time of birth. Such documents (as Gauquelin admits) are often inaccurate and, in most cases, time is given to the nearest hour, or to the nearest half-hour. This sort of timing is simply not good enough as a basis for research into horoscopes. An example is the data given by Gauquelin for the painter, Pierre Auguste Renoir. He was born on 25 February 1841, at (Gauquelin opines) 6:00 AM, in Limoges.[61] Largely because Gauquelin published these data in his influential work, they were widely adopted by other astrologers.[62]

However, the time given by Gauquelin was not correct. Progressions to the date of death (17 December 1919, at Cagnes) indicate that Renoir must have been born at 5:43 AM. The

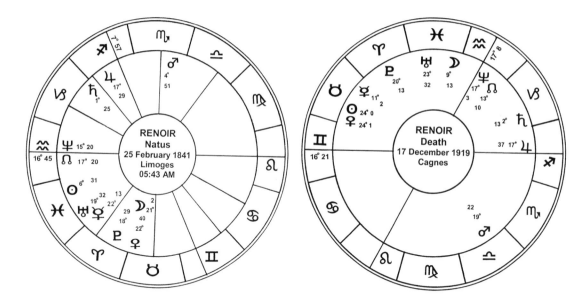

error of 17 minutes may not appear to be huge, but it is an error sufficient to change the distribution of planets in a chart – the very thing Gauquelin was studying. What I claim of the Renoir chart is intended only as an example: similar claims could be made in respect of many of the hundreds of sets of data that Gauquelin recorded.

Above is a birth chart for Renoir, alongside the progressed chart to the time and birth of death. One observes that the anaretic is Neptune and that, at the moment of death, this is on the progressed MC, sextile to both Pluto and Jupiter (which is just about to descend over the western horizon).

WEMYSS CHART DEGREES AND ARCS

Degree symbolism, which had become popular once again towards the end of the nineteenth century (see page 181), took on an important role in astrological analysis during the twentieth century. For example, the Scottish astrologer, Maurice Wemyss, constructed an extensive list of degree and short-arc influences from a huge archive of horoscopes which he had accumulated.

Wemyss was not intent on formulating a poetic image for each degree, as were Angelus and other astrologers in previous centuries. His interest lay in attempting to find what such degrees had in common in regard to human achievements and accidents. Some of his findings were astonishing. For example, after the terrible disaster of 24 August 1921, when the newly launched airship R–34 exploded over the River Humber, killing everyone on board, Wemyss cast the horoscopes of all sixteen victims. He concluded that every one of those killed had Gemini–Sagittarius 4°–5° afflicted.[63] Not unnaturally, Wemyss associated this degree with the category, Aviators. In his study of this category, he considered the charts of a number of aviators, including the renowned Lindbergh, who had been the first to fly the Atlantic alone. Lindberg's ascendant was in 4 Sagittarius.[64]

Another horoscope to which Wemyss referred was that of the famous nineteenth-century balloonist Graham, who happened to be interested in astrology, and who had been born in London on 13 November 1784, at 10:10 PM.[65] Below, is a delightful nineteenth-century chart for Graham, presented in a form fairly typical of the 'decorative' charts popular in the mid-nineteenth century. It is what we might call a 'themal horoscope', its standard quadrate form

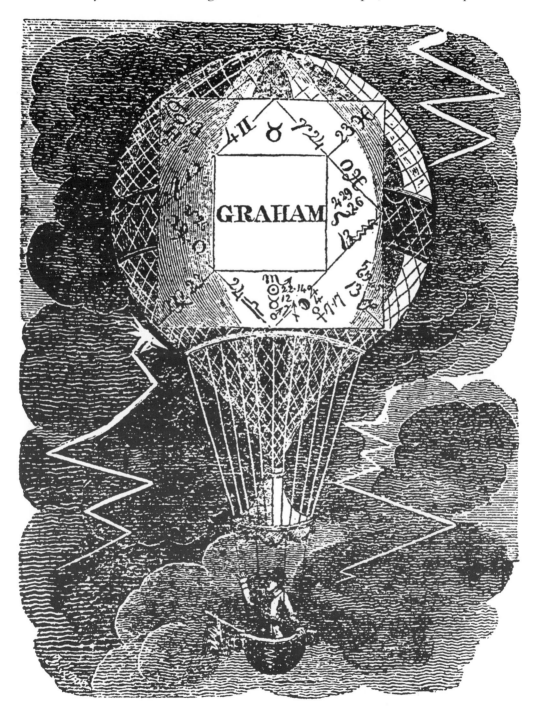

hidden behind relevant decoration. In this chart, the Moon is in 4 degrees of Sagittarius (it was actually in 3.57 degrees) – the very degree which Wemyss later linked with aviators.

The same magazine that published Graham's decorative chart also published a horoscope for Harris, the aeronaut, who had been born on 24 May 1792, in Bristol. In this chart, the Sun was in 3.35 Gemini and therefore also on the axis of the specified degree.[66]

Although I have concentrated here on Wemyss' listing of aviators, the fact is that he constructed similar significant degrees for an extremely wide range of professions, and usually supported these with valid horoscopic data.

MUSSOLINI'S VIOLENT END

When studying the final years of the nineteenth century, we noted the introduction of photo-horoscopes into modern astrology. This method, which involved inserting photographs at the centre of a chart, was adopted in a series entitled *Astro-Picture Gallery*. The first batch, published up to 1923, was cast by Robert T. Cross (that is, 'Raphael'), who furnished his own portrait-horoscope as the second in the series.[67] Altogether, this series was pedestrian in its selection of charts, and not all the predictions attached to the astro-analyses were accurate. For example, in 1916, he published the chart of Field Marshal Sir John French, and predicted that he would lead the British to victory. Unfortunately, by the time the ephemeris was published, French had resigned.[68] Later, Raphael published the horoscope of General Sir Douglas Haig, and predicted that he would 'thrash the Germans'. Unluckily, he added a rider that 'it will take him a long time to do it'. As it happened, Haig led the troops to victory in 1918, the same year as the chart was published.[69]

The penultimate of this first series was the photo-horoscope of the incumbent President of the United States, Warren G. Harding.[70] Raphael observed that, shortly, the planet Mars would be creeping up to the radical place of Jupiter (astrologese for a time of danger, and probable ill-health). 'He may [Raphael added] have a narrow escape from some personal danger.' In the following year, Harding died in office, in San Francisco, on 2 August 1923 – probably from a blood clot to the brain.

Raphael – in his everyday incarnation of Robert T. Cross – died in the same year. The replacement namesake was an extraordinary astrologer, and the following batch of astro-pictures included some of the most astonishing prophecies of the twentieth century. The study he made of the individual nativities of Mussolini, F.D. Roosevelt, Emperor Hirohito, and the two King Georges of England, left one in no doubt that there would be a world war involving not only Europe, but the United States and Japan. We shall glance at one or two of these charts shortly.

Accurate prophecy from horoscopes has always been a hazardous business. Given this, it is both surprising and refreshing to observe what the astrologer, Raphael, wrote in 1926 about the Italian dictator, Benito Mussolini (see chart opposite).[71] 'He will meet a violent end,' noted Raphael briefly, at the conclusion of his examination of the dictator's horoscope. His 'crowning

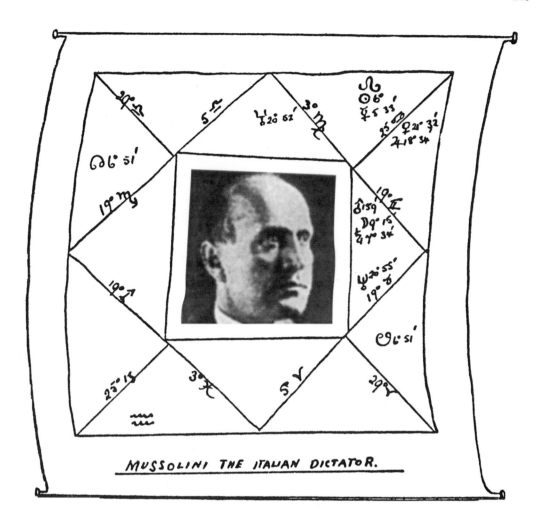

MUSSOLINI THE ITALIAN DICTATOR.

piece of egotism will be to cross the Powers of England and France, for his Saturn is conjunct of Britain's star, *Aldebaron*' [sic].[72]

Raphael did not reveal how he arrived at the knowledge of Mussolini's violent death. My own guess is that his several references to fixed stars are intended to alert us to a star in the chart which, in the traditional readings, presages a violent end.

In fact, Raphael published only half the truth about Aldebaran. What the astrologer assumed his informed readers would see was that the influence of Aldebaran was doubled: not only was Mussolini's Moon within a degree of the star, but the planet Saturn was also in a sufficient proximity to further activate the influence of the star.[73] The tabulation, based on my own calculations, makes this quite clear:

Moon in chart of Mussolini:	09.37 Gemini
Saturn in chart of Mussolini:	07.34 Gemini
Aldebaran in 1883:	08.00 Gemini

Aldebaran with the Moon brings honours at first, but usually ends in calamity. The traditional reading is that the native's death will be violent.

The most inflammatory combination of planets and stars (to which Raphael did not refer in his reading) were the extraordinary conjunctions arising from the position of the Sun. The Sun in Mussolini's chart was so placed that it stood over two fixed stars which related intimately to the character and destiny of Il Duce. These stars were Praesaepe and North Ascellus:

Praesaepe in 1883:	05.45 Leo
North Ascellus in 1883:	05.27 Leo
Sun in chart of Mussolini:	06.03 Leo

It is North Ascellus which promoted the image of the 'heroic leader', and Praesaepe which brought the evil disposition and violent death.

Mussolini was arrested on 28 April 1945. He and his mistress, Clara Petacci, were shot, and their bodies hanged from a lamp post in Milan. At the time of his death, the Moon was in 21 degrees of Scorpio, exactly opposite his radical Neptune, which had been on the unfortunate star, Baten Kaitos.[74]

DE WOHL AND THE WAR EFFORT

The chart cast in 1923 by Raphael for Mussolini (see above) has the additional interest of revealing an astrological scam. Both during and after the Second World War, the Hungarian astrologer, Louis de Wohl, had done much to invent legends about Hitler and astrology, most of which later proved to be unreliable. Fostering a number of misunderstandings about Hitler and astrology, de Wohl succeeded in obtaining for himself a minor role in counter-espionage. Unfortunately, much of what de Wohl had to say about Hitler, and his supposed interest in horoscopy, was highly questionable.

Even before the outbreak of war, Goebbels had been quick to grasp the propaganda value inherent in astrology, and in the prophetic writings of Nostradamus. It was his appreciation of this value that led him to instruct his minions to plant biased articles in popular astrological magazines. Once war had broken out, a number of German astrologers, among them Wilhelm Wulff, were employed in propaganda work. However, there seems to be no evidence that Hitler himself was interested in astrology, though (as we shall see) he did pay some attention to his own personal chart.[75]

One particular horoscope, which de Wohl calculated on graph paper, has survived. De Wohl had claimed that he cast for the birth of the Italian dictator Benito Mussolini, for which he gives the birth date 29 July 1883, at 1:54 PM near Milan. I reproduce a copy of this chart (opposite), divested of its disturbing graph lines.[76]

De Wohl claimed to have cast the figure in 1941, and to have predicted from it 'a violent and sudden end' for the Italian dictator. In fact, it is clear that de Wohl had stolen both the chart

nd the prediction from the article published by
Raphael, in 1927 – the very same chart and
analysis we have just examined, above.

So greedily did de Wohl copy the
chart of Mussolini that he transferred from it even the errors
which Raphael had unwittingly
incorporated. As a matter of fact,
Mussolini had *not* been born in
Milan – though, as we have seen,
Raphael had been led to believe
that he had. As was his wont, de
Wohl merely tagged on behind
Raphael, and made the same error.
In his own prophecy, written in 1926,
and based on the original chart, Raphael
had written, 'He [Mussolini] will meet a
violent end.' These are virtually the same words
used by de Wohl, fifteen years later.

During the first months of the war, de Wohl succeeded in persuading some officials that
Hitler had personally studied astrology, and had enlisted experts in the field.[77] He argued that
there was a need to establish a counter-astrological service to combat the Nazi use of horoscopy.
At the outbreak of the war, and on the basis of this (and other) inaccurate information, de Wohl
was set up in an office at Grosvenor House, in Park Lane, and given the impression that the
horoscopes he cast, and the astrological reports he constructed there, were being used as part of
the war effort. In fact, little of what de Wohl claimed during this period was taken seriously by
the authorities in London.

In 1943, de Wohl was part of a team faking editions of the defunct German astrological
magazine *Der Zenit*, as part of a propaganda campaign. The edition of *Der Zenit* of April 1943,
was specifically aimed at U-boat crews, with 'predictions' constructed shortly after the event, so
as to imply that the astrologer had correctly foreseen dangers to U-boats. Besides these fake
prophecies, the few editions of *Der Zenit* that were published contained more-or-less accurate
horoscopes of a number of Nazi politicians and servicemen – for example, that of Admiral Karl
Doenitz.

Overleaf, is a copy of the front cover of the April edition of *Der Zenit*, alongside a corrected
and enlarged version of the horoscope that appeared on it.[78] The latter horoscope is a computer-
generated version, cast for 3 April 1943, at 10:45 PM, local time Berlin.

One may be reasonably certain that de Wohl cast the horosope, as one of the predictions
inside *Der Zenit* was related to this chart. In the text, the reader was warned that it was not
advisable to go to sea on 4 April, 'if the horoscope of the captain is unfavourable'. There was a

sort of astrological logic behind this prediction: although *Der Zenit* was aimed at the general reader, it had to be astrologically accurate to gain the confidence of those few who were aware of astrological principles. As the Moon moves about 13 degrees in a single day, it is evident from the published horoscope that on 4 April, the Sun, Moon and Mercury would be in conjunction, in Aries. No doubt, de Wohl had selected that particular day because he already knew that a U-boat had been in difficulties, if not actually sunk, on 4 April.

THE CHARTS OF ADOLF HITLER

On 1 May 1945, besieged in his underground bunker in Berlin, and his armies utterly defeated, Hitler decided that death was better than capture. According to legend, round about 3:30 PM, he put his 7.65 calibre Walther to his right temple, and pulled the trigger. His new wife, Eva Braun, was slumped dead over the armrest of the sofa, her nostrils discoloured blue by cyanamide poison. Some years later, the legend was destroyed. The Russian, Lev Bezymenski, a member of Marshal Zhukov's staff during the final assault on Berlin, was the first to publish in the West the findings of the official autopsy report prepared for the Soviet Army.[79] The autopsy shows that Hitler had *not* shot himself, as was believed for so long in the West; he, too, had swallowed cyanamide. The distinction between a shot in the head and a rapid poison may seem academic, but the fact is that the suicide (so evident in the chart of Hitler) involved the conjunction of Neptune and Pluto: Neptune works through poisons, rather than through gunshots.[80]

A day or so before this ignominious end, Hitler had called for a couple of horoscopes which had been filed away by Heinrich Himmler.[81] Hitler knew little or nothing about astrology, but the reading attached to his own chart buoyed him up. The reversals in the war, which these commentaries predicted, were seen as persisting until the first half of April 1945. Peace would come in August, and by 1948 Germany would once again become a great nation. It is possible that the chart which offered this interpretation was based on that cast by the German astrologer, Elsbeth Ebertin. This lady knew a great deal about astrology, and it is very likely that she was aware of what would happen to Hitler in the early months of 1945, but had been too fearful to set this down in writing.[82]

Frau Elsbeth Ebertin had come to astrology by way of graphology, and within a few years found herself, in the carefully chosen words of Ellic Howe, 'the most accomplished German astrological publicist of her generation'.[83] She was, indeed, the first woman in Germany to gain a popular reputation as an astrologer.

In 1923, one of Hitler's supporters sent Ebertin a copy of Hitler's birth date (though not his time of birth), requesting a reading. Ebertin published her response (based on a reading of a noon-time chart) in her annual *Ein Blick in die Zukunft* (A Glance into the Future) – though without revealing Hitler's name. However, from her choice of words, she left little doubt about whom she had in mind. A few months after the reading was published, this man (who was 'to sacrifice himself for the German nation') was arrested in connection with the *Putsch* of 8 November 1923. Later, he was found guilty of plotting against the government, and sent to prison.

The wide misapprehension that Hitler was interested in astrology may be dated approximately to the extensive publicity which Ebertin's chart attracted. Sixteen years later, shortly before the outbreak of the war, it was being reported, on the good authority of the *Daily Mail*, that Hitler had an advisory staff of five astrologers, who counselled him when to make his *coups*. These astrologers are supposed to have advised him that the climax of his career would come in September 1939, and 'whatever he has to do to add to his fame must be done before then'.[84] Later, historians showed that this was nonsense – Hitler probably had no official adviser on astrological matters. Such articles merely fed the widespread belief that Hitler was involved in the arcane arts.[85]

In the 1934 edition of *Ein Blick in die Zukunft*, Ebertin had proposed a horoscope cast for between 6:22 and 6:26 AM, as a rectification of the recorded birth time. It appears to have been Ebertin's chart which Hitler consulted during his last days in the Berlin bunker.[86] A full survey of all the horoscopes of Hitler might be interesting for the historian, but would not further our own theme. Hitler's birth is of interest here because of the several forms of horoscopes that have been cast, which illustrate different phases in the history of horoscopy.

The German astrologer – or 'Cosmobiologist', as he was later styled – Reinhold Ebertin, developed a number of graphic devices intended to measure charted data, with a view to throwing light on the personality and fate of the native. The Ebertin system is based on the consideration of aspects between tenanted degrees and midpoints within the chart.

One popular chart that was subjected to the Ebertin analysis is that of Adolf Hitler.[87] The chart is based on the presumption that Hitler was born at 5:38 PM GMT on 20 April 1889, at latitude 48.15 North, and longitude 13.03 East. While recognising that there are other data available for the birth time of the Führer, I offer below a standard horoscope cast for this proposed time.[88] Alongside is a partial analysis of the chart, in accordance with the Ebertin system, through which, it has been claimed, the destructive nature of Hitler's personality is revealed.

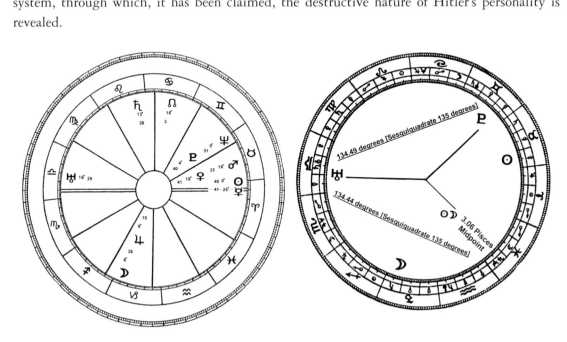

According to one analysis of the Ebertin system, the secret of the Hitler chart lies in the angular relationship of Uranus and Pluto. The two planets are in the difficult sesquiquadrate aspect (135 degrees). Since this aspect involves the slow-moving planets, it is clear that a very large number of people born in 1889 would have had it in their charts, yet not all evinced the same characteristics as Hitler. However, when this aspect is examined in the light of midpoints, in accordance with the Ebertin system, it becomes evident that the sesquiquadrate is tied down into the horoscope by the midpoints of the Sun and the Moon.

Midpoints are precisely what the term suggests – the middle point between two given planetary or nodal positions. In this particular case, the Sun is in 0.49 Taurus, and the Moon is in 6.38 Capricorn. They are separated by 114.11 degrees. The midpoint will therefore be 57.05.30 from either of the planets. When rounded off, the midpoint is in 3.06 Pisces. In the diagram above, the solar–lunar midpoint is marked at 3.06 Pisces.

I should observe that there is nothing new about the use of midpoints in horoscopic analysis. As Ebertin pointed out, the method of midpoints was used by the thirteenth-century Italian astrologer, Guido Bonatti, who had been one of the court astrologers to Frederick II. A method of midpointing was employed by the Hamburg astrologer, Albert Kniepf, at the beginning of the nineteenth century.[89] What is new about the Ebertin system is that it makes use of midpoints as an integral part of planetary patterns, which are themselves regarded as susceptible to analysis.

Now it is evident from the diagram above that neither Uranus nor Pluto falls on the solar–lunar midpoint.[90] However, the angle between Uranus and this midpoint is 139.44 degrees, which is itself close to the orb of a sesquiquadrate of 135 degrees.[91] This pattern, which depends upon a common axis, is quite acceptable within the Ebertin system. According to the theory of this system, this yoking of the Uranus–Pluto aspect into the powerful solar–lunar midpoint strengthens their union, and pulls the aspect into prominence. In the opinion of some astrologers, this prominence permits it to explain the violent and destructive nature of Hitler.

The chart analysis, which is descriptive of the midpoint relationship we have just examined, is not in itself a horoscope. In modern times, the schematic relationships of the aspect-analyses have been given many names, and have been approached from several different angles. What are sometimes called planetary patterns, or planetary pictures, are derived from the German *Planetenbilder*, as these analytical figures have been built up by a number of German astrologers intent on establishing a new approach to astrology. Since the planetary pictures are not horoscopes, they might be regarded as irrelevant to the theme of this book. However, there is an important relevance to traditional astrology, which is worth considering, and which explains why I have adopted the Hitler chart as an example of the Ebertin system.

In order to make sense of an aspect such as the sesquiquadrate (an angle of 125 degrees), the Ebertin system requires a certain amount of juggling with midpoints. Even after this juggling, the conclusions are far from satisfactory. Not only does the method demand a precisely accurate chart (when, in truth, the time of Hitler's birth is in doubt), but it is questionable whether the relatively weak sesquiquadrate (even when brought into prominence by midpoints) could account for such a violent and troubled nature as that which dominated Hitler.

However, if we turn to the traditional method of interpretation – on which Ebertin appears to have turned his back – we have an excellent explan-ation for the unfortunate destiny of Hitler. The secret of Hitler's horoscope lies in the evil fixed stars that manifest their influences through it. To the right, I repeat the chart of the Führer, this time marked with the fixed stars that fall within the permitted orb from the planetary positions.

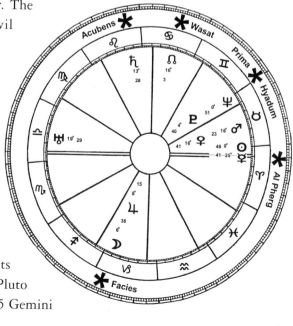

Each of these stars and nebulae is evil in its effects. Starting at the top of the chart (Cancer), and moving clockwise, the following contacts between planets and stars may be noted. Caput in 16.03 Cancer is on the evil star Wasat (16.58 Cancer in 1889). This star is infamous for its violence, malevolence and destructiveness. Pluto in 04.40 Gemini is on Prima Hyadum (04.15 Gemini in 1889). This star is recognised for its violent nature, and for the fact that it tends to bring injuries to the head. Mercury in 25.41 Aries is on Al Pherg (25.16 Aries in 1889). This is not specifically an evil star, but it tends to intensify determination almost to the point of pig-headedness. The Moon in 06.38 Capricorn is on Facies (06.46 Capricorn in 1889). This nebula is recognised by astrologers as an indicator of a violent death, and of a violent disposition. Saturn in 13.28 Leo is on Acubens (12.05 Leo in 1889). This nebula is renowned as an indicator of a violent life and a violent death.

One other 'test' of the validity of traditional astrology in relation to Hitler's birth chart may be found in the Ptolemaic teachings regarding eclipses. As we have noted, when an eclipse falls upon a tenanted degree in a chart, then some galvanic change may be expected within a few months, on either side of that cosmic event. Hitler died at about 3:30 PM on 1 May 1945, in Berlin. Two months later, a solar eclipse fell upon his Caput. As we recall, this lunar node was conjunct the evil fixed star Wasat at Hitler's birth: the eclipse of 1945 would therefore galvanise not merely the natal Caput, but also the malevolent violence of Wasat:

Caput in chart of Hitler:	16.03 Cancer
Position of Wasat in 1889:	16.58 Cancer
Solar eclipse of 9 July 1945:	16:57 Cancer

In 1934, the German astrologer Vehlow had written of the 'rain stars' – the Hyades – that when these were conjunct with Neptune, in the eighth house, they would cause confused ideas, lead to delusions of grandeur and create illusory world saviours.[92] Because of the date when this was written, Reinhold Ebertin believed that this comment was not intended as a reference to Hitler's chart. However, in Hitler's nativity, Pluto *was* conjunct with the Hyades, while the nearby Neptune was also in the eighth house.

HERMANN GOERING'S CHART

Alongside the horoscope of Hitler those of other important individuals of the Third Reich were also widely disseminated, both during and after the Second World War. An interesting example of such a chart, cast by the astrologer, Cyrille Wilczkowski, is given opposite. This is the horoscope of the former Marshal of the Third Reich, Hermann Goering. Born at 3:48 AM on 12 January 1893, Goering was directly responsible to Hitler for the Gestapo, and for setting up the extermination camps.[93]

Constructed on a method of charting that was popular in France during the twentieth century, this is a curious chart by normal standards and certainly requires some explanation. The dial of 360 degrees is fixed, like the face of a clock, with the so-called zero point of Aries to the right, which (in this particular form of horoscope) does not represent the east point. The ascendant degree is marked by an arrow head, the descendant by an arrow's feathering. In this case, the ascendant (in 27 Scorpio) is at approximately 2:0 o'clock in the figure. The Midheaven

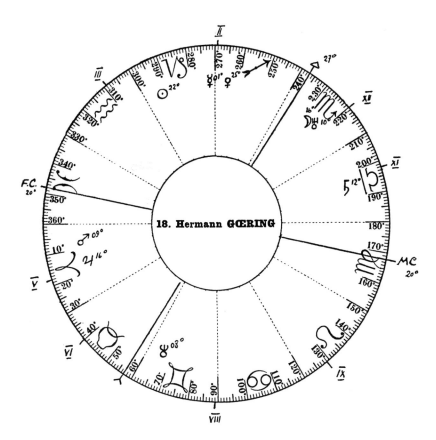

18. Hermann GOERING

s the MC (abbreviation for the Latin *Medium Coeli*, or for the French, *Milieu-du-ciel*), while the nadir is the FC (abbreviation for *Fond-du-ciel*). The positions of the planets are marked against the appropriate degrees. In this particular chart, their positions are rounded off to the nearest degree. The practised astrologer tends to lament this method of representing degrees, especially when there is a need to consider such things as communalities, as in this case.

In this particular example, research is required to determine whether a certain eclipse became operative at the time of Goering's suicide. At the Nuremberg Trials in 1946, he was found guilty of war crimes and was condemned to death. He poisoned himself on 16 October, two hours before he was due to be hanged. Given his importance in the unfolding of twentieth-century history, we would expect his dramatic passing to be signalled by an eclipse. On 30 May 1946, a solar eclipse fell in 08.49 Gemini, on or near his Neptune.

In the chart above, the position of this planet is given in a rounded-off degree, as 08° Gemini the sigil ♅ which could easily be taken as a symbol for Pluto, was used by Wilczkowski to denote Neptune). On the day of Goering's birth, Neptune was in 08.06 Gemini.

This new chart reveals something quite remarkable. Normally, Wilczkowski did not insert the position of Pluto in his charts, and this horoscope for Goering is no exception. Had he inserted Pluto in the chart, then no doubt Wilczkowski would have been astonished. The fact is that, at Goering's birth, Pluto was in 08.06 Gemini. This means that both planets were in the eclipse-degree of May 1946, the year of Goering's death:

Solar eclipse of 30 May 1946:	08.49 Gemini
Pluto in chart of Goering:	08.06 Gemini
Neptune in chart of Goering	08.51 Gemini

THE CHART OF AN ITALIAN RACING CYCLIST

The horoscopes, and horoscopic derivatives, proposed by Reinhold Ebertin in the mid-twentieth century have achieved a considerable following in Europe, especially in Germany. Ebertin was intent on formulating a rapid analysis of charts, both for the purpose of comparison and as an aid in interpretation.[94] To this end, he and his followers devised a chart system which they called a 90-Degree-Circle. This was a double system, which combined the standard 360 degree circle of the tropical zodiac with an outer circle that contained only 90 degrees.

The 90 degree circle was divided into three groups of 30 degrees, the first of which contained the cardinal signs (Taurus, Leo, Scorpio and Aquarius), the second, mutable signs (Gemini Virgo, Sagittarius and Pisces), and the third the remaining fixed signs. The advantage of this system is that when the planetary positions within the encircled chart are marked within these three arcs, the aspects of square and opposition are grouped together, and the semi-squares and sesquiquadrates fall opposite one another. As Ebertin claims, this method of charting enables one to see at a glance the aspectal factors in a chart.[95] As an example of this charting system Ebertin offered the horoscope of a well-known Italian racing cyclist, Fausto Coppi.[96]

The German sigils for Uranus ♅ and Pluto ♇ are used. The letter A stands for ascendant (which is 12° 51' Taurus), while the letter M stands for the Midheaven. The sigil which

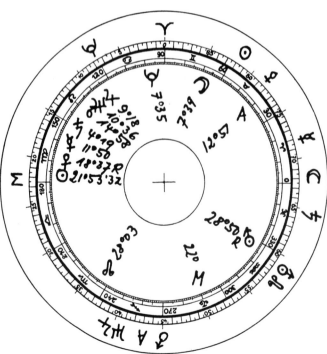

resembles Aries ♈ at the top of the figure is intended to mark the first degree of Cancer, the starting point of the 90 degree circle (this reminds us of the Aries-like pointer on the Bracken House zodiacal clock, on page 195, and figure 7).

Ebertin believes that the influence of a stellar body is determined by the synthesis of its aspects and midpoint combinations. This 'cosmic state' of a body can be determined by means of the 90 degree circle. As an example, he draws a diagram of the cosmic conditions governing Mars (from the chart of Coppi), which lies in the midpoints of the Moon and the

Midheaven, and Sun–Pluto. Mars is almost exactly at the midpoint of Sun–Pluto, and is at an indirect midpoint (that is, 45 degrees) of the Moon–Midheaven axis. The structure revealed within the 90 degree circle (below) is conveniently represented as a diagram, or 'planetary picture', in the form given alongside the circle.

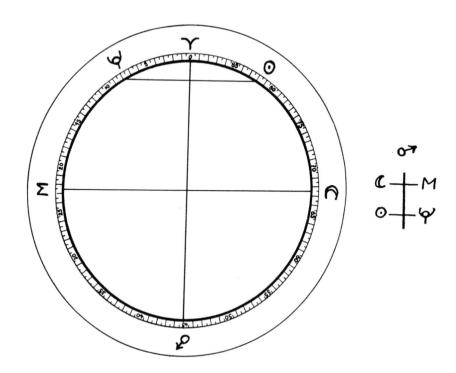

To gain a full understanding of a horoscope, the cosmobiologist draws up relevant corresponding planetary pictures for all the planets in the chart. The graphic analyses and presentations do not end with these relatively simple planetary pictures: cosmobiologists have evolved what they call a cosmopsychogram, a graphic in which the transmuted aspects are represented alongside distance-values for the cosmic bodies. However, since the cosmo-psychogram is not in itself a horoscope, it need not detain us here.

HELIOCENTRIC ASTROLOGY OF SUCHER

During the twentieth century, the urge to establish a workable heliocentric astrology, which had occupied the minds of a handful of astrologers in the seventeenth century, was felt once again. This impulse was spearheaded by a number of astrologers, or *astrosophists*, who were followers of the Austrian esotericist, Rudolf Steiner. The star-calendars, published by the Mathematical–Astronomical Section of the Goetheanum (the centre of Anthroposophy, in Dornach, Switzerland) are, within the genre, a triumph of quality, for they contain not only diagrams of the heliocentric movements of all the planets, but a superior heliocentric horoscope.[97]

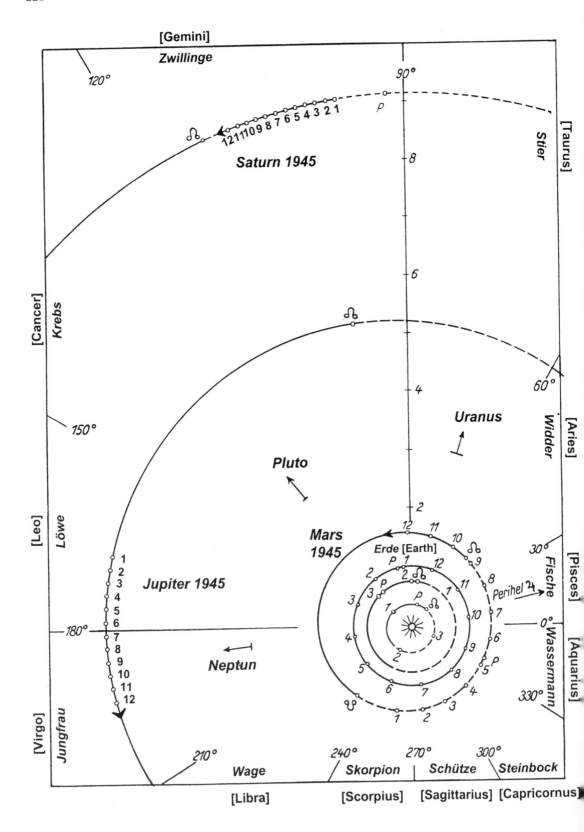

On the opposite page, is a version of the heliocentric chart from the 1945 edition of the star-calendar.[98] This is far from being a conventional chart, even within the realm of heliocentricity, for it depicts the paths of the planets, from a Sun-centred standpoint, for the whole course of the year.[99]

In the outer periphery we see a section of the pathway of Saturn, its course through the year marked by monthly incremental arcs. The short arc, marked by numbered circles, indicates the movement of the planet (in *Zwillinge*, or Gemini) during the whole of the year. Each numbered arc is the equivalent of a month. Each of the remaining sections of cycles is marked in a similar way — the central circle marks the path of Jupiter, and the numbered arcs measure its monthly movement during the year. Mars and Earth are marked in a similar way: only the Earth completes the cycle in a single year. The much shorter arcs of the planets Uranus, Neptune and Pluto are so small as to be almost insignificant: their places in the zodiacal circle are indicated with arrows.

If we wish to relate the chart to the context of ordinary astrology, then we should perhaps regard it as a comprehensive equivalent of the spring equinox charts, so popular in former times. Instead of marking the ingress of the Sun, however, the diagram charts the influence during the whole of a year. Its applicability in astrological terms is strictly limited to the outer planets.

The interest behind this heliocentric diagram lies in the fact that this — like related charts linked with the work of Steiner — formed the basis of a number of later innovatory horoscopes.

A good example of astrosophical heliocentric charting may be seen in the experimental work of Willi Sucher, who combined an interest in heliocentric charting with an interest in embryology. The correspondence between the numbered arcs on the year-chart of the figure on page 226 and the horoscope below is immediately evident. Instead of measuring the pathway of the planets in arcs, in the conventional manner, Sucher had attempted to describe visually the direct and retrograde motions of the planets. Thus the planet Mars does a retrograde swing before returning to direct motion: this is marked by a loop, and its final motion, for the horoscope in question, ends in Gemini.

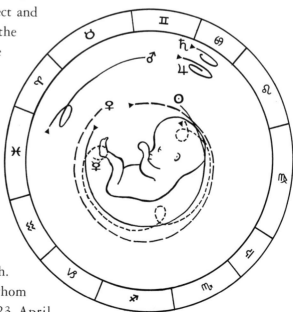

This heliocentric charting is an example of what Sucher called an *asterogram*. Like the year-chart on page 226, the asterogram above marks out an expanse of time. It is designed to mark the planetary motions during the period of gestation — that is, it relates to a nominal nine-month period, from conception to birth. It is the chart of William Shakespeare, whom Sucher believed to have been born on 23 April

1564.[100] I offer this chart merely by way of example of the kind of horoscopes that have been derived from modern heliocentric astrology. My intention is not to spell out how such a chart should be read, though it is worth observing that Sucher traced Shakespeare's sense of caprice and tenacity (even obstinacy) to the looping of Mars in its path through Aries.

On the basis of his researches, Willi Sucher decided that if astrology were to find a place in the modern world, then it should attempt to penetrate the mysteries of the prenatal realms. In his search for this new astrology, Sucher turned to the past. He examined once again the ancient rule attributed to pre-Christian astrology, to the so-called Hermetic Rule. This rule permitted the astrologer not only to rectify, or adjust, the birth chart, but also to arrive at a time of conception, which might be regarded as the literal moment of conception. Beyond the mathematical permutations of the Hermetic Rule lay a recognition that the Moon, and lunar cycles, dominated the embryonic life.[101]

Sucher's views offered a challenge to the modern concept of the nature of birth, which he regarded as a cosmic mystery. Sucher saw birth as a stage, experienced by the spirit in its descent into incarnation, and following clearly demarcated steps. Like the ancients of the Mystery schools, Sucher recognised that the incoming spirit passed through the planetary realms prior to actual incarnation into the physical womb. The last phase of this descent, which was a prelude to incarnation into the womb, was entered by way of what the ancients called the Gate of the Moon.[102]

It was the nature of the Moon, at this moment of conception, which determined something of the nature of birth that would take place approximately 273 days after the primal incarnation. The technical details concerning the effect the waxing or waning Moon has on conception and on the birth pattern (or horoscope) need not concern us here.[103] What is of interest to us is the type of chart that Willi Sucher developed to set out this new approach to astrology.

In his approach to horoscopy, Sucher introduced and developed one major deviation from traditional astrology. In the place of the standard geocentric chart, he created a design to illustrate the creative planetary and zodiacal forces at play during the prenatal period.

It will be useful to our own enquiry if we compare a chart drawn up by Sucher, to serve his system, with one cast according to standard geocentric method. The German composer Richard Wagner was born on 22 May 1813, in Leipzig, probably around sunrise.[104] The constellation chart, or sidereal chart, cast by Sucher for Wagner's birth is given opposite, alongside a standard graduated chart of traditional form.[105] The graphic differences between the two charts are, of course, fundamental. When we begin to analyse Sucher's chart, we are required to apply rules very different to those applied to a conventional chart: we must be prepared to see the chart itself as more than merely an intersection of time and space, as with more conventional horoscopes. In the terms visualised by Sucher, the chart is intended as a diagram of living cycles, culminating in a stage (admittedly an important stage) of birth: in other words, he saw birth, and the conception that preceded it, as the culmination of a process that had begun many years earlier, in the spiritual world. Sucher, recognising the fundamental difference between his sidereal pre-natal charts and conventional birth charts, called his own, *asterograms*.

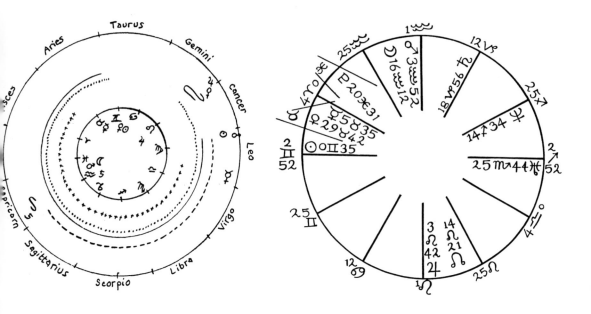

Sucher intended the asterogram of Wagner to form a basis for the study of those planetary forces which had led up to the point of birth, and which will continue, in impetus, into the lifetime. The outermost circle of the asterogram represents the twelve tropical signs of the zodiac: against this are placed the planets, at the moment of conception. The movements of these prenatal planets are set out in the asterogram by means of concentric arcs. The arcs represent the distance travelled, against the backdrop of the stars, during the prenatal period. For example, the outermost arcs begin at almost the same point, and represent the paths of Sun and Mars. At the beginning of the conception epoch, they are in conjunction in Leo. The Sun moves through almost nine months, to complete its circuit in Aries. The innermost circuit is that of Mercury (marked ++++), which is passing from Leo through to Pisces. The next arc in the sequence is that of Venus (marked . . . .), which is represented as beginning in Cancer, and, during the pre-natal period, moving towards the end of Aries. In the period of nine months, Saturn made only a relatively short movement, represented in the asterogram by the S-like form at the bottom left of the map, in the area marked by Capricorn.[107]

The cycle of the Moon is not marked. At the epoch of conception (which Sucher has calculated as 15 August 1812), the Moon was in Sagittarius. In the prenatal period, the Moon will have made ten circuits, or revolutions, and would be in Aquarius at the moment of birth.

The graphic representation of the cycles of the Moon is omitted from the chart because a spiral of ten circuits would be too complex to represent in the figure: the spiral must be subsumed by anyone considering the chart. This continual wrapping of the embryo by the Moon is seen as part of the process of embodiment of the spirit into the physical organism.

The formative importance of the chart itself rests chiefly on these lunar cycles. Each of the cycles foretells, or shadows, one of the rhythms of the following earthly life. Sucher claims that each of the cycles represents a seven-year period in the subsequent lifetime.

Within these defining formative forces of the prenatal period, the inner circle represents that moment when the spirit emerges into the world of space and time.

The diagram captures something altogether lacking in the traditional birth chart: unlike such charts, which nominally represent a static intersection in space and time, the Sucher chart represents a dynamic process in stellar space. The interpretation of such a chart involves an entirely different view of astrology to that demanded by a conventional chart. The reason for this is that Sucher tended to regard events in life as a direct consequence of cosmic events played out in the pre-natal period.

The Horoscope of Jacqueline Kennedy

Only rarely in modern times is there sufficient public interest in a personal horoscope to warrant an entire book being devoted to its treatment. In 1970, two American astrologers, Marcia Moore and Mark Douglas, published a book dealing with the horoscope and sundry related charts of Jacqueline Onassis, more famously known as Jacqueline Kennedy, the wife of the assassinated President of the United States.[108] One version of Jacqueline's chart, which appeared on the dust-jacket of the book, is reproduced below.

Altogether, this remarkable work included thirty-five charts of the famous and infamous among those who circled the Kennedy family during Jacqueline's life. In a sense, the book is the epitome of certain changes that took place in astrology during the twentieth century. As we have seen, in that century astrologers were being drawn to the study of the special relationships that could be discerned by comparing their charts with those related to them, such as through marriage or friendship. This field, which is technically called *synastry*, is based on the idea that a comparison between a pair of charts can reveal underlying and hidden issues in relationships, and offer clues to communal destinies.

The idea that when a pair of horoscopes contained a communal degree the two people would be drawn together into a special intensity or significance has long been established in the astrological tradition. However, it was not an idea that was supported by any serious research until the end of the nineteenth century.

Among the synastry charts that relate directly to Jacqueline are two that combine, in a single figure, her own horoscope with that of her serial husbands, John F. Kennedy and Aristotle Onassis.[109] In each case, there is a communality of degrees, though I shall touch here only on that relating to Kennedy.

Jacqueline Bouvier was born in Southampton, New York, at 2:30 PM, EST, on 29 May 1929. She was born when her planet of communicativeness, Mercury, was in 02.26 Leo. John F. Kennedy had the sensitive planet Neptune in precisely the same degree:

Mercury in Jacqueline Kennedy's chart: 02.26 Leo
Neptune in John F. Kennedy's chart: 02.40 Leo

Surprisingly, this simple form of synastry, expressed by a communal degree, is not at all unusual. Statistically, it should be unusual, but in reality (because human beings are guided by spiritual principles) it is not. This clear example of a unity within a single degree in the charts of two famous people should remind us of the extraordinary fact that a majority of lovers – even those who are not in any sense famous – usually have a similar communality of degrees in their charts.

Another simple example of synastry will help clarify the issue, if on a slightly different level. John F. Kennedy was notoriously unfaithful to his wife, and had an extensive list of mistresses and liaisons. Some of these relationships appear to have been important to him. In view of this, it is worth asking if it is possible to find similar 'communal degrees' between his horoscopes and that of his most famous mistress, Marilyn Monroe.

Norma Jeane Mortenson, who was to become world famous under the stage-name, Marilyn Monroe, was born at 9:06:30 AM on 1 June 1926, in the Charity Ward of Los Angeles General Hospital.[110] (Her chart is given overleaf.)

Marilyn's astrological relationship with John F. Kennedy is astonishing. It is marked by no fewer than two precise communalities, and two that are just over one degree from being exact. Powerful as these are, their synastry is far from harmonious: indeed, it is of a kind that would

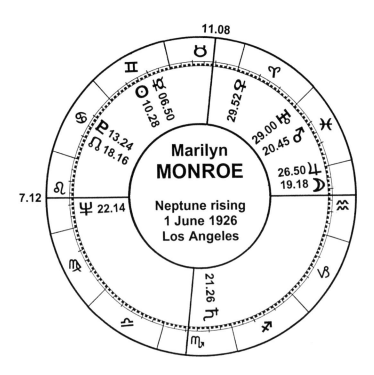

prove very dangerous for both individuals. Before glancing at these four pairs of communalities, I should observe that, in the theory of synastry, powerful effects are felt not merely through the union, or conjunctions, of planets, but also through direct oppositions. In the Monroe–Kennedy examples, two are conjunctions and two oppositions:

Monroe's Pluto:	13.24 Cancer
Kennedy's Cauda:	12. 29 Cancer
Monroe's Mercury:	06.50 Gemini
Kennedy's Sun:	07.50 Gemini
Monroe's Saturn:	21.26 Scorpio
Kennedy's Mercury:	20.06 Taurus
Monroe's Neptune:	22.14 Leo
Kennedy's Uranus:	23.43 Aquarius

According to her horoscope, Marilyn Monroe was murdered in her Brentwood home in Los Angeles shortly before midnight on 4 August 1962.[111] Astrologically, the murder seems to have been involved with the proximity of Chiron (29.52 Aries) to Venus, and the fact that Neptune was close to the asteroid Ceres, in 25.14 Leo. In the year of her death, a lunar eclipse fell on Neptune (and thus near Ceres).

Lunar eclipse of 15 August 1962:   22.22 Aquarius/Leo
Neptune in chart of Monroe: 22.14 Leo

ZOLLER'S USE OF *PARS*

One characteristic, evident among certain modern astrologers, has been a tendency to resurrect, for modern use, ideas which had long ago been rejected by traditional astrology, or which had, for one reason or another, fallen into desuetude. In this manner, many of the ancient ideas have once again found their way into astrology, even if only in specialist use and among a handful of devoted practitioners. One very good example of the resurrection of old ideas is that concerned with the Arabic Parts, or *pars*.

The *pars* are degrees originated artificially in a horoscope by projecting arcs between pairs of planets from various starting points. The most widely used *pars*, which still finds its place in many modern horoscopes (even though its significance is generally misunderstood) is the *Pars Fortunae*, or Part of Fortune. This is obtained by measuring the arc between the Sun and the Moon in a horoscope, and projecting this from the ascendant. Fortuna is the only *pars* derived from ancient astrologies that is still widely used in modern horoscopy.

By far the most learned representative in this specialist area is the American scholar, Robert Zoller, who has concentrated on the treatment of the ancient *pars* in the writings of the Italian astrologer, Guido Bonatti.[112] It is likely that there were once over 200 *pars* in use, in early medieval and Arabic astrology, but by the sixteenth century, most of these were no longer applied. However, after studying over 120 *pars* in some detail, Zoller resurrected a large number and began to use them in his own horoscopy.[113]

The main problem with this modern approach to the *pars* is identical to the problem faced by the early astrologers – the method of *pars* insertion depends on a precision of timing that few horoscopes attain. For example, the simplest of all *pars* is the Fortuna, but its accuracy depends entirely upon the accuracy of the ascendant, from which the primal arc is projected, in accordance with the traditional methods.

Due to the poverty of available tables, few early horoscopes had really accurate ascendants. As most astrologers recognise, even today, with improved time-keeping methods, surprisingly few charts exhibit totally reliable ascendants prior to accurate rectification.

A good example of this problem is evinced in Zoller's seminal book on the subject of *pars*. In this he reproduced his own version of a horoscope cast by the astrologer, Jean Ganivet, for 7:00 AM, on 7 August 1431 at Vienne, in France.[114] The purpose of this horary chart was to determine whether the Lord Dean of Vienne would survive his present illness (as a matter of fact, he died the same day the horary chart was cast). A version of Zoller's chart is given overleaf, left; Ganivet's original chart is to the right.

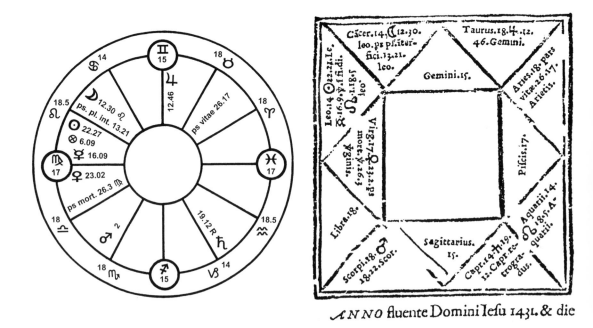

A N N O fluente Domini Iefu 1431. & die

To determine a horary response to the question, Ganivet had elected to use a number of *pars*. Among these, he resolved the degree of the part of death (*pars mortis*), which he calculated for insertion in the chart at 26.03 Virgo. In the original chart, reproduced above (right), this is indicated by the abbreviation, **ps mort. v.26.3 vginis.**[115] The three lines in the first house (below) may be resolved into the English alongside (Ganivet has needlessly repeated the word meaning Virgo).

Virg.17.♀.23.2.ps
mort.♄.26.3
♏ginis.

First house cusp in 17 Virgo.
Venus in 23.2 [of the sign]
Part of Death in 26.3 of Virgo

The rule for locating the *pars mortis* (Part of Death) is simple. The primal arc is taken from the Moon to the degree of the eighth house. To this arc is added the distance which Saturn has completed in the sign which it occupies. In this case, the calculation is as follows:

Arc of Moon to 8th:	245.30
Saturn arc:	19.12
	= 264.42

The derived arc is then projected from the beginning of the sign occupied by Saturn (in this case, from the first degree of Capricorn).

264.42 degrees from 1 degree of Capricorn: 24.42 Virgo

Now, in both the chart and in his text Ganivet places the *pars mortis* in 26 degrees of Virgo, which is a degree out in terms of the calculations. However, this small error need not concern us here. The issue in this chart involves a far more serious error. The fact is that, for the time and place given, both the Moon and Saturn as well as the cusp of the eighth house (the three determinates involved in projecting the part of death) were wrongly placed in the chart. In each case, the errors involved only a few degrees. Saturn was in 19.51 Capricorn, for example, but the ascendant degree, and thus the house cusp, was several degrees out. However, even a few degrees is of importance in calculations of this kind. Ganivet's reading might not have been changed by these errors – for example, he might still have been inclined to read an ominous omen from the fact that the part of death was in the house of life (that is, the first house).[116] Nevertheless, one feels that if the correct placing had located the *pars* on the nearby planet, Venus, then the reading may well have been different.

One placing in Zoller's version of Ganivet's chart is incorrect. Zoller, or whoever drew up the chart for him, has made a copyist error: Mars is placed in 2 Scorpio, when Ganivet had given it in 18.22 Scorpio.

As the horoscope suggests, the underlying issue is that touching upon the accuracy of charting. If the ascendant degree is questionable, then the whole edifice of *pars* begins to collapse. In this particular case, the ascendant degree and the Moon placing cannot both be accurate. The Ganivet chart gives the Moon in 12.30 Leo, and the ascendant at Vienne (France) as 17.42 Virgo. If the Moon really had been in 12.30 Leo, then the ascendant would have been 21.41 Virgo, which means that all the parts constructed from this cusp by Ganivet were incorrect. There seems to be little point in exploring how incorrect these points are: what we can learn from this figure is just how unreliable the majority of the *pars* may prove to be. However, this should not deflect us from an appreciation of Zoller's serious and scholarly attempts to resurrect a useful archaic tradition for modern astrological use.

ASTROCARTOGRAPHY AND JOHN LENNON

The most astonishing contribution to astrology during the twentieth century was Astrocartography. This system of charting was invented and developed, from about 1975 onwards, by the American astrologer, Jim Lewis, whose extraordinary talents were cut short in 1995, at the age of fifty-four. Praise for Lewis' system has come from astrologers in all parts of the world, and is perhaps best summed up in the words of the English astrologer Robert Hand, who has described Astrocartography as 'one of the most revolutionary developments in modern astrology'.[117]

Astrocartography is based on the thoroughly reasonable principle that if you move your location away from your birthplace, then you make this move within the skeletal structure of your birth chart. Thus, as Jim Lewis puts it, if your Saturn was straight overhead in Colorado where you were born, then if you move to Denver, the influence of Saturn is bound to change.[118] The chart itself cannot change – you cannot manipulate the positions of the planets in your horoscope – but if you move to a new location, then you are setting up the equivalent of the chart you would have had if you had been born there. In technical terms, you can, by making long-term moves, change the effects of angularity in your planets – the powerful relationship that planets hold to the four angles. Very frequently, moves are made in life unconsciously, in order to invite into one's life certain desired changes, but such moves can become a part of one's conscious life.

The main purpose behind Astrocartographic mapping is to identify geographical locations upon which salient lines of the birth horoscope are projected. Any given birth chart is projected for the whole of a lifetime on the world map. However, one's relationship to the horoscope changes in accordance with where one lives in relation to the projected chart.

Below is the Astrocartographic chart of John Lennon, of Beatles fame, who was born at 6:30 PM, 9 October 1940, in Liverpool.[119]

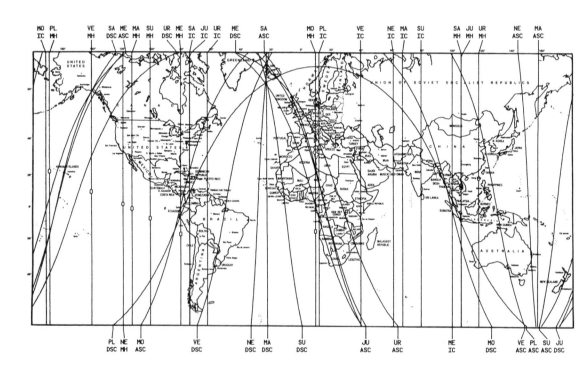

The most astonishing thing about Lennon's birth chart (opposite) is the precise conjunction between Saturn and Jupiter, and the proximity of this conjunction to Uranus, with all three hovering over the ascendant. Of course, this slow-moving arrangement of planets would have influenced the attitudes, behaviour and achievements of an entire generation, but it was in those charts that had the satellitium gathered around an angle (in Lennon's case, the ascendant) where such influences were strongest. In Lennon's chart, the gathering of Sun, Mars and Caput in Libra contributed largely to his musical genius.

When we contemplate the projected horoscope in the cartographic map, we see that the line marked VE ASC (which is the Venus ascendant line) runs upwards in the projection, to the west of Japan. The NE ASC (Neptune ascendant line) runs down to the east of that country, which means that Japan is enclosed within important lines projected from Lennon's chart. Now, in his natal chart, Venus had been a powerful force: not only were there three planets in Libra, which is ruled by Venus, but the gathering in Taurus was also influenced by Venus, the ruler of Taurus. Inevitably, this meant that the Venus line of the cartographic projection would be of profound import- ance in Lennon's life.

It was in Tokyo that Lennon met and married the Japanese artist, Yoko Ono – a relationship which completely changed his life. The couple went to live in New York City, which is almost cut through by the line marked SA IC, or the *Imum Coeli* line of Saturn. In conventional astrology, the IC governs such things as the home, and the place of nourishing. It was here that Lennon and Yoko brought up their son, Sean.

Saturn, the ancient agricultural god, is a planetary ruler of order and industry. However, Saturn also carries a scythe – a reminder that he 'cuts down', is a dissolver of physical form, and a dealer of death. It was in New York that Lennon was killed by an assassin, Mark Chapman, on 8 December 1980. I have no wish to give the impression that a Saturn line in an Astrocartographic chart is always an indicator of the place of death, or even of death itself. In Lennon's case, it is almost impossible to separate the influence of Saturn from that of Jupiter. Both planets fall on a degree occupied by two fixed stars (see natal chart, above). The first of these, Almach, was in 13.24 Taurus in 1940. The second, Menkar, was in 13.29 Taurus in that year. Almach is a beneficial star, for it brings talent, eminence and artistic ability. Unfortunately, Menkar has an evil and destructive influence. In traditional astrology, it is said that when Menkar is with Mars it brings a violent death.

In 1980, when Lennon was assassinated, Mars was transiting Scorpio, and was thus in opposition to the radical Menkar/Saturn. In his solar return chart for that year, Mars was in 28.01 Scorpio. Furthermore, on the day of the assassination, Mars (12.34 Capricorn) was square with both Jupiter (7.05 Libra) and Saturn (8.18 Libra). Thus, at Lennon's death, those factors which the astrological tradition insist lead to a violent death were operative. (I have examined the chart from a different point of view, on pages 242–3, below.)

EINSTEIN CHART IN WASHINGTON, DC

Washington, DC is the city of the stars: in or near its centre are over fifty public zodiacs in sculpted, painted or moulded forms.[120] However, only one of these zodiacs incorporates a genuine horoscope, but this is easy of access, as part of an open-air statuary in public view. Almost certainly the largest public horoscope in the United States, it is marked out on the marble expanse in front of the semi-circular bench on which is seated a statue of Einstein, sculpted by Robert Berks (figure 8). Located in front of the National Academy of Sciences, the marble surface of the platform in front of the seated Einstein is inset with stainless steel studs which mark the positions of over 2,700 stars, ten quasars, and a number of planets. The arrangement of stars and planets is far from haphazard – taken together, they represent a moment in cosmic time.

This horoscope is 28 feet in diameter, and represents the heavens at noon on 22 April 1979, marking the moment of dedication of the statue, a few days before the centenary of the birth of Einstein. The plan below sets out the schema of the heavens represented at Einstein's feet. In astrological terms, this is by no means a conventional projection of the skies. Essentially, it is a constellational chart, with the five marked planets set against the zodiac of fixed stars.

The central point marks the northern pole. Stars of first magnitude are indicated by means of the larger black circles. For example, that to the extreme left of the penultimate concentric arc represents the star Sirius, which had risen shortly before the ceremony. The star to the extreme

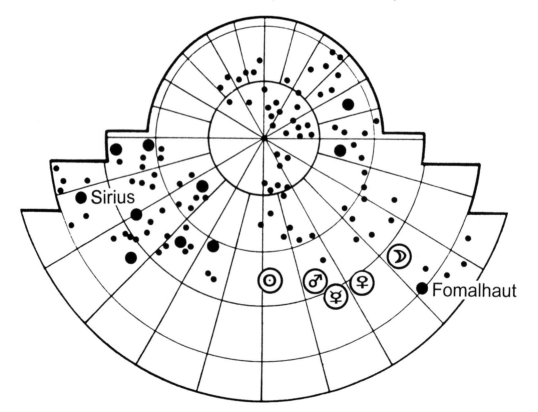

right, which falls on the line dividing the penultimate from the last arc, represents Formalhaut. This would shortly be setting.[121]

As the sigils indicate, the five planets, from left to right, are the Sun, Mercury, Mars, Venus and the Moon. Their zodiacal positions were:

Sun:	01.58 Taurus
Mercury:	04.43 Aries
Mars:	12.08 Aries
Venus:	29.29 Aries
Moon:	10.57 Pisces

Einstein was born at 11:26 AM on 14 March 1879, at Ulm in Germany.[122] Below is a copy of an early horoscope for Einstein, cast by the French-born Daniel Chennevière, who worked in the United States under the pseudonym Dane Rudhyar, and who, as we have seen, had been influenced by the esoteric writings of Alice Bailey. Alongside is an analytic diagram, which will be examined shortly.

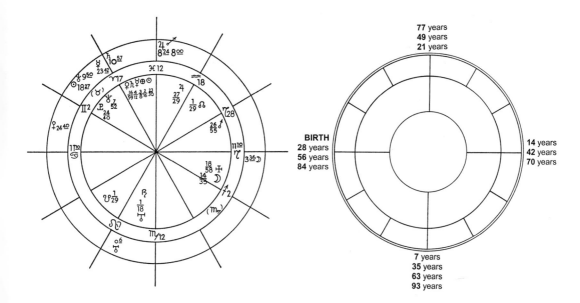

Astrologers are unlikely to be surprised to learn that there is a relationship between this marble horoscope and the chart for Einstein's birth.[123] The conjunction in Aries, between Saturn and Mercury, which contributed so much to his brilliant intellect, is in the same degree as Mercury in the marble chart:

Saturn in chart of Einstein:	04.12 Aries
Mercury in chart of Einstein:	03.07 Aries
Mercury in marble horoscope:	04.43 Aries

The outer concentric of the Rudhyar chart records the positions of the progressed planets for 1935. This horoscope is interesting for many reasons, the most important being that it is representative of a trend that became popular during the twentieth century of combining, in a series of outer concentrics, progressions and/or transits. In some cases, similar concentric chartings were used for setting out communal data from more than one chart – for example, when the chart of a married couple was represented with two combined sets of data.

Rudhyar had evolved a rule-of-thumb system for dating events in the life of the personality. This was based on the transfer of the lunar cycle of twenty-eight years (which traditionally started from the place of the Moon) to the ascendant, as a starting point. The seven-year periods, marked by the four angles, were thus useful indices of events in the life of the native. The diagram alongside Einstein's chart (right, previous page) is a summary of this 28-year cycle, which is repeated, in a lifetime of normal length, about three times.

In connection with the chart of Einstein, Rudhyar pointed to the twenty-second year – that is, to about 1901 – marked on the 28-year cycle just to the east of the Midheaven. This place was occupied by the Sun, and the period was seen as an intensification of his destiny. Rudhyar mentioned the fact that during this time, Einstein became inspector of patents in Berne, Switzerland, and shortly afterwards encountered Planck's papers on quantum theory. This impulse led to Einstein's development of the theory of Relativity, which was being formulated at about the same time as the single hand of the 28-year clock was moving over Pluto.[124]

Rudhyar had proposed that the solar–lunar arc might be projected from each of the angles – once on either side of the angle, giving eight parts altogether. Each of these parts is said to represent a function of selfhood. Rudhyar calls this 'group algebra', for he regarded each pair of planets as being susceptible to such 'nearly endless correlations and permutations'.

HARMONIC CHARTS

Harmonics is the name given to an astrological technique by means of which horoscopes are subjected to an extreme form of numerological analysis. This analysis concentrates on the radical aspects of the natus. The inventor of this system was the English astrologer, John Addey, who was deeply interested in numerology and cycles.[125]

Addey ascribed certain characteristics to numbers, characteristics that were largely supported by the numerological tradition. For example, the number four, which is linked with the Earth (originally with the four Elements), is seen as a difficult number, demanding effort. In contrast, number five – the number of the *quintessence* which enlivened and empowered the four Elements – is involved with mind, with discrimination, and the exercise of power.

The danger behind the practical use of harmonics is that students who are not thoroughly familiar with traditional astrology may be tempted to use the system as though it were sufficiently valid in itself, rather than as a tool for investigation of radical horoscopes. In reality, the true value of harmonics analysis rests completely upon the nature of the chart under analysis: the derived harmonic chart should not be used for any purpose other than as a tool for the investigation of the radical.

A harmonic chart is derived from the radical by dividing the circle of the zodiac into a specific number of equal segments, and then treating each segment as though it were itself a whole circle. The first stage in constructing a particular harmonic involves multiplying the natal position of an angle, node or planet by the designed number (or 'harmonic'), then reducing the multiples of 360 degrees until these are less than 360 degrees. The results are entered on the chart, which is then the desired harmonic chart. This chart is usually interpreted only in terms of aspects, conditions by standard orbs.

Constraints of space preclude an examination of even the main harmonics – let alone those that have accrued since the introduction of the theory into astrology by John Addey.[126] However, for the sake of revealing a harmonic derivative chart, I will examine here a seventh harmonic, or H7. In a study of the seventh harmonic, we divide the circle into seven equal segments, of approximately 51° 25′ 43″. This means that the first segment is from 0.0 Aries to 21.25.43 Taurus. Having obtained this division of seven, we then treat the segment as though it had the capability of containing an entire zodiac of 360 degrees. Thus the angular distances within the segments are multiplied by seven.

The sacred number seven is sometimes baffling to those untrained in numerology. Its inherently dangerous bipolar nature may best be understood when we consider it as the sum of the two numerical 'extremes' of 3 and 4. Three is a spiritual number, a reflection of the sacred Trinity, and of the three-fold nature of man, as a thinking, feeling and willing being. In contrast, four is a material number: it is the radical expression of the four Elements, which were once believed to underlie all natural phenomena. The seven is a bipolarity that unites, under tension, these contrasts. On the one hand, seven offers the opportunity for redemption, when the four is rendered subservient to the spiritualising impetus of the three. On the other hand, the three might be traduced and seduced by the coarsening influence of the four. One modern work has termed this bipolarity as both the 'numinous and the brutal'.[127]

The tension arising from this yoking together of opposites is often involved with an artistic outcome, which is why the H7 is essentially an index of imaginative facility. The H7 is linked to those imaginative powers that arise from within the artist himself or herself. However, the H7 does not appear to be an index of inspiration, in its classical sense, of a spiritual breath. The harmonic has been described as the index of that which inspires or captivates the soul, and as being closely associated with the native's concept of art.[128] It is by way of the H7 that one may be lifted to a higher or redemptive level of understanding, by way of one's own intuitive and imaginative processes.

Overleaf (left) is the horoscope of Henry Miller alongside a derived chart for the seventh harmonic. The chart was used, in this harmonic form, by the astrologer, David Hamblin, as an example of how the H7 relates to sexual fantasy and eroticism.[129] The chart is, of course, distinguished by the satellitium of Sun, Moon, Mars, Neptune and Pluto, all of which conspire to demonstrate Miller's concern with sexuality and sexual taboos as a means of expressing subtle

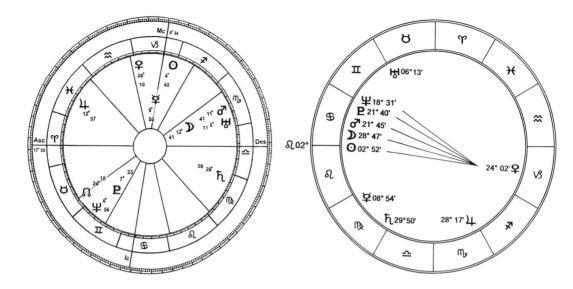

observations of human nature. The series of oppositions to Venus, which are so distinctive in this H7 chart, might suggest that the rich panorama of experiences within the conflicting realm of sexuality could be reconciled and redeemed by means of art (the Venusian impulse).

David Hamblin's study of harmonics includes examination of some of the greatest figures of recent history.[130]

THE PLANET OR ASTEROID CHIRON

Chiron has been classified as both an asteroid and a planet (even as a comet), but little is known about its nature. One American astrologer, Al Morrison, who has studied Chiron in depth, describes its nature with the aid of such keywords as 'doorway' or 'maverick': there is some basis for such epithets, as we have found the planet to relate to that ultimate doorway by which the soul returns to the spiritual realm (namely, death), and with that spiritual confusion formerly associated with the word glamour. In a chart in which Chiron is in close contact with a planet, or in which it is near an angle, its influence does seem to be involved with issues raised by the redemptive qualities inherent in death. We noted that Chiron was within a degree of Venus in the chart of Marilyn Monroe: it was this combination, manifest through Marilyn's extraordinary beauty – the exudation of glamour – which eventually led to her death. The manner of her murder was determined by the angular Neptune (see page 232, above).

Chiron was discovered on 1 November 1977 by Charles Kowal, and named after the mythological Greek centaur, who was a teacher and healer. It is in orbit between Saturn and Uranus, and seems to have a period of 50.68 years. As with the discovery of Pluto, the discovery of Chiron was predicted by an astrologer before the event.[131] Several variant sigils for Chiron are on record, the most widely use of which are the following two: ⚷ ⚷

We see the sigil for Chiron in close proximity to Pluto in the chart of John Lennon (see page 237). The opposition between Moon and Pluto attracts changes – often violent changes – into the life of the native. There is a high degree of restlessness – not just in a physical sense, but also mentally. The native is a restless searcher. In the case of John Lennon, this opposition was intensified by the fact that Chiron was within a degree or so of Pluto, with its strong connection to the Moon. In a chart, Pluto is an indication of the innermost and hidden strivings of an entire generation (Pluto is in a sign for approximately thirty years). The Moon is, among other things, an index of how one relates to people – the great audience of individuals that surrounds us in life. In the case of John Lennon, this audience was vast, and might even be described as being an entire generation. Pluto is not only in the exuberant, life-loving Leo, but is also in the fifth house, proper to the Leonine influence. This inevitably meant that Lennon was a showman, an entertainer, of the first order. The closeness of Chiron tied this impulse to entertain with a particular form of glamour. We might even say of Lennon that he cast his glamour over an entire generation.

One of the most important placings in Lennon's natal chart was the proximity of the conjunction of Saturn and Jupiter to the ascendant. This life-force, which contributed greatly to his creativity, was also linked with his death. The importance of Chiron in the life of this genius may be seen from the fact that on the day of his death, Chiron was upon exactly the same degree of the all-important Saturn–Jupiter conjunction which occurred at his birth. I have represented this placing in the outer circuit of Lennon's horoscope, below.

Although Chiron features in most astro-computer systems, little is really known about its influence. The name, chosen by Charles Kowal, is ambiguous, as it was already in use in an astrological context as one of the names of the constellation Centaurus. Furthermore, the name does not seem to fit the supposed influence of the planet.[132] Chiron (properly Pholus) was a centaur, a healer and educator of the young Achilles, and a friend of Hercules, by whose arrows, tipped with the venom from the blood of the Hydra, he was poisoned. An acute observer will note, in the charts of those where Chiron is emphasised, a special kind of fatalism at work: I have called this fatalism 'a glamour' because it seems to attract strange events. One senses it as typical of this glamour, or confusion, that some American astrologers (presumably unaware of the classical traditions) have confused Chiron with Charon, who ferried the newly dead across the Stygian river.

Like any other planet or asteroid, Chiron seems to cast its peculiar glamour when it is located on one of the four angles. This is one reason why the chart of Senator Robert F. Kennedy is so interesting from an astrological point of view. In his horoscope, Chiron was within a degree of his ascendant, and thus located in the most powerful point in a chart.

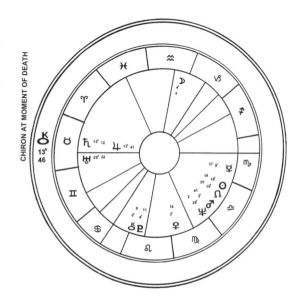

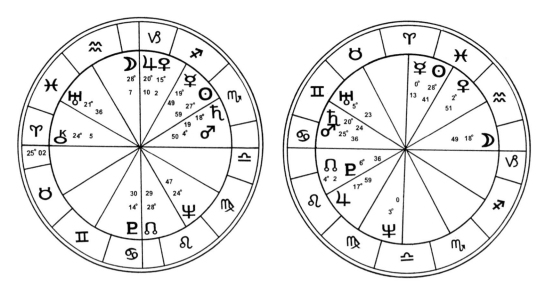

Robert F. Kennedy was assassinated in 1968. If we study his birth chart in relation to this assassination, we can learn something of the magnetic attraction of Chiron, as well as a great deal about the hidden side of astrology.[133] Kennedy's chart is given above, alongside that of his assassin, Sirhan Sirhan.[134]

By May 1968, Sirhan Sirhan had already decided that he would kill Robert F. Kennedy. We are certain of this because of what Sirhan wrote in his notebook, on a page of doodled half-thoughts. At the top of a lined page in this book, alongside a note to the effect that he was determined to eliminate RFK, Sirhan made a record of the time and date on which he wrote. The near-illegible scrawl (below) reveals the date and time as *May 18 9.45 AM–68*.[135]

No practised astrologer can fail to note the significance of the date scrawled in the notebook. At 9:45 AM on that day, Chiron was in 02.34 Aries. It had just entered the degree which placed it in diametric opposition to Neptune in the personal chart of Sirhan Sirhan (03.00 Libra). It is as though a psychical disturbed impulse was penetrating into the space of the Aries–Libra degree arc. Not surprisingly, Sirhan Sirhan's intended victim had a planet close to that degree: Kennedy's Mars was in 4.50 Libra.

Twenty-one days later, at 12:15 AM on 5 June 1968, Sirhan Sirhan shot and mortally wounded Senator Kennedy, in a kitchen pantry of the Ambassador Hotel, in Los Angeles.[136]

At the time when Sirhan Sirhan shot Kennedy, there was a gathering of three planets in Gemini: Sun, Venus and Mars. Mars was in 19.13 Gemini: this was opposite Mercury in Kennedy's birth chart (19.49 Sagittarius). Saturn, in the chart of Sirhan Sirhan, was on this same degree, in 20.24 Gemini. This means that a *single degree* tied together the charts of the murderer, the murdered, and the moment the murder took place.

Astonishingly, the date which Sirhan Sirhan scrawled at the top of his notebook was astrologically related to this same degree. On 18 May 1968, Mercury was in 19.23 Gemini. The conflux of events pertaining to this degree may be summarised in the following tabulation.

Mars at the time Kennedy was shot:	19.13 Gemini
Mercury at time Sirhan scrawled note:	19.23 Gemini
Saturn in chart of Sirhan Sirhan:	20.24 Gemini
Mercury in chart of Kennedy:	19.49 Sagittarius

ASTRO-COMPUTER CHARTING

The complexity of any chart has increased immeasurably with the introduction of computer astro-charting. The availability of computer techniques has created a modern astrology which is perplexing for the uninitiated. The following commentary on computerisation in modern horoscopy may require the non-specialist to consult, from time to time, the glossary of specialist terms on page 249.

A computerised astro-chart usually permits the calculation of up to twenty-eight of the Arabian *pars* – though in most computer systems these are listed separately from the horoscope itself. The same dislocation from the chart applies to the lists of most of the major fixed stars. If we assume a minimum of twenty-eight *pars*, and the minimum of 110 fixed stars used in modern astrology, then we see that the standard charting has already been vastly increased by the addition of 138 factors within the horoscope, as an augmentation to the standard planets and nodes. A computerised version of such a chart would be so complex as to be little more than a black mass of interweaving and overlaid symbols and sigils.

Most computer systems permit the incorporation of several hypothetical planets, such as Lilith. They allow one to move between different systems, such as the familiar tropical zodiac, the sidereal zodiac and heliocentric charting. In addition, they incorporate a number of useful adjunct tools, such as the calculations of antiscions and contra-antiscions. Most computer systems also permit adjustments for numerous house systems, so that one may (for example) change from the Placidean to the Campanean merely at the press of a button. The more versatile systems also offer such techniques as chart rotation, by which it is possible to project any planet, node or Midheaven to the zero point of Aries, and study the effects on other planets and nodes. Some systems offer the possibility of calculating relocation charts (along the lines of the Astrocartography charting, examined above). Above all, advanced computerised systems enable the astrologer to calculate progressions and transits for any chart.

The techniques on offer are bewildering, but for the competent astrologer, who knows how to limit choices of techniques, they can be a true joy. The real danger is when these sophisticated astrological techniques are used by those who have little or no idea of what they really mean, and what limits of interpretation are involved. While computers can provide complex and sophisticated charts of the most advanced kind, no computer yet developed can actually replace the astrologer and produce an accurate and living reading of such a chart.

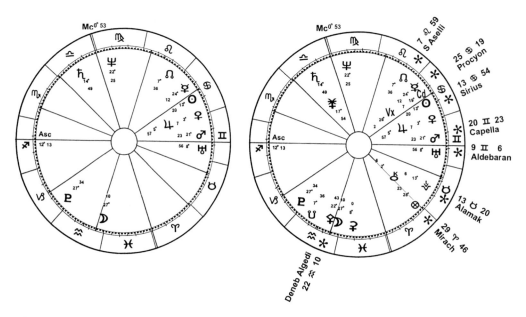

Above (right) is a computer-generated chart for the Declaration of Independence, on 4 July 1776. This chart is a more complex version of those we have already examined.

Any competent astrologer knows that the Declaration of Independence was linked with the powerful star Sirius. However, the truth is that, even if we allow only a single degree orb, there are seven other fixed stars operative within the Declaration chart. The computer system permits one to reveal these with extraordinary ease, and, in the example chart above, they have been inserted alongside the outer rim. Within the wheel itself are the four standard asteroids, the Fortuna, and Chiron. We see that, even with the addition of about a dozen extra planets or stars, the chart has become really complicated – especially so in regard to the aspects engendered by the positions. One can imagine that a super-chart, with a hundred or so hypotheticals, asteroids, nodal points, parts, and so on, would be far too complex for even a brilliant astrologer to read.

One reason why I chose this dramatic Declaration chart to illustrate something of the potential within computer astrology is that there is a specific relationship between the moment of certain major historical events involving the United States, and the chart cast for Independence. As an example of what I mean, I shall examine three major events that were seminal to the history and growth of the United States, and show how each was related to the Independence chart. All the major events I propose to examine took place during the twentieth century, and their precise time and location are well known.

The first historical event is the opening of the war between the United States and Japan, in consequence of the attack on Pearl Harbor in 1941; the second is the dropping of the atomic bomb on Hiroshima in 1945; and the third the iniquitous terrorist attack on the Twin Towers, in Manhattan, in September 2001. Each occurrence marked a milestone in the history of the United States, and each bears a relationship to the primal chart of Independence.

The opening of the Pacific War may be timed for a position 3 miles south of Pearl Harbor, at 6:37AM on 7 December 1941. The time is known from the opening salvos fired at Pearl Harbor.[137] Comparison of the chart for this event with the horoscope of the Declaration of Independence reveals a close communality of opposing planets:

Mars at attack on Pearl Harbor: 15.31 Aries
Saturn at Declaration of Independence: 14.49 Libra

For the dropping of the atomic bomb on Hiroshima, I have adopted the time given by the historian, Kurzman.[138] According to this source, the official time for this explosion was 8:16 AM. Thousands of people were vaporised at the moment of impact: an estimated ninety-one thousand lives were lost, and many thousands more were maimed or injured.[139]

When we compare the chart for this moment with the horoscope for the Declaration of Independence (opposite) we find a most astonishing communality of degrees. The position of Mars at the moment of the impact of the atomic bomb was in the same degree as the Uranus in the chart of the United States:

Mars at dropping of atomic bomb: 09.12 Gemini
Uranus at Declaration of Independence: 08.56 Gemini

The first impact of the hijacked Boeing 767 on the north tower of the World Trade Center, in Manhattan, occurred at 8:45 AM on 11 September 2001. The most important of the communal degrees were:

Mercury at impact of Boeing 767: 14.17 Libra
Saturn at Independence: 14.49 Libra

Pluto at impact of Boeing 767: 12.38 Sagittarius
Ascendant at Independence: 12.13 Sagittarius

This examination of the chart has carried us towards dramatic conclusions, yet there is a truth hidden in what we have seen which reflects on the nature of modern astrology. The conclusions we have drawn are based on the most simple of all traditional charts. We have rendered this simple chart complex only by expanding it into time and space, and seeing it as a nexus for events in a distant future, yet the data we have used for this incursion into history involve only the two planets Saturn and Uranus, and the ascendant degree. The conclusions suggest that there is really no need for super-charting, or for complex theories relating to new astrologies, new planets and new *pars*. On the contrary, the method suggests that if one has sufficient understanding of the full potential within a standard horoscope, and if one is prepared to expand this potential in space and time, then the basic data encapsulated in the traditional form are sufficient as a horoscopic tool.

Shortly before going to press, I became acquainted with Robert Powell's *Chronicle of the Living Christ* (1996), which contains a number of extremely interesting horoscopes, relating to the main participants involved in the drama surrounding the coming of Christ.

These charts include those for the Solomon and Nathan Jesus Children, relating to the tradition we examined on page 76, above. The horoscope for the former was cast 5 March 6 BC, and that of the latter for 6 December 2 BC. The charts reproduced in Dr Powell's book, offer a compendious and carefully researched astrological study, in which the data are presented in a form that incorporates, in the outer concentric of the chart, the sidereal zodiac that Dr Powell has long espoused. I reproduce as sample, below, the chart for the Solomon Child, as a good example of Powell's exquisite and refined charting.

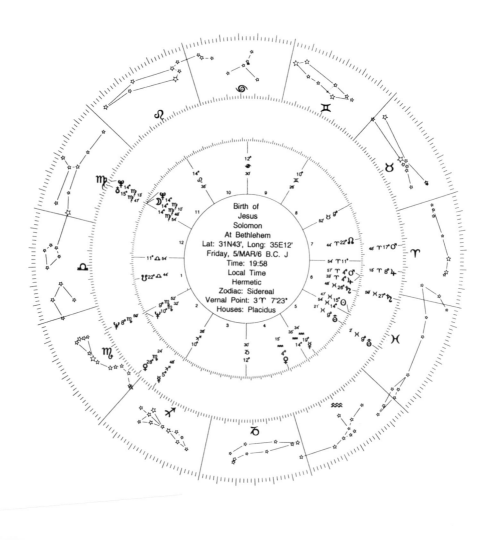

Glossary

This glossary is intended merely to provide useful definitions of terms that may be less familiar to the non-specialist. For other specialist terms, see the Index on page 292.

LORDSHIPS

ALFONSINE In the thirteenth century, Alfonso X, King of León and Castile, ordered scholars to produce a much-needed revision of astronomical tables of planetary and nodal positions. These tabulations, the *Alfonsine Tables*, formed the background for the computation of horoscopes for almost three hundred years.

ANIMODAR The name given to a method of rectifying a chart, by adjusting the ascendant, in terms of the syzygy (full or new Moon) previous to the birth. The rules are complex but involve estimating, from this chart, the most dominant planet over the sign within which the syzygy takes place. The ascendant of the chart is adjusted to be the same as the degree of that dominant planet. Ptolemy did not use the word *animodar*, which is derived from the Arabic, but he appears to have been aware of the tradition, already ancient in his day, relating to the conception Moon.

CAMPANUS SYSTEM The *Campanus*, or *Campanean* system, is the name given to an important system of house division associated with the thirteenth-century astrologer Giovanni Campano. It was based on the division of the prime vertical into equal arcs, and the projecting of this division on to the ecliptic from the pole of the prime vertical. This projection is spatial in nature. According to Campano, the cusps mark the centres of the houses, rather than their boundaries, as with most other systems.

COMBUSTION In medieval astrology, when a planet was within a certain orb of the Sun it was said to be burned up by the rays of the Sun, or in a state of *combustion*, and thereby vitiated. In some astrologies, the orb was 8° 30'; in others 5°. Few modern astrologers regard combustion as being of any significance.

CONCEPTION The *conception* chart was widely used in ancient and medieval astrology, and related to a period approximately nine months prior to birth. There is no proof that this moment of 'conception' marked the actual time of conception in a biological sense. Some modern astrologers, aware of this fact, prefer to describe the 'conception' merely as 'a certain epoch', or the Prenatal Epoch. In early astrology, conception charts were important because of the relationship they held to the TRUTINE of Hermes. It had been held, from very ancient times, that there was a distinct relationship between the moment of 'conception' and the moment of birth. Although the word *trutina* was used in medieval astrology, the technique was more usually referred to as *Rectificato per Conceptionem*, and it is evident from some texts that the words *trutina* and *conceptio* were regarded as synonymous.

CONSTELLATIONAL ZODIAC *see* TROPICAL ZODIAC

DEBILITY *see* DIGNITY

DECAN A *decan* is a third part (10 degrees) of a zodiacal sign. In traditional astrology, the 36 decans were not only ascribed influences of their own (always in keeping with the general tenor of the constituent sign), but were also associated with distinctive images. For an example of such an image, see page 56.

DECUMBITURE A *decumbiture chart* is one cast for the time at which a person takes to his or her bed, at the onset of an illness.

DETRIMENT A planet is said to be in its *detriment* when it is in the sign opposite to that which is its own sign. A detrified planet is said to operate weakly. See DIGNITY.

DIGNITY A condition whereby a planet is strengthened. There are many rules determining dignities: for example, a planet is dignified when it is in a sign which it rules. It is also dignified when in the sign of its exaltation, or when it is in a sign of the same triplicity of that of which it is ruler. Dignities were of great importance in sixteenth- and seventeenth-century astrology for determining the all-important Lordships. The following table sets out the essential dignities and debilities, as rulers, detriments, exaltations and fall.

Planet	Ruler	Detriment	Exaltation	Fall
Sun	Leo	Aquarius	Aries	Libra
Moon	Cancer	Capricorn	Taurus	Scorpio
Mercury	Gemini	Sagittarius	Aquarius	Leo
	Virgo	Pisces		
Venus	Taurus	Scorpio	Pisces	Virgo
	Libra	Aries		
Mars	Aries	Libra	Capricorn	Cancer
	Scorpio	Taurus		
Jupiter	Pisces	Virgo	Cancer	Capricorn
	Sagittarius	Gemini		
Saturn	Capricorn	Cancer	Libra	Aries
	Aquarius	Leo		

DIRECTIONAL PARALLELS *see* RAPT PARALLELS

DIRECTIONS As an astrological technique, the art of *directing*, or studying *directions*, involves the moving, or 'directing' of given planets or nodes to specific points of time-equivalence in a chart, in order to reveal the potential, for good or bad, within the natal chart. In modern astrology, the most important of these techniques is SECONDARY DIRECTIONS (sometimes, Arabian Directions). PRIMARY DIRECTIONS were used extensively in medieval astrology.

ELEVATION The *elevation* of a planet or node is its distance above the horizon, usually measured in relation to other planets in the chart. The planet nearest to the Midheaven is usually called the elevated planet. In medieval astrology, the elevated planet was supposed to cast an influence (benign or otherwise, depending upon the nature of the planet) on the chart as a whole.

EQUAL HOUSE The *equal house* system is a symbolic method of determining the cusps of the twelve houses, and the oldest known method of house division. The ascendant degree is regarded as the fiducial degree, and each of the house cusps is marked off in sequence, at intervals of 30 degrees from this point. The tenth-house cusp does not necessarily correspond to the Midheaven.

EXALTATION *see* DIGNITY

FALL *see* DIGNITY

FORTITUDES A now-archaic term, indicating the strength of a planet when it is in its own sign or exaltation: see DIGNITY.

GENETHLIACAL Genethliacal is a term derived from the Greek, meaning 'pertaining to one's birth'. The term is used to distinguish horoscopes cast for, and relating to, birth days, in contrast to charts cast for other reasons – such as horary charts.

HORARY ASTROLOGY Horary astrology is the art of interpreting a question from a chart erected for the moment the question is formulated. In medieval astrology, other names for horary astrology were *questions* and *interrogations*. The rules for interpreting horary charts are far too complex to be examined here, though a few examples are given in the main body of the text. It is usual to distinguish horary astrology from genethliacal astrology, which properly deals with birth charts.

HYLEG The *hyleg* planet is said to be the 'giver of life'. A planet was deemed hyleg when it was in one of five possible aphetic places in the chart.

INGRESS The ingress is the point where the Sun moves into the first second of arc of a sign. The word is most widely used of the ingress into one or other of the signs that mark the beginnings of the four seasons. The vernal ingress is marked by the entry of the Sun into Aries. *Ingress charts* are those cast for the moment of entry into specific signs.

ISOLATION A now-archaic term denoting a planet that is not supported by aspects.

LORD OF THE ASCENDANT The planet ruling the sign on the ascendant.

LORD OF THE HOUSE This is a term used of a planet when the sign that it rules is on the cusp of the house occupied by that planet.

MODUS RATIONALIS The *Modus Rationalis* is the system of house division associated with the sixteenth-century astrologer Regiomontanus. It was based on the division of the equator into equal arcs, and the projecting of this division on to the ecliptic from the pole of the prime vertical. This projection is spatial in nature.

MUNDANE *Mundane aspects* are those measured by the semi-arcs of the chart, rather than by zodiacal arcs. A mundane aspect between the ascendant and the MC cusp is a square (a mundane square), yet may not be 90 degrees when measured along the zodiacal arc.

MUNDANE PARALLEL *Mundane parallels* are aspects, measuring along the equatorial circle equal distances of two or more planets from a specified angle. For example, a planet on the cusp of the eighth house is in mundane parallel to one on the cusp of the twelfth, since both are of equal mundane distance from the MC cusp. *See also* RAPT PARALLEL.

NAIBOD MEASURE A measure used in DIRECTIONS. The *Naibod Measure* is based on the mean motion of the Sun, at 00° 59′ 08″. This was regarded as being the arc equivalent of a year in time.

NATIVE In astrology, the word *native* refers to the person for whom a particular horoscope was cast. It was derived from the Latin, *natus*, or birth, which also gave us the word *nativity*.

ORB The *orb* is the permitted limit within which a given aspect remains operative. The orbs vary, not only from century to century, but even from astrologer to astrologer. In modern astrology, it is normal for an orb of 8 degrees to be permitted for a conjunction; however, it was normal for sixteenth-century astrologers to allow up to 12 degrees orb for the same aspect.

OWN TRIPLICITY *see* TRIPLICITY

PARALLELS *Parallels of Latitude* refer to measurements made from circles equidistant from the ecliptic; a planet in equal declination (measured against these circles) is said to be 'in parallel' with, or in zodiacal parallel aspect with, any other planet in the same declination, whether this is to the North or South of the ecliptic. Modern astrologers tend to view the parallels of this kind as being valid only with the same latitude, or North or South. This parallel aspect is said to intensify any aspect of the two bodies: some authorities treat the parallel as an aspect in its own right. *Parallels of Declination* are measured along the equator, in terms of right ascension, the declination being measured North or South of the equator: they are used mainly in directions. Zodiacal parallels are not to be confused with mundane parallels. *See also* MUNDANE PARALLELS.

PARTILE A *partile aspect* is an exact aspect between two or more bodies.

PLACIDUS SYSTEM The *Placidean*, or *Placidus* system of house division, widely believed to have been developed in the seventeenth century by Placidus di Tito, was certainly originated by Arabic astrologers in the eighth century. It is a time system involved in the trisection of the diurnal and nocturnal semi-arcs by the equivalent sidereal time. The system becomes horoscopically invalid at latitudes higher than 66° 33′.

PRECESSION The name given to the slow backward drift of the vernal point (00° Aries) against the backdrop of the stars – properly, the precession of the equinoxes. The most obvious effect of this motion, in horoscopy, is that it changes the positions of the stars relative to the ecliptic. The 'movement' of the stars, as measured along the ecliptic, is approximately 50.25 seconds per year, or about 1 degree every 72 years. In 2,160 years, the precessional rate is 30 degrees, or the arc of an entire sign.

PRENATAL EPOCH Loosely speaking, the *Prenatal Epoch* is the equivalent of the medieval CONCEPTION, though the former is arrived at by a more complex set of rules relating to relationship between the epoch Moon and the natal ascendant–descendant, as a basis for rectification. Unlike the TRUTINE, the Prenatal Epoch is determined by such factors as the state of the Moon at birth. For example, if it is increasing in light (moving towards the full), then it will mark the ascending degree at the epoch, and the epochal Moon will mark the ascendant at birth. If it is decreasing in light, then it will mark the descendant of the epoch, and the epochal Moon will mark the descending degree at birth.

PRIMARY DIRECTIONS A method of DIRECTIONS in which a year in the life of the native is regarded as the equivalent of four minutes of time.

PROGRESSIONS The term *progressions* has two specialist meanings, both related to the original sense of the Latin, *progredior*, which implies the idea of 'moving forward'. It is used to denote the method of directing the movement (or 'progression') of planets and nodal points along their courses, for a specified period of time, to reveal future trends at that time. The word is also used to denote charts cast to reveal these directed movements.

RAPT PARALLEL A *rapt parallel* is a MUNDANE PARALLEL formed between two planets by direction, from their natal points. It is sometimes referred to as a *directional parallel*.

RECTIFICATION *Rectification* is an astrological technique involving the adjustment of a nativity in order to determine an accurate moment of birth. In modern astrology, the most widely practised method of rectification is by way of progressions, which permit the adjustment of the chart against known events in the life of the native. In former times, this was referred to as *rectificato per accidentia* (rectification by events), and was distinguished from the ANIMODAR method, which was called *Rectificato per Animodar*.

REGIOMONTANUS SYSTEM *see* MODUS RATIONALIS

RETROGRADE When a planet, or nodal point, appears to move backwards in the zodiacal belt, it is said to be retrograde ('stepping backwards'). In some astrologies, this retrograde motion was interpreted as having a sinister effect.

REVOLUTION CHARTS *Revolution charts*, or *revolutions*, are figures cast for the precise moment the Sun entered (or revolves forward to) the same degree, minute and second as in a given radical chart. It is possible to cast a revolutionary for each year of life. From each of these revolutions the astrologer can make predictions for the specific year for which it was cast.

SATELLITIUM The word *satellitium* is used to denote a group of three or more planets in a single sign. The equivalent word in modern American astrology is *stellium*.

SECONDARY DIRECTIONS *Secondary directions* are based on the theory that each day, in the sequence following birth, represents a year of life, in the same sequence. Thus the cosmic horoscopic influence in the thirtieth day after birth is said to be reflected in the thirtieth year of the lifetime of the native. This particular form of directing is usually referred to as PROGRESSIONS. Usually, the astrologer combines with this technique of investigating the future a study of the TRANSITS for the period under investigation.

SIDEREAL ZODIAC *see* TROPICAL ZODIAC

SIGIL A *sigil* is a graphic symbol – or a symbol derived from graphic forms designed to portray, within the structure of the graphic, something of the spiritual nature of the thing symbolised. For a list of zodiacal and planetary sigils, see pages 11 and 14.

SOLARSCOPE The name given to a chart cast for sunrise, in the absence of any known time.

SYZYGY The New or Full Moon.

TRANSITS The term relates to the passing over (*trans-ire*, in Latin) of a planet or node over another planet or node. Most frequently *transits* are used as a predictive support to the technique of PROGRESSIONS. In effect, transits in predictive astrology mark the combination of influences called into existence as the planets, nodes and angles pass over marked positions in the natal chart. If an astrologer wishes to establish what influences are to be experienced, through transits, for a particular future year, then he or she will cast a chart for that year, and compare it with the natal, or radical chart. Planets in the transit chart, which are in proximity to the occupied degrees in the radical chart, combine their influences and bring about specific effects in the life of the native. Transits are frequently used in connection with progressed charts, though the two methods are really quite different: a progressed chart is symbolic, while a transit chart is a graphic projection of cosmic events in the heavens.

TRIPLICITY The *triplicities* are the groups of three signs governed by a communal element. Thus the triplicities of Aries, Leo and Sagittarius are governed by the Fire signs, and are usually said to be the Fire Triplicities. A planet may be said to be in its *own triplicity* when in a sign of the same elemental nature as that sign of which it is ruler.

TROPICAL ZODIAC The zodiac directly related to ecliptic belt (wherein are marked out the tropics, or turning points of the Sun). This zodiac consists of twelve equal (30-degree) arcs, called 'signs', and is, in most cases, the zodiacal structure in the horoscope, against which are measured the planetary and cuspal positions. This tropical zodiac is to be contrasted with the *sidereal zodiac*, or constellational zodiac, which marks out the twelve unequal constellations that bear similar names to the twelve tropical signs, but which do not occupy either the same area or extent.

TRUTINE The Trutine of Hermes (*Trutina Hermetis*) is the name given to a technique designed to rectify a chart by reference to the CONCEPTION chart. The simple rule is that the degree of the ascendant or descendant at birth marks the position of the Moon at conception. Since (according to the *trutina*) the ascendant or descendant at this epoch is identical to the place of the Moon at birth, it is possible to adjust the birth chart to accommodate this fact. The simple rule has been elaborated in modern times, and is known as the *Prenatal Epoch*.

Notes

Chapter One – Introduction

1. See A. Sachs, *Journal of Cuneiform Studies* (1952),
    Vol. 6, pp. 54–7. This is not a chart in the
    modern graphic sense of the word 'horoscope';
    rather, it is a short text describing the planetary
    positions at the time of a particular birth. The
    text records data surrounding a birth that took
    place near Babylon, on 25 April 410 BC (NS).
    The name of the child is not known, but the
    record tells us that he was the son of Shuma-
    usur. The received wisdom of scholarship is that
    the Egyptian zodiac is identical with the
    Babylonian zodiac, but the orientation lore of
    the Egyptians alone proves that this is not the
    case.
2. See Cyril Fagan, 'World's Most Ancient
    Horoscope', in *Astrological Origins* (1971),
    pp. 59–74. The Irish astrologer, Cyril Fagan
    (1896–1970), was strongly attracted to the
    Egyptian culture. His works are sometimes
    difficult to follow and, while charged with both
    conviction and enthusiasm, they are not always
    accurate in detail. Even so, his general
    conclusions are often extremely exciting, and
    certainly warrant further research – preferably
    by a scholar more familiar with the Egyptian
    language and history than was Fagan.
3. The hieroglyphic is from E.A. Wallis Budge, *A
    Hieroglyphic Vocabulary to the Theban Recension of
    the Book of the Dead* (1911), p. 343.
4. For the light mysteries of Mnajdra (only one of
    the several light-temples in Malta) see Paul I.
    Micallef, *Mnajdra Prehistoric Temple: A Calendar
    in Stone* (1989). For the light mysteries of
    Loughcrew, see Tim O'Brien, *Light Years Ago: A
    Study of the Cairns of Newgrange and Cairn T
    Loughcrew Co. Meath Ireland* (1992). For
    Stonehenge, see (for example) R.J.C. Atkinson,
    Stonehenge (1956). For a general overview of
    such light magic, see E.C. Krupp, *Echoes of the
    Ancient Skies: the Astronomy of Lost Civilizations*
    (1983).
5. A dramatic picture of this precisely timed
    stream of sunlight is reproduced in E.G.
    Richards, *Mapping Time: the Calendar and its
    History* (1998), p. 142.
6. See Krupp, *Echoes of the Ancient Skies*, p. 257.
7. For the merging of the daughter Sept with the
    father Ra, and for the Denderah orientation to
    Sirius, see J. Norman Lockyer, *The Dawn of
    Astronomy: A Study of the Temple-Worship and
    Mythology of the Ancient Egyptians* (1894), pp.
    196–7.
8. The painting was executed by Sargent in the
    studio of the artist Edwin Abbey at Fairford,
    Gloucestershire, between 1892 and 1894. It
    had been painted on canvas, which was
    marouflaged on to the walls and ceiling of the
    library in Boston.
9. Sargent appears to have copied the hieroglyphic
    from John Kendrick, *Ancient Egypt under the
    Pharaohs* (1850): see the symbol representing
    the month of Epiphi, in figure 1.
10. See for example, E.A. Wallis Budge, *An
    Egyptian Hieroglyphic Dictionary* (1978 edn), Vol.
    1, p. 520b. The demotic for Gemini, which
    would have been used at about the time of the
    carving of the Denderah planisphere, was
    Na-hetru.
11. The medieval image of the Geminian Siamese
    twins is from the *Liber Albumazar*, British

Library, Sloane MS 3983, f. 8ᵛ (see also the interesting variant on f. 45ʳ). The more carnal twins are from the sphere in Nicolas le Rouge, *Le grant kalendrier & compost des Bergiers avecq leur Astrologie* (*c.* 1490) p. E.xxxv.

12. In Chapter 5, we shall examine an example of this vertical division of the head and face in the magnificent statue of *Newton after Blake*, by the modern sculptor, Paolozzi, in the forecourt of the British Library.

13. See Fagan, *Astrological Origins*, pp. 59–74. Fagan's version of the horoscope for the beginning of the Sothic era in 2767 BC (with Sirius heliacal, and Venus, Mars, Jupiter and Saturn in Cancer) is on p. 74.

14. The imagery of the two children, or twins, in relation to Gemini and Christ has been interpreted in many different ways. See, however, David Ovason, *The Two Children: A Study of the Two Jesus Children in Literature and Art* (2001).

15. In the years prior to Sargent undertaking the painting, there had been a widespread interest in Europe in Egyptian esoteric thought, spear-headed by Masonic interest in quasi-Egyptian symbolism, and by the French discovery of the meanings of the hieroglyphics. In London, the Mason, Marsham Adams, had been lecturing to general audiences on his discoveries concerning the esoteric teachings of ancient Egypt. His first published work on the subject was in *New Review* in 1894 and, in the following year, appeared *The House of the Hidden Places*, an amended form of which is now available in *The Book of the Master of the Hidden Places* (1933). Earlier publications available to Sargent and touching on Egyptian esoteric thought included Blavatsky's two masterpieces, *Isis Unveiled* (1877) and *The Secret Doctrine* (1888).

16. So far as I can determine, the American astrologer John Hazelrigg did not publish his version of the chart for Independence until 1900: for reasons best known to himself, in this chart he emphasised the position of Aldebaran, which was in the same degree as Uranus. See J. Hazelrigg, *Metaphysical Astrology* (1900), p. 16.

Hazelrigg was influenced by the English-born astrologer, Luke Broughton, who had emphasised the role of Uranus (which he called Herschel) as a contributing factor in the call for Independence. See *Broughton's Monthly Planet Reader and Astrological Journal* (1 February 1861), Vol. 2, No. 2, p. 1.

17. The chart was cast for 02:00 PM local mean time, on 4 July 1776, at Philadelphia.

18. It is from Virgil's *Eclogue* IV, line 5. For an analysis of the incorrect form of the Latin, and for a note on various works dealing with the Messianic quality of the poem, see David Ovason, *The Secret Symbols of the Dollar Bill* (2004), pp. 178–9.

19. For a Masonic text which accounts for the Masonic 'Blazing Star' as an image of Anubis, the Dog Star, alongside the proposition that Sirius had descended from ancient times to the Freemasons, see John Fellows, *Exposition of the Mysteries, or Religious Dogmas and Customs of the Ancient Egyptians, Pythagoreans and Druids* (1835).

20. See F. Gettings, 'An Ancient Sigil Revived', in *Astrology: The Astrologer's Quarterly* (1977), Vol. 51, No. 1, pp. 5–7.

21. The abbreviation is for the Greek, 'ωροσκόπος; see *Abbréviations Grecques Copiées par Ange Politien et Publiées dans le Glossaire Grec de Du Cange* (British Library press number, Ac. 5336/3).

22. Those medieval charts that located the ascendant at the top of the figure remind one of certain early maps (for example, the famous *Mappa Mundi* of Hereford) which generally located the eastern point at the top, as representative of Eden.

23. This association, between the left-hand and the ascendant, is not universal in modern astrology. I give examples of other methods among my illustrative charts.

24. The words *Imum Coeli* mean 'the lowest point in the heavens'.

25. The symbolism is sufficiently obvious to esotericists. Symbolically, the southern point of the vertical is linked with Capricorn, the oppo-

site northern point with Cancer. Porphyry called these the Gates of Death and Birth (respectively): see Porphyry, *De Antro Nympharum* (The Cave of the Nymphs).

26. Fagan, *Astrological Origins*, pp. 92–3.

27. The original planisphere was liberated by Napoleon's scholars and is now badly sited in the Louvre (Paris). A quality cast of the original has been fitted into the temple of Osiris at Denderah. An equally good quality cast, which is perfectly accessible and well lit, is in the Rosicrucian Museum at San José, California. One delightful piece of symbolism (no doubt unconscious) is that the same pot-bellied Taurit, who is the polar constellation in the Denderah planisphere, is also the guardian outside the Museum at San José.

28. The outer circle is based on the zodiacal series in C. Aq. Libra, *Astrology: Its Technics and Ethics* (1917), pp. 38–49.

29. Anthony Grafton, *Cardano's Cosmos: The Worlds and Works of a Renaissance Astrologer* (1999), p. 11.

30. For those interested in the use of horoscopy in literature, see J.C. Eade, *The Forgotten Sky: A Guide to Astrology in English Literature* (1984).

31. A useful survey of the different astrological symbols is given in F. Gettings, *Dictionary of Occult, Hermetic and Alchemical Sigils* (1981).

32. The images are from Leopold of Austria, *De Astrorum Scientia* (1489).

33. See Roger Beck, 'Interpreting the Ponza Zodiac', in *Journal of Mithraic Studies* (1976), Vol. 1, No. 1, p. 10: Beck has derived the terms from F. Nau, 'La cosmographie au VIIe siècle chez les Syriens', in *Revue de l'orient chrétien*, Vol. 15, pp. 225–4.

34. The diagram has been abstracted from the title-page of Johann Daniel Mylius, *Opus Medico-Chymicum* (1618). The position of the indeterminate Caput and Cauda, against Gemini and Sagittarius, relates to the theory of exaltations.

35. John of Seville, *Epitome totius astrologiae* (published as late as 1548).

36. The printed chart is from Junctinus, *Speculum Astrologiae* (1583); it appears to have been cast for 15 June, rather than the 14th indicated within the quadrate. The manuscript version is a copy of that given in Cardan's *C Genitura*, derived from a manuscript series bound into a copy of Luca Gaurica's *Tractatus astrologicus* (1552), and reproduced by Grafton, *Cardano's Cosmos*, p. 88.

37. By far the most useful book on different charting methods, especially in connection with the mathematics involved in the various houses, is J.D. North, *Horoscopes and History* (1986).

38. See, for example, the bordered horoscope for 17 June 1066 and 17 June 1082, from the Cairo Geniza, reproduced by North, *Horoscopes and History*, p. 91.

39. See, for example, British Library MS Sloane 428 f. 123v.

40. The chart is from Conrad Celtes, *Proseuticum ad Fridericum III Pro Laurea Apollinari* (1487), p. 6v.

41. The figure is from a German almanac for 1491, reproduced in Albert Schramm, *Der Bilderschmuck der Frühdrucke* (1930), Vol. 13, no. 43. Clearly, the astrologer who cast this chart did not have access to accurate tables. Jupiter was in 01.01 Gemini, rather than in Taurus; Saturn was in 05.44 Aquarius, rather than in Capricorn.

42. A fine horoscope which contains sigils for the fixed stars is in the manuscript made for King Wenceslas IV, *c.* 1400, Clm 826 f. 1r, in the Bayerische Staatsbibliothek, Munich. A reproduction is in Claire Fanger, *Conjuring Spirits: Texts and Traditions of Medieval Ritual Magic* (1998), p. 132. A wide number of sigils for the 'fifteen stars' was channelled into the West by way of Agrippa's influential *De Occulta Philosophia* (1534); unfortunately, some of these sigils were incorrectly copied, and have been widely transmitted in this incorrect form. For a series of unsullied medieval sigils, from a medieval manuscript in the Bodleian, see Joan Evans, *Magical Jewels of the Middle Ages and the Renaissance* (1922), pp. 246–9.

43. John Kepler, *Tabula Rudolphinae* (1627): all the planets are referred to in this work as both 'planets' and 'stars'; see, for example, *Stellae Martis*, on p. 60.
44. See, for example, Frederick H. Cramer, *Astrology in Roman Law and Politics* (1954), p. 14.
45. There is a delightful reference to Ptolemy in a fourteenth-century manuscript copy of the *Secreta Secretorum*, now in the Bodleian; this insists that while Ptolemy was certainly a 'fulle wiseman', he was 'no king'. See Bodley MS 943 f. 84.
46. The celestial globe of Jacob and Arnold Van Langren, dated 1589, is in the National Maritime Museum, London.
47. See Reinhold Ebertin, *Fixed Stars and their Interpretation* (1971), English translation of *Die Bedeutung der Fixsterne*, pp. 39–40. 'Mata Hari' was Margaretha Geertruida Zelle, born at Leeuwarden in the Netherlands, on 7 August 1876.
48. Ptolemy, *Tetrabiblos*, II.3. (The edition most widely available in modern times is that edited and translated by F.E. Robbins, for the Loeb Classical Library, in 1940.)
49. See *ibid*.
50. The mechanism of the eclipse that fell on 21 June 168 BC, prior to the battle of Pydna, had been painstakingly explained to the gathered cohorts.
51. See Cramer, *Astrology in Roman Law*, p. 114.
52. For useful notes on the horoscope of Augustus, see A.E. Housman, 'Manilius, Augustus, Tiberius, Capricornus and Libra', in the *Classical Quarterly* (1913), Vol. 7, No. 2, pp. 109–14.
53. The image is from Martin Landsberg, *Almanac for the Year 1487*. This eclipse was dealt with by the Italian astrologer, Baldinus de Baldnis, of Bologna, who concluded that its effects would last for five years. Few modern astrologers would claim so long a period of influence for any eclipse – usually, the limit is about six months on either side of the time of the eclipse. For Baldinus, see Lynn Thorndike, *A History of Magic and*

Experimental Science (1934), Vol. 6, p. 461.
54. As a matter of fact the depiction of the traditional sigils for opposition and conjunction, with their bowls darkened, appeared in some sixteenth-century charts. They have been widely adopted in modern times: for example, they are used consistently by the American astrologer Neil F. Michelsen, *Tables of Planetary Phenomena* (1990 etc.).
55. Ptolemy, *Tetrabiblos*, II.4 – what Ptolemy writes of the charts of cities is applicable to the charts of individuals.
56. The solar eclipse of 20 July 1982 fell in 27.42 Cancer (and, according to eclipse lore, activated the opposite degree, in the sign Capricorn). In the birth chart of Princess Diana, Saturn was in 27.49 Capricorn. For a summary of the effective eclipses in the life of Diana, see David Ovason, *The Book of the Eclipse: the Hidden Influences of Eclipses* (1999), pp. 153–7.
57. The horoscope cast for the moment of this eclipse of 2 September 1997 (which fell in 09.34 Virgo) is intimately linked with Diana's birth chart, as follows:

Mercury at solar eclipse 2 Sep. 1997:	06.52 Virgo
Pluto in chart of Diana:	06.03 Virgo
Uranus at solar eclipse 2 Sep. 1997:	05.26 Aquarius
Jupiter in chart of Diana:	05.06 Aquarius
Neptune at solar eclipse 2 Sep 1997:	27.32 Capricorn
Saturn in chart of Diana:	27.49 Capricorn.

58. See Cramer, *Astrology in Roman Law*, p. 190.
59. This description of the chart is discussed by O. Neugebauer and H.B. Hoesen, *Greek Horoscopes* (1959), pp. 98–9, and reproduced in horoscopic form as number L.97.II, on p. 221. I have adhered approximately to the horoscopic standardisation used by Neugebauer in my own version of the chart, and (like Neugebauer) have used only rounded off degrees.

60. The majority of the charts are recorded in Neugebauer and Hoesen, *Greek Horoscopes*. See also David Pingree, *Vettii Valentis Antiocheni Anthologiarum* (1986).

61. The original is from a manuscript collection of charts, bound into a copy of Luca Gauricus, *Tractatus astrologicus* (1552), and reproduced by Grafton, *Cardano's Cosmos* (1999), p. 35. In the manuscript chart, there are two symbols for Fortuna. That given in 11.45 Capricorn, in the sixth house, was obviously inserted in error, and (in order to avoid confusion for the non-specialist) I have dropped it from the copy. The latitude of Brunswick is given wrongly as 51° (it is 52.15 N), so the MC is out by almost 2 degrees. Otherwise, the chart is reasonably accurate, with only Jupiter out by just over a degree; all other planets are within about a degree of accuracy.

62. The woodcut is from Stabius, *Prognosticationen des Stabius* (1503).

63. The image is from Martin Landsberg's almanac for 1488. I have had the figure copied from Schramm, *Der Bilderschmuck*, Vol. 13, no. 111, and have not considered it necessary to include the Latin texts contained within the banderoles.

64. See Ronald C. Davison, *Cycles of Destiny: Understanding Return Charts* (1990), pp. 8–29. The quotation is from p. 29.

65. See, for example, Raffaella Castagnola, *I Guicciardini e le Scienze Occulte: L'oroscopo di Francesco Guicciardini Lettere di Alchimi, Astrologia e Cabala a Luigi Guicciardini* (1990).

66. Rosenberger was born on 11 May 1510 at 6:53 AM, in Augsburg. For the charting, and for the revolution charts (from 1561 to 1577), see Robert Amadou, *L'Astrologie de Nostradamus: Dossier* (1992 edn), pp. 187–97.

67. See Castagnola, *I Guicciardini*. On p. 85 is the preliminary horoscope (*figura estimativa*), corresponding to Fig. 1. On p. 87 is the syzygy chart (*oppositionis luminarium*). On p. 88 is a chart rectified by means of the animodar (*per animodar*); on p. 91 is the conception chart (*figura conceptionis*), and on p. 94, the final rectified chart (from the Trutine).

68. See, for example, the *Figura per animodar* in Castagnola, *I Guicciardini*, p. 88.

69. This rectification by the trutina illustrates one of the medieval techniques. According to the modern Prenatal Epoch, because the Moon is above the Earth, and decreasing in light, then its epochal position should be reflected on the descendant.

70. For this quotation, see G.R.S. Mead, 'The Main Source of the Trismegistic Literature According to Manetho, High Priest of Egypt', in *Thrice-Greatest Hermes: Studies in Hellenistic Theosophy and Gnosis* (1906; in the 1964 reprint), Vol. 1, p. 69. Some of the horoscopes of Vettius Valens are preserved in Neugebauer and Hoesen, *Greek Horoscopes*: see the examples studied between pp. 81 and 131.

71. The medieval work that deals most clearly with the seven planetary angels is Trithemius, *De Septem Secundadeis* (1522). Nostradamus, like many other sixteenth-century astrologers, was deeply impressed by Trithemius' work, and uniquely incorporated the dating system into his quatrains. See David Ovason, *The Secrets of Nostradamus: A Radical New Interpretation of the Master's Prophecies* (2001), pp. 101–20.

72. Henry Miller, *Big Sur and the Oranges of Hieronymus Bosch* (1958). References are to the 1962 reprint, p. 287.

Chapter Two

1. See A.L. Rowse, *Simon Forman: Sex and Society in Shakespeare's Age* (1974).

2. For example, P.I.H. Naylor, *Astrology: An Historical Examination* (1967), pp. 80–1, wrongly claims that the sculptured images are horoscopic.

3. See Alan Bott, *The Heraldry in Merton College, Oxford* (2001), pp. 202–3.

4. See John Chamber, *A Treatise against Judiciall Astrology* (1601), p. 37.

5. Porphyry, *De Antro Nympharum*; see Sections 9–11 in the Thomas Taylor translation, or sections XX–XXIII in the Greek edition, *Των Νυμφων Αντρου*, of Holstenius (1792).

6. See Rowse, *Simon Forman*, p. 33.

7. I have borrowed the symbol from H.P. Blavatsky, *The Secret Doctrine* (1888), Vol. 2, p. 591; she identifies the symbol as an image of the *septenary MAN*.

8. In the play the emphasis is humorously scatological and the scarab appears in the form of a giant dung-beetle, but Dee was familiar with the symbolism of the Egyptian variety, the *Scarabaeus sacer* (see note 10, below). For some of the underlying symbolism, see B.B. Rogers, *The Peace of Aristophanes Acted at Athens at the Great Dionysia, B.C. 421* (1913), notes on pp. 17–25.

9. The hieroglyphic for Kheper is from E.A. Wallis Budge, *An Egyptian Hieroglyphic Dictionary* (1920), Vol. I, p. 543.

10. John Dee, *Monas Hieroglyphica* (1564), Theorem XVIII: the beetle is called by Dee both *Scarabeus* and *Heliocantharis* – no doubt to differentiate its earthly and spiritual natures.

11. Rowse, *Simon Forman*, p. 188.

12. See, for example, John Heydon, *An Astrological Discourse with mathematical demonstrations … together with an astrological judgment upon the great conjunction of Saturn and Jupiter, 1603*. This appears not to have been published until 1650.

13. See Benjamin Woolley, *The Queen's Conjuror: The Life and Magic of Dr. Dee* (2001), pp. 321–2.

14. Rowse, *Simon Forman*, pp. 258.

15. *Ibid.*, pp. 260–1.

16. See James Crossley (ed.), *Autobiographical Tracts of Dr. John Dee, Warden of the College of Manchester* (1851), in *Remains Historical and Literary … of Lancaster and Chester, published by the Chetham Society* (1851) Vol. 24, p. 21 (2).

17. See Ben Jonson, *Epicoene, or the Silent Woman*, IV.i.150. For the horoscope, see V.i.17ff, where Amorous La Foole explains that Epicoene's servant carries a box of instruments. 'Like a surgeon?' asks Clerimont. 'No, the box is for *mathematics* [i.e., for astrology], that he might draw maps of every place, and person …' In Jonson's *The Divell is an Asse*, Forman is mentioned twice, once as 'Oracle-Forman' (see II. viii. 33).

18. See Bodleian Library, Ashmole MS 356, art. 5, f. 34, which is in Dee's autograph.

19. *Ibid.*, p. 1. This is the only lengthy horoscopic interpretation to have survived in Dee's hand. By modern reckoning, Sidney was born at 07:49 AM, on 30 November 1554.

20. *Ibid.*, p. 15. Dee gave Mars in 15.58 Virgo, when we know it to have been in 15.07 Virgo.

21. *Ibid.*, p. 31. The reference to *infortunata fixa violenta Gorgono seu Caput Meduse* is to the fixed star Algol. It is not always easy to understand what Dee has in mind. For example, it is not clear why he refers to Algol as being on the sixth house: in the year of Sidney's death, the star was on the cusp of the fourth (the IC).

22. In 1552, Alphard was in 22.00 Leo. Mars was not only close to Alphard, but also to Al Jabah, then in 22.35 Leo.

23. Cardan, *De Vita Propria Liber* (1501), in the opening sentences of Chapter 41.

24. This manuscript chart is from the British Library edition of Cardan's *De Iudiciis Geniturarum* (pressmark C.112 c. 5), which is replete with marginal manuscript notes from the hand of a learned, if unidentified, astrologer.

25. Hilary M. Carey, *Courting Disaster: Astrology at the English Court and University in the Later Middle Ages* (1992), p. 259.

26. Modern astrologers argue as to precisely where the Sun should be revolved: the issue does not concern us here, but see Ronald C. Davison, *Cycles of Destiny: Understanding Return Charts* (1990), pp. 25–9.

27. The date is not given in the chart itself; however, I have determined it by means of a computerised system. The chart is not strictly accurate: the Moon, given as 4.30 Taurus, should be 3.04 Taurus. Mercury (as usual) is the delinquent: the revolved position is given as 8 Leo, when it was really in 11.48 Leo.

28. I am not sure why the sigil for Mars in this section is followed by that for the Moon, save

perhaps to point to the fact that the period in question would be dominated by aspects between the Moon and this sensitive chronocrator.

29. The Sun was the ruler of the age from twenty-three to forty-two years: this was one reason why the age of forty-two was regarded with such awe by medieval astrologers – the transition from the benign rule of the Sun to the more dramatic and demanding rule of Mars usually marked some important event or change in the life of the native.

30. The 200-year cycle was called either *media* or *trigonalis*; the 800-year cycle was called *maximus* or *climacteris*.

31. The word was sufficiently new for Bonatti (see below) to play with its two meanings, as 'advancement' and as a specialist astrological term. There is a useful modern commentary on profections in relation to Bonatti's *Liber astronomiae* in Robert Zoller, *The Lost Key to Prediction: the Arabic Parts in Astrology* (1980), pp. 225–30.

32. Because we do not know the locality of the natus for 31 July 1517, it has proved impractical to calculate the radical ascendant with any accuracy.

33. This dual rulership is a manifestation of one of the many defects of the equal house system, which always posits a Geminian tenth house with a Virgoan ascendant.

34. See James Wilson, *A Complete Dictionary of Astrology, in which every technical and abstruse term belonging to the science is minutely and correctly explained* (1880 edn). The quotations are from pp. 278–9.

35. Cardan, *De exemplis centum geniturarum* (1547); this was published as the fifth part of his *Libelli quinque*.

36. See Cardan, *De exemplis*. The Cocles chart is XVIII in the series; that of Vesalius is XCIII.

37. The portrait is from Cardan's *Libelli duo* (1538), an abridgement of *Iudicia astronomica*. The chart No. XIX from Cardan, *De Judiciis Geniturarum*. The revolution for his thirty-

fifth year is on p. 89, while his conception chart is from *Segmentum IIII*, p. 246.

38. The historian Duhem has suggested that Cardan made use of certain unpublished manuscripts by Leonardo as the basis for some of his own ideas. See Pierre Duhem, *Études sur Léonardo de Vinci* (1906), Vol. 1, pp. 223–45.

39. This was *De Vita Propria Liber*, which has been translated into both English and French. For a useful translation into French, alongside the original Latin, see Jean Dayre, *Jerome Cardan: Ma Vie* (1936).

40. Venus in the Pope's chart was exactly on the star-struck *Cor Coeli*.

41. Luca Gauricus, *Tractatus astrologicus* (1552).

42. Junctinus, *Speculum Astronomiae*. The chart of Copernicus is from p. 550; that for Mary, Queen of Scots is from p. 494.

43. See, for example, Vivian E. Robson, *The Fixed Stars and Constellations in Astrology* (1969 edn), p. 133.

44. The example is from J. Rothmann, *Chiromantiae Theorica Practica* (1595). The chart relates to a birth in Uratislavia on 17 August 1567, at ten minutes after midnight.

45. For Nostradamus as an astrologer, see Jean Dupèbe, *Nostradamus: Lettres inédites* (1983). For Sumbergius as an astrologer, see René Taylor, 'Architecture and Magic. Consideration on the Idea of the Escorial', in D. Fraser *et al.*, *Essays in the History of Architecture Presented to Rudolf Wittkower* (1969 edn), pp. 81–109. For Kratzer, see E.G.R. Taylor, *The Mathematical Practitioners of Tudor and Stuart England* (1954), pp. 12–14 and 165. For John Dee, see especially Frances A. Yates, *The Rosicrucian Enlightenment* (1972), and Woolley, *The Queen's Conjuror*.

46. These are listed by Fraser, *Essays in the History of Architecture*, p. 86, note 63.

47. Junctinus, *Compendium de Stellarum Fixarum Observationibus* (1583), p. 970.

48. Equally, the ascendant was nowhere near Pollux, in the head of the southern Twin of Gemini, which was sometimes called Hercules.

49. See Rowse, *Simon Forman*. This work suffers considerably from the fact that Rowse evidently

knew little about astrology, and seems so dismissive of the little he did know.

50. The pictures appear to have been used first in the 1579 edition of the work. See Antoine du Prat, *La fondation faicte par mes seigneur et dame, les duc, et duchesse de Nivernois pour marier doresnauant par chacun an soixante pauvres filles destituees de toutes facultez & moyens* (1588).

51. See Ruth Mortimer *et al.*, *Harvard College Library Department of Printing and Graphic Arts Catalogue of Books and Manuscripts. Part I: French 16th-Century Books* (1998), pp. 236–7.

52. For example, Copernicus dedicated *De revolutionibus* to him.

53. This material is in manuscript form, in the Vatican library; see Lynn Thorndike, *A History of Magic and Experimental Science* (1941), Vol. 5, pp. 268–9.

54. The material is preserved in manuscript in the Vatican. See, however, Thorndike, *A History of Magic*, pp. 266–7. Aguilera's reference to the directions of the zodiac of 59 minutes and 8 seconds *per diem* reveals an early use of Naibod's Measure, which must have been learned from a manuscript or some astrologer familiar with Naibod's ideas.

55. Cardan's *De Iudiciis Geniturarum* in *Libelli quinque* (1547).

56. *Ibid.*

57. The following notes should throw some light on Cardan's nomenclature. Regarding the spine, or 'curve', of Pisces: in the old star charts, each of the fishes is marked, along the curve of the back, with three stars of the fourth magnitude. Junctinus, *Compendium de Stellarum*, Vol. 2 of *Speculum Astrologiae* (1583), p. 982, numbers this star 30, and described it as *media* (that is, the middle of the three) in the spine of the southern fish. He located it in 17.24 Aries (in 1583) but claimed that it was of the nature of Jupiter parallel to Venus. Regarding Betelgeuse: Junctinus, *Compendium*, p. 983, called it Bedekgense, and placed it in 23.4 Gemini (in 1583). For the star in Auriga, see Junctinus, *ibid.*, p. 972, where it is numbered 4 in the constellation, and given the same

magnitude and equivalent planetary power. In regard to Orion, I have read the corrupt typesetting of the Latin as *summitati clavae* – a description that refers to the tip of the cudgel (*clava*) held by the cosmic giant. Junctinus does not identify the star and it receives little attention in the star maps. The four numbered stars, close to El Nath, are those identified by Robert Burnham, *Burnham's Celestial Handbook: An Observer's Guide to the Universe beyond the Solar System* (1978), Vol. 3, p. 1798ff. The epsilon of Aries is now recognised as a double, of fifth and sixth magnitudes. *Iovis sextilis* is fairly meaningless as a designation of influence: the Ptolemaic classification associates the power of *Cor Leonis* (now called Regulus) with the equivalent power of Jupiter conjunct with Mars.

58. Naibod, *Enarratio elementorum astrologiae … proposita a Valentino Nabod* [*sic*] (1560), p. 417.

59. The diagram is from Naibod, *Enarratio elementorum*, n. 58, a work that lauds Ptolemy over the Arabic tradition. The vertical word *Odiosa* means 'vexatious'. The diagram itself does not do justice to my point about the extent to which Naibod was a follower of Ptolemy. However, in the nine lines of text below this diagram, no less than six lines are quotations, in Greek, from Ptolemy's *Tetrabiblos*. These are not from the section dealing with the obeying and commanding signs, but from Book I, Chapter 15 (Περί βλεπόντων καί ισοδυναμούντων), dealing with Ptolemy's doctrine of 'Beholding signs', which are opposing signs of equal hours.

60. By such reasoning, one minute of arc was the equivalent of 6 days and 4 hours: thus 42 degrees equalled 42 years and 224 days.

61. See John Angelus, *Astrolabium planum* (1488).

62. The pictorial plates have been widely reproduced in modern works on engraving. For a complete set within a modern astrological context, see Stefano Caroti, *L'astrologia in Italia: Profezie, oroscopi e segreti celesti, degli zodiaci romani alla tradizione islamica, dalle corti rinascimentali alle scuole moderne …* (1983).

63. See Du Plessis d'Argentré, *Collectio judiciorum de novis erroribus* (1755), Vol. 1, Pt 2, pp. 327–8.

64. Luca Gauricus, *Ephemerides, Recognitae et ad Unguem Castigatae* ... (1533), p. a.ii.

65. At the ingress of 1534, the Moon was in 20.48 Cancer. At latitude 45 degrees (say for Turin) the ascendant would have been 15 Gemini.

66. The chart for Suleiman (*Solymani Ottomani Regis Turcarum Nativitas*) was available in manuscript, from Arabic sources. Later Junctinus included it in his *Speculum Astrologiae* (1583), p. 669; the solar position was 05.41 Aries.

67. See Eric St John Brooks, *Sir Christopher Hatton: Queen Elizabeth's Favourite* (1947 edn), p. 28. We must recall that in those days the imagery of 'dancing' was sometimes used in a scurrilous sense: it was often claimed (quite wrongly, as it appears) that Hatton was one of the Queen's lovers.

68. The panel is now in Northampton Art Gallery; it was acquired in 1929, as a gift from Sir Algernon Tudor-Craig. It is mentioned by Brooks, *Sir Christopher Hatton*, p. 396, but with no explanation for the zodiacal circle.

69. For the naming of the *Christopher*, see *ibid.*, p. 190. For the change of name to *Golden Hind*, and Drake's quotation, *ibid.*, p. 191. For Fenton and the fall of St Paul's spire, see *ibid.*, p. 195.

70. See, for example, Junctinus, *Compendium de Stellarum*, p. 357, where the septenaries are discussed briefly.

71. See John Maplet, *The Diall of Destiny. A Booke Very Delectable and Pleasaunt* (1581). The book was dedicated 'from Northall, the last of December, 1581, to the Right Honourable, Sir Christopher Hatton'.

72. The Latin verse on the reverse, along with a poor English translation, was published in the catalogue for the *Elizabeth* exhibition at the National Maritime Museum, Greenwich, in which the Hatton portrait was exhibit 133.

73. Hester W. Chapman, *Anne Boleyn* (1974), p. 145, who quotes 'between three and four in the afternoon'.

74. This is the opening of Letter X, in Dupèbe, *Nostradamus: Lettres inédites* (1983).

75. A complete list of these almanacs is given in Robert Benazra, *Répertoire Chronologique Nostradamique (1545–1980)* (1990).

76. For the letters, see Dupèbe, *Nostradamus*.

77. For the series of charts relating to Rosenberger, including the numerous revolutions, see Robert Amadou, *L'Astrologie de Nostradamus: Dossier* (1992 edn), pp. 187–98.

78. See Amadou, *ibid.*, pp. 191–7.

79. Dupèbe, *Nostradamus*. For an example of pressure to cast charts, see letter XXV. For an example of inability of clients to understand charts, see letter XXVI. For the astrological ring, see letter XXXI.

80. It is quatrain 1.16 – that is, the sixteenth verse of the first collection of a hundred verses. See *Les Prophéties de M. Michel Nostradamus*, published in 1557 by Antoine du Rosne, in Lyon, p. 22.

81. The image of Saturn has been cut from the title-page illustration of *Practica über die grossen und manigfeltigen Coniunction der Planeten/die imfar M.D.XXIIII. erscheinen/un ungezweiffelt vil wunderparlicher {sic} ding geperen werden*. The roundel of Pisces is from an early sixteenth-century Shepherd's Calendar.

82. For reference to the *Auge*, and for the diagram reproduced, see Jaques Bassantin, *Astronomique discourse* (1562), p. 91. The word had a limited circulation in non-specialist contexts: for example, on one device of Charles V, the Sun was depicted almost on the meridian of the zodiacal circle, with the Latin motto, *Nondum in Auge*, which can only be translated as 'not yet on the zenith'. The notion is that Charles was aspiring to higher things. See Bury Palliser, *Historic Devices, Badges, and War Cries* (1870), p. 247.

83. See *ibid.*, p. 196. The heading above the volvelle indicates that it was designed to determine the movement of the auges of the planets.

84. This is Letter I in Dupèbe, *Nostradamus*, and is addressed by Simeoni (after the usual adulatory phrasing), to *domino suo et amico*, 'his master and friend'.

85. See Gabriele Simeoni, *Les illustres observations antiques* (1558).

86. See, for example, *Biographie Universelle, Ancienne et Moderne*, Vol. 29, p. 138.

87. Gabriele Simeoni, *La Vita et Metamorfoseo di Ovidio* (1559). Here, the pictorial zodiac is revealed beneath a bust of Ovid, with the cusp between Aries and Taurus at the top. Inside the inner oval are personifications of Venus, Sun and Mercury.

88. The horoscope is from Tycho Brahe, *De cometa seu stella crinita rotunda, quae anno antecedente in Octobri & Novembri apparuit* (1586). The solar position of 9.28 Scorpio could not be valid for an ascendant of 21 Virgo. With such a solar position, the Moon would have been in 07.39 Pisces, and not in the 09.10 Pisces given. The position of Mercury in Brahe's chart could be a block-cutter's error: it should have been in 18.48 Scorpio.

89. The chart is from Tycho Brahe, *De Nova et nullius aevi memoria prius visa stella* (1573).

90. This was a technique formerly used by Arabian astrologers for dealing with speculative times or dates particularly in respect of charts for comets, the timing of which was, at best, arbitrary.

91. The chart is from Conrad Dinckmut, *Practica von Paris* (1487).

92. The chart is in the Bodleian Library, Oxford, catalogued as 4° R 9 Art, p. 1. For a reproduction, see J.C. Eade, *The Forgotten Sky: A Guide to Astrology in English Literature* (1984), p. 53. The last line in the inner quadrate refers to the trutina and animodar.

93. See Robert Burton, *The Anatomy of Melancholy*, ed. Holbrook Jackson (1963 edn), p. vii.

94. *Ibid.*, I. 18.

95. *Ibid.*, 1.37. For a more general commentary on astrology, and the influences of the planets, see Burton, *Anatomy of Melancholy*, Pt 1, Sec. 3, Mem. 1, Sub. III. (Vol. 1, pp. 397ff, in Jackson).

96. Burton's knowledge of horoscopy may be gauged from his extensive library. The historian Kiessling calculated that 3 per cent of his huge collection consisted of astrological and astronomical works. These included [301] Carlton, *Astrologomania: the madnesse of astrologers* (1624); [642] Garcaeus, *Astrologiae methodus* (1576), [650] Gauricus, *Tractatus astrologicus* (1552), [957] Leowitz, *Brevis et perspicua ratio judicandi genituras*, and [1300] Ptolemy, *Quadripartium* (1519). See Nicolas K. Kiessling, *The Library of Robert Burton* (1988).

97. The ascendant of 28.16 Aries corresponds to 09:21 local time.

98. These sets of data for the Burton family are in the preliminary pages of the vellum Latin and Anglo-Norman *Statutes of England*, preserved in the Bodleian under pressmark Marshall 132.

99. See Aubrey MS 23, p. 29. This corresponds closely to that on the memorial, with the exception that the colons are generally replaced with full-stops, and certain sigils are of a late seventeenth-century form.

100. See John Gadbury, *Cardines Coeli* (1684), p. 57. The chart reproduced here is a tracing, as many of the details in the original are illegible.

101. For Burton's own prediction of his death (seemingly from the chart he erected), see F. Madan, *Robert Burton and the Anatomy of Melancholy* (1926).

102. As a preliminary survey, Burton might have directed the Sun to Mars. This would relate approximately to events in his sixtieth year. Three degrees later on in the direction, the Sun would be directed towards 2.39 Taurus. If the conversion of Naibod was used, then Burton might have calculated the passage of the Sun over Taurus as taking place in the second degree of Taurus. In the Naibod conversion, 62 years 331 days is the arc equivalent of 62 degrees. As it was, Burton's death took place at 62 years 356 days.

103. For the most widely used book on directions, see Andrea Argolus, *Primum Mobile de directionibus* (1610). Rules derived from Argol, and certainly used later in the seventeenth century, are (for example) set down by William Lilly in *An Easie and Plaine Method Teaching How to Judge upon Nativities: The Rectification of a*

Nativitie, Trutine of Hermes, Animodar, or By Accidents (1647), pp. 651ff.

104. Tycho Brahe, *Astronomiae Instauratae Progymnasmata* (1602).

105. See Rowse, *Simon Forman*.

106. For the identification of the Dark Lady, see *ibid.*, pp. 15–16.

107. The original horoscope is in the Bodleian Library. For the full page, see *ibid.*, opp. p. 162.

108. See Cardan, *De exemplis centum geniturarum* (1663 edn), p. 498.

109. Thorndike, *op. cit.*, Vol. 5, pp. 565–6.

110. In fact, many churchmen and scholars had affirmed that the human part of Christ was subject to celestial influences. They included Albertus Magnus (who is supposed to have cast a chart for the putative date of Christ's birth), and the influential Cardinal, Pierre d'Ailly, whose subjection of Christ to the stars was seen by the early sixteenth-century Flemish astrologer Albert Pigghe as a blasphemy against both God and religion; see Thorndike, *op. cit.*, Vol. 5, p. 192.

111. See Cardan, *In Themate Nativitatis Christi erigendo*, VI, p. 199. An interesting summary of the chart, alongside a crude copy, is given by Jaques Gaffarel, *Curiositez Inouyes sur la sculpture talismanique des Persans, horoscope des patriarches et lecture des estoilles* (1629), Notae 76.

112. For a survey of nineteen medieval charts relating to the birth of Christ, see J.D. North, *Horoscopes and History* (1986), pp. 163–73.

113. Urbanus Holzmeister, *Chronologia Vitae Christi quam e fontibus digressit et ex ordine proposuit Urbanus Holzmeister* (1933). According to the Gospel of Luke, Jesus was born when Cyrenius was governor of Syria, after 6 AD. According to the Gospel of Matthew, Jesus was born under Herod: however, by the time Cyrenius was governor of Syria, with an extended super-vision over what was then Palestine, Herod was dead. For a full survey of the two tradi-tions, established by Luke and Matthew, see David Ovason, *The Two Children: A Study of the Two Jesus Children in Literature and Art* (2001).

114. The horoscope is from Cardan, *Cl. Ptolemaei De astrorum iudiciis* (1578), Lib. II, p. 164.

115. See, for example, Pico della Mirandola, *Disput-ationes adversus astrologiam divinatricem*, I, 604, n. 1 in the Eugenio Garin edition of 1946–52.

116. See Cardan, *Cl. Ptolemaei ...* p. 165. In modern times the star is called Pollux, and (in 2000 AD) was in 23.14 Cancer. In the stellar tradition, the star is said to bring great honours with danger of final ruin.

117. If one progresses the Moon given in the chart (28.5 Aries), then it does conjunct with Saturn in the second revolution, on the thirty-third year.

118. John Butler's chart, cast in 1668, which we shall examine below, is based on Morin's horo-scope. A fair copy of Butler's charting is given in the *Astrologers' Magazine* (1893), Vol. 1, No. 1, p. 7.

119. A good example is in *Liber Albumasar*, British Library, MS Sloane 3983 f. 49v. The near-illegible script below mentions both Albumasar and Albertus Magnus as supposed author of the *Speculum astronomie*. See also Fritz Saxl and Hans Meier, *Catalogue of Astrological and Mythological Illuminated Manuscripts of the Latin Middle Ages* (1953), Vol. 3, p. 268.

120. North, *Horoscopes and History*, p. 165, offers a tabulation for the four most influential Arabian charts of this kind.

121. See MS Sloane 3983 f. 49v, for which it is difficult to establish even the year.

122. The chart is from Pierre d'Ailly, *Tractatus de imagine mundi et varia ejusdem auctoris et Joannis Gersonis opuscula* (1483), f. ee2v.

123. The chart is from the *Praefatio Apologetica* of Morin's *Astrologia Gallica* (1661), p. xxiii.

124. The various inexactitudes in the chart may be partly reconciled by assuming the ascendant (0.55 Libra) as fiducial, thus placing the Moon in 26.26 Aries.

125. See Ebenezer Sibly, *A New and Complete Illustration of the Occult Sciences* (1790), No. 45, opposite p. 892.

126. Many charts have been cast for the birth of Jesus during the twentieth century. Variations cast by

the English astrologers Ronald C. Davison and John Addey are for 25 August 7 BC, at 08:24 local mean time, and give Aries on the Ascendant: see Clive Hounsome, 'Significators of Religion?' in *Astrology: The Astrologers' Quarterly* (1978), Vol. 52, No. 1, p. 9. One chart, based on the conjunction of Jupiter and Saturn in Pisces in May 7 BC, has been given by the English astrologer Dan Lloyd in the *Mercury Star Journal* (Christmas 1976); Lloyd gives the date of the conjunction of Jupiter and Saturn in Pisces as occurring on 27 May 7 BC. See also Robert Powell, *Christian Hermetic Astrology: The Star of the Magi and the Life of Christ* (1991), esp. p. 204. For the Jesus described in the Gospel of Matthew, Powell proposed a birth of 6 March 2 BC.

127. Laurence Humphrey, *The Nobles: or, of Nobilitye* (1563), sig. y vi verso; quoted by Keith Thomas, *Religion and the Decline of Magic* (1971), p. 290.

Chapter Three

1. See Michael Hunter and Annabel Gregory, *An Astrological Diary of the Seventeenth Century: Samuel Jeake of Rye 1652–1699* (1988).

2. For example, Jeake made every effort to test the validity of the Measure of Time attributed to Naibod, which constituted a very necessary adaptation of the ancient Ptolemaic principle of directing planets and angles.

3. The chart is discussed, in some detail, as being visible on the façade of the house; cf. Hunter and Gregory, *Astrological Diary*, p. 198. For Jeake's own admission that he laid the first stone, and for his own version of the foundation chart, see *ibid.*, p. 197.

4. I have been privileged to examine the stone closely, from a distance of a few inches, and I can confirm that there is no trace of a carving.

5. Although witchcraft and its attendant trials were on the decline by 1689, a series of famous trials of the Exeter Witches had been conducted in that city as late as 1682. For a view of foundations charts (that is, elections) as a

dubious spiritual activity, see Hunter and Gregory, *Astrological Diary*, p. 13 and (for Jeake) p. 230.

6. See Henry Coley, *Clavis Astrologiae Elimata; or A Key to the Whole Art of Astrology New Fil'd and Polished* (1676) and, in particular, the synopsis of contents on the title page of the Second Part (p. 135).

7. Jeake read Morin's *Astrologia Gallica* between 3 April 1684 and 22 January 1685, and was sufficiently enthused to put some of the precepts into action. For example, on 5 September 1686, he noted in his diary that he had just completed his wife's nativity, following exactly the method and principles set out by Morin. See the Selmes papers (mss. 53/1) in Rye Museum.

8. The historian, Bernard Capp, quotes the sentence in a well-constructed summary of Gadbury's position: see Bernard Capp, *English Almanacs (1500–1800): Astrology and the Popular Press* (1979), p. 184.

9. Ann Geneva, *Astrology and the Seventeenth-century Mind: William Lilly and the Language of the Stars* (1995), p. 9.

10. For 'Astrall Causes', see Hunter and Gregory, *Astrological Diary*, p. 18.

11. For Jeake's horoscope, with 28.38 Aries on the tenth, see *ibid.*, p. 263. Caput was in 5.19 Aries.

12. For the chart of 8 June 1680, to mark Jeake's visit to Mrs Barbara Harteshorn, see *ibid.*, p. 150. The cusp of the seventh was 9.00 Aries. Cauda was in 5.27 Aries.

13. For the chart of 14 June 1680, to mark the actual proposal of marriage, see *ibid.*, p. 151. The cusp of the seventh was 19 Aries.

14. For the marriage chart, see *ibid.*, p. 155, where the correction of the sigil for Venus to one for Taurus is still quite visible. Uranus was in 18.25 Aries – an invisible placing, so far as Jeake was concerned, that was to inexplicably haunt his marriage.

15. See Selmes MS 56/1, fols 35v and 37, in the Rye Museum.

16. Henry Coley was born in 1633, and had published his *Clavis* in 1676. There are

indications that Jeake knew Coley and had read his influential book, which was essentially a collection of selected texts from Guido Bonatti and Cardan.

17. For notes on Evans, see Capp, *English Almanacs*, p. 305.

18. See Hunter and Gregory, *Astrological Diary*. The quotation is from p. 154. The chart for his first approach to his future mother-in-law is on p. 150. That cast to elect a time for him to propose is on p. 151.

19. Among the most outstanding elements, engineered by the choice of this time and date, is the rising Jupiter in Gemini, the triple conjunction of Sun, Cauda and Mercury in Pisces, trine Saturn in 16.01 Cancer, and the opposition of Jupiter with the Moon, in Sagittarius. Jeake may have realised that Saturn was on the star Castor (then in 15.47 Cancer). In the tradition to which Jeake subscribed, this placing was held to be unfavourable to marriage and to bring about the early sickness of children. As a matter of fact, in the tabulation of the fifty principal fixed stars in the fold-out plate of Henry Coley's *Anima Astrologiae* (1676), the position for Castor was given as 16.30 Cancer for 1700, which means that an astrologer using this text would have assumed that, in 1681, Castor was in 16.14 Cancer.

20. The abbreviation *g* stands for *gradus*, or degree.

21. William Lilly, *Christian Astrology: Modestly Treated in Three Books* (1647), Bk 1, p. 112.

22. Jeake's own question concerning Saturn (posed beneath the placing for Saturn) – is the planet retrograde or is it static? – is easy to answer. At the time of his marriage, Saturn was in 15.39 Cancer, and retrograde.

23. See Hunter and Gregory, *Astrological Diary*, p. 155. The word 'detrified' is an adaptation, for oral use, of the specialist astrological term 'detriment' – that is, 'rendered detrimental'; see Glossary, p. 249.

24. Francis Crow, *The Vanity and Impiety of Judicial Astrology* (1690), A2r–A2v.

25. John Gadbury, *The Jamaica Almanack: or, an Astrological Diary for the Year of Our Lord God,*

1673. Gadbury's tables are calculated for 16.00 N latitude, whereas the actual position of Port Royal is 17.55 N. The quotation is from the foot of the page tabulating the essential dignities.

26. For a sample chart, see British Library, MS Sloane 1684, f. 46v.

27. See, for example, Dryden's comedy, *An Evening's Love, or the Mock Astrologer* (1668), which was an adaptation of Corneille's *Le Feint Astrologue*. See also his delightful ambiguity concerning the chart and birth day of Charles II, in the poem, 'Astraea Redux'.

> That Star that at your Birth shone out so bright
> It stain'd the duller Suns Meridian light . . .

The truth is that, at about noon on the day of Charles' birth, a star (perhaps a Nova) had shone visibly in the skies over London. It was naturally taken as a propitious omen by Royalists, such as Dryden. The delightful (and oft unrecognised) ambiguity in the reference to the star rests on the fact that, at the birth of the prince, the powerful star Capella was within a degree of his Sun. In 1630, Capella was in 16.50 Gemini: Charles' Sun was in 17.24 Gemini.

28. Kenneth Young, *John Dryden: A Critical Biography* (1954), p. xvi. Young saw astrology as representative of the romantic and suppressed side of Dryden's nature (*ibid.*, p. 37).

29. *Ibid.*, p. 62.

30. The first is in Ashmole, MS 243 f. 209: this was cast for 5:33:16 PM. The second is in Aubrey MS 23, f. 87, and seems to have been cast by John Gadbury: this gives an ascendant of 25.07 Capricorn.

31. The engraving is after the frontispiece to J.B. Riccioli, *Almagestum novum* (1651).

32. The tables of houses for London, Berlin and Brussels are from Luca Gauricus, *Ephemerides Recognitae et ad Unguem Castigatae* (1533).

33. The method of house division was only one of the fields of astrology he sought to reform. He adjusted the Ptolemaic system of directing (for which he had a profound respect) by introduc-

ing what is now called the solar arc. He rejected the method of solar returns. See *Quaestionum physiomathematicarum libri tres* (1650).

34. The manuscript, entitled *Collectio geniturarum*, is preserved in the Bodleian Library as Aubrey MS 23.

35. These are the charts for Carleton, on pp. 54r and 54v.

36. Even in specialist histories, Hollar's birth is recorded merely as taking place in 1607 – see, for example, Vladimír Denkstein, *Hollar: Drawings* (1977), p. 6. According to Aubrey MS 23 (f. 121v), he was born on 23 July 1607, at about 08:00 AM. Hollar seems to have given the data directly to Elias Ashmole, in the 1650s: see Ashmole MS 3, f. 12. Penn's Moon was recorded as being in 21.36 Leo, but was in 21.50 of that sign. It is possible that Penn's chart (f. 90a–v) was cast for sunrise, to meet an unknown time of birth.

37. I have abstracted these aspects from the somewhat confused commentary in Coley, *Clavis*, pp. 14–16.

38. Joshua Childrey, *Indago Astrologica: Or, A Brief and Modest Enquiry into Some Principle Points of Astrology ...* (1652), Sect. 17, p. 9.

39. See M.L. Todd, *Total Eclipses of the Sun* (rev. edn 1900), pp. 112–13.

40. At certain periods, and in certain countries, the two artificials were each divided into six two-hour periods, confusingly still called 'hours'.

41. See C.R. Cheney, *Handbook of Dates for Students of English History* (1948), p. 10. I have selected Trafalgar to some purpose: this was the last important sea-battle to be so recorded by the Navy. Shortly afterwards log-books were initiated in accordance with the now-familiar midnight-time commencement of day.

42. Nelson was born on 29 September 1758: the data are given for midday.

43. An excellent synopsis of the reforming movement may be found in Capp, *English Almanacs*, pp. 180ff, who recognises the contribution made by almanacs to the reform of astrology.

44. J. Goad, *Astro-Meteorologica, or Aphorisms and Discourses of the Bodies Coelestial* (1686). For the suicide rates, see pp. 506–7.

45. Keith Thomas, *Religion and the Decline of Magic: Studies in Popular Beliefs in Sixteenth- and Seventeenth-Century England* (1971), p. 327.

46. Among the influential reformers whose horoscopes remain pedestrian, in spite of their reformative tendencies, are William Ramesey, whose reforms were set out in *Astrologia Restaurata* (1653), and whose critique of the inept and mercantile astrologer is near-hilarious in its invective: see *The Character of a Quack-astrologer: Or, the Spurious Prognosticator Anatomiz'd* (1673). Godson's reforms are set out in *Astrologia Reformata* (1696). Both Jeremy Shakerley, who not only observed the transit of Mercury (the second man ever to do so), but discussed the phenomenon in his *Almanac* for 1651 (B7 vff), and John Partridge, the title of whose book, *Opus Reformatum* (1693) and the contents of another, *Tabulae Britannicae*, reveal his attitude to astrology, were of great service to their contemporaries. It was Partridge who recommended that Ptolemy's *Tetrabiblos* be made available in an English translation – thus aiding popularisation of the art. Unfortunately, this was not achieved until the first year of the eighteenth century, when the Irish astrologer John Whalley brought out his translation of Ptolemy's *Quadrapartite*.

47. The chart itself, alongside a more conventional version, is in the Bodleian Library, Aubrey MS 23, f. 54v. It was cast for 12:18 PM on 12 February 1620 at Shepton Mallet, Somerset. Here, I have reproduced my own version of the latter chart. For further details of the horoscopes, see J.D. North, *Horoscopes and History* (1986), pp. 182–4.

48. It is possible that Brouncker was experimenting with the old Greek system of the *oktopodos*, or eight-house system which entailed marking the centre of each house with a cusp, designed to indicate its primal power. However, it is more likely that the chart was derived from the medical tradition.

49. John Gadbury, *The Nativity Of the Late King Charls Astrologically and Faithfully Performed ...* (1659).

50. See [I. Boulliau], *Ismaelis Bullialdi Astronomia Philolaica* (1645), II. *Tabulae Philociaca*, p. 226, which is from Chysococca's *Catalogus Tabulis Persicis*.

51. See Gadbury, *Nativity of King Charls*, p. 22.

52. Antonius Bonattis, *Universa Astrosophia Naturalis* (1687), p. 44: his actual words were, *... Antiscium suum vibrabit*.

53. Gadbury, *Nativity of King Charls*, p. 29.

54. In the *Astronomical Tables* of George Hartgill, which John Gadbury had helped revise for 1670, the alternative names of Cal and Alatrab were given to the star. In these revised tables, it was located in 5.14 Sagittarius – a few minutes deviant from modern tables (*ibid.*, pp. 14–15).

55. The Sun in Charles' chart was actually closer to the evil Rastaban than to Antares: in 1600, Rastaban was in 6.19 Sagittarius.

56. Gadbury, *Nativity of King Charls*, p. 14.

57. Strangely enough, Gadbury seems to have missed one of the secrets of the beheading star, Algol, in respect to the King's natal chart. The fact is that Algol (20.39 Taurus) was much closer to the antiscion of Saturn (23.52 Taurus) than it was to the Midheaven.

58. See for example, C.V. Wedgwood, *The Trial of Charles I* (1964; in the 1970 edn, pp. 188–93).

59. See 'Kepler's Horoscope of Wallenstein', translated by W. Becker, from Otto Struve, *Beitrage zu Festellung des Verhältnisses von Keppler zu Wallenstein*, in *Modern Astrology* (1911), Vol. 8, pp. 71–83.

60. For the 1652 eclipses, see William Lilly, *Annus Tenebrosus, or the Dark Year* (1652); the 1645 chart was published in Lilly's *The Starry Messenger*, and is discussed in Geneva, *Astrology and the Seventeenth-century Mind*, pp. 248–51. For the mock Suns, see *ibid.*, pp. 227–8: a sample chart, from *The Starry Messenger*, is given on p. 233.

61. For the vermin chart, See C.H. Josten, *Elias Ashmole (1617–1692)* (1966), Vol. IV, p. 1698, entry for 18 December 1681. For the Golden Age, see Martin Harvey, 'Predictive Astrology in the Golden Age', in the the *Astrological Journal* (Autumn 1968), Vol. 10, No. 4, pp. 5–11.

62. This is now Bodleian manuscript Aubrey 23, from which I have already given a number of charts. See Josten, *op. cit.*, IV, p. 1698, entry 20 December 1681.

63. The statute was 5 Elizabeth, c 16. For an account of the background to the statute, see Rossell Hope Robins, *The Encyclopedia of Witchcraft and Demonology* (1970 edn), pp. 156–9.

64. Culpeper, *Catastrophe Magnatum, or The Fall of Monarchie . . .* (1652).

65. See Capp, *English Almanacs*, pp. 79–80.

66. See Culpeper, *Catastrophe Magnatum*, pp. 65ff.

67. See William Hunt, *Demonstration of Astrology. Or, A Brief Discourse, Proving the Influence of the Sun, Moon, and Stars, over this Terraqueous Globe* (1696). See esp. p. 27.

68. See *ibid.*, p. 28.

69. For an interesting comment on the motto, see the cipher note on the title-page of Ashmole's copy of Lilly's *Christian Astrology*, now in the Bodleian (Ashmole MS 312). The cipher has been translated by Josten, *Elias Ashmole*, Vol. 1, p. 23, note 1.

70. For Lilly and the Regiomontanus *Modus Rationalis* house system, see Lilly, *Christian Astrology* (1647), Bk 3, pp. 519–24.

71. See John Gadbury, *Collectio Geniturarum: or, A Collection of Nativities, in CL Genitures* (1662 edn), p. 188. As a matter of fact, Gadbury seems to have been writing the truth. In his almanac of 1645, Lilly *does* claim to have had the Moon in Pisces – which would have given him a birth day on 5 or 6 May 1602. However, in several other places he recorded his birth as 'Diseworth, seven miles south of the town of Derby, on the first day of May, 1602'. The quotation is from 'Life of William Lilly', which prefaces Lilly's *An Introduction to Astrology* in Zadkiel's reprint of 1853.

72. For *New Model Astrology* (a sly, if outdated, dig at the New Model Army of Cromwell), see Coley, *Clavis*, p. 265.

73. Try as they might, they would not understand (at least, this side of the grave) what astrological factors could drive them apart. The disruptive Uranus in the horoscope of Gadbury was in 5.28 Virgo, and dangerously close to Lilly's Mars, in 6.31 Virgo.

74. Cromwell's chart is preserved in Gadbury, *Collectio*, p. 145.

75. *Ibid.*, p. 145.

76. See, for example, Geneva, *Astrology and the Seventeenth-century Mind*.

77. All the charts are from Lilly, *Christian Astrology* (1647), Bk 2: for death of husband, p. 415; battle of Alsford, p. 399; lady's marriage, p. 385; Canterbury hanged or no, p. 419; whether he would obtain parsonage, p. 437; and whether the sailor would return, p. 417.

78. For the analysis, see Lilly, *Christian Astrology*, Bk 2, p. 438.

79. For a full definition of the term, see *ibid.*, Bk 1, p. 111.

80. For a full definition of the term, see *ibid.*, Bk 1, p. 112.

81. The chart and analysis are from *ibid.*, Bk 2, pp. 162–4.

82. The horoscope is from *ibid.*, p. 162. It is worth recording that Lilly (no doubt due to the poor quality of the tables available to him) has obtained an incorrect ascendant degree. I point to this error because the correct ascendant would have changed radically (for example) the cusp of the second house, which plays an important role in his analysis.

83. A few of Childrey's manuscript notes, relating mainly to the comet of 1652, are preserved in the S. Hartlib Collection of manuscripts in the British Library (pressmark Sloane 427).

84. See Childrey, *Indago Astrologica*.

85. See Renée Simon, *Henry de Boulainviller: Historien, Politique, Philosophe, Astrologue 1658–1722* (1946), p. 664.

86. Childrey, *Indago Astrologica*, Section 21, p. 11.

87. See Joshua Childrey, *Syzygiasticon instauratum, or, an Ephemeris of the Places and Aspects of the Planets, as they respect the Sun as Center of their Orbes* (1643).

88. *Ibid.*, p. A.4v. Gadbury mentions Fitzsmith in *Britain's Royal Star* (1661), p. 20.

89. See Childrey, *Indago Astrologica*, p. 7.

90. The graphic of the Tychonian system is from Andrea Argolus, *Ephemerides Ab Anno MDCXL Ad Annum MDCC*, p. 13.

91. Childrey, *Syzygiasticon*, p. A.3r.

92. *Ibid.*, p. A.3v.

93. *Ibid.*

94. The word triplicities, as used by Childrey, has not exactly changed its meaning, yet its application has changed entirely – it is no longer regarded as a validation of Dignity.

95. See Charles Coulston Gillispie (ed.), *Dictionary of Scientific Biography* (1971), Vol. 3, p. 248.

96. See British Library MS Sloane, 1684, f. 25r. The chart preserved by, and perhaps originally cast by, John Partridge, in Egerton MS 2378, f. 178v, is for 2 September 1616.

97. For two charts cast by Bernard for the foundation of London, see British Library, *Bernard Nativities of Eminent Persons*, Sloane 1683, p. 22v, and Sloane 1797, f. 37r.

98. See, for example, Sloane 1707, ff. 35–8. For a brief exposition of Bernard's method, see homas, *Religion and the Decline of Magic*, pp. 327–8.

99. The 'hieroglyphic' appeared, like that of the bull, in Lilly's *Monarchy or No Monarchy* (1651).

100. See, Sloane 1683, fol. 178v. In order to make the delicate script legible, I have had the entries copied.

101. See *A Catalogue of the Library of the Late Learned Dr. Francis Bernard, Fellow of the College of Physicians, and Physician to S. Batholomew's Hospital* (1698).

102. See Richard S. Baldwin, *The Morinus System of Horoscope Interpretation: Astrologiae Gallicae Liber Vigesimus Primus* (1974), unpaginated introduction.

103. *Ibid.*, p. 13.

104. L.F. Alfred Maury, *La Magie et l'Astrologie dans l'Antiquité et au Moyen Age, ou Étude sur les superstitions païennes qui se sont perpétués jusqu'à nos jours* (1860), p. 215.

105. The chart is from p. 4 of the anonymous, *The Nativity of the Most Valiant and Puissant Monarch*

Lewis The Fourteenth King of France and Navarre (1680). I have selected this figure from the numerous available horoscopes because it contains a number of interesting fixed stars. It was cast for 23:03, according to the contemporaneous French time system, which is the equivalent, in modern terms, of 11:57 AM local time, Saint Germain. This work contains a very useful speculum of directions for every day of the native's life, up to 1691, as well as a number of revolution charts.

106. Morin actually noted a birth time of 23:11 PM (according to the method of Paris); the circular chart I have reproduced gives a time of 23:03 PM. For the Morinus version, see *Astrologica Gallica*, p. 555. See also John Gadbury, *Obsequium Rationabile, Or, A Reasonable Service Performed for the Cælestial Sign Scorpio; In XX Remarkable Genitures of that Glorious, but Stigmatized Horoscope ...* (1675), p. 84.

107. In that year, the progressed Moon fell within a 5-degree orb of Uranus – a planet then un-known to the world, yet now recognised as an institutor of dramatic change. The fact that the progressed Midheaven and the progressed Sun were within a 2-degree orb might help explain the unexpected transition to kingship.

108. See Morin, *Astrologica Gallica* (1661), *Praefatio apologetica*, ap. xxvii.

109. Thus, Morin merged two celestial orbs which had been regarded as entirely separate in the medieval system.

110. Robert Fludd, *Tomi Secundi Tractatus Secundus: De Praeternaturali Utriusque Mundi Historia* (1621), p. 157.

111. John Evans, *An Ephemerides for Five Yeares to Come. Calculated by the Most Learned and Excellent Mathematician, M. David Origanus* [actually for 1633–7] (1635), p. 87.

112. The first of Morin's twenty-six books of *Astrologica Gallica* was dedicated to defending Catholic beliefs, mainly against Protestantism.

113. See Lynn Thorndike, *A History of Magic and Experimental Science* (1958), VII, p. 491 who gives an excellent summary of the strengths and weaknesses of Morin's approach to astrology.

114. Morin, *Astrologica Gallica*, Bk 23, Caput 3, p. 600.

115. *Ibid.*, Caput 4, p. 600, is headed with the question, *Ad quem locum figura Revolutionis fit erigenda?* (For which place should the revolution figure be erected?)

116. The two charts are from *ibid.*, Bk 23, p. 612.

117. As the Cinq-Mars conspiracy was being hatched, Richelieu had been ill at Tarascon, in the South of France, but appears to have gone to Lyon to oversee the matter. Morin lists only two of the conspirators (Effiat and de Thou), but six aristocrats were discovered and punished by Richelieu.

118. Cambridge University Library, MS 18/2r. Several versions of the chart are in circulation, based on the hand-drawn version in A.J. Pearce, *The Text-Book of Astrology* (1911 edn), p. 18: see, for example, the National Astrological Library edition, *The Textbook of Astrology* (nd), p. 16. Neither reproduced the Latin tag from Horace; both reproduce an inaccurate Cauda.

119. See Pearce, *The Text-Book of Astrology*, p. 19.

120. In fact, another degree would have brought the less desirable star, Raselhague, to the ascendant.

121. See H. Howard, *A Defensative against the Poyson of Supposed Prophecies ...* (1583), p. i. The Latin phrase, *Risum teneatis amici*, was certainly used by Robert Burton in his *Anatomy* (P. II, Sec. II, Mem. III) but not in an astrological context. The general interpretation of Flamsteed's use of the quotation has led some writers on the history of astrology (particularly A.J. Pearce) to assume that the snippet from the Horatian Latin was added by a later hand, in a cynical commentary on the chart itself. However, I think there is little doubt that the words were written (perhaps later) by Flamsteed, intended as an insistence on the *validity* of the chart.

122. Capp, *English Almanacs*, p. 188.

123. See *Diary of John Evelyn*, ed. J.S. de Beer (1955), Vol. 3, p. 249.

124. According to seventeenth-century astrological theory, the latitudes were of importance in the precise calculation of antiscia and contra-antiscia. An understanding of this technical

relationship is not essential for our study of charts examined in this present book. For a number of derived ambiguous terminologies, see James Wilson, *A Complete Dictionary of Astrology, in which every technical and abstruse term belonging to the science is minutely and correctly explained ...* (1880), pp. 300–1. This historical view of parallels must not be confused with the modern astrological theory of parallels.

125. See Josten, *Elias Ashmole*, Vol. I, p. 11.

126. The whole edifice of planetary hours seems to have been derived from horary astrology, and it has proved difficult to determine at what point in history it was merged so intimately with the personal birth chart, where it has no valid application.

127. The words in quotation marks are from Henry Coley's treatment of planetary hours; see his *Clavis*, p. 264.

128. I must report that I have encountered several different methods of determining the planetary hours, and of how the various rulers are extrapolated from these: however, the method I have just described is certainly that used by Ashmole. See Lilly, *Christian Astrology*, pp. 474–86.

129. See Coley, *Clavis*, p. 272.

130. See *ibid.*, p. 273.

131. See *ibid.*, p. 265.

132. See Lilly, *Christian Astrology*, Vol. 3, pp. 489–91, inclusive of tables.

133. The series of fifteen stars appears in several medieval manuscripts that came into the Bodleian Library by way of Ashmole's collection. In general, however, astrologers were familiar with the fifteen stars from Agrippa, *De Occulta Philosophia* (1534), Vol. 2, p. cxcvii. A reliable modern short survey of the tradition is Joan Evans, *Magical Jewels of the Middle Ages and the Renaissance* (1976 edn); see esp. Appendix G, pp. 246ff.

134. John Gadbury Εφημερις: *or, a Diary Astronomical, Astrological, Meteorological for the Year of Our Lord*, 1703, fol. A.1v.

Chapter Four

1. See Robin Spencer, *Eduardo Paolozzi: Writings and Interviews* (2000), p. 322.

2. For a study of the horoscope of Newton, see A.J. Pearce, 'Sir Isaac Newton and Astrology', in *Urania: A Monthly Journal of Astrology, Meteorology and Physical Science*, April 1880, pp. 97–105.

3. Blake was born on 28 November 1757 at 07:45 PM. Newton was born on 25 December 1642 at 02:00 AM, at Woolsthorpe, south of Grantham: see Michael White, *Isaac Newton: The Last Sorcerer* (1997), p. 11.

4. For a concise account of Blake's interest in Newton as a symbol, see S. Foster Damon, *A Blake Dictionary: The Ideas and Symbols of William Blake* (1973 edn), pp. 298–9. Newton was for Blake one of the infernal trinity (see his poem 'Milton', 41:5). Along with Bacon, the initiator of an experimental approach to the world, and Locke, who expounded the philosophy of the five senses, Newton was the inventor of the godless material world of science.

5. See Spencer, *Eduardo Paolozzi*, p. 332.

6. White (*Isaac Newton*) deals adequately with Newton the alchemist. Blake's interest in alchemy was of a different kind – as a follower of Jakob Boehme, he regarded both astrology and alchemy as arcane sciences, rich repositories of symbols relating to the discovery of the spiritual life, or 'inner' gold.

7. The left-hand print is the frontispiece to Boehme's *De Signatara Rerum*, the other to his *Dreyfaches Leben*, both published in his *Theosophische Wercken* (1682).

8. The two outstanding Boehme scholars were William Law, *The Works of Jakob Behmen, the Teutonic Theosopher* (1764), and Dionysius Andreas Freher. For the latter, see Charles A. Muses, *Illumination on Jacob Boehme: the Works of Dionysius Andreas Freher* (1951), and Adam McLean, *The Paradoxical Emblems of Dionysius Andreas Freher* (1983), being material edited from the British Library, Additional MS 5789.

Freher was born on 12 September 1649, in Nuremberg, under a conjunction of Moon, Uranus and Neptune in Sagittarius, opposed by Pluto in Gemini. His Saturn was in the same degree as Blake's ascendant, in 29 Cancer.

9. Bernard Capp, *Astrology and the Popular Press: English Almanacs 1500–1800* (1979), p. 283.

10. J.C. Eade, *The Forgotten Sky: A Guide to Astrology in English Literature* (1984), pp. 215–16, discusses the sigillisation of the Hudibras horoscope.

11. The sacred word *AGLA* is a Cabalistic acronym for the Hebrew *Attah Gibor Leolam, Adonai* (Thou art powerful and eternal, Lord).

12. Urban VIII issued an anti-astrological bull in 1631. The bull followed on from many others, promulgated during the previous century, but in this case it seemed to reflect the intellectual spirit of the Enlightenment, with its quasi-mechanical cosmo-conception that stands in such contrast to the vision of astrology. Even before the bull of 1631 was issued, all the Italian universities had done away with their chairs of astrology.

13. See Patrick Curry, 'John Worsdale and Late Eighteenth-Century English Astrology', in Annabella Kitson (ed.), *History and Astrology: Clio and Urania confer* (1989), pp. 237ff.

14. A number of pre-printed intaglio horoscopes are pasted down among the horoscopes in the manuscript *Schemes and Nativities* once owned by Partridge, and now Egerton MS 2378 in the British Library.

15. For Thwaites, see David C. Douglas, *English Scholars* (1939), pp. 78–81. For the quotation, see p. 79.

16. George Parker (ed.), *Eland's Tutor to Astrology: or Astrology Made Easy* (1704, 10th edn).

17. See Herbert Leventhal, *In the Shadow of the Enlightenment: Occultism and Renaissance Science in Eighteenth-Century America* (1976), p. 58. Leventhal has the story from William P. Sheffield, *An Address Delivered by William P. Sheffield before the Rhode Island Historical Society in Providence, February 7. A.D., 1882* (1883), p. 18.

18. For the John Gadbury chart of 1666, see *Nauticum Astrologicum: Or, The Astrological Seaman* (1691), p. 82. In 1745, Scheat was in 26.05 Pisces. In 1666, it was in 25.02 Pisces. An orb of 3 degrees was quite acceptable to seventeenth- and eighteenth-century astrologers.

19. See Capp, *Astrology and the Popular Press*, p. 263.

20. See Leventhal, *Shadow of the Enlightenment*, p. 59.

21. See John W. Farwell, 'A Horoscope of Joseph Warren', *Publications of the Colonial Society of Massachusetts*, 20 (1917–19), pp. 18–20.

22. See *ibid.*, p. 20. The chart of John Hancock cast by Rintoul and mentioned by Farwell may have been genuine, but that for Warren was not only wrong astrologically, but seems to have premised a death in 1785 ('in the fourth yeere of the natives fourth decade'). Charts cast for this erroneous date reveal the analysis to have been just as inept as for the correct time of death: the entire astro-reading was spurious.

23. The cut is from the ephemeris-almanac published by the Afro-American mathematician, Benjamin Banneker, for 1795; it had been borrowed from one used earlier by Benjamin Franklin. See William Mille, *Benjamin Franklin's Philadelphia Printing 1728–1766* (1974), Appendix B, fig. 11.

24. See *Poor Robin. 1774. An Almanack After the Old; yet nevertheless as agreeable as Hands can make it to the Newest New Fashion.*

25. Henry Season, *Speculum Anni: Or, Season on the Seasons, For the Year of our Lord 1776*, p. C2ᵛ.

26. Francis Moore, *Vox Stellarum: Or, a Loyal Almanack for the Year of Human Redemption 1774*, p. 14.

27. Tycho Wing, Ὀλύμπια Δώματα, *Or, An Almanack for the Year of Our Lord God, 1776*.

28. See Moore, *Vox Stellarum: Or, a Loyal Almanack For the Year of Human Redemption MDCCLXXVI* [1776], p. 11. Quatrain II.89, from Nostradamus, *Prophéties* (1555), is incorrectly quoted by Moore. For the reference to the enmity with North America, see *ibid.*, p. 12.

29. Theophilus Garcencières, *The True Prophecies or Prognostications of Michel Nostradamus* (1672).

30. John Gadbury, Εφημερις: Or, a Diary of the Celestial Motions for 1679: both the reference to Nostradamus and the prophecy appear in the section dealing with Astrological Observations for the year.

31. John Partridge, Merlinus Liberatus. Being an Almanack for the Year of our Redemption, 1775 (final page). The chart for Louis XVI is from Francis Moore, Vox Stellarum: Or, a Loyal Almanack for the Year of Human Redemption, MDCCLXXVI, p. 44.

32. Robert White, Ἀτλας Οὐράνιος. The Coelestial Atlas; Or, A New Ephemeris for the Year of Our Lord 1774.

33. White, Isaac Newton. Only the first four registers are reproduced from the total of nine in the original plate.

34. Henry Season, Speculum Anni: Or, An Almanack For the Year of our Lord 1734, f. A.2.

35. See John Gadbury, A Brief Relation of the Life and Death of the Late Famous Mathematician and Astrologer, Mr. Vincent Wing (1670): the birth chart is on p. 6, the revolution for the year of death is on p. 32. See also Ebenezer Sibly, A New and Complete Illustration of the Celestial Science of Astrology; or, the Art of Foretelling Future Events and Contingencies (1817), plate no. 25, p. 882.

36. Some of the details given here are abstracted from the alphabetically arranged 'Biographical Notes', in Capp, Astrology and the Popular Press, pp. 293–340.

37. See ibid., p. 242.

38. See for example, W.S.B. Woolhouse, 'Ἀτλας Οὐράνιος, White's Coelestial Atlas; or, an Improved Ephemeris for the Year of Our Lord 1848. This is listed as the ninety-ninth yearly impression; that for 1849 was not quite so extensive or liberal with the asteroids.

39. The cave was discovered by accident in August 1742 and shortly afterwards was investigated by the antiquary, William Stukeley, the friend of the astrologers Tycho Wing and Edmund Weaver. For the cave, see Sylvia P. Beaumon, The Royston Cave (1992).

40. See, for example, the chart of Prince Alfred, born 6 August 1844, in William Seed, An Almanack and Weather Guide for the Year of Our Lord, 1847, p. 44. This chart is accurate to one minute of arc!

41. The chart is from Thomas White, The Beauties of Occult Science; or, the Celestial Intelligencer (1810), p. 398.

42. I refer to it here, briefly, as An Illustration because the title changed over the years. For example, see note 35 above, which gives the title of the 1817 edition. The work appeared in parts during 1784 under the title The Complete Illustration of the Celestial Art of Astrology.

43. Sibly's version of the Erasmus chart appeared in An Illustration, plate 7, opposite p. 889. As the inscription within the Erasmus chart indicates, Sibly acknowledges that he had copied the figure from David Origanus: however, the latter had certainly copied his version from Junctinus, Speculum Astrologiae, Universam Mathematicam Scientiam (1583), p. 542.

44. Sibly recognised that many of the sixteenth-century charts were inaccurate; it was indefensible of him to re-present such horoscopes without correcting their errors.

45. Conjurer's Magazine, March 1792.

46. See Cyriel Odhner Sigstedt, The Swedenborg Epic: The Life and Works of Emanuel Swedenborg (1952), p. 20.

47. See ibid., p. 1.

48. Ibid., note 1, p. 446.

49. The data for Swedenborg given in the Astrologers' Magazine, ii 484 and v. 16 is more accurate: it reflects the chart given by Sibly, but recognises that the data are for 1688.

50. Sibly, An Illustration, p. 825.

51. Ibid., p. 826. Sibly's mention of Newton in regard to Swedenborg reminds me that the two scientists had a communality of degrees in Taurus. Swedenborg's Caput was in 07.25 Taurus: Newton's Mars was in 07.30 Taurus.

52. Ibid., p. 827.

53. Ibid., p. 825.

54. Ibid., p. 826.

55. Ibid., p. 809.

56. For an interesting example of drugs and suicide
in relation to Fomalhaut, see the chart of the
Austrian poet Georg Trakl (born 3 February
1887), who became addicted to morphine and
committed suicide on 3 November 1914. At his
birth, Trakl's Mars (2.27 Pisces) was on
Fomalhaut (2.11 Pisces), and in square to Pluto.
See Ebertin-Hoffmann, *Fixed Stars and their
Interpretation* (1971 edition of *Die Bedeutung der
Fixsterne*), p. 79.

57. Ellic Howe, *Urania's Children: The Strange World
of the Astrologers* (1967), p. 21.

58. In Swift's personal library were a number of
astrological works, ranging from those authored
by Cardan to those of Enschuid (Eastwood); the
most notable was Jean-Baptiste Morin,
Astrologia Gallica. For other astrological works,
see William LeFanu, *A Catalogue of Books
Belonging to Dr Jonathan Swift* (1988).

59. The scholar, George Mayhew, has put to rest the
notion that Partridge was named Hewson.
Partridge was born in 1644 in East Sheen. See
G. Mayhew, 'The Early Life of John Partridge',
Studies in English Literature, 1 (1961; Rice
University), pp. 31–42.

60. See Irvin Ehrenpreis, *Swift: The Man, His Works,
and the Age* (1967), Vol. 2, p. 199.

61. Initially, Swift had not intended to subject
Partridge to a spoof, but the full story cannot be
told here. See Ehrenpreis, *Swift*, Vol. 2,
pp. 197–209.

62. Jonathan Swift, *Predictions for the Year 1708, by
Isaac Bickerstaff. Written to prevent the people of
England from being further imposed on by vulgar
Almanack Makers.* It is hard to believe that Swift
did not intend us to cast a horoscope for the
date (29 March 1708) to see how far the spoof
went. In the late evening, the Moon fell into a
direct opposition with Saturn (13.54 Gemini),
both planets being in square to Mars (9.33
Pisces). As if this were not enough, the next
lunar eclipse (on 29 September of that year)
would fall in 06.39 Aries – on the Caput of the
chart.

63. Jonathan Swift, *The Accomplishment of the First of
Mr. Bickerstaff's Predictions. Being an Account of*

the Death of Mr. Partridge, the Almnack-maker,
upon the 27th Instant.

64. See for example, *Merlinus Liberatus. An
Almanack for the Year of Our Redemption, 1848*. In
the nineteenth century the almanacs were still
being attributed to John Partridge.

65. For the horoscope of Partridge, see Sibly, *An
Illustration*, plate 25, opp. p. 882.

66. John Partridge, *Mene Tekel, Being an Astrological
Judgment on the Great and Wonderful Year 1688*,
p. 10. For the after-analysis, see Partridge, *Mene
Mene, Tekel Upharsin. The Second Part of Mene
Tekel: Treating of the Year MDCLXXXIX* (1689).

67. W.S., *Sidrophel Vapulans: Or, The Quack Astrologer
Toss'd in a Blanket* (1699), p. 28.

68. For an account of Franklin's spoof, see
Leventhal, *Shadow of the Enlightenment*,
pp. 51–4.

69. The French instrument of death had been
constructed by a German mechanic named
Schmidt, following the instructions of Dr
Antoine Louise – which explains why it was
called a 'Louisette' long before the name
'guillotine' became popular. See A.S.E.
Ackermann, *Popular Fallacies: A Book of Common
Errors: Explained and Corrected with Copious
References to Authorities* (1950 edn), p. 494.

70. See Sibly, *An Illustration*, p. 244.

71. The drawings of Andromeda and Perseus have
been adapted from Samuel Leigh, *Urania's
Mirror* (1823), plates 5 and 6, respectively.

72. See, for example, the chart of Robespierre in
André Barbault, *Traité Pratique d'Astrologie*
(1961), p. 266 (the date is wrongly given as
8 May, but the chart is correctly cast for 6 May
1758). A similar figure is given in the curious,
Aleister Crowley with Evangeline Adams, *The
General Principles of Astrology* (2002), p. 512.

73. The most astonishing thing about the
proliferated charts is how inaccurate they
usually are. So far as it is possible to tell, Marie
Antoinette was born on 2 November 1755 in
Vienna, Austria, at an official time of
07:30 AM. Louis was born on 23 August 1754
in Versailles at what I estimate to be 06:14 AM.
It is not possible to list all the appearances of

the charts, but the following are of interest, if only because it proves possible to trace their sources: Cyrille Wilczkowski, *L'Homme et le Zodiaque: Essai de Synthèse Typologique* (1947); for Louis XVI, see p. 204; for Antoinette p. 187. The chart for Louis gives an ascendant in 14 Virgo, and a Moon in 8 Scorpio, which suggests that the source was the chart given in *Raphael's Prophetic Messenger* for 1877. The chart for Marie Antoinette gives 4 Cancer as the ascendant, with Moon in 21 Libra, and is thus close to the Sibly version. Barbault, *Traité Pratique*, gives Marie Antoinette, p. 265; Louis XVI, p. 262. The former is derived from the time given in the family literature, and corresponds closely to the Sibly version; the latter from the *Gazette de France* and *Le Mercure de France*, which give 06:24 AM as time of birth. Sibly had given 03:50 PM as time of birth, but with a lunar placing that suggested a much later time of birth.

74. See Sibly, *An Illustration*, opp. p. 1054.

75. Progressions for the moment of her violent death call for an adjustment of her birth time to 06:02 PM. The progression to her moment of death gives progressed Mars (15.43 Cancer) on the ascendant, and on its own natal position. This position of Mars was an important influence on her life, for it was on the beneficial fixed star Propus (in 1755, this was in 15.32 Cancer). Progressed Moon (20.12 Pisces) was on the Midheaven. Progressed Pluto (16.08 Sagittarius) was 2 degrees from the Sun. Neptune (10.45 Leo) had progressed to the radical IC.

76. The birth date is recorded in Jeanne L.H. Campan, *The Private Life of Marie Antoinette, Queen of France and Navarre* (1884), Vol. 1, p. 69. The astrologer Cyrille Wilczkowski, *L'Homme et le Zodiaque*, p. 187, followed the official time, giving an ascendant of 04.00 Cancer and a Midheaven of 03.00 Pisces. However, it is evident that this time needs some adjustment.

77. The official time of birth (06:30 AM) clearly needs some adjustment, even though it has been used by a number of proficient astrologers: for example, Wilczkowski, *L'Homme et le Zodiaque*, p. 204, appears to have adopted it without any rectification, though the official time does require rectification by 16 minutes.

78. See John Corfield writing under the pseudonym 'Cardanus' in the *Urania; or The Philosophical and Scientific Magazine*, 1 June 1814, p. 13.

79. The secret of the identity of 'W. E.' was unveiled in the *London Correspondent* by the professional astrologer, James Wright, who took it upon himself to reveal the identities of those who wrote in the *Conjuror's Magazine*.

80. Madame Campan (*Private Life of Marie Antoinette*, Vol. 2, pp. 323–4), the former lady-in-waiting to the Queen, tells us that the carriage stopped by the scaffold at 10:10 AM. Refusing the aid of the executioners, Louis took off his own clothes. After a moment of indignation, he allowed them to bind his hands behind his back. Once on the scaffold, he delivered a few words by way of speech, and was placed beneath the guillotine. I estimate that, at most, 10 minutes may have elapsed between his arrival at the scaffold and the fall of the blade.

81. The *Conjuror's Magazine* for February 1793. The two charts have received some notice in Patrick Curry, 'Astrological Literature in Late Eighteenth-century England', in Kitson (ed.), *History and Astrology*, pp. 243–52. Curry is of the opinion that the precision of the data suggests that the astrologer rectified the horoscope.

82. Curry, *ibid.*, p. 248.

83. This suggestion seems reasonable, as both charts have suffered from a seeming inability to distinguish the font for the sigil for Virgo from that for Scorpio.

84. See Thomas White, *The Beauties of Occult Science Investigated; or, the Celestial Intelligencer: in Two Parts* (1810).

85. The title is very long, being designed to read as an advertisement for the text. Above, in note

84, I have given only the first thirteen words of the title.

86. The story of the fight waged by astrologers in Britain and the United States to legitimise their art, and to mitigate the persecution of unfortunate astrologers, is really no part of this present study. In England, the pro-astrology camp was spearheaded by the astrologer Richard James Morrison ('Zadkiel') and supported by the astrologer–solicitor Christopher Cooke. Ultimately, it was the 'legitimisation' of astrology in middle-class circles, mainly by the Theosophists, that gradually put an end to police persecution in Britain. In the United States, it was the tireless campaigning of the English-born astrologer and medical doctor, Luke Broughton, which had the most powerful effect. The dramatic case mounted against Evangeline Adams, in New York – a case rooted in the illegality of 'pretending to tell fortunes' – helped sway public opinion away from persecution of astrologers: see Evangeline Adams, *The Bowl of Heaven* (1926), pp. 52–5.

87. The chart is from White, *Beauties of Occult Science*, p. 425.

88. See *ibid.*, p. 427, penultimate line in tabulation. Of course, since Uranus was given the wrong position in the figure, White's directions could not be accurate, in historical fact. My interest does not lie in the accuracy or inaccuracy, but in the conclusion that White clearly drew – that the directed opposition should have such a destructive effect. The progressed Uranus was on 8.15 Pisces on the day of Louis XVI's execution.

89. John Corfield wrote a short article on the nature of Uranus in *Urania*, June 1814, but it is evident that by this time the leading astrologers were in fair agreement as to its significance.

90. See White, *Beauties of Occult Science*, pp. 426–7.

91. The chart is from Sibly, *An Illustration*, p. 891. Charles Brent was a well-known mathematician and astronomer who dabbled in astrology. He was author of *The Compendious Astronomer* (1740).

92. See Henry Season, *Speculum Anni: Or, Season on the Seasons, For the Year of our Lord 1771*, p. C.7^v c6. The lines are quoted by Capp, *Astrology and the Popular Press*, p. 262.

93. Sibly, *An Illustration*, p. 892. The chart itself was printed as an engraving between pp. 890 and 891.

94. See, for example, Susan Manuel, 'Making Sense of Sibly', in *National Council for Geocosmic Research Journal*, Vol. 13, no. 1 (1994), pp. 35–40. Manuel argues that the chart is set for London, and is based on the time of the angles for the Cancer ingress on 20 June 1776. In fact, the angles on Sibly's chart for American Independence do not correspond with the Cancer ingress, which occurred at 22:34 PM with the ascendant in 13.08 Aquarius and the Midheaven in 9.44 Sagittarius. My own view of this vexing horoscope takes into account just how slipshod Sibly was when it came to casting charts. If we assume that the chart is horary, and that Sibly posed a question about the new nation at 21:53:45 PM, then the angles and houses (Placidean) would have been fairly close to those represented in the engraving. However, the Moon would have been out by 3 degrees (nothing exceptional in Sibly's charting). The Sun would have been out by 11 minutes, and Saturn by 1 minute. The fact is, there is no time or place wherein the chart given by Sibly for that date could be absolutely accurate. If we take the fiducial as the Sun (13.08 Cancer in the chart), then this would occur at 17:10 London time, and the Moon would be in 24.09 Aquarius, but the other planets would be out by a degree or so. For such a time, Mercury would be in 24.18 Cancer, over 2 degrees from the position given by Sibly. Personally, I think that the chart, howsoever originated, is nothing other than run-of-the-mill inaccurate Sibly.

95. The revolution chart of George III for 1776 is cast for 23 May 1776, at 12:17:30.

96. Charles Brent's natal chart for George III was cast according to the Regiomontanus tables of houses, for 24 May 1738, at 07:05:40 AM. In the corresponding revolution chart for 1776,

the Regiomontanus system gives a second-house cusp of 12.30, while the Placidean gives 13.30. We must recall that Sibly tended to use the Placidus tables.

97. See Alfred T. Story, *James Holmes and John Varley* (1894), pp. 245–8.

98. *Ibid.*, p. 246.

99. *Ibid.*

100. *Ibid.*, p. 247.

101. For an account of these clairvoyant sessions, see F. Gettings, *The Hidden Art: A study of occult symbolism in art* (1978), pp. 111–18.

102. The horoscope was printed in *Urania: or, the Astrologer's Chronicle, and Mystical Magazine* (1825), No. 1. In fact, this chart was cast for 07:31 PM, and not for 07:45 PM, as the text in the internal box claims.

103. The differences between the computer-generated chart and Varley's version are slight. The most surprising placing is that given by Varley for Mars, which he places in 29.15. I suspect that this is a typographical error for 20.15.

104. According to Blake, the original 'old' Moon was in the heart of man. However, when man was divided into *animus* and *anima*, the Moon separated. He seems to have equated this separation with the destruction of Atlantis: see *Jerusalem* 49:19. See Damon, *A Blake Dictionary* (1973), pp. 285–6.

105. Several other examples of eclipses effective in the personal life of William Blake may be studied in David Ovason, *The Book of the Eclipse: The Hidden Influences of Eclipses* (1999), pp. 134–9.

106. For examples of eclipses in works by Blake, see *ibid.*, pp. 134–8.

107. The charm was reproduced in *The Proceedings of the Historical Society of Lancashire and Cheshire* (1852).

108. See Ralph Merrifield, *The Archaeology of Ritual and Magic* (1987), p. 148.

109. All the sigils and the magic square of the Sun may be traced to Cornelius Agrippa, *De Occulta Philosophia* (1533), p. cl. The first three sigils represent the Sun and Leo. The second sigil

along is a copy of the sigil for the *Intelligency of the Sun*: the line of letters running along the top of the sigil is a pseudo-Greek version of the Latin 'intelligency'. The complex sigil to the bottom left is the symbol of the archangel Michael, the ruler of the Sun; the letters below offer a pseudo-Greek version of the archangelic name. The symbol at the end is a poor copy of a more complex symbol for the Sun given by Agrippa. The sigil within the top enclosure represents Leo, ruled by the Sun. The other sigils appear to be an attempt to spell out the solar name *Eloh*, in Greek letters.

110. The Roman was adopted for the first three letters to suggest, in a clumsy yet artful way, the numeral 666 (see note 111).

111. Revelation 13:18. According to the biblical text, the number is that of a man, or of mankind: however, the magical tradition assigns the number to a demon, or daemon. The magical numbers of the letters in the Hebrew word Sorath (סורת) is: 60 + 6 + 200 + 400 = 666.

Chapter Five

1. For an account of this curious bronze horoscope, see David Ovason, *The Secret Architecture of Our Nation's Capital* (2000), pp. 207–15.

2. The six planets, listed in order within the sign, on 2 July 1881, were Mars 07.47 Taurus; Saturn 10.06 Taurus; Neptune 15.58 Taurus; Jupiter 18.22 Taurus; Venus 25.33 Taurus; Pluto 28.46 Taurus.

3. Allan Peskin, *Garfield*, 1978, p. 6.

4. James Abram Garfield was born at 02:25 AM, on 19 November 1831, at 'Orange township on the edge of a ravine sloping down to the Chagrin river, today the plush urbanite community of Moreland Hills', Ohio (this I have taken as 081W23 41N25). See A.J. Pearce's *Urania: a Monthly Journal of Astrology, Meteorology and Physical Science*, January–September 1880, p. 287. Pearce, with his usual expertise, predicted from the chart that Garfield would be elected President. I have rectified the chart to a

number of progressions, including the assassination and death. Garfield died at 10:35 PM, on 19 September 1881, at Elberon, New Jersey.

5. I have cast the chart of Charles Julius Guiteau for 07.24 PM on 7 September 1841, at Freeport, Illinois. There is some confusion as to the day of birth. R.J. Donovan, *The Assassins* (1952), p. 17, gives 8 September 1841: this date was used by the English librarian–astrologer, A.G. Trent, *The Soul and the Stars* (1893), p. xii. However, the nineteenth-century Detroit astrologer, Henry Clay Hodges (who wrote under the pen-name Alvidas), gave Guiteau's birth as 7 September 1841, at 07:13 PM. See Alvidas, *Science of Life*, Vol. 2, *Planetary Influences* (1902), p. 439.

6. *Urania*, Vol. 1 (January 1880), p. 287.

7. For an example of A.J. Pearce's interest in eclipse lore, see *The Text-Book of Astrology* (1911 edn), pp. 326ff.

8. Uranus on Armus (10.22 Aquarius), and Neptune on Terebellum (23.28 Capricorn) tend to be overshadowed by the benefits of the star Bungula (27.13 Scorpio).

9. The name is said to be from the Arabic *Al Mankib dhi'l Inan*, meaning 'the Shoulder of the Rein-Holder', in reference to the charioteer in Auriga.

10. See Trent, *The Soul and the Stars*, p. xii.

11. Abraham Lincoln was born at Sinking Spring Farm, at 01:32 AM on 12 February 1809. The date and place of birth are derived from Louis Austin Warren, *Lincoln's Parentage & Childhood. A History of the Kentucky Lincolns Supported by Documentary Evidence*, 1926, p. 82. When asked about his place of birth, Lincoln himself mentioned Nolin Creek, which was on Sinking Spring Farm. This appears to have been about 15 miles south-east of Elizabethtown, at what is now called Hodgenville, in Larue County, at 37 33N85 49W. The most interesting versions of Lincoln's charts are the assassination and death charts in Raphael's *Guide to Astrology*, Vol. 2, which is replicated in the *Astrologer's Magazine* (September 1893), No. 38, Vol. 4, No. 2.

12. John Wilkes Booth was born on 10 May 1838 at Bel Air, Maryland. The date of birth is

recorded by Stanley Kimmel, *The Mad Booths of Maryland* (1940), p. 58, and in Richard J.S. Gutman and Kellie O. Gutman, *John Wilkes Booth Himself* (1979), p. 11. I offer two sources, because I have seen alternative dates offered – for example, 26 August 1838. The time has not been recorded. However, it has proved possible to rectify the chart (to 04:22 AM) by Booth's assassination of Lincoln, and his own death, both of which have been timed to within a minute or so of accuracy. Booth was shot in the head, in a barn on Garrett's farm, near Bowling Green (077W27 38N04), on 26 April 1865. The *Rochester Daily Union and Advertiser*, 1 May 1865, p. 2, refers to the sun rising as Booth began to die, and being the 'height of a man' (whatever that means) at the time of his death. If this is to be taken seriously, then the death would have taken place between 5:34 and 5:50 AM. At this later time, with the Sun well over the horizon, the Moon was on Booth's natal Sun, in 18.52 Taurus.

13. John Wilkes Booth shot Abraham Lincoln at 10:15 PM on Friday, 14 April 1865 in Ford's Theater, Washington, DC. For an account of the sequence of events after 10:10 PM, when Booth entered the lobby of the theatre, see David Miller Dewitt, *The Assassination of Abraham Lincoln and its Expiation* (1909), pp. 46–7. Lincoln died at 7:23 AM on 15 April 1865, in the Petersen house opposite Ford's Theater, Washington DC. For the timing, see Francis Wilson, *John Wilkes Booth. Fact and Fiction of Lincoln's Assassination* (1929), p. 135.

14. The flag itself has a curious history. It was the Treasury Guard flag, with stripes, thirty-four stars and an eagle. After the tragedy of that Good Friday, it disappeared, and was discovered in 1998, in the collection of the Connecticut Historical Society.

15. The predictions are in *Broughton's Monthly Planet Reader and Astrological Journal* for the last three months of 1864, and (in the same issue) in the article, 'Fate of the Nation for 1864'.

16. The method is interesting. There would be eclipses on 11 and 25 April. That of 11 April

would fall on the 22-degree axis of Aries–Libra, while that of the 25 April would fall on the 6-degree axis of Taurus–Scorpio. In the horoscope of Lincoln, Broughton had marked the position of Mars in 26 Libra, and Uranus in 10 Scorpio. Being uncertain as to which of the two would be more powerful, he elected to mention a two-day period between them.

17. *Broughton's Monthly Planet Reader and Astrological Journal*, Vol. 1, No. 6, 1 September 1860. On p. 42, Broughton tells us that 'After careful examination of his Nativity, we are of the opinion that he was born near two o'clock in the morning.'

18. *Ibid.*, December 1860.

19. *Ibid.*, Vol. 5, No. 1, October–December, 1864, p. 2.

20. For example, it is the progressed Pluto that falls precisely on the IC of the chart, when this is rectified to 01:37 AM. This would be explosive enough under normal circumstances, but we must recall that Lincoln's Pluto was on the fixed star Achernar (in 1809, this star was located in 12.37 Pisces).

21. Broughton's assessment of malign aspects was only partly correct. Saturn was 80.07 from the Sun, well out of orb for the quintile of 72 degrees. However, Saturn *was* 50.53 degrees from the Moon, and *just* within orb of the afflictive semiquadrate (45 degrees) aspect.

22. For a modern version of the horoscope of Edwin Booth see Marc Edmund Jones, *The Sabian Symbols in Astrology* (1953), p. 346.

23. *Chicago Post*, 16 April 1865.

24. See A.B. Clarke, *The Unlocked Book. A Memoir of John Wilkes Booth by His Sister Asia Booth Clarke* (1938); in 1971 reprint, pp. 56–7.

25. This was one of the billings at the Grover's Theater, in Washington, DC, on 11 April 1863. Robert J. Donovan, *The Assassins* (1952), used it as the heading for one of the chapters dealing with Booth, pp. 217ff.

26. Richard Hinckley Allen, *Star Names. Their Lore and Meaning* (1963 reprint), p. 35. (Formerly, *Star-Names and their Meanings*, 1899).

27. In that same year, the star Zosma was in 9.03 Virgo, on Booth's Jupiter (8.50 Virgo).

28. Oswald was born on 18 October 1939, in New Orleans. His Mars was in 11.07 Aquarius: Armus was in 11.53 Aquarius.

29. W.H. Chaney, *Chaney's Primer of Astrology and American Urania* (1890).

30. See Evangeline Adams, *The Bowl of Heaven* (1926), pp. 27ff. Heber is mentioned by Egbert Cleave, *Cleave's Biographical Cyclopedia of Homoeopathic Physicians and Surgeons* (1873).

31. Christopher Cooke, *Curiosities of Occult Literature* (1863), p. 168.

32. *Ibid.*, p. 176.

33. For notice of the prefabricated charts, see R.J. Morrison in *Zadkiel's Almanac and Herald of Astrology for 1852* (henceforth *Zadkiel's*).

34. See Nils William Olsson and Erik Wikén, *Swedish Passenger Arrivals in the United States 1820–1850* (1995), item 4511, p. 429.

35. Dr C.W. Roback, *The Mysteries of Astrology, and the Wonders of Magic: Including a History of the Rise and Progress of Astrology . . .* (1854), p. ix.

36. *Ibid.*, p. xii. One wonders who had been around in the 1830s to read the hieroglyphics for Roback, and to demonstrate their astrological contents.

37. *Ibid.*, p. xiii.

38. *Ibid.*, p. 78. The chart of Henry VIII, from which Roback copied his own inept version, was from E. Sibly, *A New and Complete Illustration of the Occult Sciences . . .* (1790), opposite p. 853. Henry was born in 1491, not 1641.

39. John Gadbury, Γενεθαιαλογία or *The Doctrine of Nativities* (1658).

40. George Wilde and J. Dodson, *A Treatise of Natal Astrology* (1894). The reading for Antoinette is on p. 157; that for Coleridge on p. 162; that for Davy on p. 164; that for Frederick on p. 149; and that for Washington on p. 153.

41. See *Broughton's*, Vol. 1, No. 6, 1 September 1860. The horoscope is from the front cover.

42. Pearce, *The Text-Book of Astrology* (1911, 2nd edn), pp. 171–2.

43. At 01:34 AM, Washington, DC time, on 5 September 1861, the following conjunction would be operative in Virgo: Jupiter: 08.47; Mars: 08.40; Sun: 12.39; Saturn: 12.51; Mercury: 12.57; and Moon: 17.13. The combined Sun and Saturn were in opposition to Lincoln's radical Pluto; Jupiter and Mars were in opposition to his radical Mercury.

44. The horoscopes of the Tsar, which appeared in *Urania*, Vol. 1, p. 41 and in the *Horoscope*, Vol. 2, p. 240, are based on the officially promulgated birth time of 10:00 AM. Although this time was used by Pearce (*Text-book of Astrology*, p. 171), it is a rounded-off figure, and requires rectification to 10:32 AM. The progressed chart for the moment of assassination, at 03:30 PM on 13 March 1881, is highly dramatic. At the moment his legs were destroyed by the blast, progressed Pluto (26.28 Pisces) was setting over the descendant, square Neptune (24.45 Sagittarius). Uranus (17.19 Sagittarius) was exactly on the IC, opposite Mercury (21.29 Gemini) on the Midheaven.

45. The prediction had been made in *Zadkiel's for 1881*, pp. 9 and 12, and *Zadkiel's for 1882*, pp. 53–63.

46. See James R. Wallace, 'Horoscope of the late Dr. Broughton, Astrologer and Medical Practitioner, New York', in *Coming Events. The Astrological Monthly*, pp. 178–82.

47. See *Broughton's*, Vol. 5, No. 1, 1864.

48. See John J. Broughton [*sic*], 'What the Stars Tell. Major McKinley will be the next President', in the *Baltimore American*, 26 July 1896, p. 14.

49. See Yarmo Vedra, *Heliocentric Astrology or Essentials of Astronomy and Solar Mentality …* (1899).

50. See *ibid.*, p. 34.

51. See *ibid.*, p. 38.

52. Alice Bailey, *A Treatise on Cosmic Fire* (1925; 1962 edn), p. 156.

53. For a possible origin of this device, see J.C. Street, *The Hidden Way Across the Threshold* (1888), esp. p. 47.

54. The chart appeared in *Modern Astrology: The Astrologers' Magazine*, Vol. 8, July–December 1900.

55. For the 'wives', see Fawn M. Brodie, *No Man Knows My History. The Life of Joseph Smith the Mormon Prophet* (1954 edn), pp. 434–65.

56. See *ibid.*, p. 7. The data given by Trent, *The Soul and the Stars*, p. xiii, are based on a birth time of about 8:00 AM for the 23 December. The secret of Smith's complex personality may be assessed from the fixed stars called into prominence in his chart – Lesath and Manubrium.

57. The exact time of Smith's death is known from the fact that a companion, murdered alongside him, wore a watch that was broken by a bullet, and had stopped at 05:16 PM. See George Q. Cannon, *The Life of Joseph Smith the Prophet* (1907 edn), p. 527.

58. See Sepharial's chart in *Coming Events. The Astrological Monthly*, October 1899, pp. 455–7. Unfortunately, Sepharial wrongly erected the chart for Rome: the difficulties are resolved when we accept Sepharial's ascendant and adjust the time for Turin, at 09:52 AM.

59. The data are from B. Anatra, *Dizionario Biografico degli Italiani* (1972), p. 168.

60. In a piece of brilliant detective work, Edvard Radzinksy, *Rasputin. The Last Word* (2000), pp. 25–6, has shown that Rasputin was born on 10 January 1869 – the day of Saint Grigory, after whom he was named.

61. The above information is derived from *The Great Soviet Encyclopedia* (1978), Vol. 30, p. 456.

62. The chart given by Wilde and Dodson, *A Treatise of Natal Astrology*, p. 177, is cast for 04:00 AM. I have rectified to 03:28 AM, based on details in Gene Smith, *Maximilian and Carlota. The Habsburg Tragedy in Mexico* (1974 edn).

63. The data are given by Jones, *Sabian Symbols in Astrology*, pp. 355 and 386–7. For the few letters from Chaney to his son, see Irving Stone, *Sailor on Horseback* (1938).

64. Thomas White, *The Beauties of Occult Science Investigated; or, the Celestial Intelligencer* (1810); the horoscope appears on p. 429.

65. Vincent Cronin, *Napoleon* (1971), pp. 19–20.

66. John Corfield, *Destiny of Europe!!! The Nativity of Napoleone Buonaparte, Emperor of France* (1812).

67. In addition to those horoscopes discussed in this section is that cast by Thomas Orger, *The Nativity of Napoleon Bonaparte* (1805). This figure is replete with fixed stars, yet stymied by the fact that Orger located Uranus in Aries, when it should have been well into Taurus. His prophecy of Napoleon's death was out by seventeen years! Another interesting chart, with an incorrect prophecy, is that reproduced by White, *The Beauties of Occult Science Investigated*, p. 428.

68. John Worsdale, *The Nativity of Napoleon Bonaparte, Emperor of France* (c. 1807). The chart is the frontispiece.

69. *Ibid.*, p. 78.

70. Thomas Oxley, *The Celestial Planispheres, or Astronomical Charts* (1830).

71. *Ibid.*, p. 117.

72. These directions are listed by Oxley, *ibid.*, p. 121.

73. The only difference between the two charts is that the first gives an elaborate sigil for the Part of Fortune, thus: ♓ *21. 40* The typographer who copied the chart mistook it as a sigil for Pisces, which explains why, in the chart of 1814, there appear to be two cusps for the sixth house, one in Aries, the other in Pisces.

74. Corfield, *Destiny of Europe!!!*

75. *The Urania; or, the Philosophical and Scientific Magazine*, 1 June 1814. The horoscope appeared on p. 29.

76. See Corfield, *Destiny of Europe!!!*, p. 12.

77. See Ben Weider and Sven Forshufvud, *Assassination at St. Helena Revisited* (1995 edn).

78. *Ibid.*, pp. 161–2.

79. Montholon was born in Paris on 21 July 1783: I have cast the chart for noon.

80. The manuscript notes are in the autograph of the nineteenth-century astrologer, Abraham Beresford, here reproduced from the margin of his personal copy of John Partridge, *Merlinus Liberatus. An Almanack for the Year of Our Redemption, 1848*, p. 17.

81. Abergilly Bay is a nineteenth-century version of Abergele Bay.

82. Details of the disaster are presently from Benjamin Vincent, *Haydn's Dictionary of Dates and Universal Information Relating to All Ages and Nations* (1885 edn), p. 601.

83. The quotation is from Vivian E. Robson, *The Fixed Stars and Constellations in Astrology* (1969 edn), p. 200.

84. See Partridge, *Merlinus Liberatus*, p. 18: the date, Wednesday 13th, is marked *Moon {sigil} eclip. vis.* The eclipse is discussed as 'a total Eclipse of the Moon' … 'visible in these parts' on pp. 40–1.

85. The diagram is from *ibid.*, p. 40.

86. See 'The Tay Bridge Catastrophe', in *Urania*, February 1880, pp. 38–9.

87. *Zadkiel's for 1878*, p. 27. The hieroglyphic appeared on the final page.

88. See Ellic Howe, *Raphael: or, The Royal Merlin* (1964). Morrison and Smith had both been born in 1795: Morrison on 15 June, at 09:45 AM, and Smith on 19 March, at 09:07 AM. The charts were published in *Modern Astrology* (1891), Vol. 2, Smith's at p. 295, and Morrison's at p. 315.

89. *The Horoscope: A Weekly Miscellany of Astrology* (1834).

90. The prosecution was brought in 1851, after the police had set up a sting following an advertisement in *Copestick's Prophetic Annual, Celestial Intelligencer and Weather Guide*. Copestick was found guilty, and imprisoned for a month.

91. See Cooke, *Curiosities of Occult Literature*. For Copestick, see pp. 30ff. For the trip to America, see p. 162. For Mr Lister, 'an English professor of Astrology', see p. 168, and for the Chicago astrologer, see p. 176.

92. *Zadkiel's for 1845*, p. 44.

93. See *Urania*, Vol. 1, January 1880, p. 284.

94. Wellington's Mars (7.10 Cancer) was on Napoleon's Venus (07.02 Cancer).

95. *Zadkiel's for 1844*.

96. Cooke, *Curiosities of Occult Literature*. The British Library pressmark is 8610 bbb 10.

A manuscript note implies that the figure appeared originally in the *Horoscope* for 1834, and in *Zadkiel's for 1846*.

97. However, the ascendant suggests a birth at about 09:24:10 AM.

98. In 1795, Regulus was in 26.58 Leo: whosoever cast Morrison's chart specified it as being in 27.37 Leo, within 1 degree of the ascendant.

99. The copy of this badly mutilated chart is from my own collection. The chart gives Venus in 13.35.

100. This self-advertising served to call attention to his work as a homoeopathist.

101. See W.H. Chaney, *Astrological Definitions: Being an Accompaniment to the Nativity* (1872).

102. The internationally agreed system of alpha-numeric abbreviations was adopted in 1975. See, for example, Charles Harvey, *Astrological Journal*, Vol. 19, No. 2 (1977), pp. 51–2.

103. The abbreviation chart is from Chaney, *Astrological Definitions*. The sigillised version is from the opening title of Part 3 of *Chaney's Primer of Astrology and American Urania* (1890), p. 102.

104. My own copy is dated 1890, and is a bound accumulation of partworks.

105. Chaney, *Chaney's Primer*, pp. 10–11.

106. *Ibid.*, p. 2, in the *Dedication*, to John W. Beckmann and Milda J. Beckmann.

107. In particular, he was critical of Albert Victor, son of the Prince of Wales, whose precise birth data he published. See Chaney, *Chaney's Primer*, pp. 21–2.

108. *Ibid.*, p. 133.

109. *Ibid.*, p. 134. Technically, a planet is 'burned up by', or *combust*, the Sun when it is within 8 30' of the body of the Sun. In the charts of both Beecher and Edison, Mercury was about 3 degrees from the Sun.

110. Chaney, *Chaney's Primer*, p. 144.

111. The couple had separated on 3 June 1875. See *ibid.*, p. 118. See also Andrew Sinclair, *Jack: A Biography of Jack London* (1978), p. xv.

112. The decans figure in the surviving fifteenth-century astrological frescoes of Francesco del Cossa and Cosmè Tura, in the Palazzo Schifanoia, Ferrara: see P. Ancona, *The Schifanoia Months of Ferrara* (1955).

113. See 'Charubel', *The Degrees of the Zodiac Symbolised* (1898).

114. These experiments encouraged later astrologers to research degree symbols. See for example Isidore Kozminsky, *Zodiacal Symbology and Its Planetary Power* (1913); Adriano Carelli, *The 360 Degrees of the Zodiac* (1951); the series first set out by Dane Rudhyar, *The Astrology of Personality: A Re-formulation of Astrological Concepts and Ideals, in Terms of Contemporary Psychology and Philosophy* (1936), pp. 343–78, dealt with more expansively by Jones, *The Sabian Symbols in Astrology* (1953), and E.C. Matthews, *Fixed Stars and Degrees of the Zodiac Analyzed* (1968 edn). It is important to note how the degree-readings, intended originally to relate only to the ascendant, were appropriated in the twentieth century, to apply to all tenanted degrees.

115. 'Charubel', *Degrees of the Zodiac Symbolised*, Preface to Second Edition, p. ix, quoting from *Astrologer's Magazine*, April 1893. The death reading is in the March issue, p. 175.

116. Charubel, *Degrees of the Zodiac Symbolised*, p. ix.

117. The best account of the death of Shelley, of the finding of the bodies and of their disposal, is undoubtedly Edward J. Trelawny, *Recollections of the Last Days of Shelley and Byron* (1906), pp. 76–83: but see also Phyllis Grosskurth, *Byron. The Flawed Angel* (1997), pp. 409–10. For the burning, which took place on the day of the eclipse, see the report of Domenico Simoncini in Edward J. Trelawny, *Records of Shelley, Byron and the Author* (1858; 2000 edn), pp. 302–3.

118. See 'Terminus Vitae. – Percy Bysshe Shelley' in *Modern Astrology*, Vol. 3, p. 175.

119. Shelley was born at Field Place, near Horsham, England, on 4 August 1792, at 10:39 PM. The accurate time was recorded by the English astrologer and novelist Jean Overton Fuller, 'Profile. Percy Bysshe Shelley', in *Astrology: The Astrologers' Quarterly*, Vol. 40, No. 3 (1966), pp. 85–92. Fuller refers to a letter from Shelley's father sent to Whitton, the family solicitor,

recording that Percy Bysshe was born at 10:00 PM. A rectification, to 10:39 PM, offers a powerful progression for Shelley's drowning.

120. The two horoscopes are from the series 'Horoscopes of Notable Astrologers', in *Modern Astrology*, Vol. 2 (1891). That for Sibly is from p. 363; that for Morrison (Zadkiel) from p. 315.

121. See E.H. Bailey, *The Prenatal Epoch* (1916), p. 178.

122. The birth chart for Princess Alice Maud Mary is from William Seed, *An Almanack and Weather Guide for the Year of Our Lord 1844*, p. 41.

123. The truth is that Seed (*ibid.*) – one of the most accurate technicians of his period – erroneously inserted a Moon placing that had been cast for exactly 15 hours *after* the birth time (that is, for 05:05 PM).

124. See L. Edward Johndro, 'You and Your Eclipses', in *Horoscope*, Vol. 4, No. 6, June 1939, p. 7.

125. See 'Fomalhaut' [Charles Nicoullaud], *Manuel D'Astrologie Sphérique et Judiciaire* (1897), p. 316.

126. As a matter of fact, the difference of several minutes of arc in the directions led Nicoullaud to conclude that the time of birth was out by a few minutes; see *ibid.*, p. 249.

127. According to the *Astrologers' Magazine* (August 1894), No. 49, Vol. 5, pp. 28ff., Carnot was born at 6:00 PM.

128. The *Astrologers' Magazine* gives a version of his death chart. He died at 00:45 AM on 25 June 1894.

129. I have taken the birth time from the article on Caserio by A. Coletti in Giuseppe Alessi *et al.*, *Instituto della Enciclopedia Italiana Fondata da Giovanni Treccani* (1978 edn), pp. 339–40. I have rectified by the progressions to the assassination, which took place at 9:30 PM on 24 June 1894, at Lyons. If this rectified time is correct, then Caserio's Moon was exactly on Carnot's Pluto.

130. The **pr** is short for the French, *conjunction précédente*. In his own astrology, Nicoullaud treated this point of syzygy as being a nodal point, which could receive aspects and which was influential to transits and progressions.

In the detailed speculum, which he published alongside the two charts (see Nicoullaud, *Manuel D'Astrologie*, p. 133), the letter *a* is meant to represent antiscion: thus *a. pr* indicates the antiscion of the preceding syzygy, which is 21.03 Taurus. The letters *c. a.* are abbreviations for contra-antiscion.

131. Sepharial, *Coming Events*, October 1899, p. 45, which is clearly referring to Nicoullaud.

132. See Bessie Leo [*et al.*], *The Life and Work of Alan Leo: Theosophist – Astrologer – Mason* (1919), p. 26.

133. See *ibid.*, pp. 42 and 177. The variations on the given time of 06:00 AM seem designed to place Saturn on a Leonine ascendant.

134. See *ibid.*, pp. 20ff.

135. *Ibid.*, p. 43. He did read H.P. Blavatsky's works, *Isis Unveiled* (1877) and *The Secret Doctrine* (1888), which probably gave him the erroneous idea that he knew something about esoteric astrology.

136. See E.H. Bailey, *Destiny* (June 1904–October 1905).

137. By any standards of astrology, this explanation is nonsensical. The transits for 1903 permitted no such oppositions, Neptune being in Cancer throughout the year. Nor did the progressions for 1903 permit such opposition.

138. However, given that the place of birth was Stockholm, the MC should have been 2.12 Scorpio.

139. A recalculated chart suggests a local time of 01:51:30 AM on 19 February 1865 at Stockholm.

140. The series began in the *Astrologer's Magazine*, No. 37, August 1893. The data for Leo's chart are given as 7 August 1860 at 05:49 AM, in Westminster (London), with Regulus on the ascendant.

141. See Adams, *The Bowl of Heaven*.

142. See *ibid.*, p. 37, where she gives the time when she cast the chart (16 March 1899, at 20:00 PM), but not the data relating to Leland.

143. See *ibid.*, p. 39.

144. Leland had been born on 1 June 1845 at 05:45 AM, at 72W 43N. The chart I have

reproduced here is from Sepharial, *Coming Events*, October 1899, Vol. 3, p. 345.

145. I write of Hazelrigg as a nineteenth-century astrologer because he was born in the middle of that century. However, he died, well into his nineties, in 1941.

146. The most impressive collection of US charts are the thirty or so related figures in Nicholas Campion, *The Book of World Horoscopes* (1996 edn), pp. 397–424. These include a survey of the data for such events as the Boston Tea Party of 16 December 1773, the first Continental Congress of 5 September 1774, the outbreak of the War of Independence on 19 April 1775, the Mecklenburg Declaration of 20 May 1775, timed to 2:00 PM (which had also been used as a basis for astrology by Hazelrigg), and the hallowed 4 July 1776, with its several variant times.

147. See John Hazelrigg, *Astrosophic Principles: {etc}* (1917), p. 112. The chart is on p. 111. See also Adelyn Richardson, 'In Search of the True Horoscope of the U.S.A.', *American Astrology*, July 1994, pp. 16–52.

148. It was published in John Hazelrigg, *Metaphysical Astrology* (1900), p. 16.

149. Hazelrigg had been introduced to the significance of Gemini for the United States by Broughton. Broughton seems to have been the first to recognise the intimate relationship between the future of America and 9 degrees of Gemini. See *Broughton's*, 1 February 1861, Vol. 2, No. 2, p. 1.

150. Hazelrigg, *Metaphysical Astrology*, p. 15.

151. Hazelrigg's studies of cycles have greatly influenced American astrology. Some of the Jupiter–Saturn cycles described by him in his monthly, the *Astrological Herald* (November 1901, p. 88), and related by him to presidential deaths and assassinations, surfaced in a short article by Jerry Klutz, dated 7 January 1960 in *American Astrology*, Vol. 28, No. 12, February 1961. The future president being considering, under the provocative heading 'Statistician Fears Next President Faces Fatal Curse', proved to be John F. Kennedy.

152. The image of Taurus reproduced here is from *Globi Coelestis in Tabulas Planas Redacti* (1729), Part 3, based on the calculations of Johann Dopplemayr.

153. For Ptolemy, see *Tetrabiblos* I:9. Ptolemy did not use the name Aldebaran, which is of later Arabic origin: he called it Λαμπαδίας (Lampadias) or 'Torch'. For the destructive power of Aldebaran, see Robson, *Fixed Stars and Constellations*, pp. 119–22.

154. Hazelrigg seems to have cast this version of the national chart sometime during the last two decades of the nineteenth century.

155. I have taken this time from William C. Davis, *Battle at Bull Run: A History of the First Major Campaign of the Civil War* (1977), p. 4.

156. In Hazelrigg, *Metaphysical Astrology*, p. 19, he specified the beginning as June 1942 and the culmination as October 1943 ('when *Aldebaran* will be in partile conjunction with the radical place of Uranus'). However, Uranus went into Gemini on 15 May 1942.

157. See Ellen McCaffery, *Astrology: Its History and Influence in the Western World* (1970), p. 349, where (incorrectly) she refers to the passage of Uranus through Gemini between 1940 and 1949.

Chapter Six

1. The exact time of Churchill's birth was unknown until 1966. On 11 September 1966, a private letter from Lord Randolph Churchill to his mother-in-law was published in the *Sunday Telegraph*, indicating that his father's birth had taken place at 1:30 AM. See *Astrology: The Astrologers' Quarterly* (1968), Vol. 42, No. 1, p. 17.

2. See R.C. Davison, 'The Horoscope of Sir Winston Churchill', in *Astrology: The Astrologers' Quarterly* (1965), Vol. 39, No. 1, p. 5.

3. *Ibid.*, p. 7.

4. William Butler Yeats was born at Sandymount, near Dublin, on 13 June 1865. From unspecified 'private sources', Leo's *Notable Nativities* gives an ascendant of 00.01 Aquarius

(see p. 98, No. 960). Yeats set down his symbolic system in *A Vision* (1925), pp. 95–184, where his twenty-eight phases, and the related tinctures, are discussed. For a later astrological approach to these symbols, see Marilyn Busteed *et al.*, *Phases of the Moon: a Guide to Evolving Human Nature* (1974).

5. His interest in astrological ideas can be discerned scattered among his writings: see Sydney Omarr, *Henry Miller: His World of Urania* (1960).

6. Henry Miller, *Big Sur and the Oranges of Hieronymus Bosch* (1958; references are to the 1962 reprint), p. 261.

7. *Ibid.*, p. 259.

8. See Omarr, *Henry Miller*.

9. Miller, *Big Sur*, p. 247. See Moricand, *Miroir d'Astrologie* (1928), of which Miller had a copy. Moricand showed Miller the manuscript of his own essay, 'L'Oeuvre et le génie de Balzac devant l'Astrologie'. Jay Martin, *Always Merry and Bright: The Life of Henry Miller* (1978), p. 318, recognised that Moricand was a far greater influence on Miller's imagination than had hitherto been appreciated.

10. Miller, *Big Sur*, pp. 246 and 254.

11. *Ibid.*, p. 246.

12. See Omarr, *Henry Miller*, p. 34.

13. The chart of Krishnamurti (known as 'Alcyone') had been published in *Modern Astrology* (1911), Vol. 8, p. 268. For the birth date of Joan of Arc see Perceval de Boulainvilliers, *Procès*, V, 116: Joan was born on 6 January 1412 at Domrémy.

14. The quotation is from Martin, *Always Merry and Bright*, p. 3.

15. See Vivian E. Robson, *The Fixed Stars and Constellations in Astrology* (1923): the quotation is from the 1969 impression, p. 132. In 1891, Alphecca was in 10.46 Scorpio.

16. Moricand was born in Paris on 17 January 1887, at either 7:00 or 7:15 PM: see Miller, *Big Sur*, p. 243, on the title-page of *Part Three. Paradise Lost*.

17. Miller, *Big Sur*, pp. 274–5.

18. After the actress Tallulah Bankhead had discussed her chart with Evangeline Adams, she described herself as 'An Aquarian in the skin of a Scorpion'. See Tallulah Bankhead, *Tallulah: My Autobiography* (1952), p. 40.

19. Miller, *Big Sur*, p. 274.

20. H.P. Blavatsky, *The Secret Doctrine* (1888), Vol. I, p. 219.

21. See for example, Willi Sucher, *Isis Sophia: an Outline of a New Star Wisdom* (1951), Part 2, p. 35.

22. Furze Morrish, *Outline of Astro-Psychology* (1952), pp. 213–14, was one of the earliest astrological writers to deal with the obvious polarity between rigidity and fluidity.

23. For Miller and Moricand, see Omarr, *Henry Miller*, pp. 44–50. See also 'The Books in My Life', abstracted from *New Directions* (1952), *ibid.*, pp. 92–3. For an indication of Rudhyar's esoteric background, see Dane Rudhyar, *The Astrology of Personality* (1936).

24. The French astrologer, Barbault, constantly referred to the methods of Morin: see André Barbault, *Traité Pratique d'Astrologie* (1961), pp. 56ff.

25. Eudes Picard, *Astrologie judiciaire* (1932).

26. Jean-Pierre Nicola, *La Condition Solaire* (1964; but see the 1971 edn). For Goya, p. 90; Vlaminck, p. 100; Dali, pp. 120–1; Beethoven, p. 173; Paganini, p. 165; Louis Armstrong, p. 90.

27. See Michel Gauquelin, *L'Influence des Astres: Études critiques et expérimentales* (1955).

28. André Barbault, *Traité Practique*, pp. 51–6, gives an assessment of the methods of the Gauquelins.

29. See *ibid.*, p. 228, which refers to P. Anselme, *Historie genéalogique et chronologique de la maison royale de France*.

30. See *ibid.* For the chart of Colbert, see p. 258; for that of Richelieu, see pp. 49 and 252.

31. J.H. Holden, *A History of Horoscopic Astrology: From the Babylonian Period to the Modern Age* (1996), pp. 236–7, records that this system was used in *The Gauquelin Book of American Charts* (1982), which contained over 1,400 sets of data.

32. I cannot resist quoting from that enjoyable work, Owen Gingerich, *The Book Nobody Read:*

Chasing the Revolutions of Nicolaus Copernicus (2004), p. 136.

33. L.H. Weston, *The Planet Vulcan: History, Nature, Tables* (1920?).

34. See Patrick Davis, *Revolutionizing Astrology with Heliocentric* (1980).

35. See Eleanor Bach and George Climlas, *Ephemerides of the Asteroids: Ceres, Pallas, Juno, Vesta 1900–2000* (1973).

36. See B. Hubner and L. Hubner, *Lebensuhr im Horoskop* (1980–5).

37. See Ronald C. Davison, *Cycles of Destiny: Understanding Return Charts* (1990).

38. See M. Harding and C. Harvey, *Working with Astrology: The Psychology of Midpoints, Harmonics and Astro*Carto*Graphy* (1992 edn).

39. Marc Edmund Jones, *Guide to Horoscope Interpretation* (1941).

40. William J. Tucker, *The Principles, Theory and Practice of Scientific Prediction* (1936).

41. See Robert Powell and Peter Treadgold, *The Sidereal Zodiac* (1979).

42. 'The First Selenocentric Horoscope', in the *Astrological Journal* (Autumn 1969), Vol. 11, No. 4, p. 1.

43. See, for example, L. Kolisko, *The Total Eclipse of the Sun, 15th February, 1961 Studied in Bordighera* (1961).

44. See Agnes Fyfe, *The Signature of the Planet Mercury in Plants: Capillary Dynamic Studies* (reprinted from the *British Homoeopathic Journal*, January 1974, Vol. 43, pp. 40–1.

45. *Ibid.*, p. 40. My own chart, for London, gives conjunction at 10:44:55 AM.

46. Among the most appropriate chartings I have seen is that for the autumnal equinox of 1978, in the *Cincinnati Journal of Ceremonial Magick* (1978), Vol. I, No. 3, p. 11.

47. Percival Lowell had begun searching for the planet as early as 1908 after observing a small perturbation in the orbit of Neptune. The Lowell Observatory (perhaps even Lowell himself) dubbed it 'Planet X', and a systematic search for its location began as early as 1914. See Ferris Greenslet, *The Lowells and their Seven Worlds* (1946), pp. 364–5.

48. See *Raphael's Astronomical Ephemeris of the Planets' Places*. The horoscope of George V is on p. 40 (1932 ephemeris); that of the Duke of York is on p. 41 (1933 ephemeris).

49. Manley P. Hall, *Astrological Keywords* (1959), p. 138, speculated that Pluto represents a higher octave of Mars, and mentions that the Alexandrian Pluto was Serapis, patron of the Mystery schools. He concludes that Pluto heralded the re-establishment of the Mystery schools of the ancient world.

50. See Isabelle M. Pagan, *From Pioneer to Poet: or the Twelve Great Gates* (1911), p. 255.

51. See Raphael, *Ephemeris for 1934*, pp. 40–1.

52. See note 49 above.

53. The article and chart appeared in the *Sunday Express*, 24 August 1930, p. 11.

54. *Sunday Express*, 5 October 1930, p. 21.

55. See *Prediction*, July 1938, for Naylor's earlier prophecy of 'difficulties' in the London Underground, signalled by the eclipse of 14 May. The crash occurred three days after the lunar eclipse of 14 May.

56. In September 1936, the astrologer William Tucker was asked by the *Sunday Dispatch* to contribute a weekly article on astrology. See W.J. Tucker, *Autobiography of an Astrologer* (1960), pp. 250–3.

57. A.F.L. Deeson, *An Illustrated History of Airships* (1973), pp. 98–102.

58. This datum is given for noon local time, at Nasik, Maharashtra.

59. The diagram is based on that in Gauquelin, *L'Influence des Astres*, p. 161.

60. For a record of the data, see *Astrology: The Astrologers' Quarterly* (1969), Vol. 43, No. 2, p. 62, and the correction in *ibid.*, Vol. 43, No. 3, p. 90.

61. See Gauquelin, *L'Influence des Astres*, p. 289.

62. See, for example, *Astrology: The Astrologers' Quarterly* (1968), Vol. 41, No. 4, p. 10.

63. Maurice Wemyss, *The Wheel of Life or Scientific Astrology* (c. 1930), Vol. 2, p. 49.

64. According to Weymss, *ibid.*, p. 48, Lindbergh was born in Detroit at 2:30 AM on 4 February 1902.

65. See *The Straggling Astrologer of the Nineteenth Century; or, Magazine of Celestial Intelligences* (11 September 1824), No. 15, title page and pp. 226ff.

66. *Ibid.*, p. 61.

67. See *Raphael's Astronomical Ephemeris ... for 1912*, p. 41. Cross had been born on 15 May 1850 at 02:35 AM, 'in East Anglia'.

68. See *Raphael's Ephemeris ... for 1916*, p. 41. French was born on 28 September 1852 at 09:35 AM, in Walmer, Kent.

69. See *Raphael's Ephemeris ... for 1918*, p. 41. Haig was born on 19 June 1861, at 09:45 PM, in Edinburgh.

70. See *Raphael's Ephermeris ... for 1922*, p. 41. Harding was born 2 November 1865, at 02:30 PM, at Blooming Grove, Ohio.

71. See 'Raphael's Astro-Picture Gallery. No. 15', in *Raphael's Astronomical Ephemeris of the Planets' Places for 1927* (1926), p. 41. Unfortunately, Raphael believed that Mussolini had been born in Milan, whereas he had been born in Predappio, in Romagna.

72. Raphael made an error of more than 2 degrees in his calculation of the position of Mars. At the time of birth, Mars was in 13.09 Gemini.

73. When the planets involved are in conjunction (as in this case) an orb of 2 degrees is permissible.

74. In 1883, Baten Kaitos was in 20.10 Taurus. The opposing Moon was on the evil star Unukalhai.

75. I am indebted for some of the facts in the following assessment to Ellic Howe, *Urania's Children: The Strange World of the Astrologers* (1967), pp. 204–18, and to Louis de Wohl's unreliable works, *I Follow my Stars* (1937) and *The Stars of War and Peace* (1952).

76. The chart is reproduced in colour, above a photograph of de Wohl, in Louis MacNeice, *Astrology* (1964), p. 216.

77. De Wohl is usually described as a Hungarian Jew, but he was born in Berlin on 24 January 1903; he changed his German familial honorific Von to De when he left Germany. In his work, *I Follow my Stars*, he claimed a birth time of 7:45 PM. However, after the war he told a well-known American astrologer that the correct time was 3:30 PM. He was introduced to astrology by Baron Harald Keun von Hoogerwoerd in 1930, and had only a short time to master astrology, one of the most time-consuming of all disciplines. See Howe, *Urania's Children*, pp. 205–6.

78. A copy is necessary as the original *Der Zenit* cover does not lend itself to reproduction in line.

79. Lev Bezymenski, *The Death of Adolf Hitler. Unknown Documents from Soviet Archives* (1968). The archival forensic report (Document No. 12 – Berlin-Buch, 8.V., 1945. *Mortuary Chirurgisches Armeefeldlazarett No. 496*) is given on pp. 44ff.

80. In Hitler's natal chart, Pluto was 0.51 Gemini, close to Pluto in 04.40 Gemini: both were on the star Prima Hyadum, which generally brings a rapid and violent death.

81. John Toland, *Adolf Hitler* (1997 edn), p. 860. Himmler had an interest in astrology, in consequence of which numerous charts were cast for Hitler and other Nazi leaders. See Howe, *Urania's Children*, p. 109.

82. In *Ein Blick in die Zukunft*, published in 1934, Elspeth Ebertin had proposed a horoscope for Hitler cast for between 06:22 and 06:26 PM. The progressions for her chart using 06:22 PM. suggest that Hitler would be under great pressure in 1945.

83. See Howe, *Urania's Children*, p. 88.

84. See the *Daily Mail*, 12 July 1939, p. 13, reporting Dr Nicholas Murray Butler, President of Columbia University.

85. There is no historical support for the conflated stories of Hitler's initiation into esoteric circles or of his interest in astrology. However, many influential Nazis *did* aspire to occult knowledge and magical empowerment. See Nicholas Goodrick-Clarke, *The Occult Roots of Nazism: The Ariosophists of Austria and Germany 1890–1935* (1985), esp. pp. 217–25.

86. See Toland, *Adolf Hitler*, p. 860.

87. Geoffrey Dean [*et al.*], *Recent Advances in Natal Astrology: A Critical Review 1900–1976* (1977), p. 421.

88. Adolf Hitler was born on 20 April 1889, in Braunau, Austria. After he became Chancellor, a number of horoscopes for his birth were published, each with a different time. For example, in 1933 Frank Glahn published a horoscope in his *Astral Warte*, with a 05:45 AM birth. For other examples, see Howe, *Urania's Children*, pp. 109ff.

89. See Reinhold Ebertin, *Kombination der Gestirneinflüsse*, in the 1972 English translation, *The Combination of Stellar Influences*, p. 21.

90. The figure I have evolved here is loosely based on that given in Dean *et al.*, *Recent Advances*, p. 421. However, I should point out that the textual analysis of the figure in this work is faulty: the two planets, Uranus and Pluto, do *not* fall on the Sun/Moon midpoints, as claimed. Furthermore, it is misleading to claim that the Hitler chart presents a problem for traditional methods of astrology: on the contrary, in his case the fixed stars reveal all.

91. In most modern astrological systems, the orb for this aspect is rarely more than 2 degrees: however, in the Ebertin system, an orb of 5 degrees is permitted for major aspects.

92. Joananes Vehlow, *Lehrekursus der wissenchaftlichen Geburts-Astrologie* (1934) Vol. 2; quoted by R. Ebertin, *Die Bedeutung der Fixsterne* (1971), p. 28.

93. The chart is from Cyrille Wilczkowski, *L'Homme et le Zodiaque: Essai de Synthèse Typologique* (1947), p. 224. Goering was born in the early hours (*c.* 04:00 AM?) on 12 January 1893, in Rosenheim, Germany.

94. Reinhold Ebertin, *The Combination of Stellar Influences: Supplement 1, 1961*, p. 5.

95. See *ibid.*, p. 4.

96. Infuriatingly, Ebertin tends to refer to his own archives for data – in this case, the reference 'epa-154'. Coppi must have been born at 20:18:30 PM, on 15 September 1919, in Rome.

97. See L. Locher-Ernst, *Sternkalender Erscheinung am Sternenhimmel im Jahre 1945*. Among the authors of articles included within this star-calendar is Joachim Schultz, whose work

Rhythmen der Sterne: Erscheinungen und Bewegungen von Sonne, Mond und Planeten (1963) has become a classic in the field.

98. I have had this diagram redrawn to incorporate essential translations of astrological terms into English and to preserve the original clarity of the presentation, which was in colour.

99. Precise co-ordinates for the geocentric positions are tabulated in Locker-Ernst, *Sternkalendar*, p. 97, whereas precise heliocentric positions are tabulated on p. 100.

100. The chart is from W.O. Sucher, *Man and the Stars* (1953), p. 36. My own copy of this work is cyclostyled, and is of poor quality; accordingly, I have had the chart copied, as accurately as possible. The birth date of Shakespeare is not known, though he was baptised on 26 April 1564 (NS).

101. The method of determining the time of conception, which is loosely based on the Hermetic maxims, may be seen in E.H. Bailey, *The Prenatal Epoch* (1916, but generally available in the Weiser reprint of 1970). For a cogent account of the ancient view of the descent through the spheres, see 'The Seven Zones and their Characteristics', in G.R.S. Mead, *Thrice-Greatest Hermes: Studies in Hellenistic Theosophy and Gnosis* (1906; in the 1963 reprint), Vol. 1, pp. 288ff.

102. For the Gate of the Moon within the context of ancient esoteric thought, see Porphyry, *On the Cave of the Nymphs* (the Thomas Taylor translation is available in the 1991 Phanes Press edition).

103. The rules are set out, in brief, by Willi Sucher, 'Looking Through the Horoscope of Birth: the Significance of the Pre-Natal Events among the Stars', in the *Mercury Star Journal* (1976), Vol. 2, No. 3, pp. 64–75.

104. The article on Richard Wagner, in *Astrology: The Astrologers' Quarterly* (1967), Vol. 41, No. 3, pp. 79–83, gives 'sunrise' as the time of birth, without recording a source.

105. The original chart was reproduced by Willi Sucher, in the *Modern Mystic*, Vol. 1 (1937), pp. 44–6.

106. Sucher, *ibid.* (1967), p. 68, wrongly describes it as passing from Leo to Virgo.

107. Sucher appears to have made a mistake when drawing up this asterogram, for he placed the loop-curve of Saturn in Sagittarius. I have amended the original asterogram to reflect its true position.

108. Marcia Moore and Mark Douglas, *An Astroanalysis of Jacqueline Onassis* (1970).

109. See *ibid.* The combined charts for Jacqueline and John F. Kennedy are on p. 161; those for Jacqueline and Onassis are on p. 281.

110. The time of birth is recorded as being just past 9.00 AM by A. Gregory and M. Speriglio, *Crypt 33. The Saga of Marilyn Monroe – The Final Word* (1993), p. 5. According to Jane Ellers Wayne, *Marilyn's Men. The Private Life of Marilyn Monroe* (1992), she was born at 9:30 AM. This latter time was adopted for the chart in Jim Lewis and Ariel Guttman, *The Astro*Carto*Graphy Book of Maps: The Astrology of Relocation* (1989), p. 71, with an ascendant of 13.04 Leo. See also Alexander Markin, 'Pre-Natal Influences in the Birth Chart', in *Astrology: The Astrologers' Quarterly* (1977), Vol. 51, No. 4, p. 120, which offered an ascendant of 14 Leo.

111. For want of a more precise time, I have rectified the chart to 11:30 PM, on that day. The result of such rectification is astounding in terms of progressions to her death: progressed Pluto in the same degree as progressed Sun. The solar eclipse of 5 February 1962 (15.43 Aquarius) fell on the progressed Cauda.

112. This is the *Liber Astronomiae, or, Guidonis Bonati Forliviensis Mathematici de Astronomia ...* Part 4, 2, cols 616–64.

113. See Robert Zoller, *The Lost Key to Prediction: The Arabic Parts in Astrology* (1980).

114. The revamped chart is in *ibid.*, p. 185. It is copied (not altogether accurately, as we shall see) from Iohann Ganivet, *amicus medicorum magistri ioannis ganiveti* (1496), Cap. VI, p. 305.

115. In the Ganivet chart, the signs are represented in words rather than sigils. The sigil for Mercury is upside-down. For a discussion of the *Pars Mortis*, see *ibid.*, pp. 270–98.

116. The errors in the chart led Ganivet to conclude that the part of death, and the part of life were in opposite degrees, and in the terms of the malefics: however, this was not the case. See Zoller, *Lost Key*, p. 185.

117. See introductory page to Lewis and Guttman, *Astro*Carto*Graphy*, (1989).

118. *Ibid.*, p. 2.

119. This date is from Alan Clayson, *John Lennon* (2003); the astrological time of 6:30 is from Lewis and Guttman, *Astro*Carto*Graphy*, p. 91. The combined horoscope of John Lennon and Yoko Ono, in Alan Oken, *Astrology: Evolution and Revolution* (1976 edn), p. 218, gives (for Lennon) an ascendant in Libra and the Moon in Capricorn.

120. For a survey of these zodiacs, see David Ovason, *The Secret Architecture of Our Nation's Capital: The Masons and the Building of Washington, D.C.* (2000).

121. The stereographic projection has been resolved into its component constellations in *ibid.*, pp. 274–5.

122. The chart is from Rudhyar, *The Astrology of Personality* (1936), p. 273.

123. Einstein was born at 11:30 AM, on 14 March 1879, at Donau, Germany. See John Stachel *et al.*, *The Collected Papers of Albert Einstein* (1987), Vol. 1, item 1. His horoscope, for 11:36 AM, is printed in Davison (1971 edn), p. 147.

124. See Rudhyar (1936), p. 275. As a matter of fact, in the segment of the 28-year clock following the age of twenty-two, the following planets were transited by the hand of the clock, in the sequence Mercury, Saturn, Pallas, Venus, Juno, Chiron, Ceres and Pluto.

125. In the 1930s, the Swiss astrologer Karl Krafft subjected a large number of horoscopes to analyses resembling the harmonics. However, his approach has been criticised because of infelicities in his statistical methods. See Karl E. Krafft, *Traité d'Astro-Biologie* (1939).

126. John Addey, *Harmonics in Astrology* (1976).

127. Michael Harding and Charles Harvey, *Working with Astrology: the Psychology of Midpoints,*

Harmonics and Astro*Carto*Graphy (1998 edn), p. 225.

128. *Ibid.*, pp. 230ff.

129. This H7 chart was discussed by David Hamblin, *Harmonic Charts: Understanding and Using the Principle of Harmonics in Astrological Interpretation* (1987 edn), p. 72.

130. See *ibid.* Among the more interesting harmonic charts are those of the following: Ludwig van Beethoven (pp. 165–71); Georges Braque (p. 54); Edgar Cayce (p. 82); Winston Churchill (p. 40); Jean Cocteau (p. 58); Le Corbusier (p. 72); Salvador Dali (p. 68); Albert Einstein (p. 50); Uri Geller (p. 84); Ernest Hemingway (p. 54); Adolf Hitler (p. 74); Wolfgang Amadeus Mozart (p. 52); Richard Nixon (p. 75); Pablo Picasso (p. 240); and Rudolf Steiner (p. 82).

131. See Charles Jayne, *In Search*, Spring 1961.

132. It was also used for the constellation Sagittarius. For useful notes, see Richard Hinckley Allen, *Star Names: Their Lore and Meaning* (1963), pp. 18, 149, and 353.

133. Robert Francis Kennedy was born at 02:38 PM on 20 November 1925 at Brookline, Massachusetts: see David Heymann, *RFK. A Candid Biography of Robert F. Kennedy* (1998), p. 16.

134. Sirhan Bishara Sirhan was born on 19 March 1944, in Jerusalem. The date and place are from Dan E. Moldea, *The Killing of Robert Kennedy. An Investigation of Motive, Means and Opportunity* (1995), p. 101. I have given a noon-time chart. The chart for Sirhan given by Moore and Douglas, *Astroanalysis of Jacqueline Onassis*, p. 180, was for *circa* sunrise.

135. I have had the top part of the page from Sirhan's notebook (the original of which is preserved in the California State Archives) copied from the plate in Moldea, *Killing of Robert Kennedy*, and between pp. 124 and 129.

136. See Moldea, *ibid.*, p. 13.

137. Nicholas Wapshott, in *The Times* of Friday 30 August 2002, p. 17.

138. Dan Kurzman, *Day of the Bomb* (1986).

139. For further astrological material relating to the dropping of the bomb, see David Ovason, *The Book of the Eclipse: The Hidden Influence of Eclipses* (1999), pp. 108ff.

Index